Eric Moon, Sarasota, Florida, 1981

A DESIRE TO LEARN

Selected Writings

by

ERIC MOON

"Where there is much desire to learn, there of necessity will be much arguing, much writing, many opinions; for opinion in good men is but knowledge in the making."

—John Milton, *Areopagitica*

The Scarecrow Press
Metuchen, N.J., & London
1993

British Library Cataloguing-in-Publication data available

Library of Congress Cataloging-in-Publication Data

Moon, Eric, 1923-
    A desire to learn : selected writings / by Eric Moon.
      p.   cm.
    ISBN 0-8108-2686-0 (acid-free paper)
    1. Library science—United States.
Z665.2.U6M66   1993
020'.973—dc20   93-15146

Copyright © 1993 by Eric Moon
Manufactured in the United States of America

Printed on acid-free paper

TO

E.J. and Dorothy

Two Profiles in Courage

Would that they faced more often
in the same direction

Acknowledgments

In addition to those who have granted me permission to reprint many of the articles and editorials included in this collection, there were a number of people who assisted me in a variety of ways in tracking down items of which I no longer had copies, and in some cases of which I was unaware.

I wish to express my gratitude to the following friends and colleagues for their assistance on this journey back through so many words and so many years:

John N. Berry III
Arthur Curley
Richard Dougherty
Edward Dudley
Wm. R. Eshelman
Judith Farley
Mary Sue Ferrell
Joseph Green
Irene Hoadley
Norman Horrocks
E. J. Josey
Michael Malinconico
Ronald G. Surridge
Jana Varlejs

Especially, I want to thank my wife, Ilse, not only for compiling the very thorough index to this volume . . . but for everything else.

Table of Contents

Foreword, by Arthur Curley … ix
General Introduction … xiii

Part I. Politics and Public Policy

Introduction … 1
A Clear Choice *(1964)* … 4
Voices on Vietnam? *(1967)* … 8
The Central Fact of Our Times *(1965)* … 10
Hungry and Not Very Scrupulous Lions *(1967)* … 21
A Matter of Values *(1976)* … 32
Data Bank Is Two Four-Letter Words *(1977)* … 42
Education Without Libraries = Catastrophe *(1977)* … 53
Money in the (Data) Bank *(1978)* … 61
Our Commission, Our Omissions *(1984)* … 69

Part II. Discrimination

Introduction … 85
The Silent Subject *(1960)* … 87
The Process of Dilution *(1963)* … 91
Access and the Supreme Court *(1966)* … 96
The Issues That Confront Us Now *(1984)* … 98
A "Chapter" Chapter *(1992)* … 110

Part III. Censorship

Introduction … 119
The Right to Write *(1960)* … 121
Courage and Cowardice *(1962)* … 123
The Benefit of the Doubt *(1965)* … 130

To Disagree Is Not to Destroy *(1981)* — 138
A Priori Censorship *(1985)* — 151
Living the Library Bill of Rights *(1990)* — 155

Part IV. Collection Building

Introduction — 169
Critics, Awake! *(1951)* — 171
The Assistant and the Bookish Habit *(1954)* — 175
Stock Control in Public Libraries *(1957)* — 189
Confusion and Conviction *(1962)* — 199
The Blue and the Grey *(1969)* — 201

Part V. The Library Profession

Introduction — 215
A Jungle Tale *(1963)* — 218
Fire from the Maddened Crowd *(1965)* — 228
RTSD and the Big Wide World *(1966)* — 235
High John *(1968)* — 245
A Conspiracy Against the Laity? *(1969)* — 264
A Potpourri of P's *(1976)* — 280
Who's Larry Powell? *(1986)* — 295

Part VI. Library Associations

Introduction — 305
Potential for Power *(1960)* — 307
Library Association Agonies *(1971)* — 309
The State of the Union, Jack *(1977)* — 321
The Lacy Commission Report *(1985)* — 335

Part VII. The Library Press

Introduction — 345
Hello, Out There, or Let's Communicate *(1962)* — 347
The Library Press *(1969)* — 352
The Journalist and the Writer *(1970)* — 366
Hook, Line and Sinker *(1977)* — 369
The Library Press and Eric Moon *(1987)* — 377

Part VIII. General Articles and a Review Sampler

Introduction	395
The Province Nobody Knows *(1959)*	397
Blimey, a Limey! *(1967)*	402
Writer of the People (John Steinbeck) *(1957)*	405
Too Hot to Handle (Henry Miller) *(1958)*	409
From the Twosome, a Quartet (Miller/Durrell) *(1963)*	413
New Blacks in Notting Hill (C. MacInnes) *(1969)*	416
Simenon's Magic *(1966)*	419
Interpretations of the First Amendment *(1985)*	422
Emergence of a Free Press *(1985)*	425
Index, by Ilse Moon	427

Foreword

On Guy Fawkes Day, 1959, there arrived in New York a young Englishman of wit, charm, and pyrotechnic propensities; this time, an explosion *would* occur. When asked by his prospective publisher, Daniel Melcher, what he thought of *Library Journal,* the soon-to-be editor, Eric Moon, had replied that "it looked tired and middle-aged and badly needed livening up." Judging by his widespread influence in the years since, he might as well have been speaking of the entire library field.

It is clear from his earliest writings—railing against the profession's obsession with gadgetry and calling for a social revolution in librarianship—that Eric Moon was no establishmentarian. His passion for the world of ideas and literature as the true basis of librarianship is also evident, but few clues suggested the remarkable impact he would exert on the most fundamental issues affecting the role of libraries in society.

The year 1959 did represent, of course, the eve of the most turbulent decade in recent American history. The editorial pages of *Library Journal* would soon address the Civil Rights crisis with a fervor and forcefulness that electrified (i.e., both shocked and galvanized) the library profession. Next, the staff of *Library Journal,* backing its intrepid leader, literally took to the streets, forsaking armchair journalism for active on-site coverage of experimental library projects in urban ghettos or rural outbacks.

By 1964, if any doubt still existed that library journalism and librarianship itself were undergoing a sea change, it was shattered by the unprecedented intrusion of *Library Journal* into the political arena through open endorsement of a U. S. Presidential candidate. This bold and controversial action represented not an attempt to align the profession with one political party, but rather a principal tenet of the Moon doctrine calling for a politically alert and active profession. Not content with the power of the pen, Eric Moon's compelling eloquence would inspire a growing movement as he responded to frequent requests to speak at conferences, library schools, or impromptu gatherings of budding activists.

Throughout the selections in this volume, drawn deliberately from papers presented before diverse audiences and from articles in disparate publications, one encounters the themes with which Eric Moon challenged an emerging generation to a virtual redefinition of librarianship: political activism as a requirement for effective promotion of library services, assertion of the social role of libraries as fundamental to democratic values, alignment with humanistic and socially progressive causes, fierce defense of intellectual freedom and free access, witty but devastating attacks on complacency and hypocrisy, aggressive and experimental outreach to broaden the borders of the library's target audience, and democratization of the library profession.

The foundations of this activism had been laid in the early career of Eric Moon in Britain. He began at the Southampton Public Library in England in 1939, the year war broke out in Europe. He served in the Royal Air Force in the Far East before returning to study at the Loughborough College library school in the immediate postwar years. These were exciting times as libraries were in the forefront of the social rebuilding of the newly elected Labour Government. Eric became a leader in the Association of Assistant Librarians and was soon leading the charge of the younger members of the profession against the "establishment" of the elders of the British Library Association. He honed his debating skills at Association meetings and practiced a lively and thus, by definition, pioneering sense of journalism in *Liaison,* a newsheet issued with the official *Library Association Record.* It was an excellent training ground for what was to follow in the American context.

Describing his initial reception in America, Eric Moon suggests that "among most of the ALA establishment and a good many other prominent members of the profession, I was during that time as much a public enemy as those gentlemen whose photographs adorn the walls of local post offices." The rapid rise in *Library Journal* readership, on the other hand, suggested a far more magnetic response from librarianship at large. By the mid-sixties, Eric Moon's growing national following had elected him to the ALA Council, where he promptly positioned himself at the back bench, that symbol of political dissidence. Throughout the following turbulent decade, that focal point became the major force for change and progressive action in ALA, moving inexorably from dissent to leadership until self-proclaimed back-benchers soon seemed a near majority of the Council.

Ironically, Eric seems never really to have sought such a leadership role. As the movement for change took concrete form, he invariably deferred to and encouraged younger potential activists eager to try their wings. On the floor of Council, as in his writings, his eloquent voice represents far more a search for truth and clarity than an appeal to followers. His frequent successes in Council resulted often from forcing a grudging respect from even his fiercest opponents and then engaging them in a search for reasonable compromise: that this was usually on his own terms is just further tribute to his intellectual and negotiating skills. It would be difficult to enumerate the ALA crises that have been resolved by Eric's behind-the-scenes diplomacy.

Eric also never sought the Presidency of ALA; a decade of pressure from friends and admirers was the driving force. But his resounding election to that office in 1977 represented a stirring triumph for the values and ideals he so eloquently champions. By this time he had left *Library Journal* and was President of Scarecrow Press, to which he brought his enthusiasm and dedication while continuing his deep involvement with libraries and their readers. He continued to seek out librarians with something worthwhile to say in print, whether as commentators, compilers, or contributors to useful knowledge. Fulfilling his declared aim to retire from full-time work at the early age of 55, he stepped down as Scarecrow President in 1978 but remains an active editorial contributor. His work for ALA has continued with appointments to key committees. The Association has honored him with the Lippincott Award and Honorary Membership (ALA's highest award).

All in all it has been a remarkable journey—an extraordinary search for knowledge. Eric Moon has brought excitement and inspiration to a generation and more of librarians. Read on and discover why.

Arthur Curley, Director
Boston Public Library

General Introduction

The idea of compiling this collection of writings—mostly ancient and occasionally modern—arose during my many discussions with Ken Kister, who has been saddled with the task of writing my biography. He picked up the task because I was unwilling to attempt that autobiographical exercise I had persuaded a number of my professional colleagues to undertake during my decade at the helm of The Scarecrow Press.

Ken and I were agreed, I think, that no matter how skillful or penetrating the biographer, there are likely to remain some subtleties about the subject that may become apparent only through an examination of the subject's own words and opinions. Certainly this seemed likely in my case, writing and speaking having played such a central role in my professional career. Whatever influence, if any, I may have had upon the profession of librarianship, and the changes wrought in it over the past forty-odd years, most probably derives from the many thousands of words I have committed to paper or sent winging through a microphone.

This selection, then, is intended to complement Ken Kister's biography of me. With that objective in mind it was decided not to attempt to cull the "best" of a very large output. Rather, I have tried to include some articles, editorials, etc. ranging over nearly the whole of my career. Some not so polished juvenilia are therefore to be found here and there throughout the volume.

One other objective was not to include too much material which is very easily accessible to most potential readers. Clearly, a publisher might not be too eager to bring out a volume the contents of which are already known to most probable readers. Therefore, although the largest part of my writings appeared in *Library Journal* during the fertile decade of the sixties, not much of that appears here—with the exception of a few key editorials and one or two other pieces I could not bring myself to omit. My two earlier collections—*Book Selection and Censorship in the Sixties* (Bowker, 1969) and *Library Issues: The Sixties* (Bowker, 1970)—take care of much of the *LJ* material that is excluded from this volume.

The principal concentration has been upon speeches and other pieces which have not previously been published or that have appeared in sources considerably less accessible than *LJ*—for example, state library association periodicals, other limited circulation publications, or journals from abroad (England, Canada). In case this might lead to the inference that what is included consists solely of "lesser" material or the dregs of my output, it should be noted that these categories include, for example, my ALA Presidential Inaugural Address ("Data Bank Is Two Four-Letter Words"), never before published, and my address to the Centennial Conference of the (British) Library Association ("The State of the Union, Jack"), which was published in England but not in the U.S.

The arrangement of the articles and editorials within each topic area is, for the most part, chronological, the hope being that this might reveal changes (even growth!) in philosophy and opinions and style. There is one slight departure from chronological order in Part I, in order to lead that opening section with two key *LJ* editorials of the sixties, and the miscellaneous Part VIII is arranged by sources of publication.

Many of the pieces included have been edited, in greater or lesser degree, to avoid repetition as far as possible, or to remove "speech" aspects or irrelevant asides from an article. I have resisted the temptation to rewrite extensively, to remove examples of less than felicitous style, to update opinions I have outgrown or no longer hold, to bury some early revelations of chauvinism of one kind or another, etc. A good many warts are left on display.

I hope that some items in this volume will still have pertinence, particularly for students and newcomers to the profession, and that some of my more senior colleagues will find something here other than nostalgia. I am distressed that so much of the fire has disappeared from the library literature (and from our professional gatherings). We need far more opinions hung out on the line so that others may react to them. Not only would this be more interesting than much of the benign pap placed before us today, but opinion, ideas, argument, debate are, in the words of Milton that grace the title-page of this volume, "knowledge in the making." We can all use a little more of that.

Eric Moon

PART I

Politics and Public Policy

Introduction

This section, on Politics and Public Policy, otherwise in chronological order, begins with two *Library Journal* editorials of the sixties. "A Clear Choice" was, I believe, a genuine "first" in library literature: the first public position taken by a library periodical in a political election. We made sure that readers would not miss the editorial by clothing that particular issue in a cover featuring Senator Goldwater, framed in gold. Below the photograph of the Senator appeared, with page reference, the first sentence of the editorial.

In a subsequent editorial ("End of the Story," December 15, 1964), John Berry said that the editorial had "brought more letters and reaction than any recent position we have taken." Some "60 per cent of those who wrote were against the editorial, the remaining 40 per cent for it," and "among the 'antis' there were three basic opinions: they favored Goldwater, they were against federal aid, or they opposed professional journals 'dabbling in politics'."

"Voices on Vietnam" is another example of *LJ*'s unrepentant penchant in the sixties for taking political positions. In retrospect it seems to me that we took this one much later than we should have. This editorial was prompted by a lunchtime discussion with my friend Richard Bye of *Publishers' Weekly* (and later publisher of *LJ*). He was organizing support from the publishing community for a statement opposing the Administration's policies on Vietnam. Why not ask librarians, too, I suggested. How many of them would join such a public effort? he asked. I said I didn't know but I'd find out. Hence the editorial. When the protest page appeared in the *New York Times* it was encouraging to see a united front from the book world. And true to form, here was *LJ* attacking the person (President Johnson) it had supported in the earlier editorial attacking Goldwater. No inconsistency there—just keeping abreast of the times

The other two items from the sixties ("The Central Fact of Our Times" and "Hungry and Not Very Scrupulous Lions"), both conference speeches, were further efforts to persuade the library community that political awareness and involvement were vital if libraries and the profession were ever going to be able to make the kind of contribution to society that they should.

The next four pieces all cluster around my Presidency of the American Library Association in 1977-78. The first state library association gathering I had attended after entering the U.S. in 1959 was California's, so it was perhaps appropriate that the first conference I addressed as ALA's President-elect was also California's. "A Matter of Values" was really a communal effort: I was still searching for a theme for my Presidential year and had asked a number of friends and colleagues for their ideas about what I should do. A number of those ideas appear in this paper.

"Education Without Libraries = Catastrophe" was the result of a request by my good friend E. J. Josey, then employed at the New York State Library, that I represent librarianship at a gathering sponsored by the Regents of the University of the State of New York. It was the first time I had waxed autobiographical in a speech, but I wanted to convey how important libraries and books had been to my own life, as a way of conveying to the Regents how important libraries could be, given adequate support, to the people of New York.

The centerpiece of this group of writings is, of course, my ALA Inaugural Address, "Data Bank Is Two Four-Letter Words." I worked on it longer and harder than on anything else I have written, but for some reason no library periodical seemed prepared to pick up this piece for publication (not even *LJ!*), perhaps because it was too long. Interestingly, one library school (in Britain!) wrote asking me for a copy, and later informed me that it was being used as required reading for one course there. The paper was, I believe, the first real attempt to focus ALA's and the profession's attention on the vital matter of national information policy—an area in which I felt it important for us to exercise some influence, if not leadership. At the recent (1991) White House Conference on Library and Information Services national information policy was still a very hot issue, but it was clear that our efforts to influence it had not progressed as far as they should have in the intervening 14 years since that inaugural address in Detroit.

The last item in this section, from the 1980s, continues a concern that was apparent in the California speech in 1976—and well before that in the pages of *LJ*. I was asked by John Berry to do an assessment of the achievements of the National Commission on Libraries and Information Science since its inception. Judging from the response, either nobody gave a damn about NCLIS or "Our Commission, Our Omissions" was the most resounding failure I had ever penned. I received two letters from librarians but there was not one response in *LJ*.

Some years later, however, in 1988, the ALA Executive Board, concerned (no, angered) by recent statements by NCLIS chair Jerald Newman and other NCLIS members, asked the Washington Office and the ALA Legislation Committee to report on the history and effectiveness of the National Commission. The resulting 26-page report (plus extensive appendices) declared that "The most complete assessment of NCLIS, and one which summarizes published views to that time, is the *Library Journal* article by Eric Moon, 'Our Commission, Our Omissions'." The article is quoted throughout the ALA report, the apparent dull thud of 1984 still producing reverberations four years later.

A Clear Choice

"It will become, I suspect, harder and harder to be both a Goldwater Republican and a friend of the library." This comment was made by Dr. Robert A. Dentler of the Institute of Urban Affairs, Teachers College, Columbia University, in a paper delivered to the Westchester Library Association conference in May, 1964.

Dr. Dentler raised what he called "five outrageous questions about suburban libraries." He expressed the belief "that suburban libraries, like most other public library systems, will come for the remainder of this century to require increasingly massive state and federal aid in order to adapt to changing conditions." His implication, clearly, was that if Senator Goldwater becomes President such aid is not likely to be forthcoming.

This set us to examining the political record. As far as the major political parties are concerned the recorded evidence reveals no great chasm. In 1960 the platforms of both parties included a good word for libraries. The Republican platform said: "Toward the goal of fullest educational opportunity for every American, we pledge. . . . Support of efforts to make adequate library facilities available to all our citizens." The Democrats, in their 1960 platform, pledged "further Federal support . . . for libraries." If the Democratic statement is rather less equivocal than the Republican, let us not quibble about that—equivocation in platform writing is a fact of life. In their 1964 platforms the parties still remained somewhat in harmony—neither one even mentioned libraries. But there has been strong bipartisan support for most library legislation in Congress in recent years, and we must assume that it is still there.

So we have to get beyond the parties to the individuals who are running for President and Vice President (remember, Dr. Dentler's comment refers specifically to Goldwater Republicans).

Reprinted by permission from *Library Journal,* October 15, 1964. Copyright © 1964, Reed Publishing, USA.

Let's take a look at the record of the four candidates on a few specific pieces of legislation of vast importance to libraries, and on which there were roll-call votes.

The Library Services and Construction Act of 1964 was passed by a vote of 89-7 in the Senate; clearly, it received support from a very large majority of both parties. But not, as Senator Humphrey's campaign chorus has it, from Senator Goldwater. He was one of the seven dissenters. Senator Humphrey, who in 1960 had been a sponsor of the bill to extend the old Library Services Act, voted for LSCA in 1964. Representative Miller did not vote when the House passed LSCA, but according to the *Congressional Record* of January 21, 1964, he was recorded by the clerk as paired against the bill. President Johnson, of course, was in no position to vote, but when he signed the legislation on February 11, he said: "There are few Acts of Congress which I sign with more pleasure, and certainly more hope, than this new Library Services and Construction Act. . . . The library is the best training ground for enlightenment that rational man has ever conceived."

The Higher Education Facilities Act passed the House in 1963 by a vote of 107-56. Again, Representative Miller did not vote, but this time he announced for the bill. In the Senate, Humphrey voted for the measure which received strong bipartisan support, passing by 60-19. Senator Goldwater was not only one of the 19 against the bill but he also submitted an amendment which would have eliminated $900 million in grants for academic facilities. He was still, thankfully, in the minority, and his amendment was heavily defeated.

The National Defense Education Act was first passed in 1958. In the Senate both Johnson and Humphrey voted for it. In the House, again Miller did not vote. Senator Goldwater, of course, voted against it, but he then launched into a curiously inconsistent record on NDEA in the years to follow. In 1961, when a bill to extend the NDEA (as well as the impacted areas education program) passed the Senate by 80-7, Goldwater voted for it. Two years later he was back to his original position, and on October 8, 1963 did not vote, but was paired against a bill authorizing new grants for vocational education, a three-year extension of NDEA, and federal aid to impacted areas.

Finally, the Economic Opportunity Act. This is by no means library legislation, but there is no doubt, in Dr. Dentler's words, that it can help libraries "adapt to changing conditions." President Johnson's position on this war on poverty hardly needs to be mentioned. In the Senate, Humphrey voted for the legislation; Goldwater flew in specially from Arizona to vote against it. And in the House, Miller not only voted against it, but supported a motion by Virginia's Howard Smith which, had it been successful, would have killed the bill.

One could add much more, but on these four crucial pieces of legislation, each of which has, or can have, a vital impact on library service in this country, the position of at least three of the four candidates is crystal clear. President Johnson and Senator Humphrey have demonstrated, time and again, in words and actions, their support for library services and their awareness that the kind of progress which is urgently needed is only possible with greater aid from both federal and state sources. Senator Goldwater certainly has no record to indicate support for library legislation, and he has demonstrated, time and again, in words and actions, that he is opposed to all forms of federal aid to education, including libraries. Representative Miller's position is the cloudiest of the four. The *Congressional Quarterly* recently said: "Miller has voted consistently against federal aid to secondary education. His record on federal aid to higher education is mixed." We can only add that his record on library legislation is almost nonexistent.

Magazines of many other professions have taken political positions at election time, but no library periodical, to our knowledge, has done so. We propose to make a dent in what we regard as a lamentable record of unnecessary neutrality.

Let it be clear that the choice between the two major parties as such is no concern of ours here. Both parties, as we have said, have strongly supported legislation affecting libraries, and in the election of individual Congressmen and Senators there are too many factors, including local ones, influencing the librarian-citizen's vote to make generalities on a party basis valid. Perhaps our publication—in this issue—of a lead article by a Republican Congressman will make it the more obvious that we are not waving any particular party banner.

The Presidential election is another matter. Even if one discounts all other issues, many of which are of frightening concern to all of us as individuals, we feel that we have a strong responsibility to speak out on an election in which the candidates offer us "a clear choice" on the future direction and health of library service in the United States. On these grounds alone, this magazine must declare for President Johnson and Senator Humphrey, because we do believe, with Dr. Dentler, that libraries will require "increasingly massive federal and state aid" and that they must "adapt to changing conditions" if they are to fulfill their proper role in society. If Senator Goldwater becomes President, we cannot feel sanguine that these things are likely to happen.

Voices on Vietnam?

Dissent—or more particularly, the lack of adequate representation of dissenting voices in library collections—has often been a topic of discussion in these pages. But what of librarians themselves? As citizens concerned with social issues they seem unable or unwilling to escape from anonymity; as dissenters they are scarcely visible.

True, a few did turn out to demonstrate when Maxwell Taylor spoke during the ALA Conference in San Francisco, though the librarian few were well outnumbered by the peacefully passionate youth of the Bay Area.

As the U.S. government's Vietnam "policy" malingers on, taking those defensive bombs ever nearer the China border, ruining the land from which a peasant people draws its meager sustenance, alienating our friends abroad as well as heating up even our cooler cold-war opponents, the indignation and protest at home begins more and more noticeably to swell.

The voices of opposition to the Administration's nebulous policies come from an incredible number of directions. Demonstrations have been held and statements made by churchmen, civil rights groups, teachers, housewives, veterans, writers, businessmen, the academic world (faculty and students alike), and a host of others. Sadly and strikingly absent thus far among the voices of dissent have been representatives of major segments of the book world of America—publishers, booksellers, and librarians.

We have noticed before when public protests have been made—even in areas closely related to library interests, such as censorship—that while the names of writers, publishers, editors, illustrators, and photographers can be counted on to appear in support of such statements, the names of

---

Reprinted by permission from *Library Journal,* October 15, 1967. Copyright © 1967, Reed Publishing, USA.

librarians have stood out only because of their rarity. Among the possible reasons for this phenomenon are:

First, that because librarians properly assert that the library is neutral ground—in the sense that it represents (or should represent) all sides of public issues—the conclusion has been drawn that librarians themselves are all neutral, and they are therefore rarely asked to participate in public protest.

Second, that librarians really do not care, that their concern with social, political, and international issues is less than that of other members of society or members of other professions.

We are not prepared to accept the latter grim conclusion, nor to believe—if the first of the assumptions above has any validity—that the anonymity of librarians among the voices of dissent need continue.

This matter came up a week or two ago when we heard that a group of prominent publishers was preparing a statement opposing the Administration's policies on Vietnam. They intended gathering the names (and financial support) of several hundred individual people in the publishing and book trade fraternity. Why, we asked, not make this a united front on the part of the book world? Librarians and publishers may have had their disagreements on other matters, but the public and private sectors might well find some common ground in this conflict. Why not ask librarians too?

How many are there, we were asked, who are prepared to put their names—and their cash (perhaps $10-$15 a head to finance a full-page ad in the *New York Times*)—on the line? We said we didn't know, but we imagined there were quite a few, and that we were prepared to find out more precisely. This editorial's purpose is to do just that.

The statement being prepared by our publisher friends will be a broad one, appealing to President Johnson to stop the bombing of North Vietnam and to start serious and purposeful negotiations for an end to the conflict. The statement is, in essence, an attempt to add to the chorus of other responsible citizens from the worlds of business, the professions, and the arts, the voices of those men and women of the book world who can no longer tolerate in silence the Government's apparent conclusion that the Vietnam conflict will yield only to military "solutions."

Any librarian who is prepared to support and sign such a statement is asked to send his name and address to the editor of *Library Journal*. As soon as it is completed, a copy of the statement will be forwarded to all respondents, so that they may see it before making a final commitment.

The Central Fact of Our Times

I am willing to bet that, even among dedicated friends of libraries—a phrase which, in its broader sense, must include library trustees—one could produce a whole rainbow of answers to the simple question: What is a library?

I am willing to bet also that a good many of the answers would be serious underestimates or devaluations, if not of what a library is, of what it should be. Some answers might convey an image of the library as a place of polite recreation to provide for the leisure hours of bored housewives; some would give a picture of it as a sort of mass study hall for desperate students; others might see it as a kind of subsidiary educational instrument.

I can almost sense the doubts already. "What is a library?" some of you may be saying, is a pretty mundane topic. Surely everyone agrees about what a library is, or should be; what it does, or should do; what its purpose is, or should be. Somehow I doubt it. I can still hear ALA president Ed Castagna saying: "It should be safe to assume that everyone in this group has known from childhood what librarians do. But it is sometimes surprising to find big gaps between what the practitioners think they do and what the consumers think is being done."

Even people who have lived a good part of their lives in and around libraries will nurture very divergent images. Even the editors of our two most widely read library periodicals see the library through quite different lenses.

Kathleen Molz, editor of the *Wilson Library Bulletin,* describes the library as "a peaceable kingdom where the lion lies down with the lamb, and does not devour him." In the article in which she said that, she was disagreeing, politely but pointedly, with my earlier description of the

---

Originally a talk to the Trustees and Friends Luncheon at the Alabama Library Association Conference, Mobile, Alabama, May 7, 1965, this article is reprinted from the *Alabama Librarian* 16: 3-8, October 1965.

library as "a hotbed, a dangerous, exciting, challenging jungle. No soporific place, no place for easy equanimity or myopic self-delusion . . . [a place where one finds] the bared claws of ideologies, the bared teeth of conflicting beliefs."

I believe it was John Ciardi, the brilliant poet and *Saturday Review* columnist, who called the public library—approvingly—"revolutionary headquarters, the most dangerous place in town." I must say that the historical record seems to lend more support to the aggressive masculine views of Ciardi and Moon than to Miss Molz's alternative blend of femininity and Biblical language. To illustrate, there is no need to go back through all the ages to the dreadful destruction of the library at Alexandria which wiped out the records of a civilization. Nor is it necessary to go back even a century and a half to an act of British barbarism, the burning of the Library of Congress in 1814.

The more recent record will show that American libraries abroad have been violently attacked on no less than 80 occasions since 1947. In more than 30 countries around the globe the libraries of the United States Information Agency have been stoned, burned, bombed, or demolished; and last year, new records in library devastation were set, with somewhere between 15 and 20 such incidents. The most crucial climax to any of these incidents occurred in Indonesia, where a complete takeover of all USIS libraries was effected by the government of that country early this year.

Now, a great many people, legislators and others, have expressed deep concern over these repeated depredations, with some obvious justification. I do not, myself, regard attacking libraries as a particularly constructive or desirable sport. Nevertheless—and I hope you will not regard this as a seditious, un-American thought—my own concern over these events has been tempered curiously with a kind of satisfaction and even hope.

Why? Well, in the first place, these attacks are a very clear admission by some elements in Indonesia, Bolivia, Egypt, Yugoslavia, and various other countries, that they are afraid of these libraries and what they contain. They are, of course, right to be afraid. What these libraries contain and promote is propaganda (that is not intrinsically a disreputable word)—propaganda for what we believe is a better way of life, a better system of government. Books, films, and other informational materials are the weapons of this propaganda effort; the library is the arsenal.

There is, as I suggested at the outset, nothing new about attacks on books and libraries. Censorship is older than printing by many hundreds of years. Closed societies, dictatorships, insecure people and their representatives, have always—very early in the game—tried to put a clamp on dissident opinions; that is, opinions other than those they hold or share. Widespread ignorance is the ally of such governments or people, widespread knowledge their deadliest enemy. And books, magazines, and other communication media not only contain the world's store of knowledge but also the world's rainbow of opinions and beliefs—all the "isms" and "ologies," all the heresies and great and vulnerable "truths." This is what Ciardi meant about the most dangerous place in town; this is what I was referring to when I called the library a jungle.

Fear and suspicion of the library and of its potential impact upon society are not, of course, foreign monopolies. It can, it does, happen here. It is the same inherent fear and suspicion which provide the basic motivation for the attacks upon libraries by the Birch Society and other domestic extremist groups, that prompts their efforts to restrict what shall appear on the shelves of school and public libraries. These armies of library invaders usually march under a flag of protective and patriotic righteousness, but what they really want to protect and perpetuate is their own narrow vision of life and what they mistakenly call Americanism. Their basic objective is to prevent the exposure of other people to alternative ideas and opinions. Their success would mean the defeat of all that America—and certainly all that the public library—has ever stood for.

Southern public libraries seem not so often to have fallen under the lengthening shadow of the Birch tree as have their counterparts in the Far West, the Midwest, and the Northeast. But libraries in the South have nevertheless had more than their share of pressures; although the violations have seemed to be of a different kind, at base they have the same motivation: the preservation of a kind of status quo of ignorance because knowledge breeds a less easy acceptance of things as they are.

A notable example of fear of the library's arsenal of knowledge and the tragicomic results of that fear is the case of "Judge" Leander Perez of Plaquemines Parish in Louisiana. He refused to allow the librarian of that parish to buy any book by or about Franklin or Eleanor Roosevelt, any book about or published by the United Nations or any of its agencies, any book by a Negro or which might reflect Negroes in a favorable light—and imposed a host of other limitations to exclude anything which might conflict with his own rigidly narrow ideas. This is local totalitarianism at its most obvious, absurd, and repellent.

Among the fearful also are those who have burned or bombed the nascent libraries being established by the Mississippi Summer Project workers in the Freedom Schools in that state. What real distinction is there between this kind of activity and that of communist mobs in Indonesia?

I am well aware that I have chosen two extreme examples. However, without the violence, but for not very different reasons, a great many Negroes have, for many years, been denied access to strong collections, or to libraries at all, in some areas of the country. Only ten years ago, two-thirds of all Southern Negroes were entirely without library service. I am also aware, of course, that a great many white people in many areas of the country have similarly been without library service, but the reasons for this have been somewhat different—and I'll get to those in a moment.

The last decade has brought great, although insufficient, improvement to the situation I have been describing. And one of the reasons for the improvement may well have been the recognition, increasingly, of the library's potential. What is even better is that this recognition, clear for so long to those who would restrict the library's power and influence, has also dawned upon those who are still seeking a place in society's sun. Thus libraries in the sixties have sometimes become targets of sit-in or read-in demonstrations—actions which are themselves a recognition that knowledge, and access to it, are like food or the right to vote, basic to the betterment of the human condition.

When such a sit-in occurred in 1961 at the public library in Danville, Virginia—to take just one of many examples—the Danville City Council committed the ultimate absurdity: it closed the library altogether rather than admit Negroes. Even the *Richmond News-Leader*, whose James Jackson Kilpatrick could scarcely be depicted, even by his worst enemies, as an integrationist, commented:

> In Danville and elsewhere, the fairly incredible view is being expounded that it would be better to close the libraries than to admit Negroes to them. Such a position is simply absurd . . . a LIBRARY is something special. The treasures a good library can make available do not belong to a community except in a narrow and legalistic sense; the accumulated inheritance of the mind belongs to mankind. To deny Negro citizens free and equal access to books is an indefensible act of discrimination. The City of Richmond recognized this more than 15 years ago, and never has had reason to regret the policy that now admits both races to our Library freely. We hope Danville will consider this course.

Danville did, of course, reconsider after a while and after playing around with something called "vertical integration," which meant removing the furniture from the library, declared itself open for business and use by the public at large.

Another, more pervasive, subtle, and often almost unconscious form of discrimination (not inherently racial) has been at work in perhaps the majority of our public libraries—North and South, East and West—for a long, long time. Despite the noble, and sincere, pronouncements of the library profession—in the Library Bill of Rights and elsewhere—that libraries shall be available to all people and that they shall contain material representing "all points of view concerning the problems and issues of our times, international, national, and local," many libraries, in fact, do not measure up on either count. A majority of our public library services (and book stocks) have been geared, if not exclusively, certainly emphatically, to the expressed needs and demands of one major stratum of our society (in essence, of course, another minority group) which might be broadly described as the middle-class.

The kind of effect this has had upon library collections was aptly summarized by *LJ*'s assistant editor, John Berry, after he completed a survey recently of public library holdings of a number of periodicals which, in some cases, are the only adequate representation of certain contemporary "dissident" opinions. He said: "We are left with the feeling that public libraries in the United States continue, very cautiously, to cling to the middle of the road."

Some of the reasons for this state of affairs are fairly obvious. It is the middle sector of society which has traditionally made most use of public library service; so, like businesses, we have gone on putting our limited resources where the largest returns are (or where we have thought them to be). But the shaping of public library service more and more to the most vociferously expressed needs becomes a self-perpetuating process. And this process has been aided yet more (sometimes unconsciously, as I said before) by the fact that most librarians—and of course a great many trustees and friends of libraries—are themselves products of this middle layer of society; and many of them, naturally, envisage the library, its collections and purpose, in pretty much the same way as do the traditional patrons the library has acquired over the years.

Ralph Blasingame, former Pennsylvania State Librarian, put into a nutshell the basic problem and the ultimately suicidal effects for libraries if they allow this pattern to continue:

Communication with the middlebrow class is easy for us; with the lowbrow it is difficult and unrewarding. Yet, clearly, the library's atmosphere of "culture" puts a rather small percentage of the former and almost none of the latter at ease. What if the trend to serve the few continues while the percentage of non-users in the population rises? The public library, to keep its claim to tax support, may then have to shift its entire focus. It might, for example, become an arm of government with the primary purpose of supplying the bureaucracy with information. The matter of dealing with the needs of the non-reader may then pass into the hands of an agency not now in existence. The library, in these circumstances, might alternatively become a cultural high water mark and guarantee its failure as a socially useful institution. In many communities, the library has already achieved this status; indeed, it was begun as such: that is, as an evidence of culture, not as a creative or moving force.

Society today is alive and *humming* with change. What seems not yet totally obvious to everyone connected with libraries is that some of our accepted concepts of what library service is all about are also going to have to change at the same rapid tempo—or maybe faster, since in many respects we start way behind other social institutions. If such drastic change does not come about, if libraries do not become what Blasingame calls "a creative force" in society, they can expect to be neglected and under-supported, comparatively, as they have always been, in general throughout our public library history.

This is where I get, belatedly, to the reasons why I take some mild cheer from the unpleasant things which have been happening to some of our USIS libraries.

First, I cherish the hope that patriotic Americans, as well as being incensed by these incidents, will glimpse in this overseas mirror the reflection and the danger of some of their own anti-library and book-restrictive actions on the home front. Less tentative than this hope are the signs that the awareness of the effectiveness of books and libraries is no longer all on the negative side of the Sukarnos and the Nassers, the Perez's and the Birchers. There is nothing like a crisis to wake up a democratic government, and nothing like attacks on government property to make them do something about it. I believe it is quite possible that some legislators, who have rarely whispered the word "library" in public before, have been persuaded, by virtue of the library's recent persistent position as a central and primary target, that libraries are a more potent weapon than they have hitherto considered.

Such negative lessons have not been necessary around the White House for some years. Under President Kennedy, libraries finally began to emerge from a long twilight of federal neglect. JFK it was who said: "The library is not only the custodian of our heritage but the key to progress and the advancement of knowledge." Under President Johnson, libraries are moving into more fiscal sunlight than some of them are suddenly prepared for. When he signed the Library Services and Construction Act, LBJ said: "The central fact of our times is this: Books and ideas are the most effective weapons against intolerance and ignorance."

Today, really for the first time in our history on such a massive scale, books are being enrolled in an all-out war on the basic enemies of mankind—poverty, ignorance, intolerance, and all the evils that stem from these human diseases. Legislation already passed and legislation under way will pour, in the next few years, over half a billion dollars of new money into books and libraries.

Not all librarians or trustees are jumping for joy at their new-found recognition. There are a good many people who are afraid of this federal outpouring. They see all around them the spectre of federal control. The truth of the matter is that the federal authorities are equally as afraid of this spectre, and they have bent over backwards to avoid even a hint of it, certainly so far as the books provided with money are concerned. True, there have been *some* controls such as the insistence that state and local governments accede to the Civil Rights Act and make federally-supported services available equally to *all* people. But this is control with a broadening purpose; it is the limiting kind of control we should be afraid of.

The federal agencies have refused consistently to produce lists of books or materials eligible for purchase under the National Defense Education Act; in fact specific guidance has been absent to the point where they have appeared to encourage waste rather than expose themselves to the charge of control. When books were wanted for the Appalachia program, it was the librarians of that region who were asked to select them. When books were wanted for the Job Corps, professional librarians at the Boston Public Library were asked to produce a suitable list. When a broad selection of books was wanted for the War on Poverty, Sargent Shriver brought together top librarians to select them.

Apart from the selection of materials, the most rigid control of library expenditure has also not come from the federal level. Speaking from personal experience, as one who has been on the receiving end of federal funds, Walter Brahm, State Librarian of Connecticut and former Ohio State Librarian, said recently that federal control is "practically nonexistent... As far as Washington goes, state libraries enjoy more freedom and enjoy more flexibility in the expenditure of federal library funds that the states themselves permit after the funds are received, or with funds appropriated to match them from local or state sources. No, it is the state and local governments," he said, "who hamstring the expenditure of federal money with the same straitjacket in which they imprison their own funds."

Despite these sentiments, with which I agree, I do recognize the great danger of using books and libraries as any kind of government weapon, for whatever cause. But we *must* recognize that democracy is in itself a dangerous way of living. So long as government power and money are used to broaden the scope of what is available and to ensure that it is available equally to all, we are headed in the right direction. We are headed for the kind of wisdom that Leo Rosten described when he said that "wisdom is not much more than the capacity to confront dangerous ideas with equanimity." To restrict a library's holdings to any narrow set of beliefs or to one side of any or every question is no better than rewriting history (and this is still being done because of textbook adoption pressures in some states). To restrict library service, consciously or unconsciously, to any one section of the public, is to maintain for the excluded a kind of intellectual concentration camp.

To get practical for a moment (why is it that some people only consider you practical when you talk about money?), it is not, of course, only the kind of idealistic or political factors I have been describing which have restricted what is available in our public libraries. We have also lived through a continuous history of economic neglect of public libraries, and certainly Southern libraries have suffered more from fiscal starvation than have many others. Recent unofficial estimates from the US Office of Education, for example, showing a ranking of states by per capita expenditure on public libraries (based on a 1962 survey), found Alabama in 49th place—in actual fact, last among the states, since Idaho did not furnish figures for this survey. Also, South Carolina was 48th, West Virginia 47th, and Mississippi 43rd. Alabama's per capita expenditure was 66 cents; the national average $2.15. In short, most of the Southern states are still well at the bottom of the list when it comes to public support of public libraries.

It is logical that they should also be at the bottom of the heap in the library resources that they can make available to the public. The ALA *Access to Public Libraries* study (although dismally discredited in many of its other findings) did present useful figures showing the regional distribution of library resources. Again, the South was the exceptional area. The Southern and the North Central States, for example, each account for about 30 percent of the total US population. But while the North Central states have 35 percent of the nation's volume and account for 33 percent of the national expenditure on libraries, the South has only 17 percent of the volumes and 15 percent of the expenditures—less than half in each case.

I quote these depressing facts perhaps only to underline and emphasize the obvious—that the South has further to go, and will need more help, than most other parts of the country if it is to achieve some kind of public library adequacy. Even in some of the states where libraries have been more generously supported, librarians know that their services are doing little better than standing still in the face of the many explosions—of population, of knowledge, of the student body. They are going to have to run much faster to have a hope of catching up. If this is true, and all the evidence points that way, the states where the backlog of neglect is longer will have to fly.

I do not mean to overlook or undervalue in any way the herculean efforts that many individuals have made at all levels, national, state, and local, and in all parts of the country. I don't mean to ignore that spotlight that the Library Services Act threw on the rural library deserts, nor the way in which it strengthened state library influence and moved the thinking of many librarians and trustees toward cooperation, coordination, system development, and a broader concept of library service.

I do mean to insist, however, that the battle has hardly begun. While the federal aid will help tremendously, it can't solve all the problems alone, and we shall have to keep in focus the fact that the needs and demands upon library service are likely to grow even faster than federal aid. For example, while the money poured into school and academic libraries will undoubtedly take some of the student load off public libraries eventually, at the same time the new efforts to eradicate poverty and equalize opportunity will put back many new and heavy burdens and many new pressures where they belong—square on the shoulders of libraries.

If public libraries are to play the part they have been allotted in shaping LBJ's Great Society, they will have to be much more strenuously supported—and not at the federal level alone. Even at that level, federal support of public library service, compared to federal support of libraries in more formal educational areas, is still miserably low. But the weakest of the three levels, beyond any measure of doubt, if one looks at the picture nationwide, is the state government level. Nor has local government, in general, any proud record to boast of. After 100 years of public library development, local government left us with yawning chasms where no library service existed, or where what was available barely deserved the name of library service.

It took us many years to discover that economic growth of the nation was unlikely to continue unless it was aided by educational growth. Today, education is still fighting for fiscal support, but it is getting it a bit more spontaneously than ever before. What we have not yet learned fully is that formal education is not the whole story: it covers too small a part of the human span of life. And also, the world progresses too fast for us to be able any longer to stop learning at 16 or 18 or 25. Education has got to be a permanent, continuing process, and one of the most vital elements in the continuity of that process is library service.

We have not yet—and by we, I mean librarians and trustees in particular—been sufficiently insistent in pushing for a higher priority for libraries. We know now that education, although not expensive if we take the value of the product fully into account, costs a lot of money. We have got to be adamant in talking to governmental authorities and to the general public that libraries, also not expensive if we understand what they can do, cost a lot of money too. And we must be insistent, as well, that libraries are not frills, but are as essential as parks or roads or sewers. Our mental health is as important as our physical well-being.

But in getting tough and competitive, as we must, we must also be careful about what we compete with. Janice Kee, Wisconsin's State Librarian, made the essential point at a recent conference: "I think we cannot afford to engage in competition for funds for education. We cannot afford the folly of fragmentation of educational objectives. I do not mean that special interest groups (and librarians are one of them) should not lend their maximum effort to gain support for their particular function. I do mean that these separate interests should find their place in a great harmonious voice that can affect educational expansion and improvement in every part of the country."

It is not, you see, only in relation to fiscal provision that we must change the scope and character of our thinking about libraries. We must be less parochial in thinking about separate types of libraries, or of communities, areas, regions, or states. ALA president Edwin Castagna has pointed the direction in which our planning and thinking must go:

> Traditionally, libraries were separate, isolated units, each serving a community, a campus, a school, a business. Theoretically they were related because they all belonged to the great world of

books and ideas. But actually there was no real relationship that was meaningful for most of the users of library service. The ideal situation, real access to the total body of the nation's pool of knowledge, was a dream, possibly to be realized in the distant future. But now . . . what is theoretically and mechanically possible is the creation of a network to include all the nation's libraries, linked together in an organized, systematic way, with the objective of getting knowledge, information, and ideas to people.

There, I think, is the only objective which is worth shooting for, which should be at the forefront of the mind of every library trustee and every friend of libraries. That goal, the nation's total library resources easily accessible to all the people of the nation, may still seem to be far off in the future—and if you don't focus on it, it will stay out there in some distant twilight zone. But actually, you have very little choice. The future now moves in on the present so fast that unambitious planning for a here-and-now today can get you nowhere except into a quickly superseded, dying yesterday.

Hungry and Not Very Scrupulous Lions

I cannot refrain from observing, at the outset, that the majority of our libraries still cling tenaciously to the middle of the rainbow, and in doing so, for a long period of time, they have left many of our services far shorter of one of the profession's most cherished objectives—as the Library Bill of Rights puts it: "the fullest practical provision of material representing all points of view concerning the problems of our time, international national and local." We are, in fact, so far from that objective that I know I am safe in declaring that only a very small minority of our libraries today give even minimal representation to the views and philosophies, for example, of Mao Tse-Tung, the Black Muslims, the Birch Society, or even the Beat school of poets and novelists.

Censorship is older than printing by many centuries. What is new is the intensity and frequency of attacks upon libraries. I mention these attacks, not to make you feel sorry for yourselves and your fellow afflicted librarians, but to support the perhaps paradoxical view that, disturbing and uncomfortable as all this aggressiveness may seem, it may really be a very healthy and encouraging development from the point of view of our profession. What can be seen in all this sordidness, if you look through a clear, cold glass, is a quite concrete, if not very pretty, illustration of growing political awareness of the importance and effectiveness of libraries, of their potential for effecting or assisting change, of whatever kind, upon society.

Not all the new political awareness, of course, has been expressed as negatively as in the instances I have cited. The reverse of the coin may be seen in the early efforts of civil rights workers in the South to establish libraries to aid their cause and nourish their workers and constituents; or in the "sit-in" or "read-in" attempts to open up libraries to readers who

---

Originally the keynote speech at the Ohio Library Association Conference, Toledo, October 13, 1966, this article is reprinted from the *Ohio Library Association Bulletin* 37:5-6, 8-14, January 1967.

for many years have been denied access to them; or in the picketing of libraries, college and public, by students who are tired of being regarded as a library "problem."

Political candidates at various levels in different parts of the country have begun to take up libraries as a serious issue in their campaigns. In New York City, Ed Koch, a Democratic-Liberal candidate from Greenwich Village for City Council sent out a press release headed "Koch Warns of Peril to N.Y. Public Library System; Forecasts Continued Cut in Services." The Koch statement focused on the alarming number of staff vacancies in the New York Public Library, the difficulties caused by Mayor Lindsay's job freeze, the delays in processing books, and the curtailment of library services this summer, when 17 of NYPL's branches were closed down (actually, four were reopened after loud public protest).

This is not the stuff that political campaigns have traditionally been made of. Formal education has been made an issue for quite some time but libraries, until fairly recently, merely ranked with sewers and parks, highways and rent control, welfare and sales taxes. This new political interest in our activities appears to have seeped from the top down. The word "library" has been a common one in the White House lexicon for most of this decade.

It was under President Kennedy that libraries at last began, perhaps, truly to emerge from the long twilight of federal neglect. JFK called the library "not only the custodian of our heritage but the key to progress and the advancement of knowledge." Under President Johnson, libraries are moving into more fiscal sunlight than some librarians' economy-accustomed eyes can suddenly stand. In fiscal 1966, authorized federal expenditures for library services, construction, and programs totaled $610 million. When he signed the Library Services and Construction Act, LBJ said: "The central fact of our times is this: Books and ideas are the most effective weapons against intolerance and ignorance."

LBJ's statement may be tinged with political hyperbole—I would say that the central fact of our times is that everyone on earth lives daily under the threat of potential annihilation—but, taken in context, the President's statement is not too irrelevant, and is certainly of major importance to the library profession, because here we have, from the highest pulpit of our government, words indicating that libraries are an integral factor in the social and economic planning and development of our nation. Actually, one of the great lessons to be learned from the developing nations of the world—as my friend John Berry pointed out in an *LJ* editorial not long ago, and as State Librarian Joe Shubert indicated in a talk to the Montana

Library Association a few months ago—is that libraries have a real role to play in the mobilization of a society for its own improvement, but that they will only be able to play their part successfully if they get in early and at the highest levels, and with full knowledge of their own plans and objectives.

But not all the members of our profession are ready to accept the challenge and the opportunity implicit in the President's words. Their new-found recognition has not set all librarians and library trustees jumping for joy. Many cower back from the federal outpouring; they cannot see the purse for the strings; they see nothing but the spectre of federal control. They forget that those in federal authority have been reared by the same social, educational, economic and political system, conditioned by the same fears. And they ignore the ample evidence in certain essential areas—for example, the selection of books purchased locally with federal money—that the federal authorities have bent over backwards, to the point of absurd wastefulness, to avoid even a hint of "control."

This is not to say that there have been no controls. There is, to cite one example, the federal insistence that state and local governments accede to the provisions of the Civil Rights Act and make federally-supported services equally available to *all* people. But this is surely in accord with our professional objectives and, in any case, this is control with a broadening purpose; it is the limiting kind of control we should be afraid of.

The difference seems to me to have been spelled out rather cogently by Harold Howe II, the U.S. Commissioner of Education—and in the following quotation you can read "public libraries" for "public schools" without any loss of relevance: "Localism in education gives communities the right to have both good and bad schools, and the right has been liberally exercised in both directions. What the federal government is now about—and what the states have been about for some years—is to curtail the right to have bad schools."

All of this leads me to the central assertion of this paper—"the central fact of our times" for libraries—which is that the most fundamental and far-reaching changes in the structure and patterns of library service in this country will be brought about, in the next several years, not by computers or any brand of technology, not by "cooperative" projects, so much as by legislative and political action. And, increasingly, that political action will come down from the highest levels of government—federal and state—rather than upward from local units of government.

New functions needed to meet new situations are neglected by most local units, and old functions are conducted without benefit of new techniques. By default, initiatives have commonly been left to more resourceful federal forces. Cast in an archaic mold, unable to cope with new issues, many—if not most—local governments are centers of strenuous resistance to change.

Sweeping initiatives by the national government, and to a lesser degree by a few state governments, have helped to fill the partial vacuum created by failures at the local level. Resulting changes have altered the basic character of the American federal system. Local governments tend to become administrative mechanisms for implementation of national policies, rather than dynamic centers of authority in their own individual right.

That sad verdict is not mine, though I share it. It comes from a recent report by the Committee for Economic Development, an influential nonprofit research and educational organization of 200 top business executives and educators. The report calls for a major modernization of local government, including the reduction of the present 80,000 local units to no more than 16,000. I wonder how many librarians have read it—or even have it on their shelves?

I say I wonder, but I really know the answer, at least in general terms. Few librarians will have read this report because, to so many of them, political reorganization or infighting are divorced from the proprieties, even the realities, of professional life. Henry Reining, Jr., dean of the public administration school at the University of Southern California, said recently that library politics has too often meant staying out of politics. The attitude has been that the library is no place for fierce tactics but a place of professional decorum. "Unfortunately, these tendencies have put the library in the cellar of the house of government," said Reining. He argued that public libraries have lost considerable money by trying to keep their local control, that they have consistently been at the bottom of government spending. . . .

The whole job can't be done in the District of Columbia, and of course it can't be done either by a handful of leaders alone. The profession as a whole needs to see and understand the changes that have come about and the further changes that will inevitably come in the political and power structure of library service. Only by being fully involved can we hope to influence the direction of change as it affects libraries. Otherwise, change will be imposed upon us without benefit of our professional knowledge or our understanding of local needs.

But being involved will only help if we are equipped to give both advice and *answers.* There is little doubt that we are less well-equipped than we should be. We are hazy about our objectives, divided in our professional ranks by pettiness and jealousies, and abysmally deficient in reliable research data about our operations. We draft high-sounding, generalized documents which we call standards, but we have little scientific evidence to support our declarations of needs. Ed Castagna made a stab at providing us with a few answers with his *National Inventory of Library Needs,* but this was, perhaps necessarily, a fragmentary, rushed, and not altogether convincing piece of work.

Whether or not we are ready with the answers, the questions are already beginning. The President, himself, has acknowledged that "money alone will not do the job." He said: "We need intelligent advice and planning to see that our millions are spent wisely and well. We need to take a close look at the future of our libraries. We need to ask some serious questions."

He asked a few himself: "What part can libraries play in the Nation's rapidly developing communications and information-exchange networks? . . . As we face this information revolution, we want to be satisfied that our funds do not preserve library practices which are already obsolete.

"Are our federal efforts to assist libraries intelligently administered or are they too fragmented among separate programs and agencies? Are we getting the most benefit for the taxpayer's dollar spent?"

To answer some of his questions, LBJ appointed (in September 1966) a President's Committee on Libraries and a National Advisory Commission on Libraries, and announced: "I have asked the Commission to evaluate policies, programs, and practices of public agencies and private organizations—and to recommend actions which might be taken by public and private groups to ensure an effective, efficient library system for the nation."

We now know one of the major sources from which the federal administration will gather advice and information about the nation's library services. It might be revealing to know where the President gets his advice on the composition of such advisory bodies. The National Commission is entirely dominated by representatives of research library interests and institutions of higher education. Nowhere in the list of names is there any very obvious recognition of the place in the national picture of school or public libraries, unless one accepts Carl Elliott, former

Congressman from Alabama and one of the original sponsors of the Library Services Act, as adequate representation of public library interests. Nor does the composition of the Commission make any bow to the importance of the state level in the hierarchy of library service. There is no representative of state government, a state library commission, or a state library. But I have yet to discern any indication that the profession has voiced concern to the White House about the imbalance in the Commission's membership.

The role of libraries as research facilities is obviously a matter of major concern at the federal level in view of the vast amounts of federal money which are expended on R & D. And the make-up of the Commission may be partly the result of ALA emphasis and criticism, during Robert Vosper's presidency, of federal support for libraries in this area. But if the Commission is to provide the President, in his own words, with "a national perspective on the problems that confront our Nation's libraries," it needs to be so balanced that it is itself capable of a perspective that recognizes the importance of library services of all kinds—not just those which serve research or higher education needs.

The composition of this Commission, I believe, is just one more indication of a pronounced lack of coordination, perhaps prompted by understandable opportunism, in our profession's political and legislative efforts. Libraries have for so long been invisible at higher legislative levels that one can understand the present tendency to grab what we can get when we can get it. And we need the immediate, short-range coup, to be sure. It would be reassuring, however, to be able to sense some master plan, some evidence of long-range planning and objectives behind the glittering facade of federal legislation for libraries.

We have had some powerful legislative victories in recent years, and those who have worked so hard for them are to be praised rather than criticized. Yes it would be foolish for us not to recognize that most of the library legislation is fractured along the lines of our traditional administrative walls and boundaries. We get legislation for school libraries, for public libraries, for academic libraries, for medical libraries—all in separate packages, as though these were still unrelated activities—rather than legislation for library service.

Even in these legislative packages which have been delivered, we do not always discern evidence of foresight or coordinated planning, though the Medical Library Assistance Act is a superbly-designed exception. But massive aid for school library materials is received before any funds are available to provide facilities in which these materials can be properly used or exploited. A federally-supported centralized cataloging program gets into the Higher Education Act, more perhaps because the Association of Research Libraries pushed for it than because the benefits of such a program are applicable to academic libraries alone. And even in a decade of federal support for public libraries, there is no adequate legislative recognition that the major crisis in public library service is in the metropolitan areas, where the rapid population changes have left old administrative alignments irrelevantly adrift.

There has been much talk in and around library circles about a national system or networks of libraries or statewide systems, but little of this is reflected in our political achievements to date—nor in that National Commission. The problem, at least in part, is that most of us think and act as though our present administrative structure is sacrosanct. We do not see beyond our own tight little islands. Libraries are not libraries, but college libraries, public libraries, school libraries, special libraries. If we are ever to see libraries whole, we are going to have to work back from the people who are (or should be) served by the various institutions, rather than planning always in the opposite direction. Hard as it may be to extend our concerns beyond parochial interests, we shall have more chance if we start with the library user and his needs, than if we begin with the administrative form or the type of institution.

To cite a local example, I'm quite sure that many academic librarians in Ohio are concerned that this state should have squeezed past Mississippi and Rhode Island to capture 50th place in the nation in per capita academic library operating expenditures. But how many public librarians share their academic colleagues' concern or are fighting to improve this lamentable record. It is surely in their own interests, if it has to be put on that kind of basis, to do so. Where do all those dissatisfied college students go when they can't get adequate service from the institutions in which they are enrolled? You know where they go—to public libraries. Which then complain about the student problem.

The burgeoning political interest in libraries will, unquestionably, bring about changes in the structure of librarianship, in library policies, in patterns of service. Whether these changes will be imposed—or brought about with the library profession's help and advice—will be determined by our ability to catch up with (or get ahead of) the thinking of politicians and the higher-level social and economic planners. Legislators depend upon votes for survival, and this mundane fact carries the implication that their questions are likely to be phrased more in terms of the public interest than are the questions that librarians sometimes debate among themselves.

The legislators will think of people first and the interest of institutions only secondarily.

As an example, let me cite a column written for *LJ* by former Ohio State Librarian, Walter Brahm. Brahm was writing about nonresident fees, which he called "the vestigial appendix of 19th Century library service." He pointed out that the most compelling reason presented by librarians in favor of nonresident fees is that "taxpayers of their community should not pay for another community's library service." Brahm says: "Such rationalization had merit in the days before federal and state aid. As librarians today, we place ourselves in a most untenable position if we withhold the fruits of our own taxpayers' bounty while at the same time seeking a greater share in federal and state funds. If there were a taxpayer's suit, we have some doubt that, where a library accepts state aid, the courts would uphold the legality of the fee."

Brahm goes on to report that "At a recent hearing before a state legislative committee considering an increase in state aid for libraries, the chief interest evinced by questions on the part of legislators was whether the funds would permit residents of the state to use libraries of neighboring communities wherever they found them. The library services division of the U.S. Office Education reported the same thread of interest appearing in Congressmen's questions on federal aid."

The implications of this kind of legislative questioning are, of course, vital for other than public librarians. Academic and school librarians, who are increasingly beneficiaries of state and federal aid, need to do some thinking about their attitudes and policies on community use of their institutions' facilities and resources. Some of the attitudes of college librarians were exhibited in all their gruesomeness during an all-day meeting of ACRL's College Libraries Section at the recent ALA Conference in New York. But there, again, E. J. Josey, who chaired the sessions, asked: "Could not residents of the community argue that they had a right of free access to college and university libraries receiving generous support from state and federal funds to which their taxes had contributed?"

Josey went on to cite a report by the Legislative Analyst to the Joint Legislative Committee of the California Legislature, which contended that "the university library system exists not only to serve the educational needs of students, but also is the major resource center in the state for research by resident faculty and faculties from other educational institutions, *and also for industry and other community users.*"

One of the repercussions of the new political interest in libraries is already with us: a fairly sudden and significant realignment of the power lines in librarianship which has already, to some extent, taken place, and for which we were, judging by the evidence, totally unprepared. As the federal floodgates have opened wider, it has become increasingly obvious that the dams which must control and distribute much of the emerging power are the state library agencies. It is at these points, in such national power structure as we have, that more can be done to reshape—or wreck—the future of librarianship than anywhere else in the profession.

It is, in a sense, a frightening thought. If we had planned the way things have developed over the last decade, we would have to have searched very hard to find a weaker foundation stone upon which to build our future. No one needs to tell you, in Ohio, that legislators still need to be convinced that the state library has a major coordinating and leadership function to perform in late 20th-century library service. Nobody needs either to tell you that the State Library, in this and most other states, is far from being equipped to perform that role. But we have got to cope with this fast about-face of history and unite in an effort to strengthen and support this weak link on which so much of our future hangs.

I was glad to see Bob Vosper arrange a special President's Program at the last ALA Conference focused on the state level, because it has seemed to me that the profession has far too long been behaving as though it were unaware of this crisis in our midst. Vosper, however, said that "we (and I suspect that's an editorial we) have been increasingly aware of serious disabilities at the state level." Historically, the state, he said, "has been a weak element in the total pattern." He called for a look at statewide library services to be "the next order of business for the library profession, for the several states, and for the federal government." I think it came in a little low on this proposed agenda, at least for the library profession, but it's on there now. How much gets done about it will depend on the amount of political unity and determination the library profession can bring to bear on the situation. And how far this is forthcoming will depend in turn, I guess, on the profession's own understanding of what the state's role is.

The latter was spelled out pretty clearly, it seemed to me, by one of the participants in Bob Vosper's program—Ewald B. Nyquist, deputy commissioner of education at the State University of New York in Albany. Said Nyquist:

> The role of the State is to provide diversity in leadership; to organize and coordinate an effective library system; to establish

a sound program of financial support; to provide effective coordination and distribution of funds; to establish quality controls and minimum standards for achievement, to lead in long-range planning; to conduct and cooperate in research; to stimulate innovation; to develop good informational systems on the facts and conditions of libraries and librarianship; to assist local agencies in coordinating results. The State is the key to securing a proper balance of strength amongst the local, State, and Federal agencies composing what will increasingly become a calculated interdependence. There is a bright future for complexity. No one can afford to go it alone any longer. Library service too long has been a many-splintered thing.

Nyquist was reporting on the long and frustrating history of effort to gain legislative support for New York's "3-R's" program. The first glimmer of success came in this year's Legislative session. As Nyquist put it (with help from Victor Hugo): "There is nothing like the power of an idea whose time has come." He educed several morals from his brief history of the New York library community's legislative efforts, and they are worth repeating as a capsule lesson in political principles for librarians everywhere:

1) First, there are two ways to get to the top of an oak tree: Climb it, or sit on an acorn. We tried climbing and settled for long-term incubation.
2) Persistence with a good idea pays off. A mighty oak is just a little nut that held its ground.
3) These days, education is everyone's business. Education and books are too important to be left to the sole custody of educators and librarians. In the modern day, professional people must learn to relate to the political process, to interpret the political instincts of legislators and chief executive officers, for politicians have discovered that education pays off in political income and is indispensable to the social and economic well-being of their constituents.
4) Above all there is something to be said for learning the art of insinuating a new idea into State Government without getting detected at it.

So, my message, if you have been unable to detect it in this morass of words, is simply this: As you go about reshaping your objectives, do not be too remotely or sternly professional, or too concerned with minor questions of administrative or other techniques—many of which the profession has debated tediously, without end and without profit, for more than a century. Think first of people, not institutions or institutional forms, and do your reshaping in terms of political realities and probabilities.

If librarianship is to fight its case with some hope of winning, it has got to do it—as education has, as the unions and big business have, as science has—in the political arena. It's a tough place, full of hungry and not very scrupulous lions and you can get eaten if you're not well armed and equipped. But if you stay outside the arena, you will just wither away and die listening to the crowd roar inside as others with more nerve and better equipment fight for the big prizes.

A Matter of Values

A lot of people, after recovering from the shock of seeing one of ALA's most vociferous critics elected as President, have asked me what I'm going to do. I tell them I don't know. I complained for years that membership doesn't have enough input or influence upon what happens in the corridors of ALA power, so I want to spend a good piece of my vice-presidential year finding out what members are concerned about. What I'm concerned about is not the only, nor even the main, issue.

The other thing I'm asked is: now *you* are a member of the establishment, are you too just going to move around blowing the PR horn for ALA? In short, have the critical fangs been removed by this elevation to office? The answer is NO, to both questions. But I did say, even in the days of my most vitriolic sermons from the *LJ* pulpit, and shall go on saying, that ALA, for all its foibles and weaknesses, is the best political weapon the library profession has. And if you want to change it, make it better, make it do what you want, you have to join it, have to get involved. Sideline bitchers and crybabies get no free tissues from me.

That ALA hasn't met the needs and desires of the majority of our profession is obvious. You only have to consider that its membership is no more, and perhaps lower, than it was ten years ago. Less than a third of the profession belongs. Nevertheless, none of the other associations—not even the ARL, composed of the volume-fat titans of the research library world—has the power or the influence of ALA, in Washington, worldwide, wherever. And no new breakaway organization has a hope in hell of building to ALA's potential in less than a quarter of a century.

An edited version of a speech at the Opening General Session of the California Library Association Conference, Los Angeles, December 2, 1976.

Troubles and a Target

I open with what may sound like a standard membership plug because I believe we ought all to be focussing on one principal concern: that library service in this country is in desperate trouble. I said in my ballot statement that that was why I was running for an office I didn't want, and I meant it. If we're going to dig out of that trouble, we need strength, and in the political world strength means the unity of numbers. We only get weaker, more ineffective while we keep bickering among ourselves, keep splintering, keep focussing on special or narrow interests and losing sight of the main target, the overall good, the *general* interest.

So, what is the target? It was brought into focus for me just recently with devastating simplicity by a marvelous old man, Dumas Malone, a brilliant Jefferson scholar but real down home in manner, like Robert Frost without the arrogance. I was attending the dedication of the Jefferson Building of the Library of Congress—what used to be called, with appalling lack of imagination, public relations sense or respect, the Annex. Professor Malone, rambling on about the beginnings of LC, mentioned that when the new Congress left Philadelphia for the wilderness village of Washington, almost the first thing that Congress did was set about putting together a working library. It had to have a library, Malone said, simply couldn't operate without it.

That's where we've got to get to, or strive to get to. In other spheres of current activity, it's called consciousness-raising. Congress still knows it needs a library; what we've got to do is convince them that not only they, but everyone, needs a library—poor people, rich people, business and labor, young and old, the scientist and the student, even *my* special interest group, the middle aged. That they can't, whether they know it or not, operate fully or adequately in this society without it.

The interesting thing is that the politicians in developing countries are often so much more aware of this than are the pols who occupy our state houses and the halls of Congress. They know that real growth and development are simply not possible (just as did those early Congressmen) against the brick wall of ignorance, and they know too—many of them—that libraries are the cheapest, fastest, most economical devices —because they can be made accessible to all the people—for the dissemination of information, and of broad-based education. That's why libraries often feature large and early in the plans of new governments in struggling countries.

If ours is not exactly a struggling country today, there can be little doubt that many of its people are struggling, and I believe that libraries could achieve greater priority support if they will demonstrate that they have a vital contribution to make to society—not just in general motherhood and God terms, but in terms of the specific, sometimes desperate, needs of many and varied individuals and groups. We are going to have to get a lot more aggressive in asserting what libraries are, what they can do. For some in our society, libraries are (or can be and should be) the most accessible, cheapest source of a whole range of what has come to be called (without too much hyperbole) survival information. For others, libraries are the most accessible, cheapest form of truly liberal education beyond the school years (perhaps even *during* those years). For yet others, libraries are among our mightiest research tools, the repositories not just of our past but of our future. And for many, let us not forget, they remain the most satisfying avenue of relaxation (and leisure is one of our society's growing problems), particularly for those whose budgets are not as elastic as today's prices.

We need to launch our message not only at the white dome in Washington, D.C., but with equal precision and force at the state houses in all fifty of our states. If ever there were a cause in which ALA and the state associations should unite in joint effort, this is it. State support of libraries is perhaps the place where we have made our least progress the past couple of decades.

The Individual Librarian

With all this talk about institutional needs, I don't want you to think that I have forgotten, or that I rate as a lesser priority, the condition and needs of the individual librarian. Our profession shares with the rest of society one of the ripe fruits of the Nixon and Ford administrations—large-scale unemployment, particularly in the urban areas.

Nor have I forgotten that we share another problem with society—discrimination against minorities and against the majority of our profession, women. And this problem, particularly discrimination against minorities, has been vastly aggravated by the economic neglect of libraries and the consequent unemployment of librarians. Because it wasn't too long ago that we began to make our first feeble efforts to correct our wrongs in this area, and as soon as the fiscal crunch arrived, what little progress we had made was virtually wiped out by the "last in, first out" philosophy of employment. And we saw the birth of a new racist slogan: "reverse discrimination."

These problems, however, are not separable, not—as the classificationists would have it, "mutually exclusive," not capable of being ranked as priorities. They form a very real, if unholy, unity. We shall not find more jobs for librarians without improving the health of the institutions in which those jobs can exist. And social progress is infinitely more likely in a healthy society, a healthy profession, than in a sick one.

As we look for solutions to some of these problems, however—and here I must say, like Carlyle, "Brothers [and I would add, sisters], I am sorry I have got no Morrison's pill for curing the maladies of society"—as we look for solutions, there are perhaps a few things we should subject to particular scrutiny.

One is library education and recruitment. Are we today (the profession and the schools) recruiting young people with false promises? Is there truth in our advertising? Is there really a realistic prospect of a decent job for all those people we are luring into library schools to collect that MLS piece of paper? What kind of doors, and how many, will it open for them? Should the schools be continuing to pour out a flood of graduates each year onto an already saturated market? Is the welfare of the profession any part of the school's real motivation, or are they chiefly concerned with their own survival? And should ALA, given this situation, continue to swell the ranks of accredited schools across the country? Personally, I think not.

We need, too, to take a fresh, hard look at our legislative stance. Are we lobbying for the right needs, the greatest urgencies, or are we still locked into a strategy which proved effective ten and twenty years ago? Is that strategy, despite diminished relevance, continued perhaps for reasons of expediency, or for reasons of self-interest among certain power blocs, or because of the self-perpetuation of the legislative power structure; or is this simply another example of the "we've always done it this way" psychology which is still too pervasive in our profession?

Should anyone really need telling that the most severe and intractable problems in our society are urban problems? And can it not be apparent, to all but those who do not want to see, that the necks of the urban centers and their swelling collars of suburbia are *both* within the same noose of economic fate.

While we're thinking about our legislative posture, we need to give some thought, too, to our weaponry. ALA has been the spearhead for a long time in the profession's legislative effort, at the federal level anyway.

And whatever reservations one may have about ALA's legislative policies—and I have plenty—it has been and is still the most potent force we have in the legislative arena. It needs now, though, to watch its political flank. In the past couple of years it has deferred too easily and too often, or perhaps not tried hard enough to exercise sufficient influence upon a new library force on the Washington scene: NCLIS.

Nobody would deny that we need all the lung power, all the influence, all the connections possible in Washington, and it would be foolish to dismiss the potential of NCLIS for aiding the cause of libraries. Nevertheless, we ought to think very carefully about its role, and about what voice we want expressing the needs of libraries, their patrons and their staffs, to the Congress and the Administration.

Here is a Commission which is charged, in the words of Public Law 91-345, to "advise the President and the Congress on the implementation of national policy. . . . " This same Commission, of 14 members, is to include only five professional librarians or (and here's the kicker) information specialists. I personally think that librarians ought to be the major shapers of legislative recommendations affecting library service, as ALA has been hitherto, not a token minority representation.

There is, I think, another serious potential hazard in relying too much on NCLIS as the voice of library policy, a potential that may well emerge into reality as a result of the events of last November 2. How much influence can a Commission, all of whose members were appointed by Richard Nixon or Gerald Ford, be expected to exert on the new Administration and a solidly Democratic Congress? With our political destiny in such hands, is there not a very real danger that we may end up once again with no more than peanuts?

I don't believe my qualms about NCLIS are a personal hobby horse. In preparation for a couple of years back on the speech circuit, I contacted a couple of dozen friends, librarians whose minds and abilities and views I greatly respect, and asked them to write me about their concerns, to tell me what issues they'd like to see me spotlight, what they thought about where we are and where we should be going, what ALA ought to be doing, and so on. About half of them mentioned NCLIS in one way or another, usually with unease, to put it mildly. Here, for example, is one of them on that topic:

> . . . on the subject of activism, one problem lies very close to home: the National Commission on Libraries & Information Science. Here is an entity which has claimed as its jurisdiction

nothing less than the matter of how library service in America will be defined, structured, delivered and paid for. Now, one would assume that these are questions in which the library profession should have something of an interest. Yet, the American Library Association has behaved toward NCLIS as though its subject of concern were rat-lice. When the Commission was preparing its report, many voices pleaded with the ALA Executive Board and Legislation Committee to seek an active role for ALA and its units. The ALA response was to do just about nothing until there was a final report to which to react. Not only is that point in time far too late for meaningful input, but the 'information industry' was abiding by no such wait-and-see policy. It not only sought aggressively (and successfully) to influence the Commission at every turn, but through its excessive representation on the Commission itself the industry virtually wrote the report.

I might add that the ALA Council endorsed the Commission's report with about as much consideration and integrity as the Congress exhibited in rejecting the report of another National Commission at the behest of Richard Nixon, that of the National Commission on Obscenity and Pornography. In both cases, it was transparently obvious that most of those voting could not possibly have read, never mind considered, the final report.

That's the negative part (much abbreviated, let me say). Now let's try to revert to the presidential role and be a bit more upbeat. We must, despite the foregoing remarks, strive to retain the political advantage that the presence of a permanent National Commission in Washington can offer. But we need to make perfectly clear to Jimmy Carter and the pols on the hill that such a Commission is badly needed on the national scene as a research arm for library and information services. As such, a Commission, with its funding potential, could be a giant advance for us, a great hope for our future. We also need to make very clear, however, that the *policy* recommending voice for the future of libraries is ALA, broadly representing libraries and library service as it—and only it—always has. Let's get NCLIS out of the lobbying business.

I'd like to zoom off here for a while into some mistier, more philosophical areas. If we're going to tell the library story convincingly and more aggressively, I think we're going to have to strive for a little more balance, a little more continuity in our thinking and our propaganda. Our profession, perhaps not too unlike other professions, has a penchant for leaping aboard bandwagons, sometimes without checking to see whether or not the axle's cracked. When the wheels fall off, we just step to the side of the road and wait for the next likely-looking vehicle to come along. Let's just take a quickie look at a couple of the current hot-rods.

The first, the biggest, the one with the most tempting chrome, is the network concept. In introducing this, I'm reminded of a cover of *LJ* I once ran to dramatize an issue of the journal questioning some of what was then going on in the devising of what we now know as the Anglo-American Cataloging Rules. The title of that issue was "Holes in the Network."

Today the word network pervades our professional talk as inexorably and abominably as the words super and colossal once attached themselves to everything emanating from or connected with Hollywood. But I wonder how many of us have thought seriously about what we're trying to achieve, whom these networks are designed to benefit. Are we not envisaging a mountainous and prohibitively expensive solution to the problems of a minority of library users? I have little doubt that the network concept will go forward, and I am not sufficiently a Luddite to believe that it should not. What I do believe is that its real target is solution of the "research" problem, and that its primary beneficiaries will be those who are pushing hardest for it—the large research libraries and, of course, their users (or some of them).

I have seen little, however, in the reams of words and dreams about networks that convinces me that the majority of library users or potential users will benefit much: those whose needs are basic and relatively simple, even mundane perhaps as seen through the remote consoles of some of these network planners. In what ways, and with what, will the networks reach the aged, the housebound, the poor, the student in elementary school, or even the underprivileged undergraduate? What of the small public library user, the community college, the rural resident? Read the National Commission report and see how tuned in it is to the problems of school libraries.

Let's, by all means, not be Luddites about networks, but while we're hitching a ride on this jazzy bandwagon, let's not forget that there are still many bicycle riders on the road. Why not, for example, think constructively about some late—rather than early—twentieth century legislation, with financing that would give impetus to coordinated (not, for god's sake, cooperative—another abused and feeble word) endeavor at local levels, involving, for example, cities and suburbs jointly, and certainly involving all types of libraries. Type of library divisions in our thinking and our practices have, I believe, had as pernicious an effect on our services as national, religious, language and other divisions have had on our lives. These divisions are not relevant to our users, only to our own prejudices about status and turf.

Another bandwagon—still a compact compared with the V-8 we've just been considering—is continuing education, which as one of its first creative acts brings us another ringing acronym: CLENE....

Continuing education, of course, is not a bad idea per se. It is obvious, at any meeting, in any library, that there is great need for it. But, as usual, we need to get our priorities straight. Walter Brahm in *LJ*, exaggeratedly as a good columnist should, saw the continuing education movement bringing us another parade of pathetic workshops, like some of the nonsense we indulged in during the sixties in the flush of federal largesse. I hope it will do better than that. Might we not, for example, look for some trade-off between continuing the education (or re-education) of our present librarians and controlling the excessive over-supply of new librarians who can't find jobs? In other words, a redirection of effort rather than another straw on the camel's back.

Where do we need to concentrate the C.E. effort? Can it be used to help strengthen not just the capacity but the job potential of those in our profession who are unemployed, or to remove some of the disadvantages of those who are victimized by minority status or by the long-term effects of our accreditation system, among other causes? In what ways can it help to counteract the deadening impact of the nineteenth-century parochialism of some of the long-serving middle management of our libraries?

When we talk priorities, we are dealing essentially with our morality, our motivation, a subject that has been of great concern to me (and I think to many others in our profession) for a long time. Money has a more devastating effect on morality than almost anything else, in our profession no less than in other areas.

This dawned on me most clearly in the sixties, as the sun of federal aid to libraries first rose high in the sky and then sank rapidly (in the East). At high noon, the skywriting was full of slogans like outreach, service to the disadvantaged, libraries to the people. Some of us felt hope and joy that social consciousness was finally upon our profession and its services, And the pilot projects and "special" services blossomed.

But then came Tricky Dick and the faucet was turned off, and we began to realize that, alas, many librarians really did see these breakthroughs of the sixties as pilot projects, as special services—as something that could only be tackled with federal funds, and perhaps in some cases created only to take advantage of those funds. Normal service, i.e, service to our faithful middle class, continued and continues apace. The rest we went on talking about as something the feds had abandoned, not us. Our priorities were showing. This, folks, is expediency, not morality.

And now, today, after eight years of passage from what my friend Bill Eshelman calls "from benign concern to malignant neglect," our fiscal crunch is worse and we are heading into another money vs. morality clash—over the fees for service philosophy. This one is really dangerous, because it feeds upon and draws strength from the march of technology, the support of the largest and most powerful in our ranks, and the network propaganda. When we buy the philosophy that information should be available only to those who can pay for it, we have renounced social concern and professional responsibility, the public welfare, and all of our perennial holiness about intellectual freedom. We might then just as well leave library and information service entirely to the commercial world. What a journey we shall then have traveled from the Unesco Public Library Manifesto's simple, moral declaration that a public library "should be maintained wholly from public funds, and no direct charge should be made to anyone for its services."

Apart from the morality of it, this expediency, like others, is just not smart tactically if one takes the long view. As Eshelman said in a speech to the Virginia Library Association: "It seems incontrovertible to me that charging fees for library use or service would soon erode the tax base."

The last little bit of morality I want to preach is "truth in advertising." I don't know how many of you saw the supplement on libraries which ALA prepared for the Sunday *New York Times,* in October (1976), to celebrate its centennial. It was a bold, imaginative idea, the kind of thing we have often been a bit short on. But it painted a picture of libraries and library service I didn't recognize in the flesh. That, too, would have been fine if it had stressed more openly that this is what we can do if, in the words of that terrible old Tory, you give us the tools to do the job.

I think we've got to start admitting that, by and large, we have not done the job as we should have done, and that some of this, at least, is due to lacks that exist in our own ranks—lacks of sufficient imagination, energy, and commitment. Nothing is more disarming than a little *mea culpa.* But let's stress also that major reason why 90% of blue collar workers, 85% of the retired, almost 70% of the unemployed and, what is most startling, well over half of all students (primary, secondary and college) are among the library unserved (the figures are from a report to NCLIS out of Berkeley's Institute of Library Research in 1973)—and perhaps the primary reason—is that library service for all the people of this country has been seen and understood and considered as a lesser social priority than the survival of Lockheed or some other defense contractor.

A couple of weeks ago, my seven-year-old grandson came to visit us. As soon as he burst through the door, he said: "Grandpop, I think I like Chardin better than Goya." Before I got my dropped jaw back in place, to ask him why, and what brought that on, he did one of those rapid switches that are only possible in computers and seven-year-olds and said, "Do you think a Jaguar's better than a Lincoln Continental?"

Well, grandfathers get pretty confused dealing with stuff like that, but after a while I figured out that what he was really doing was exploring values (priorities, if you like) and was taking some soundings to see what mine were like.

My good friend Arthur Curley was on this theme, too, in a letter he sent me recently. He said:

> My major concern for libraries remains, as it has been since I entered the field two decades ago, a matter of values. Of course the functional role of libraries is a basic one (or at least it would be, if we did the job even moderately well). But I think the abstract, even symbolic role of libraries is equally important. In other words, what we stand for is as important as what we do.

I hope that "what we stand for" will be a major concern of many library conferences in the years ahead. If we resolve that, we may well find out, perhaps for the first time, how important, how damned vital, we really are.

Data Bank Is Two Four-Letter Words

... When I started, some time ago, to think about what as President of ALA I could do that would be useful, I wasn't short on ideas (there are altogether too many things that need doing) but I was hard-pressed to decide among many alternatives what was most important, or possible to achieve in one year, or likely to encompass the interests of the many fragments that make up what we call our profession. I was sure of one thing: that in one presidential year, one could only concentrate on a single target. The buckshot approach, typical of many of my speeches on the circuit, would not do.

Though I've never been convinced that two heads are better than one, I was sure in this instance that I needed not only help but advice. So I brought together about 40 heads, not selected according to any Machiavellian scheme (some always seem to suspect me of that) but as a sort of brains trust, a group of people whom I knew to have ideas. Many of them, I knew, were likely to disagree with each other on most anything, so I put them together in a room to see what would come to the surface when the brew boiled.

If we don't exactly have a master plan firmly nailed down yet, at least I have an idea of what I'm going to concentrate on for the next year, with the culmination of that effort at the 1978 Chicago conference.

What I want to do might be described as building a bridge between historic occasions—between the celebration and enthusiasm of last year's centennial conference and what I hope will be the landmark achievements that can come out of the White House Conference on Libraries in 1979, if we prepare for it adequately.

There were several factors that led us in the direction we finally chose, not least among them the fact that Clara Jones had already moved us part

---

An edited version of the ALA Presidential Inaugural Speech, ALA Conference, Detroit, June 21, 1977.

of the way with her fine Presidential program on the Post-Industrial Society and its implications for us as librarians.

But there were other factors. Nations around the world, and the examples come from those countries we call underdeveloped as well as from the industrial giants, are beginning to pay significant attention to what may be both the most crucial and the least understood energy source of all for our troubled world: information, an energy source we have never properly harnessed in the service of humanity.

Our own nation is not ignoring the problems and challenges of information production, dissemination and use, but there is some doubt in my mind (and I don't believe I'm alone with these doubts) about our country's focus on the subject. What, that is, do we mean by information? What kinds of needs do the governmental and other power structures perceive? And where are they getting their advice?

And finally, to finish ticking off the factors that persuaded me about the focus of my year's program, there was a new man in the White House. A man who started his career of public service as a library trustee, who came out of Georgia with a record of support for education and libraries, who talked constantly of the need to communicate with the people, of public access to information. After years of not so benign neglect, here, we have to hope, is an opportunity to make ourselves heard, to stem the tide of degradation of our facilities and our collections; for us to lay claim to the significant contributions this profession has made, and can make, to the health, education and welfare of this nation.

But we must speak up. And more than that—we must think, and having thought, move on—to action. And not action prompted by short-term expediency, but action motivated by principle. For if we do not, there is nothing more certain than that others, and particularly those who see the material potential in information as a commodity, will move before us to grab off this energy source as they have oil and gas and coal, and who will use it and develop it with perhaps no more social concern than the record from the Industrial Revolution on down should lead us to expect.

We need, urgently, before it is too late and the scene is mangled by piracy and greed and fear, a national information policy which addresses and respects the real and multifaceted needs of all the people of our society. This is what I have determined to move toward in my presidential year because here is a matter, I believe, on which it is vital that the voice of the librarian be heard in the land.

Other voices can already be heard. In the past few months I have read two reports which address this issue directly. One, published a few months ago by NCLIS and entitled *National Information Policy,* is a report to the President of the United States submitted by the staff of the Domestic Council Committee on the Right of Privacy, which was chaired by Nelson Rockefeller. In some ways it is not too bad a report and, certainly, its major focus is on an issue with which we should be vitally concerned: the dangers that technology in the information field pose for individual privacy. Its view of libraries, however, is condescending, if not downright demeaning. The Foreword, for example, discusses the many connotations of the term "information policy" and outlines what it may mean for the FCC, the Justice Department, the National Science Foundation, the businessman. Then it says, "to the library community it may mean policy with respect to postal rates for the distribution of books throughout the country." Now neither as a librarian nor as a publisher am I about to decry the importance of postal rates, but what a vision of our role in society this statement implies—or of our need for any more advanced information technology than a bag slung over the shoulder of one of Uncle Sam's mail carriers (weekdays only of course)! If a national information policy means no more to us than that, or if the powers in this land think that's all it means to us, we are looking extinction in the face.

The second report is called *Scientific and Technical Information: Options for National Action.* This one was prepared for NSF's Division of Science Information and was published by the Mitre Corporation in McLean, Virginia. It is a dismal hack job of consultant-type "research," which "analyzes" eighteen other reports and endlessly reiterates three profound lessons it has learned in the process:

> 1. STI (that's sci-tech information) is important. Why? Because it's the "*primary* means by which research results are translated into useful applications for the well-being of the nation."
> 2. STI is big business, representing billions of dollars in annual expenditures (ah, there we have it).
> 3. There are problems—among them lack of coordination of policies, duplication, waste, etc. Also, the report admits, "the ability of STI systems to serve the needs of users has been questioned."

Do tell? I told you this one was profound. Only on one page of this report is there any acknowledgment that STI is no more than one part of a larger information problem. I quote: " ... can STI policies be formulated without taking into consideration broader information policies? The doc-

uments reviewed by Mitre do not specifically address this concern. . . .
However . . . it seems certain that the field of STI will also be affected in
the future by a growing awareness of the economic and social significance
of a broad spectrum of information activities. . . . "

Well, friends, that future into which the Mitre Corporation peers so
dimly had better be now, or awareness of the economic and social
significance of information may not have a chance to grow.

I'm rather well aware, from various reactions during the past several
months, that on the face of it, national information policy may not be a
theme or a topic which all of you will see as an immediate turn-on. But
given the circumstances that surround us, the temper of the times, the
plight of our profession and its services, the looming competition we face
in what should be our own bailiwick, and the social, educational and
economic needs of millions of people, I cannot believe there is a more
urgent issue for us to address. We are all of us concerned (or should be),
not only as librarians but as citizens, as human beings. The topic is not
only of paramount importance to our profession, but I suggest it is relevant
to every unit of ALA, to its chapters and to every other library and
information-related organization in this country (or, for that matter, the
world).

The issues tucked under the broad umbrella of this large topic are so
various and so multitudinous that there is a corner of concern for each of
us, individually or as organized units. In the rest of my time I want to
sketch in a few of my own concerns, not because I think they are the only
or the most important ones, but because I hope that one or another may
touch or activate others of your own. We need a total effort, and a unity
of purpose, if we are to carry our influence to where a national information
policy will be shaped and implemented. We are very late out of the starting
gate.

The first question we must grapple with is the one that should always
come first, as any young child knows: Why? Why is a coordinated national
policy on information necessary? What do we want to accomplish? And
here I'm going to quote, because I can't possibly say it better than it vas
said in a 1972 Conference Board publication titled *Information Technology: Some Critical Implications for Policy Makers:*

> No wonder many thoughtful people believe that the new information technology will prove as important to human development as all the inventions and innovations introduced during the first 150 years of the Industrial Revolution. Looking back, we

can think of the massive horrors that would have been averted or, at least, ameliorated if the Industrial Revolution had been guided more intelligently by the societies that gave it birth and nurture. None of these societies proved vigorously enough or soon enough to foresee the indirect consequences of the steam engine, the dynamo, or the automobile. Because policy-making was inadequate, industrial societies slipped into patterns of action that no one had designed or intended—least of all the scientists, engineers, and the businessmen who were most directly responsible for the innovations that changed society. Neither the nineteenth century's squalor nor the twentieth century's record of social conflict and environmental pollution had to happen.

And, also from 1972 (and it's worth emphasizing that both these statements were made five or more years ago, to illustrate how far we are *not* progressing) is an article in *Science* by Edwin B. Parker and Donald A. Dunn entitled "Information Technology: Its Social Potential." The most interesting proposal in this article is "the creation of an 'information utility' for the purpose of fostering equal social opportunity in the United States." The authors, optimistically perhaps, declare that "The main difference between the present period of technological change and the earlier periods is that our society now has a greater opportunity to direct the development of the technology *to meet positive social goals,* instead of becoming the beneficiary (or victim) of uncontrolled technological change." Well, opportunity often knocks, but it isn't always answered.

What is important about both these pieces is that they recognize the inevitability of technological growth and change, and the potential benefits and dangers. But both, essentially, are warning us that it will all be for nought (or less) if the social good and educational progress are not controlling factors in our use of information technology.

One of the things that disturbs me most about all the current obsession with technology is that it may be having a distorting effect on our thinking, even about what information is. There is a growing tendency to equate information with data, to see it as something that comes in discrete "bits" or units. There are too many voices that sound like Mr. Gradgrind's in *Hard Times:* "Now, what I want is, Facts. . . . Facts alone are wanted in life." This mind-set directs our attention, ever-increasingly, toward the information needs of science and technology, of business, of something generally and loosely called "research."

These are not unimportant areas of activity in society, but undue obeisance toward them and a narrow concentration on them as the only important (or even the most important) beneficiaries of an improved information capacity is a good way to ensure that the Information Revolution will be as great a social disaster as the Industrial Revolution was before it.

Such a route can only lead us to the sad terminal so vividly described by Pete Hamill in a recent *New York Daily News* column, in which he wrote movingly about the Park Slope Branch Library in Brooklyn. "When we were young," said Hamill, "this library was the very best of America: a free, breathing institution, its doors open to the immigrants and their children, a place that said, Here, pick up these books, the universe lies within. And when we opened those books, which were given to us with no questions about incomes or religion, we started down the long road to becoming human."

Hamill goes on to talk about the decay and neglect of that library—a symbol perhaps of the potential fate of all libraries, unless some priorities are changed—and concludes:

> Somewhere in that neighborhood, there is a poor kid who will never hear Dickens speak. He will never sit on that hilltop with Robert Jordan, killing Fascists. One day, 10 years old, he will walk up to this strange decaying building. Someone will have told him that they have books inside and you can take them home and they are free. And when he gets there, the door will be locked. And the roof caved in. And the remaining windows punched out. The Count of Monte Cristo will have moved to a better neighborhood. And while the banks get paid, and the federal government collects its taxes, we'll be that much closer to the most terrible poverty of all.

I would hate to see librarians, of all people, becoming fogged or bedazzled by words like information and data, to the point where they fail to emphasize with pride the broader things for which libraries stand and have always stood: knowledge, ideas, art, creativity, understanding, pleasure, awareness of self and the world around us—even, by God, wisdom. Or, as Hamill so beautifully puts it, a way of becoming human.

All of that may be perhaps a rather high-flown way of saying that if we are to carve out a niche for ourselves in the formation of a national information policy, those are the kind of values we must accentuate, not the values of the searchers for material advantage in this pursuit. It is not that sci-tech and business and some other areas are not important, but that they will not be overlooked in any case. They are too profitable, too important for economic and political reasons to be ignored. But who, if not us, will remember the information needs of that poor kid in Brooklyn?

We must argue and establish the position, I believe, that we and our institutions and services should be the citizenry's protectors in the information arena, ensuring that this vital energy source is not, as others have been, drained off into private storage tanks to which the only key is money. We must fight not only for the production of information geared to the needs of individuals at all levels of society, but for their right of unlimited access to it. And we can make a strong argument, if we get our principles in order, for being the best agency in society to accomplish that role.

There are other issues we need to examine which fit with this role of guardian of the public interest in the information arena. A variety of human rights can be jeopardized by the impact of technology on information gathering and dissemination. The oil companies know the power potential that lies in controlling both production and flow, and have demonstrated that profit is a more likely partner for power than human rights.

Among the endangered species as information technology marches on is individual privacy. The Privacy Act of 1974 was a small step forward, but a vague and gingerly one which, as the Rockefeller Commission admits, leaves many problems mired in confusion. This is a topic of worldwide concern, since technology has the capacity to cut sharply through such plastic barriers as national borders. Thus we see Sweden, among other countries, passing new legislation designed to rather firmly regulate the availability of personal information about Swedish citizens.

There is, of course, a sort of Catch-22 question here. How do you argue the cause of maximum access to information and then turn around and say there are *some* kinds of information to which access should be severely limited? You have to be very careful about principle here, or you can easily wind up sounding like Nixon arguing executive privilege where none applies. The Rockefeller Commission took a look at this question from a slightly different angle: "How to preserve a sense of individuality and privacy against a massive government which demands more and more information from individuals and businesses, and which argues that its restricted use promotes efficiency?"

But is efficiency the real question? Should there be more accessibility to information about public persons than others? And how do you define "public"—those who work for the public and are responsible to it? What about the Rebozos and Geneens and Shankers, who work behind the scenes and exert massive influence on those responsible to the public? Even in their cases, whether we like them or not, is their privacy less a right than ours? Are perhaps the nub questions: What *kinds* of information about individuals are private? Who if anyone should have access to personal information? And to what uses may such information be put? The solutions to such dilemmas are not likely to be easy, but because they are both difficult and important, because they have direct impact upon our work and our services and the credibility of our institutions and ourselves, they deserve more than passing or surface consideration.

Other broad rights than can be put in jeopardy by the "information-as-product" mentality and by the increasing ability to control information production and flow include the right of dissent and the rights of creators—writers and artists and others who deal with thought and consider questions rather than answers. I think it's at least debatable whether factual information is or ever has been as important as what is produced by the imagination of creative talents. Think back over the written record and remember those who have left you with indelible images of other times and places, of other societies and lifestyles, even of historical events. I'll wager that many, if not most, of the names that come floating to the surface out of the wells of memory are of poets and novelists and dramatists. As V. S. Naipaul said recently "The novel is a form of social inquiry."

What does all this have to do with information policy? Only the need to stress that this kind of information is as vital to the intellectual and imaginative health of our nation, of the world, as any data-type information that may further contribute to the ruin of our lungs, our cities, our rivers, fields and forests in the name of progress. Yet we librarians have not waged any very convincing campaign for massive support of the arts—as they have not for us.

This is one of many areas where we have potential natural allies, most of them in trouble like us, and most of them like us fighting their survival battles alone. And thus far, rather unsuccessfully. Both business and the unions know better than that.

I have a small news item to insert at this point, which is *to* the point. I have recently been asked to serve on the national board of a new organization, the American Arts Alliance, which has been set up to launch a heavy lobbying campaign for support for the arts. It is made up of a very impressive group of people from the opera, theatre, symphony, ballet, literature, etc., etc. I was invited by pure chance. A young woman from the Metropolitan Opera Association happened to be present at a New York

Library Club dinner at which I was speaking a few months ago. In the course of my remarks I was urging, as I have before, that we need to form alliances if we are to save our embattled cultural institutions in New York City and other cities around the country. To that point, the founding group of the Arts Alliance had not considered inviting anyone from the world of libraries and books, but in subsequent discussions I think I managed to persuade them not only that we were natural allies but that libraries provided the best national information network they could find, without money, to promote their cause. We need to find friends like this wherever we can, and so do many other organizations and institutions which are in danger of decline in an increasingly anti-intellectual climate. We must go out and find them, offer them our support, and ask for theirs.

To get back after that digression, one other area of information rights we need to take a hard look at is the rights of the young to access to information. It is an issue we have avoided for far too long. And what seems to have become our traditional stance—that it is up to parents to control the reading and viewing of their offspring—may be politically expedient but it isn't particularly principled.

The arrival of compulsory education provided one escape route for those children whose parents seemed determined to establish a dynasty of ignorance. Some parents still struggle to protect their children from education but, by and large, society has come to accept education as among the rights of the young. Society usually does things for selfish reasons, however, and this may be no more than acceptance that the need for an educated next generation to continue or improve upon what we have wrought is so important that it must even supersede the rather despotic rights we have customarily accorded parents.

The question for us, though, is, do we then accept that the child's or young adult's right of access to knowledge stops when the school doors close at three, or four? Do we believe that education happens only in school, that libraries are not educational, that they are less important, less relevant than schools? If we do not believe these things, then how come we do not protest as strongly when an individual parent bars the door of the library (or the adult section) to his or her child as when the governor of a state stands in the schoolhouse door and bars entry to children who seek nothing more dangerous than an equal crack at a decent education?

Something is wrong here, either with the consistency of our principles, or with our belief in the educational potential of libraries. Or is it really just a failure of nerve? Even the flag has had its detractors these past couple of decades; even apple pie perhaps has its rivals in the coke and the hamburger, but motherhood (let's not be sexist—fatherhood, too) is a fearsome opponent to challenge. Nevertheless, anything that pretends to be a national information policy must address the needs and rights and problems of all people—and all people includes the young.

I have saved until the end what for me is the most serious and fundamental issue we must deal with in forging any national information policy. That issue—one which gnaws at the philosophical foundations of library service—is nowhere more clearly posed for us than in the title of an October 1975 article by Eugene Jackson in *Sci-Tech News:* "The End of Free Library Service Is at Hand." That title, for me at least, has the ring of Doomsday about it. "I do see the time coming," says Mr. Jackson, more honest than some equivocators in our midst, "when all library service will be for a charge levied on the user." Unless we shake loose from our laissez-faire attitudes toward the fee-brokers' encroachments upon our services, I am afraid that Jackson may indeed be right.

How did we get to such a point of horrendous surrender of principle in scarcely more than a quarter-century since the simple moral declaration in the Unesco Public Library Manifesto, that a public library "should be maintained wholly from public funds, and no direct charge should be made to *anyone* for its services."

Let us not get into that ridiculous argument about library services never really having been "free." That's playing with semantics. It's a question of *who* pays, as that Unesco statement makes abundantly clear.

If we sit back and allow present trends to gather momentum, we shall be silently acquiescing in their inevitable conclusion: that information will, in the end, as Jackson predicts, only be available to those who can pay for it. That seems to me a total renunciation of all the things we have ever said we believed in: social responsibility, public access, a professional concern for the public interest, and all of our perennial holiness about intellectual freedom and the rights of the individual.

It is also specious, I think, to claim that we can for long operate, side by side in public institutions, fee-based and "free" services. How long do you think that can last? When any fiscal crunch comes along, where will governing bodies press for cuts—in services that produce a return they can see, or in those whose return, while perhaps of equal value, is nothing so obvious or concrete? In the end of this process, shall we not then be pressed, as Jackson forecasts, to produce a hard-cash return for all our services?

Here is a splendid example of what technology ungoverned by principle can do to us. There is little doubt that we shall build in the next few years the most impressive network of bibliographic apparatus the world has ever known. But if the cost of doing that (and of maintaining it), and if the intensity of effort to achieve that goal is so blindered that it leads to a paradoxical decline in information available locally, and access to the rest filtered through a means test to fewer and fewer people, what shall we have achieved with our technology other than an Orwellian spectre?

The financial and political implications of this issue are surely not simple, and we are going to have to grapple with them to find practical solutions. But let us not do it on the basis of short-term expediency, or our future as instruments of civilization rather than of commerce may be short-term too. We must loudly, insistently, affirm that free access to information for all is the very foundation, not only of our profession and our services, but of individual liberty. If this is not the central principle of any national information policy, we shall indeed, as Pete Hamill says, "be that much closer to the most terrible poverty of all."

Libraries, we must tell all those who have not been convinced, have more real wealth than Fort Knox. "Give us," as old Winston said in the darker hours of World War II, "the tools to do the job," and we'll spread that wealth around.

Education Without Libraries = Catastrophe

Although as President of the American Library Association I am called upon often to speak for and of libraries and librarians, I am not at present (and have not been for many years) a practicing librarian. At least at the outset, therefore, I'd like to take a look at the topic of concern here—whether libraries are essential to education—as a representative of a group whose voice and viewpoint needs to be heard, and too rarely is, in gatherings of this kind. Let me open, then, as that supreme generalist: the library user.

Generalists have a depressing habit of beginning always with autobiography, perhaps because there is no better fuel for generalizations than personal experience. Bear with me for a while; I'll indulge the pattern only briefly.

When I was twelve, in England, my stepfather, a Scottish carpenter with an honors degree from Edinburgh University (who liked to work with his hands and could not bring himself to separate entirely from the working class), offered me a bribe. If I could bring off some unprecedented (unprecedented for me) feat of scholarship—I believe the requirement was that I had to finish at the top of my class in at least four subjects that year—I should receive for my thirteenth birthday a present, he said, I would remember all my life.

Powered by visions of a bicycle that was at least two-thirds chrome, I conquered my usual laziness and a few time-consuming passions and somehow achieved the impossible goal. On the morning I was to receive my Oscar, I raced around the house searching for the gleaming vehicle

---

Edited version of a speech at a Seminar held by the New York State Library, in Albany, October 26, 1977, in honor of the inauguration of Gordon Ambach as President of the University of the State of New York and Commissioner of Education.

that was to be the materialist envy of my friends, and even more particularly of my enemies. Nothing was in evidence except a square brown-paper package on the kitchen table. In those days, bicycles came from the shop all in one piece, so I knew my saddled dream could not be compressed into any packet so unprepossessing. What that package did contain, though I did not know it then, and would not for some time, consumed as I was by chagrin and the certainty that I had been well and truly had, was however a vehicle that would take me much further than ever the gleaming two-wheeler of my fantasies could. It was a volume containing the complete plays of Bernard Shaw.

That was the day my education really began. As my anger and frustration cooled, curiosity started to do its insidious work. I had to find out what my stepfather (whom I regarded with a certain affection and respect) thought was so special about that fat brown volume, and for weeks I ploughed doggedly through its pages.

Some months later, my English teacher (a marvelously entertaining man who later went into politics and wound up as the Speaker of the House of Commons), surprised on several occasions by my penchant for quoting the irascible Irishman, invited me home for tea, and we talked Shaw for an hour or two. The next day he asked me if I would give a talk to the class on Shaw. That was one of the terror events of my life but it gradually began to dawn on me that the square brown-paper package might indeed be more valuable than the chrome-plated bicycle. It had already given me a kind of grudging status and recognition among my fellows as the possessor of something more mysterious than a bicycle: I knew something none of them knew. What I had was knowledge. A little piece, to be sure, but the genuine article nevertheless.

From that time on I became a library gourmand. I simply could not get enough books to read. And it was just as well. These were the thirties and a poor boy from the working class, no matter what his academic and scholarship potential, could rarely afford the extravagance of elite and expensive institutions like Oxford or Cambridge. His early contribution to the family budget—or the removal of his drain upon it—was mandatory. I left school at sixteen—and it was perhaps more than coincidence that I became a librarian, because I already knew, with instinctive conviction, that it was only on those dim and dusty old shelves that education, or my only chance at it, really lay.

I give you that unexciting slice of autobiography not out of ego but because the topic I was asked to discuss seemed to me faintly absurd. Given my personal experience and conviction, asking me to speak about the essentiality of libraries to education was rather like asking me to talk about the essentiality of oxygen to breathing. Indeed, I felt that someone had simply made a mistake, had put the emphasis on the wrong end; that the more pertinent topic, surely, was the educational road to libraries—or, if you like the essentiality of education to libraries!

More than a quarter of a century ago, H. G. Wells said "Human history becomes more and more a race between education and catastrophe." Nothing that has happened in the intervening years seems to have done other than to prove him, for once, to have hit the nail squarely on the head. I am a little more optimistic than Mr. Wells, however, and I think that human history, given our dogged instinct for survival, even on the constant brink of catastrophe, is likely to be a fairly long race. To win a race of that nature, though, you need a sturdy long-distance runner, and libraries, I suggest, are the best long-distance runners on the education team. Even when educational or other institutions fold or fail, their libraries are usually transferred to other teams; they are too valuable to be retired. From Alexandria and before, down to the present day, libraries, usually lacking star quality, have nevertheless been the backbone, the staying power, the record-holders of education. No university ever became a great university without a great library. No great scholar ever became one without a good library behind him or her. No great breakthrough in social or technological progress, no spark of genius was ever ignited without someone, somewhere, rubbing a couple of books against the human mind. One may well wonder where the Soviet Union might be today without the British Museum.

I am convinced that if education, at all levels, were doing its job with flair, with understanding, superbly as it should, libraries would be among the most popular, most used and appreciated institutions in our society—places which could compete on equal or better terms with what John Leonard calls the "air-heads" who gabble over the pictures on the television screen. I see education (formal education, that is) as a mechanism for drawing back the shutters from the unchallenged human mind, a way of revealing the panorama of opinions and options and facts and philosophies and dreams that are there for the taking if only one is once given an irresistible taste (like my Shaw volume, which I have to this day) for the real adventure of life: the unpredictable voyage of the intellect. If they do their job at all well, among the first discoveries educators must reveal is that there is a map, a guidebook, to this ever-expanding frontier. That map is called a library.

No matter how brilliant or far-ranging a faculty any university or college or school has, its collective knowledge, imaginative potential and ultimate wisdom will always fall far short of the incredible brilliance and scope of the formidable faculty whose common room is the library's shelves. What other faculty can hope to recruit *every* Nobel Prize winner, everyone in science from Philolaus to Pauling, in philosophy from Aristotle to Russell, in literature from Homer to Hardy? It is perhaps in homage to that faculty of the shelves that administrators of educational institutions so often reiterate such pious phrases in reference to the library as "the heart of the university," or that politicians so blithely refer to the public library as "the university of the people."

Thus the link between libraries and education, it is clear, is recognized—or rather, acknowledged—by virtually everyone. But it is a long leap from piety to commitment, to recognition that education without libraries is scarcely education at all. If libraries are the hearts of our universities, they are soon—unless they receive considerably more generous transfusions from government (local, state and federal)—going to need transplant operations beyond the skill and capacity of even a Dr. Christian Barnard. And if public libraries are really the university of the people, the people are headed for functional illiteracy unless their "university" receives massive emergency aid and a real recognition of its educational function.

This is in no way an exaggeration. Indeed, eighteen months ago the Regents of the State University of New York released a statement which vividly recognized the critical plight of libraries (and of museums and other cultural institutions) in the state, and deplored the "meat-axe" approach of shortsighted budgeters who were (and still are) chopping the guts out of these institutions. The Regents called for what has long been necessary, if our belief in education is more than skin-deep: a substantial re-ordering of priorities which would translate lip-service into budgetary commitment. As the Regents said:

> Municipal administrators must recognize, either intellectually or viscerally, that a major segment of our population depends on cultural resources not only for emotional or intellectual stimulation but also as resources to make better communities and to make people better members of their communities. Our current and future culture can only be diminished . . . by the drastic reductions projected. . . . They will contribute as well to the foreclosure of the right of the individual citizen to attempt to

reverse or improve his present economic state through low-cost self education.

The Regents in that comment appear to be talking about public libraries primarily, but fiscal deprivation which leads to a degradation of resources can have just as pernicious an effect upon our institutions of formal education, from school through university—and upon those who go there in search of an education.

The editors of the *Journal of Academic Librarianship,* discussing the current financial squeeze in a recent editorial, asked: "What course then should the institution follow?" And, as good editors should, they answered their own rhetorical question, thus:

> One could cite the policies adopted by Harvard during the depression of the 1930's, when it chose to pursue aggressively the development of its library collections at the very time when most institutions had opted for a more conservative posture. Book and periodical budgets elsewhere were slashed, thus creating permanent gaps in library holdings. Forty years later one can better assess the impact of Harvard's decision to build rather than retrench.

In his assessment of higher education, made toward the end of the sixties, the late Alan Cartter concluded that there was indeed a link between the quality of library resources and perceived academic program excellence. Today, one has to join the editors of the *Journal of Academic Librarianship* in wondering how different Cartter's rankings might have been if other institutions had pursued library policies similar to Harvard's.

Today, access to information (and I use information in the broadest possible sense, as including not just facts and data but anything which leads to knowledge and understanding or even, we might hope, to wisdom)—access to knowledge, let us say, is perhaps more crucial and more difficult, and in some ways in greater jeopardy, than ever before. Without such access, not only is the individual denied full economic, educational and cultural opportunity, as the Regents noted, but national progress, social progress, business progress, educational progress will inevitably be retarded.

The National Commission on Libraries and Information Science recognized the paramount importance of such access when it set as its basic goal: "To eventually provide every individual in the United States with equal opportunity of access to that part of the total information resource which will satisfy the individual's educational, working, cultural and leisure-time needs and interests, regardless of the individual's location, social or physical condition, or level of intellectual achievement."

The central focus of my presidential program in the American Library Association is to concentrate the attention of our profession upon the urgent need for a national information policy, the issues and priorities to be addressed in the formation of such a policy, and the over-all part that libraries can play in providing the individual citizen the kind of access to our knowledge resources that he or she needs. Only within the parameters of such a national policy, I believe, will it be possible to attain the kind of reordering of priorities that is necessary if our libraries are to play the part they can and should play in the educational and informational structure of the nation.

This is an urgent concern not only for librarians, but certainly for educators—indeed, for all who still see a role in our future for what we have known as "liberal" education, for the humanities or, if you like, for humanitarian values. Information has become our biggest industry and as it expands, the danger is that the commercial entrepreneurs will further narrow the concept of what information is, simply by placing greater and greater emphasis on that information which is profitable. And what is most profitable, clearly, judging from the allocation of resources, is information which feeds and nurtures science and technology.

Only a Luddite fool would assert that science and technology are not important, that what happens in these fields will not have a profound effect upon our individual and collective futures.

But an unquestioning faith in technology as a panacea for all our problems can only lead in the nightmare direction Orwell warned us of many years ago.

It became clear to librarians as the twentieth century began to engulf them in the swelling knowledge output that no single institution—not the Library of Congress nor Harvard nor the New York Public Library, even—could any longer hope to keep abreast of the total massive output in all media. That it never could is perhaps beside the point. Whatever, we reached the conclusion that our only road to adequacy was via sharing resources wherever and in whatever ways we could.

The public, of course, as always was well ahead of the professionals. They do not care how we segregate our institutions or resources—whether we call something a public library, a school library or a college library. They want what they want when they want it, wherever it is—which is why an ill-equipped library in one institution only brings greater pressures on another better-equipped library, of whatever kind, somewhere else in the area. The public demonstrates for us what we should have known all along; that libraries, like people, are interdependent—they need each other.

Thus we began truly to think in terms of cooperation, of sharing, and New York State, with its library systems development, its 3R's program and other developments, was a leader in that kind of progress. Now, however, there are dangerous signals that our focus may have been skewed by the twin influences of fiscal shortages and too much hopeful faith in technological solutions.

The great paradox of the library scene at present is that we have learned to use technology to the point where, for the first time in our history, we shall really know what knowledge resources we have in the nation's libraries, and where they are. We are building and will soon have, I am convinced, the greatest bibliographic network the world has ever seen. In this sense everyone—educators, students, government, businessmen, ordinary citizens—will have greater access to knowledge than has been true at any time in the past.

The Catch-22 is that while we pursue this technological nirvana and pour more and more of our fiscal resources into it, local library collections and services are declining rapidly all over the country, and the ability of individual libraries or of all the libraries of a community to meet even the most immediate needs of that community is on a fast downhill slope. If the pattern continues, we shall wind up with greater and greater access to less and less, and since our ability to deliver the actual documents of knowledge is not in the same ballpark as our capacity to locate them, we may eventually reach the point where we can offer knowledge-seekers catalog entries on consoles or printouts for almost everything, but rarely the books or other documents these entries record. I can't remember how many years ago it was that I first told a library school class that I never knew a reader to leave a library deliriously happy with having found a catalog entry when what he wanted was a book.

The message is that while cooperation, sharing, technology are all important, and we must have them—if we do not preserve strong libraries at the local or immediate institution level, our networks will only be links between voids.

This paper may be getting a bit remote from what I was asked to talk about, so let me wind up and underline what I've been trying to say by quoting something that puts the case with the kind of dramatic simplicity that is perhaps only possible in the *New York Daily News*.

There, a few months ago, Pete Hamill wrote a moving column about the Brooklyn Public Library's Park Slope Branch. "When we were very young," he said, "this library was the very best of America: a free, breathing institution, its doors open to the immigrants and their children, a place that said, Here, pick up these books, the universe lies within. And when we opened those books, which were given to us with no questions about incomes or religion, we started down the long road to becoming human."

Hamill went on to talk about the decay and neglect of that library—clearly a symbol of the potential fate of many libraries unless some priorities are changed—and concluded:

> Somewhere in that neighborhood, there is a poor kid who will never hear Dickens speak. He will never sit on that hilltop with Robert Jordan, killing Fascists. One day, 10 years old, he will walk up to this strange decaying building. Someone will have told him that they have books inside and you can take them home and they are free. And when he gets there, the door will be locked. And the roof caved in. And the remaining windows punched out. The Count of Monte Cristo will have moved to a better neighborhood. And while the banks get paid, and the federal government collects its taxes, we'll be that much closer to the most terrible poverty of all.

The most terrible poverty of all. Are libraries essential to education? Hamill thinks so. I think so. And for any among you who believe that putting people "on the long road to becoming human" is a desirable objective of education, I don't think there can be any doubt about it.

Money in the (Data) Bank or, User, Can You Spare Ten Bucks?

I think we should begin by pushing aside the semantic nonsense which makes it difficult to see the shape and texture of the real issue. The swelling debate of the past few years seems to have led to the adoption of one of those slogan-like umbrella titles: Fee vs. Free. This is neat as a title, pleasing perhaps to the journalistic eye and ear, but it is self-evidently a distortion.

We all know—even the often despised lay citizen knows—that those millions of volumes that occupy the shelves of thousands of institutions staffed by many more thousands of librarians throughout this country, and the variety of services that spring from these staples, did not materialize as if by a simple wave of a magic wand. They were not, and are not, free. They have been paid for already, largely by that same unfortunate lay citizen in one way or another (but mostly one way—through taxation). And the real question before the house is whether John Q. or Mary Y. Citizen shall pay yet again, via the device of a fee for the use of what he or she has already bought and continues to maintain through regular payments which are as relentless as alimony or child support.

In short, the simple question is not whether new or different or expanded services shall be free. It is, rather, how shall they be paid for? And here we come upon, as we so often do with societal questions, a confrontation between principle and expediency. We have been there before, and the record of the past should not make us too sanguine that we shall choose the right fork in the road this time.

Why are we suddenly facing this dilemma? The answer (or answers) to that question can be complex, but I have always had a reputation, particularly among those who disagree with me, for shooting for what they

---

Edited version of a speech given at the Spring Banquet of the District of Columbia Library Association, at the Capitol Hill Club, Washington, D. C., May 1978.

regard as idiotically simple answers to tough questions, so I will suggest that we are where we are because of two or three fairly apparent but overlapping circumstances, and it is only the overlapping that makes it all look complex.

The first of these circumstances is that technology, that Genghis Khan of the twentieth century, in its quest for conquest, decided a few decades ago that even our relatively insignificant territory should not be overlooked. Since in such peaceful terrain violence was inappropriate, it used the other weapons of conquest—bribery, propaganda and fear.

It promised us that its modern mechanical marvels would enable us to do things we had always dreamed of but which had always been beyond our grasp. Visions of Browning! "Man's reach should exceed his grasp, Or what's a Heaven for?" What librarian could resist such a dream? In a few short years we should be able to store encyclopedias on the head of a pin. We could locate information of whatever kind, in whatever format, wherever it might be. We could transfer this information with the speed of light from point X to point Y, no matter how far apart they might be.

All of this, at first, the producers and exploiters of these visions admitted with a poignant touch of honesty (not often to be repeated thereafter), would be expensive, but as their markets expanded and their efficiency multiplied, the costs would zoom downward and we should be able, while vastly improving the quality and range of our services, to solve many of our perennial problems and resolve their fiscal implications. We'd be able, for example, to avoid the continuing expense of huge multi-million-dollar buildings, because storage would be so much more efficient. And there was the very special advantage for what they called a "labor-intensive" operation like library service: machines would be cheaper than people.

Meanwhile, back on the ranch of reality, the world's economy began to go into a tailspin. Oil began to surpass gold as the world's most valuable item of barter and the corridors of power became misty with confusion. Inflation dropped its bombs as indiscriminately upon some of the rich nations as the poor. Now, if there is one sure thing in this world, it is that matters economic have more immediate and more visible impact upon our lives than any other kind. And, as has happened so often before when the economy has gone out of control, the social conscience began to fog—and in some cases, virtually to black out.

On our domestic front (i.e., libraryland), the effects of all this chaos were quickly apparent. The poor are always among the early victims of economic turmoil and, in terms of social and government support, libraries were always, compared with many other communally-supported agencies and services, in the lower economic strata. In the sixties, for a few brief years, we had begun to imagine or hope, thanks largely to the powerful and beneficent wand of fairy godfather Lyndon Johnson, that our economic status might be changing rapidly for the better, but the wicked witch of Watergate soon scuttled that dream. And now, in the seventies, we see our costs, like everyone else's, soaring skyward, and the rain from Plains [Georgia] shows no sign of falling mainly, or even very steadily, on that institution called library.

While our federal support cupboard begins to resemble Mother Hubbard's, however, technology has really whetted our appetites and our imagination, and though far from delivering on its visions of rescuing us from space, staff and fiscal problems, it continues to spread a banquet before us. Eat, it says, enjoy, participate. There's just one thing—you might call it a cover charge, and it's steep. They've done a good job of selling, though, and we can really taste those goodies now, and we want, desperately, to perform the wonders technology has promised us, even though the elected representatives of society show little inclination to help with picking up the tab.

The answer to the dilemma, some among us decided, was simple. We'll make this banquet, these increased benefits, available only to those who can pay the freight. Those who use these services shall pay for them. We'll charge fees. Nor was this, I think, an answer out of context with much else that was in the air; it was perhaps just another manifestation of a growing worldwide malaise, a burgeoning conservatism and elitism, an abandonment of the goal of the public good in favor of the private gain.

One reason that it poses such a dilemma for some of us is that *we* see librarians as people whose roots are sunk deep in the concept of the public good. Whatever other reason could there have been for the formation of our institutions and collections and services? *Per se,* they are the result of socially philanthropic motivation. There were always among us people who could afford to build private information castles that would satisfy both their needs for grandeur and self-satisfaction and their own pursuit of knowledge, or even wisdom. But is was equally apparent that for the vast majority this was an impossible dream. Libraries, along with mass education—and you may quail at the term if you like—are among the preeminent examples of socialist thought and activity in this country's brief history.

That this was understood, not just here but internationally, even as recently as thirty years ago, is evident in the simple, moral declaration of the Unesco Public Library Manifesto, that a public library "should be maintained *wholly* from public funds, and no direct charge should be made *to anyone* for its services."

To demonstrate how far we have come from that conviction, today we hear pronouncements like Eugene Jackson's (and I quote him because he equivocates less than most of the fee-boosters), that "The End of Free Library Service Is At Hand." Jackson sees the time coming when "*All* library service will be for a charge levied on the user.*"

Unless we take—and soon—a firm stand for principle (perhaps the one solid principle on which most library service has stood for more than a century), and against expediency in the face of economic pressure, I believe that the fulfillment of that forecast is inevitable. And because I believe that what he proposes represents the certain demise of one of the greatest institutions for the public good in our history, I am greatly heartened by the fact that the association over which I preside this year *has* adopted a clear statement of principle. It says:

> The American Library Association supports the principle of equal access to information through the maintenance of publicly funded institutions providing library and information services. The charging of fees and levies for information services, including those services utilizing the latest information technology, is discriminatory in publicly funded institutions providing library and information services.
>
> The American Library Association through its membership will promote the concept of equal access to information in a free society. The Association calls upon all concerned citizens to join in developing the kind of public support for libraries and information agencies which will ensure the utilization of the latest technological developments in information delivery without placing additional fees and levies upon the individual seeking access.

This is not the first time in our history that we have not been able to supply all the services we'd like to provide, or that some of our users or potential users need. In fact, there is no time I can think of when that has not been the norm. Our answer, even if rather misty in practice, has been to adopt priorities (sometimes, perhaps, the wrong ones)—to decide that we can do this more effectively than that, or that this user's need is more important or pervasive than another's. Or, often, some among us have decided not to make such judgments and have wound up doing nothing very well.

That same range of policy and administrative decision and indecision is in play today, but the difficulty of decision-making has escalated under the impact of technology and rising costs. Because technology has vastly enlarged our potential capacity to do certain things, there are some who argue that we *must* do them, no matter the cost, or we shall miss the bandwagon that will drive us into a grander future. Worse, they say, if you do not get aboard, the wagon may run over you.

This kind of philosophy of panic can result not only in a dulling of conscience but also seems to lead to a decline in perception and logic. For example, instead of regarding data base services as a technologically-facilitated expansion or improvement of bibliographic or reference service, many among us are now talking of them as *new* or *different* or *specialized* library services—and this is made part of the rationale for adopting a new or different economic base to support them.

There is, in my mind at least, a marvelous parallel to this kind of thinking in what happened in the sixties when Lyndon Johnson waved wads of greenbacks before our eyes in order to attract our attention to the Great Society. We quickly became aware that among the poor and in the ghettos and slums of our country was a vast public that libraries had never reached, and in many cases had made little effort to reach. Given the new and surprising development that the Fed seemed prepared to bankroll an effort in this direction, local communities suddenly discovered people whose existence they had hitherto hardly recognized. (It was, for example, the first time in the living memory of many that Scarsdale, N.Y. even admitted to having any poor people within its boundaries.)

Library service to "these people" (remember that phrase?), since it had not been part of our normal pattern, was *obviously* something new or different or specialized—so we made up names like "outreach" to emphasize its separateness. Further, we came to persuade ourselves (and I don't mean just librarians, but trustees and local councils and the panoply of local government) that since these were not "normal" services they could not be supported out of "normal," i.e., local, funding sources. And when Uncle Sam—or rather, Uncle Richard—tightened the purse strings, many of these services, still experimental or at the special project stage, were abandoned or emasculated, and we returned once more to "normal" library service.

The parallel does not seem so clear to some people I've talked to, but I think it's valid. Simply put, service to minorities and the poor was seen, as data base services are seen, as specialized—services to special publics with special needs. And since we have a hard time finding the funds for regular, normal, ordinary library service, we can only undertake these "extras" if we have special financing. In the case of the poor, the special funding was to come from the Fed; in the case of the data base services, since the Fed door seemed to be closed, it is to come from the pockets of those who are able and willing to pay for their information.

The most frequent question those of us face who oppose the concept of charges to individuals for information goes something like this: "Are you saying that if we have the capacity to deliver a service which cannot be supported out of regular library funding, but which some users want and are willing to pay for, we should deny those users access to that service because there are others who cannot pay for it?"

My answer to this, which seems to shock some who ask the question, is a simple yes. For these reasons:

1) I do not buy the bit about services we cannot support out of regular library funds, as I've tried to explain. We make policy decisions every day about what we can or cannot do, can or cannot supply. The question is, is this a priority or not? If it is, given the finite quality of budgets, what do we drop that is of lesser priority? Or, the other answer, if it is a service of major importance, why do we not make a solid pitch for increased funding in order to supply it?

2) It is also a basic and traditional tenet of library policy, in public institutions at least, that we do not discriminate among users, and here perhaps we can begin to discern an omission in the Library Bill of Rights. This document tells us: "The rights of an individual to the use of a library should not be denied or abridged because of his (!) age, race, religion, national origins or social or political views." In view of recent developments I would add: "Or his (or her) financial status."

The real danger of the present debate, as I see it, is that it is focusing all of our attention on one surface manifestation of the *major* issue, most of the ramifications of which still lie below the water-line of our profession's active concern.

Perhaps the two most important driving forces in our society today are energy and information. Both significantly affect not only our present condition but the shape of our future. Both, in a sense, are out of control, disorganized, their direction motivated not so much by human needs as by human greed. And access is a key factor in both cases, since both are sources of tremendous power, and access to power *is* power. Power has always been the most explosive influence upon the human condition, and whether its effect has been disastrous or beneficial has depended largely upon public policy. The quality of our policy-making with regard to these power sources will, I believe, more than anything else determine the quality of most people's lives for perhaps centuries ahead.

The current administration is struggling rather desperately to get a hold on policy to regulate energy and its use, and access to it, so that our society will not be crippled either by lack of access or gross misuse and waste of energy. I think we can begin to see signs of similar attention to national policy as it relates to information and its potential effect on our society—though the higher levels of the administration appear not to have adopted this as a matter of great concern yet, even though the information components of the U.S. economy account for almost half of our Gross National Product.

What concerns me more than the administration's apparent lack of interest is that the library profession has not demonstrated much concern over national information policy. There are others, though, who have recognized the dimensions and the potential of this "other" energy source—information. As Lee Burchinal, director of the Division of Science Information at NSF, said at the recent Pittsburgh Conference on the On-Line Revolution in Libraries:

> The driving forces for these changes—present and projected—lie outside the library field and its on-line suppliers. The major impetus is derived from the dynamics of the major elements comprising the U.S. information economy. Information processing requirements of business, banking, and other commercial enterprises are immense.

So they are, so they are. And they should and must be met. And I have no doubt that they will be met. But do we want information production, dissemination and availability in our society shaped entirely by such forces?

There is a need, a desperate need, for public policy in the information field, before it is too late, before this power source goes out of control like others before it; before information, like oil and gas, is drained off into private storage tanks to which the only key is money, and of which the beneficiaries are only a privileged few.

This, I think, is the real issue facing the library profession. Are we prepared to do the thinking and carry on the in-fighting that will be necessary to preserve *public* rights and services to meet *public* needs in an arena which has such profit potential that the private sector is determined to annex as much as it can for its own purposes. We have never, I believe, had a better opportunity to demonstrate the public utility and value of our profession, our institutions and our services; we shall not demonstrate it by adopting the tactics and motivations of commerce itself.

A long time ago, Bernard Shaw said, "All professions are conspiracies against the laity." Having witnessed the social responsibility of those bastions among the professions, medicine and law, these past years, the irascible Irishman's witticism sounds prophetic. But much as I love Shaw, I'd like to see the library profession prove him wrong. We have a chance. Will we take it?

Our Commission, Our Omissions

An Assessment of the National Commission on Libraries and Information Science (NCLIS)

In the history of American government the batting average of national commissions is not such as to produce many Hall of Fame candidates. For the most part commissions have acquired a deserved reputation as delaying devices, mechanisms for inaction, or fronts for presenting, with contrived impartiality, the views of whatever administration is currently in power.

One shining exception to this sad record for many years was the U.S. Commission on Civil Rights. Under administrations of both parties it stood firm and independent, strongly espousing and fighting for the principles inherent in its name. Then along comes a celluloid cowboy from the West, three commissioners whose dedication to civil rights could scarcely be faulted are dismissed, and a "neoconservative" (to use the term applied by the current chair, Clarence M. Pendleton, Jr.) fifth column is established. As we moved into 1984 we witnessed the Orwellian specter of the Commission advocating the denial and total reversal of much that its distinguished predecessor had ever represented.

The obituary of the Commission as believers in civil rights had known it was written, vividly and appropriately, by Mary Frances Berry (one of the original Reagan targets, later reinstated as part of a dismally unsuccessful "compromise"): "The Civil Rights Commission has become a twin of the civil rights division of the Justice Department, and the bank of justice, as Martin Luther King used to say, is now bankrupt. The Civil

---

Reprinted by permission from *Library Journal* 109, No. 12: 1283-1287, July 1984. Copyright © 1984, Reed Publishing, USA.

Rights Commission is no longer the conscience of America on civil rights. I despair for women and minorities in this country."[1]

NCLIS and Reagan

In 1981 President Reagan attempted, illegally, to dismiss three members (all of them women, and one a former President of the American Library Association) of the National Commission on Libraries and Information Science (NCLIS). Looking back, this appears uncannily like a preview of the successful experiment which transformed the Civil Rights Commission from a decent and generous Dr. Jekyll into a malevolent Mr. Hyde. Actually, in the case of NCLIS the Administration's plan misfired badly: after many protests the Senate sat on the President's recommendations, the process of investigation and confirmation had to begin all over again, and the three "fired" Commissioners wound up serving an extra six months beyond their originally allotted terms.

Among those who best expressed the fears aroused by this arbitrary White House raid on NCLIS was Frederick Burkhardt, the first, and perhaps most distinguished, chair of the Commission. Testifying before a Senate committee, he warned that the premature dismissals violated Congressional directives specifically designed to "insulate the Commission from shifting political winds," and cited three precedents (two Supreme Court decisions and one district court ruling) to support his contention that "There are some offices that by their nature and function are meant to be independent of control. direction and interference from the President."[2]

This event, despite its ominous ramifications, elicited no great outpouring of comment or criticism in the library press. It may well, however, have exacerbated some of the doubts and uncertainties about the Commission's direction and purpose that have rumbled, mostly below the surface, in many areas of the library profession since NCLIS became a legal entity.

Early doubts about NCLIS

Reporting on the first NCLIS press conference, back in the early 1970s, for example, *LJ* commented that "Both the makeup of the Commission and the tenor of its first utterances suggest that libraries will be of peripheral concern,"[3] and pointed to the absence among the

Commission's membership of anyone concerned with the information problems of children and youth, anyone from the publishing industry, anyone concerned with the information starved urban poor, anyone from the Office of Education or the American Library Association . . . and so on.

The makeup of the Commission continues to be a problem of serious concern. Throughout the dozen or more years of NCLIS, perhaps only Clara Jones, former director of the Detroit Public Library and former ALA President, could truly be described as a member drawn from the mainstream of librarianship, a person widely known and respected in library circles and deeply involved in professional activities. Over those years, too, ALA has had a consistently dismal record in gaining representation on the Commission.

Political naïveté

Today, for the first time, two librarians, both women, front for the Commission. On the staff side, Toni Carbo Bearman serves as Executive Director. Serving as chair of the Commission (the first woman and first librarian in this seat) is Elinor Hashim from Connecticut, a former public librarian who is now a special librarian. I asked the politically astute Hashim why she thought ALA was so ineffectual with its nominations for the Commission. Her response, in essence, was that too few librarians are actively involved in politics (and certainly in the Republican camp), that ALA puts forward too many names each year, and with little regard for their political affiliations. She was talking about political naïveté. Her analysis is shrewd and on the button. And I speak as a left-wing Democrat who has been nominated at least twice to a very right-wing Republican administration.

Another early critic of the Commission was Dan Lacy, surely one of the most respected voices from the book world. In the mid-seventies when NCLIS unveiled its first, and only, basic policy and program document, *Toward a National Program for Library and Information Services: Goals for Action,* Lacy criticized the report for "its primary emphasis not on strengthening the resources of individual libraries but on largely electronic networking." Said Lacy: "One had the impression that the report was seeking problems for the solution rather than the other way about."[4] His comments found little support because in this NCLIS had jumped on a bandwagon already occupied by many leaders of the profession. The vehicle remains crowded today, but the resources of many libraries are in poorer shape than when Lacy made his comments.

By the mid-'70s John Berry saw NCLIS as one of "three potential sources of library legislative leadership." His other choices were, obviously, the ALA Washington Office and, curiously, Librarian of Congress Daniel Boorstin. "The problem with NCLIS," however, said Berry, "is that we are not yet sure to which library body that arm is connected" . . . and "before we accept the well-intentioned leadership of such an agency, we'd better be sure we can influence the results."[5] In the next few years there were some who began to wonder whether the arm was connected to a library body at all.

Private forces

For example, in 1980 two leaders in the Illinois Library Association questioned "the oblique direction the National Commission . . . has been taking with regard to its constitutional charge," and declared that " . . . private interests have been allowed to be the overwhelming force in the conduct of the Commission."[6]

This apprehension gathered steam when the Commission, in early 1982, issued its Task Force report on *Public/Private Sector Interaction in Providing Information Services.*[7] Carol Tauer, a professor of philosophy in Minnesota, said: "When I first tried to read the report . . . I was dismayed. Frankly, I couldn't figure out what it was all about . . . the Task Force report was nearly incomprehensible to me . . . There must be a hidden agenda, I thought . . . It occurred to me that perhaps the Task Force had been assigned the task of formulating an information policy that would be consistent with Reaganomics."[8] And, in the best balanced and most thoughtful article yet to appear on that report, Patricia Schuman concluded that the approach advocated by the NCLIS Task Force was "simplistic, but dangerous."[9]

Over the years of the Commission's existence, *LJ* has been by far the most frequent and insistent critic of its directions, purposes, and motives. Most of the quotations above have been drawn from its pages because there is little elsewhere in the library press other than regurgitations of NCLIS press releases as news. When I was commissioned to prepare this assessment of NCLIS past and present, I suspect that the editors of *LJ* knew I shared some of the doubts and concerns that they have repeatedly expressed.

Before coming to any conclusions in print, however, I set off in search of more balance, to test some of my gut feelings against the views of knowledgeable people who are or have been deeply involved with the Commission and its work. Some of their views are reflected in what follows, although few of them are identified; many would not have talked so freely had their comments been for attribution.

Bureaucratic styrofoam?

So where stands the Commission in relation to the library field today? Is it friend or foe, giant or pygmy, advocate or fifth column? Is it a leader, a catalyst, an honest broker (the Commission is fond of those last two terms) or just another layer of bureaucratic styrofoam, in place to deaden noise and impact? How do those who are or have been involved with the Commission see its role, its mission, its purpose?

The two women, Elinor Hashim and Toni Bearman, who stand on the bridge of the Commission as it sails into whatever future lies ahead for libraries and information services, are clearly and emphatically agreed upon one point: the limitations of NCLIS, its inability to do all that its critics or its proponents would wish of it. With a total staff of ten and an annual appropriation hovering consistently around $700,000, NCLIS is clearly not in much more than the rowboat class among the vessels of the Federal Fleet. Even though that budget is cushioned by something like $200,000 from other sources (contracts such as one with the Department of Commerce for about $66,000, and "in-kind services" such as the loan of two professional librarians from IBM), a disproportionate amount of the Commission's effort the past few years has had to be expended on insuring its own survival.

Some political cynics have seen the constant pressure from the Office of Management and Budget as a calculated device to keep the Commission in line with Administration policies and objectives. Hashim denies this strenuously. She points to the fact that this year the Administration, for the first time, has recommended an *increase* in the NCLIS budget. Even though the increase is minuscule, *any* increase in the present Washington climate can be fairly judged a minor miracle. It is, I think, the *only* increase proposed by the Administration for any library program in the past year.

This does perhaps support the view, propounded by one informed observer, that NCLIS has been gradually winning the support of individuals in government, proving its worth agency by agency, and has gained sufficient political backing that it can now be regarded as pretty well established. This is not to say that all threats have vanished, but that NCLIS security is more nearly normal on the federal agency hazard scale.

No degree of security, however, seems likely to convert the Commission into the kind of advocacy or lobbying leader that some of its critics want it to be. It still sees itself primarily, as it was set up to be, as an advisory body, providing informed and "independent" information when and where it can along the labyrinthine corridors of government. My strong impression is that it has done, and continues to do, that job rather well—if one accepts the limitations it seems to place upon its interest range. A recent example of its growing acceptance as a source or gatherer of information is the request made by a Senate Committee that NCLIS develop technical advice on the reauthorization and redesign of the Higher Education Act as it impacts on libraries.[10]

Issues for NCLIS

But whatever successes it has had in this direction, there are many who are not satisfied, who want NCLIS to act rather than react, to be more up front on serious issues with strong potential effect on libraries and librarians. Among such issues which came up repeatedly during our interviews were:

1. The continuing incursions by the current Administration upon access to and dissemination of information. Even the ALA Washington Office, which for years has made almost a fetish of "bipartisanship," has issued three chapters in a continuing chronology of government misdeeds in this area.

2. The standards proposed by the Office of Personnel Management, which would severely downgrade federal library and information positions, the fallout from which could be expected to reach into all areas of the profession. One observer commented that NCLIS had been "supportive" on this matter but had not exercised much influence. When I asked Elinor Hashim about the OPM issue she seemed to confirm that observer's evaluation. "We couldn't come out as strongly as we wished," she said.

3. The OMB Budget Circular A-76 which, if its proposals were adopted, would result in more and more federal library services being

contracted out to private companies. Again, one of our interviewees said, "NCLIS has never gotten involved in this."

4. The emerging campaign for a National Lending Right. Here is a case where the Commission could get in early and formulate some common sense approaches and attitudes before the debate sinks to the level it achieved during the British battle on the same issue.

If issues of this scope and import have failed to turn the Commission on, what *has* it been doing all these years? I asked everyone I talked to: "What do you think has been the Commission's greatest single achievement?" All of them, without exception, answered, "The White House Conference in 1979." Which leaves one with the old political question: "What have you done for me lately?" I also asked, in deference to the President's campaign rhetoric, "Are libraries better off, or worse off, than they were before the Commission?" That, of course, is a loaded (not to say unfair) question, given the variety of forces that have had an impact on libraries in the past dozen years, so it's no surprise that no one was prepared to declare that things are rosier now than they were pre-NCLIS.

Information without evaluation

One of the proud boasts of the Commission is that is has assembled, in the form of Task Force reports and other commissioned studies, a vast repository of information and testimony related to specific areas of library and information services. And so it has. But it is in connection with this "achievement" that some of the real problems and questions begin to come to the surface. Information without assessment and evaluation, leading to concrete policies and positions, is not necessarily particularly valuable; it is, perhaps, no more than what the information technologists call "raw data." It is when one asks what the Commission has learned from all this paper, and what positions have evolved from its accumulation, that one finds oneself immersed in a miasma of uncertainty. As Marilyn Gell Mason notes, "Although NCLIS . . . and other federal agencies have sponsored numerous reports and held countless planning meetings, it is not clear what these efforts have accomplished."[11]

According to Hashim, it is only since she assumed the chair that NCLIS members have been asked to vote on specific recommendations made by reporting Task Forces. Previously it seems to have been policy for the Commission *not* to take positions on anything, but simply "receive" whatever was presented to it. "The Commission now feels an obligation to decide on report recommendations." says Hashim.

If this is one small step toward clarification of its positions, and away from such marshmallow phrases as "catalyst," "honest broker," "forum" and "resident expert" to describe the Commission's apparently amorphous view of its role, there was an even firmer stride in January this year when NCLIS issued its statement on "Libraries and Information Skills in Elementary and Secondary Education." This firm statement in support of school libraries was issued in response to "an important void" in reports such as *A Nation at Risk,* prepared by the National Commission on Excellence in Education. Said the NCLIS statement: "A major criterion for the determination of excellence at any college or university is the quality of its library and information resources; and, yet, NCEE omitted any such criteria from the determination of excellence in elementary and secondary schools."[12]

In talking to Bearman and Hashim (separately) I applauded this public affirmation of the value of school libraries and asked whether similar statements would be forthcoming on the contribution that public and other types of libraries make to education. One said yes. The other said no, the school libraries statement was *it*. NCLIS may not yet be familiar enough with advocacy to have learned that a united front is helpful.

NCLIS & UNESCO

Another recent example of NCLIS position-taking, one which offers some refutation of the claim that NCLIS is under the thumb of Reagan administration policies, occurred at the ALA midwinter meeting last January in Washington, D.C. ALA's International Relations Committee was battling in the ALA Council for a resolution in favor of continued U.S. participation in UNESCO and deeply regretting the President's decision to issue notice of U.S. withdrawal from membership in that body. To the microphone came Elinor Hashim to report, surprisingly to some, that the Commission supported the intent of this resolution.

[Apparently those who were surprised had a point, or that presidential thumb was in motion after Midwinter. On May 21, long after Eric Moon wrote the paragraph above, Sarah G. Bishop, the Acting Executive Director of NCLIS, prepared a statement on the NCLIS role regarding UNESCO. According to that statement, NCLIS "reviewed its dual responsibility as secretariat for the U.S. National Committee for the UNESCO General Information Program (PGI) and official advisor to the State Department on matters relating to the program." According to the Bishop statement, NCLIS has been asked by the State Department to "1) encourage full and active U.S. participation in the UNESCO/PGI for the remainder of the year; 2) monitor any changes in the program during the year; and 3) draft a proposal for alternative mechanisms to accomplish the objectives of the PGI, should the U.S. carry out its intent to withdraw from UNESCO . . ." Bishop also reports that in an April resolution on the subject, NCLIS said that " . . . if the U.S. does actually withdraw from UNESCO, NCLIS will adhere to official U.S. policy." The statement adds that, "The Commission is deeply committed to the objectives of the PGI and will continue to help further them through whatever means are available."—[*LJ* Editor]

Public vs. Private Sector

If there are critics who are unhappy about the Commission's inaction on issues, there are others who believe that the Commission *has* developed positions (even if rather mistily) that they regard as pernicious and in opposition to policies espoused by both the White House Conference and the American Library Association. One insider we talked to felt that there has been a pronounced negative policy change, that NCLIS has "reneged on the long-range plan" presented in the old blue book[13] without replacing it with any new plan.

These kinds of doubts about where the Commission really stands are most virulent in relation to the two most pervasive and powerful issues involved in library and information services today: the respective roles of the public and private sectors, and the application of fees for various services in libraries.

On the first of these, the NCLIS report, *Public Sector/Private Sector Interaction* . . . was perhaps the most controversial document yet to emerge from NCLIS, and it heightened the fears that a policy direction had developed—and that it was distinctly in favor of the private sector. The reappointment (yet again) of Carlos Cuadra, unquestionably the most ardent and perhaps most able and influential Commission supporter of the private sector, exacerbated those fears and seemed, to the fearful, to have added confirmation of a growing conformity between the views of the

Commission and the Administration as to the respective roles of the public and private sectors.

The Commission, nevertheless, declares that it has as yet taken no firm public positions on this issue. There are many who disagree, including some we have quoted earlier in this article. Another whose opinion seems unequivocal is Marilyn Gell Mason who, as former director of the White House Conference, is certainly familiar with Commission currents. She says: "Even NCLIS, the agency responsible for the White House Conference and thought to be sensitive to the public need for information, has issued a report that recommends the shifting of responsibility away from the public sector to private industry."[14] Earlier in the same volume she notes: " . . . there is no doubt that the administration's actions have resulted in a deliberate shift of power from the public to the private sector."[15]

Also, among those we interviewed, one person with close connections to NCLIS declared flatly, "The Commission has moved toward the interests of the private sector." Another said, "I feel that in the Commission the private sector view has prevailed," attributing this result, at least in part, to the imbalance in the Commission's membership, and added, "With the Reagan appointments continuing . . . the imbalance will probably continue."

NCLIS on fees

When we raised the question of fee-based services with both Hashim and Bearman they declared absolutely that to date the Commission has taken no position. Indeed, incredibly (to this observer at least), they indicated that the Commission did not have enough facts to take a position and that they were considering a "literature search" to find out what was happening in relation to fees in libraryland. This would be hilarious if the issue were not so vital to the future of library services and to the public good. Given years of constant and loud debate on this issue in all corners of the profession, one has to wonder whether the Commission has been locked in a very remote ivory tower or whether it is being evasive in the best political manner.

One Commission document which brought the fee issue into the full glare of the spotlight was the recent *Report of the Task Force on Libraries and Information Services to Cultural Minorities.*[16] Only a month before its appearance the Commission issued another Task Force report on

Community Information and Referral Services.[17] That one NCLIS had happily "received, accepted and endorsed" at its meeting in April 1983, apparently without reservations.

Unprecedented rejection

By contrast the Commission reacted strongly to the report from the Cultural Minorities Task Force and even seemed to take some pains to dissociate itself from the recommendations therein: "It is important to note that this is a report *to* the Commission from an independent Task Force... We have not assisted the Task Force substantively in the preparation of the report..."[18] The foreword by the chair Elinor Hashim notes that the Commission endorses "the majority of the 42 recommendations in this report," but "we have declined to support eight of the 42 recommendations at this time."[19] Three of the eight rejected recommendations dealt with financial barriers to information access, and two of these addressed the fee question directly.[20] The Commission's response to these three was: "The Commission supports, in general, the concept of 'free' basic library service. However, in order to take advantage of the enormous power of technology. it may be necessary to pass on certain related costs to users."[21]

As John Berry notes in an *LJ* editorial on this report, the NCLIS-sponsored White House Conference had voted that "... all persons should have free access, without charge or fee to the individual, to information in public and publicly-supported libraries." Similar positions have been adopted by the NCLIS precursor, the National Advisory Commission on Libraries, by the American Library Association, the Public Library Association, and numerous state and national organizations. "In that sense the NCLIS Task Force recommendations echo widely accepted principles of public library service."[22]

We asked E.J. Josey, the chair of the Cultural Minorities Task Force, how his group had reacted to the rejection of eight of its recommendations. He was clearly upset that neither he nor any member of the Task Force had been informed about the rejections and learned about them only after the report was in print. "We were given no opportunity to respond," he said, "not even given a chance to explain more fully why the recommendations were made." He added: "Once again minorities were treated as minorities." To the best of our knowledge, the Commission's response to this report is unprecedented, and it's possible, again, that lack of experience with position-taking may have contributed to the Commission's discourtesy in not even informing the Task Force chair of its actions prior to publication.

NCLIS no shows

Not all of the blame for the uncertainty about the Commission's role, activities and positions (if any) can be laid at the door of the Commission itself. The press coverage of its activities over the years has been lamentable. The library press hardly ever shows up at Commission meetings, we were told by both Hashim and Bearman, even though these meetings are open and attempts are made to hold them in conjunction with or adjacent to meetings of library or information associations. It should perhaps be noted, in passing, that one prominent library periodical editor, some years ago, was fired for, among other things, being apparently *too* interested in reporting what the Commission was doing.

If the library press can be faulted for inattention (and here one might except Berry, who has maintained a steady editorial barrage of questions and criticisms), the profession itself has not been much more active in Commission watching *or* pushing. Both Hashim and Bearman acknowledged that Bob Wedgeworth and Eileen Cooke both maintained a steady top-level ALA contact with the Commission, but both bemoaned the fact that few librarians ever attend Commission meetings or otherwise make much direct contact. Certainly the ALA Council, usually involved in a feast of parliamentary minutiae, has paid little or no attention to the activities of NCLIS.

A year or so ago Bob Wedgeworth spoke to me (and I believe to one of the annual dawn breakfast gatherings of past ALA presidents) about his concern over the dwindling content of both Membership and Council meetings at ALA conferences. I asked everyone I interviewed about the Commission how they would react to the idea of ALA calling upon the Commission to send representatives for a public exchange of views at an ALA membership or Council meeting. The Commission could receive ideas and input directly from more librarians at such a session, and, one hopes, this might lead to some constructive consideration, by ALA Council particularly, of Commission activities in major issue areas that affect us all. The response to this suggestion was positive, indeed enthusiastic, and both Hashim and Bearman said they would welcome such an opportunity.

Simmering discontent

One person I talked to about the Commission said that one reason for the Commission's increasing tilt toward private sector interests was that they had done a better job of getting their views across and that the library field had done comparatively little to lobby or pressure the Commission effectively. Said this person: "Either ALA doesn't think the Commission is important (which is sad), or it believes that it can't influence it (which is equally sad), or it is simply apathetic."

If there is a prevailing discontent with, or unease about the Commission in the library field—and I think there is—it is not enough for it just to simmer below the surface; it should be communicated strongly and effectively. If the Commission advocates or supports positions which are in opposition to widely held beliefs in the profession, ALA should make it clear that it will not support the Commission uncritically and unconditionally at budget time.

Like the Commission, the American Library Association. and its policy-making body, the Council, have been criticized in recent years for lack of leadership. Here is an area where leadership could, and should, be demonstrated. The Commission is in a very prominent position to affect library services, for good or ill, and it deserves, at the very least, our scrutiny and forceful attention. It seems to want it. Let's see that it gets it.

References

1. New York Times News Service Story, Jan. 18. 1984.
2. "Burkhardt challenges White House for terminating NCLIS appointments," *LJ*, June 15, 1982. p. 1166.
3. "National Advisory Commission Meets the Press," *LJ*, January 15, 1972, p. 139.
4. "Memos to NCLIS," *LJ*, November 15, 1975, pp. 2107-14.
5. Berry, John, "NCLIS: Accountable to Whom?" *LJ*, January 15. 1976, p. 297.
6. Simpson, Betty J. and Deborah Miller, "NCLIS and the Private Sector," *LJ*, June 1, 1980, pp. 1240-41.
7. National Commission on Libraries and Information Science. *Public Sector/Private Sector Interaction in Providing Information Services.* GPO, Feb. 1982.

8. Tauer, Carol A., "Social Justice and Access to Information," *Minnesota Libraries,* Summer 1982, pp. 39-42.

9. Schuman, Patricia Glass, "Information Justice," *LJ*, June 1, 1982. pp. 1060-66.

10. "NCLIS committee to seek input on HEA revision for Congress." *LJ*, March 15, 1984, p. 526.

11. Mason, Marilyn Gell. *The Federal Role in Library and Information Services.* Knowledge Industry Publications, 1983, p. 133.

12. NCLIS. "Statement on Libraries and Information Skills in Elementary and Secondary Education." Approved unanimously by the Commission, January 6, 1984.

13. NCLIS. *Toward a National Program for Library and Information Services: Goals for Action.* Washington. D.C., 1975.

14. Mason, *op. cit.,* p. 147.

15. *Ibid.,* p. 99.

16. *Report of the Task Force on Libraries, and Information Services to Cultural Minorities.* Washington, D.C.: NCLIS. 1983.

17. *Community Information and Referral Services.* Final Report to the National Commission on Libraries and Information Science from the Community Information and Referral Services Task Force. Washington. D.C.: NCLIS, 1983.

18. *Minorities Task Force Report,* p.v.

19. *Ibid.*

20. *Ibid.,* p. vii.

21. *Ibid.,* p.viii.

22. "NCLIS and Fees," *LJ,* November 15, 1983, p. 2110.

PART II

DISCRIMINATION

Introduction

The brevity of this section is by no means a measure of the importance of this topic to me, nor of the amount I wrote on the subject. However, almost everything I wrote about discrimination appeared in *Library Journal* in the decade of the sixties, and it seems sufficiently accessible there not to repeat it all in this volume.

The only pieces included here from *LJ* are three editorials. The first, "The Silent Subject," is by far the most significant. It was this editorial, accompanied by an article by Rice Estes (to which the editorial refers), that really launched publicly the battle that would be fought throughout most of the decade to integrate libraries and library associations which were chapters of the American Library Association. I have always been proud of this editorial and I was overjoyed to read an assessment of it by E.J. Josey, Mr. Civil Rights of the library field. In *Activism in American Librarianship, 1962-1973,* he said: "That editorial alone was worth a million dollars, if we were to give monetary value to the fight for equal opportunity and equal access for Black people to libraries in the civil rights battle in librarianship."

The second editorial, "The Process of Dilution," was prompted by ALA's abortive Access Study, which was so irrelevant and so suspect in its muddy findings that it served only to set back temporarily our progress toward true civil rights in libraries and librarianship. And the third editorial dealt with a Supreme Court decision in a case involving discrimination in a southern public library. The decision demonstrated among other things that the highest court in the land found it as difficult to deal with decisions on access to libraries as ALA had done to that point.

"The Issues That Confront Us Now" was a speech to a group of Black librarians in New Jersey who were gathered together to honor E.J. Josey for his many contributions to the profession. My good friend Cheryl McCoy of the Montclair Public Library asked me to tell some of the history of the civil rights battles in which E.J. and I had participated and to take a look at discrimination and access problems from an eighties perspective.

The final item in this section is a contribution to a Festschrift for E.J. Josey, recently published by The Scarecrow Press. This edited version tells briefly the story of the struggle, sometimes heated, occasionally comic, to integrate a number of southern state library associations, and the central role that E.J. played in it all.

The Silent Subject

It is common knowledge in the library profession that segregation is not something that happens only in schools and lunch counters; that it happens in libraries too. It is common knowledge that libraries have closed their doors and their bookstocks, not because they were short of funds or readers, but because certain members of the public with the "wrong" pigmentation wanted to read.

All of which goes to prove that word of mouth is a pretty effective medium of communication, for any librarian looking at our library periodicals over the past five or six years would find it difficult to divine that libraries were involved in such problems, or even that a "segregation" problem existed.

Segregation and integration are two words which appear not to have crept into *Library Literature,* but there are two headings which seem to relate to the subject. They are "Negro and the library," and "Public libraries—services to Negroes." In the seven issues of *Library Literature* for 1959-60 we found no single item from a library periodical indexed under either heading, though there was a short news item about black and white rabbits from *Publishers' Weekly* and an editorial in *America.* There were, of course, plenty of entries under "Services to students," "Services to business and industry," and "Services to senior citizens," but services to Negroes yielded nothing except some library school theses. The 1958 *Library Literature* also revealed seven library school theses touching the subject and a few articles in *South African Libraries.* But we had to delve back as far as 1955 before we discovered any treatment of the subject in an American library periodical. An article on "Library Service in Mississippi," by Dorothy McAllister appeared in the March 1, 1955 issue of *LJ,* and an editorial feature entitled "No Segregation Here" appeared in the November 15 issue of *Junior Libraries* the same year.

Reprinted by permission from *Library Journal*, December 15, 1960. Copyright © 1960, Reed Publishing, USA.

After these years of vacuum it is encouraging to see at least two of our library periodicals becoming aware that segregation is a social menace that inflicts itself upon libraries as well as other institutions. Even reporting without comment what has been happening recently in Danville, Petersburg, and other places is an improvement. Even the bland, benign and tentative discussion of segregation in the September editorial in the *Wilson Library Bulletin* is a big step forward. But something more is needed, and we welcome the forthright and honest statement by Rice Estes. We hope that it will be the beginning of a much wider expression of opinion on a situation which is improving, if at all, desperately slowly, a situation of which the profession can hardly be proud.

With Mr. Estes we challenge the assumption of the editor of the *Wilson Library Bulletin* that "ALA's record is that of an organization opposed to segregation, and *as effective against it as its structure permits.*" Even if he is right, doesn't the opening sentence of ALA's *Goals for Action* state: "The American Library Association recognizes its obligation as an organization devoted to the service of our society *to adapt its program of action* to the changing needs and problems with which our nation contends"? If the structure doesn't permit action, then it should be changed. Here is one goal that demands action.

We recognize that ALA's Federal Legislative Policy states that libraries "have direct responsibilities in making good books . . . available in quantity to all Americans of all ages, races, creeds and circumstance." But why does the Library Bill of Rights feel that it is more important to condemn the exclusion of "any book . . . because of the race or nationality, or the political or religious views of the writer," than to condemn the exclusion of any reader for the same reasons?

Even the admirable *Newsletter on Intellectual Freedom* skirts the subject of segregation in favor of Mrs. Granahan, the Postmaster General, Lolita and Lady Chatterley. These are interesting subjects, we admit, but since when did intellectual freedom involve the book but not the reader? Is it any more an infringement of intellectual freedom or an application of censorship to keep one book out of a library than to bar the door to hundreds of people?

Why does ALA need to set up yet another committee to study the question of civil rights when it already has an Intellectual Freedom Committee? And why the stand announced by President Benjamin Powell at Montreal that the Association "cannot and does not attempt to intrude upon local jurisdiction." What constitutes "intrusion"? And how long does a question remain "local"? This is an issue which affects thousands of would-be library users in perhaps a third of the country. In any case, even at a local level the profession has been more demonstrative when someone has tried to keep a book out of a library than when a reader has been excluded.

We would agree that ALA's attitude toward segregation is clear. We do not agree that it is positive enough, nor that it is voiced either frequently enough or at the most appropriate times. And we are not convinced that an attitude is enough to offer. Some Southern librarians are opposed to segregation and are working, as John Wakeman says, "with all deliberate speed" to end it. But we are equally sure that there are some Southern librarians who are not going to stick their necks out on this issue because they can expect no visible or concrete means of support from the rest of the profession.

How many segregated libraries are there today? How many public libraries are there where Negro readers are still not allowed to borrow under any circumstances? In 1955, Dorothy McAllister, in the article referred to above, found that of 50 Mississippi communities providing public library service only 12 provided that service for Negroes, and apparently all these 12 served Negroes through separate branches or rooms, thus cutting off Negro readers from the main central book collection. The other article previously referred to, "No Segregation Here," revealed that two-thirds of the Negro population of 13 states were entirely without library service in 1953. It requires an elastic definition of "local" to cover this situation.

There has been improvement. But the recent eruptions at Danville and Petersburg illustrate that there is still much to be done before public libraries are free in the most important sense of the word. So long as there remains one place where any reader is denied the right to read and borrow freely from a public library, it is not enough for the profession to stand upon an attitude. The individual reader, and the librarian who is fired for fighting for the rights of that reader will not find an attitude very comforting.

What actions should be taken to support the attitude? Mr. Estes suggests several approaches. One we particularly like is that ALA might urge trustees of libraries in the South which have desegregated to use their persuasive powers upon the trustees of those libraries which have not made this elementary advance. The local chapters of ALA could certainly be asked to bring more pressure to bear in protesting the closing of libraries.

Most urgent, in our opinion, is the need for the profession to find some way to give legal as well as moral support to librarians—and if need be, groups of citizens—who at present fight alone to keep libraries open and free. How actively does the profession support other bodies involved in the struggle for civil liberties when libraries and library readers are involved? Is it considered unprofessional to associate with "dangerous" bodies like ACLU or NAACP?

The world today is full of deterrents: don't we have any? What about federal and state aid to libraries? Is it reasonable that federal funds made available under the Library Services Act should be apportioned to libraries whose services are not available to *all* the people who wish to use them?

We feel sure that there are many avenues of persuasive action which have been left unexplored. ALA, as Mr. Estes points out, has done some great things. But we cannot be satisfied while there are great things left undone, and the profession should lend all possible aid to the cause of "free" libraries.

The Process of Dilution

An article on "Segregated Libraries" by Rice Estes—the first of its kind in library literature for at least several years—appeared in *Library Journal* in the December 15, 1960 issue. It was clear from the letters we received that the article had opened many eyes, and that there were many librarians who had previously been unaware that discriminatory practices were as deeply rooted in libraries as they were in schools and other public institutions.

Immediately following the Estes article there began the demands for a survey which would elicit some of the facts about discrimination in libraries, since this lack of knowledge, some people claimed, was what made it difficult for the library profession to take appropriate action in this area. Within a few months came an editorial in the *California Librarian* by William Eshelman, a letter in *LJ* (February 15, 1961) from Dorothy Bendix, later to be one of the sponsors of the Access Study, and an editorial in this journal (March 15, 1961), whose publishers also became one of the principal sponsors of the Access Study. Here was the real beginning. Promptly after the *LJ* editorial, Archie McNeal, chairman of ALA's Intellectual Freedom Committee, expressed interest in our proposal, and the wheels began to turn.

We record this chronology for one reason only: to make it quite clear that we were in favor of a study from the beginning, if only to remove "lack of facts" from the scene as an excuse for inaction. Our publishers backed our words with financial support for the Study, despite some reservations about the outline proposed for survey. If we now join the ranks of the critics of the report, we do so as clearly interested and involved parties.

It is worth noting that all these early advocates of a fact-finding study urged a survey of *Southern* libraries, where it was clear that direct

---

Reprinted by permission from *Library Journal*, December 15, 1963. Copyright © 1963, Reed Publishing, USA.

discrimination was most prevalent and stringent. The objective was not to apportion blame but to find out more, in Dorothy Bendix's words, about "the factors responsible for the successful transition from segregated to integrated libraries in some Southern communities." This, our March 15, 1961 editorial commented, "is perhaps the most vital [information] of all." The thought was that if enough information could be compiled about the ways in which some Southern communities had been able successfully to integrate their libraries, this evidence might be used diplomatically to persuade still reluctant Southern librarians, library boards, and other authorities that similar progress was possible in their communities too.

As the Access Study began to emerge from idea to concrete proposal, it became obvious that ALA did not intend to pursue this reasonably clear and manageable goal. The very term "access" was the beginning of the process of dilution (like so much that was to follow, and like the phraseology of the report of the Access Study, the term had many connotations): the real purpose, it seemed, had to be camouflaged in some kind of research neutralism and respectability. The proposal finally approved by the ALA Executive Board expressed concern "about the Negro and the restrictions still imposed on him in certain areas," but added, "the problem is not limited to one minority group or to one geographical area."

In a sense this was true, but it was also an avoidance of another truth, that the most acute and obvious problem was precisely the restrictions placed upon the Negro reader in particular, and particularly in one geographical area. Nevertheless, diplomacy quickly prevailed over common sense, and we found ourselves faced with a study involving all 50 states and bringing under the research umbrella a variety of digressions such as restrictions upon students, variations in regional resources, etc. It is almost a wonder that ALA did not include some aspects of censorship, which restricts "access" as surely as some of the other factors with which the Study was burdened.

As it was, we already seemed to have on our hands a study blown up to nearly the proportions of the Public Library Inquiry—and the vast, nebulous territory of this newly "defined" inquiry had to be covered for little more than carfare, some $35,000 to $40,000. Then, having found International Research Associates, Inc. to bite off this impossible task, ALA demonstrated a commendable but rare urgency and asked that the job be done as quickly as possible. In barely more than six months the job was "done," the report issued, and the tumult began.

Given the dilution of purpose and the spread in scope of the study, the limited financial resources, a tight deadline, plus the survey team's (later to be revealed) obvious unfamiliarity with library service and practice, it is little wonder that the final result is as disappointing and dismal as it is. The fault lies not nearly entirely with INRA.

Many specific criticisms of the report have been made by the contributors to our symposium, and we do not intend to repeat any of those here. We intend to concentrate only on an aspect of imbalance in the report which stems perhaps from the original shying away from the focal problem.

With the wave of Negro protest expanding rapidly northward in this past eventful year, it seems that the surveyors decided, or were persuaded, to jump on this bandwagon, to prove, at all costs, that discrimination is not a someplace thing, it is everywhere. This scarcely needed proving, but in their attempt to do so the surveyors have eliminated the shadings and have given the spotlight a sharp 180-degree spin to leave it focussed on the places where, if discrimination does exist in library service, it certainly is not as strenuous or adamant or extreme as in some places on the other side of the arc.

The emphases and attitudes in this report vary subtly but considerably, and nowhere more so than in the methods of study and reporting of the Southern situation as opposed to that in the ten selected cities. While protecting the anonymity of Southern libraries, the surveyors erect a signpost prominently pointing to Washington, D.C., Detroit, Philadelphia, *et al.* While concentrating properly on the services and resources of the main library when studying Southern libraries, the researchers omit all mention of the main library when making their peculiar assessment of de facto discrimination in library service further North. And while sending in interviewers to back up and verify questionnaire findings in the South, Detroit and others get their treatment on the basis of statistics only.

This is not to claim that all is roses and purity north of that famous line, only to insist that the treatment of the libraries surveyed should be as fair and equal as one hopes the services of all libraries might be when discriminatory practices are finally stamped out. Thus, when the surveyors point out with some deliberation that Philadelphia has more branches in "white" tracts than in "black" ones, they surely invoke the obligation to point out that Philadelphia's "black" tract branches contain more volumes than those in the "white" tracts. But there is no need to delve further into the absurdities of the survey team's methods of evaluating branch provision—which bring to mind a delightful little book published some years ago, entitled *How to Lie with Statistics*—for even the Advisory Committee, in its guarded way, seems to have written off this piece of the report.

If the report is suspiciously invalid in this section, it gives hints of being quite as inaccurate on the South. Here, we see the difference in attitude. While rooting for malpractice in the North, determined to find it whether it is there or no, the surveyors have done their best to present the Southern situation in a kindly light. No one objects to sympathetic reporting of course, providing it is done within the bounds of reasonable accuracy. But is it?

In an appendix, the report provides a "List of Integrated Public Libraries," all located in "the eleven states of the Confederacy." Now admittedly, the report also defines its terms—in a footnote, as follows: "The term 'integrated' is used in this listing to indicate library systems in which the main library is accessible to members of all races. Many of these libraries, however, are not *fully* integrated in the sense that they provide more restricted services for one group of the population than for another."

The surveyors are not kidding! But they don't indicate in any way which of those libraries on the list impose some of the most unpleasant restrictions or perpetrate various indignities on their Negro readers. There in the appendix, proudly listed as "integrated," are Albany, Georgia, Montgomery, Alabama, and Danville, Virginia, where various forms of insidious maneuvering like so called vertical or horizontal "integration" are still in force to remind Negro readers that they use these libraries on sufferance. Footnote or no, the use of the word "integrated" to describe these situations is laughable.

The information upon which this list is based, says the report, was "received from regional informants in the South, visits to the South by interviewers from INRA-New York, and a wide variety of research studies, journals, magazines, and newspapers." Did anyone, we wonder, ask *Negroes* in these communities whether they regarded such libraries as integrated?

The thoroughness of the research may be illustrated by a couple of other comparisons between this bald listing in the Access Study and the evidence in another recent study titled *Integration in Public Library Service in Thirteen Southern States, 1954-1962*. This latter is a master's thesis completed at the School of Library Service, Atlanta University in August 1963: its evidence was collected also by a combination of questionnaires, correspondence, interviews and a literature search.

Two libraries listed as "integrated" in the Access Study are those of Lafayette, Louisiana, and Concord, North Carolina. Of these, the Atlanta study records:

1) "The city of Lafayette supports a library system composed of seven branches and the main library. The branches are still operated on a segregated basis. Six of the seven are operated for use of white patrons and one provides service for Negroes. *The Main library does not offer fully integrated service for Negroes.* A Negro reader must be in high school before he is permitted the use of the main library facilities."

2) "No change in the policy of serving Negroes at the Concord Public Library . . . has been made by the library board. The arrangement which permits Negroes to secure circulating materials from the main library through a segregated branch is still the general rule. A few Negroes have been permitted the use of the reference room. This is an exception to the general rule of the library, and it is not generally known by the Negroes that this can be done. *The library board has maintained that library cards are not to be issued to Negroes at the main library.*" (Our italics in both the above items.)

These are just a couple of samples, but perhaps they are sufficient to demonstrate our point. The report is suspect in its "findings" as regards both North and South, and even more suspect in the contrasting tenor of its presentation of those "findings" in the two cases.

What, then, should the next step be? Ralph Shaw suggests that ALA should: a) reject the INRA report; and b) set in motion "studies that would be meaningful and helpful." Drastic as this sounds, we see little alternative.

One of the original proposals on the Access Study was that, after completion of the survey, there should be "A conference on 'access to libraries' involving *lay* persons as well as library personnel. The purpose of such a conference would be to discuss information gathered, to make recommendations for improvement, and to define problems for further study . . ." These may very well be listed in the wrong order: first we surely need to look at those "problems for further study"—particularly at some of the problems raised by this study, and how to avoid a similar disaster in any further attempts to seek out the real story of discrimination in libraries.

Access and the Supreme Court

Access to libraries has been high on the agenda and the conscience of the library profession, consistently, for a number of years. In its latest attempt to grapple with the problem, the ALA Council made a difficult decision—so difficult that it left uneasy even those who agreed with it—against closing the membership doors to those institutions which are still guilty of discrimination.

Only a few weeks after that Midwinter meeting, it became abundantly clear that decisions on access to libraries are not easy no matter at what level they are taken. A much higher body with somewhat more authority than the American Library Association—the United States Supreme Court—has divided five-to-four on the case of five Negro "stand-in" demonstrators who tried in 1964 to integrate the Clinton (La.) Public Library.

There was a measure of satisfaction in the Supreme Court decision for those who had argued, during the ALA Midwinter debate, that the law of the land could better take care of discrimination in libraries than could ALA with any further statements or constitutional amendments. Certainly, the latest decision of the Court appears to establish that Negroes may not be ejected from public libraries simply because they are Negroes.

But the unfortunate narrowness of the Court's decision may possibly herald the testing, again and again in various states, of even this clear-cut issue. If this happens, those who oppose racial discrimination in libraries may be subjected to the same continuing, tedious, expensive legal battle that has plagued and harassed the opponents of censorship. In this kind of situation, one wins only the immediate battle, never quite the war.

If that's not enough of a wet blanket of gloom to throw over a significant milestone decision, let us conjecture a little about some other problems that may be in store for libraries as a result of the views

---

Reprinted by permission from *Library Journal,* April 1, 1966. Copyright © 1966, Reed Publishing, USA.

expressed by the dissenting minority on the Court—Justices Harlan, Clark, Stewart, and, most notably, Black.

These four held not only that the Clinton case involved no racial discrimination, but that the state has a right to put people out of its libraries if it wants to. Taking off from this shaky foundation in logic, Justice Hugo Black saw the majority view as a "threat" to "public buildings such as libraries" and concluded that "The states are thus paralyzed with reference to control of their libraries for library purposes."

We are inclined to agree with the *Washington Post* that Justice Black's is a somewhat "spongy premise" and that he has inflated the issue out of all proportion. But some libraries may well have cause to share the Justice's fears.

The Supreme Court decision, in this particular case, was a clear ruling against discrimination in access to libraries on *racial* grounds. If the majority of the Court disagrees with Justice Black on this specific issue, however, does it also disagree that the state has a right to put people out of libraries for *any* reason?

Whenever the profession had discussed access, it has always been in terms of discrimination on grounds of race, religion, or personal beliefs (though ALA's "Access Study" did, sketchily, concern itself with other kinds of limitations). Do the comments of the court's dissenters not now raise the issue of discrimination on grounds other than the usual big three? What of discrimination on grounds of age (the student "problem") or of residence (the non-resident issue)?

Is there not cause to believe that students might demonstrate—successfully—against some of the restrictions which have been placed upon their access to libraries? Could not nonresidents argue that they had a right of *free* access to libraries receiving generous support from state and federal funds to which their taxes had contributed?

It begins to appear that the line between an administrative decision on services to readers and discrimination against readers is becoming as hazy as the line that has never been adequately defined between book selection and censorship. We do not share Justice Black's view of this as a "threat" to libraries, but see it as another opportunity to clarify our objectives. If it makes us think—and do—more about solving the problems of access by all people to all libraries, perhaps we should welcome what some will only dismiss as a new parcel of problems which we should avoid until they are insuperable.

The Issues That Confront Us Now

In a good many years on the speech circuit I believe I have only once indulged in a bout of autobiography. The occasion took place in Albany, N.Y., a prestigious gathering called by the Regents of the State of New York. Among the four or five other speakers, I remember, was the irresistibly charming dancer-choreographer Jacques d'Amboise. In fact there was so much histrionic talent on that platform that I felt like a small, grey cloud, barely visible in an iridescent sky. Each of us was to talk about his own field, and with the Regents present one had the feeling that there were future dollars out there whose distribution might be affected by how well we convinced them of the social and educational worth of our various professional endeavors. I had been invited as the salesman for librarianship by E.J. Josey.

It was not easy to compete with the flamboyant Jacques and his heart-warming stories of what dance and his inspirational guidance had done to revitalize the spirit and hope of poor kids in New York City, and to get across what books and reading and libraries could mean to people's lives. The only way I knew was to dramatize how my own life had been totally changed and in large part determined by the people and experiences I met on bookshelves. How well it worked I don't know, but one Regent at least told me afterwards that she had never understood before how really vital libraries were.

If I launch into a little autobiography again it is because I know of no other way to deal with this occasion. Or perhaps you should blame E.J., since he has been a guiding force in both instances where I have given way to public confession.

When I came down from Newfoundland, Canada at the end of the fifties to be interviewed for the *Library Journal* editorship, Dan Melcher,

---

An edited version of a speech at a meeting organized by the New Jersey Black Librarians Network, May 19, 1984, New Brunswick, N. J., to honor E. J. Josey for his contributions to the profession.

who would be my publisher, asked me what I thought about *LJ*. I said it looked tired and middle-aged and badly needed livening up. (You must remember, I was young then. Middle-age looks pretty good from my current perspective.)

When I got the job Dan and I decided that it might be helpful, since I was a newcomer to these shores and to the American library scene, to put together a group of distinguished American librarians who would be on tap for a couple of years whenever I felt the need for advice or contacts or help of some kind. And an outstanding group it was, including among others the profession's greatest missionary, Lawrence Clark Powell, and one of our finest Librarians of Congress, Luther Evans.

I mention this group to demonstrate how much I had to learn. Distinguished it was indeed, but no less certainly was it totally unrepresentative. Well, not totally; like ALA ballots it was geographically pretty good, and type of library representation was adequate. But the group included no minority person, and no woman. Nobody advised me of the enormity of the error; in fact, I'd be surprised if anyone at that time even noticed.

As I began to move around the country in that first year on my new job it seemed to me that you didn't have to be particularly acute or understanding to see that something important was under way in America. A few years behind us already were the Montgomery, Alabama bus boycott and the Supreme Court decision in *Brown vs. the Board of Education of Topeka, Kansas*; sit-ins in restaurants and other public places were hitting the headlines with growing frequency, and the voice of Martin Luther King was being heard, and sometimes listened to, throughout the land. Even to this newcomer it was obvious that a social revolution was gathering steam. So what impact, I asked myself, was all this having on libraries?

I spent several weeks scouring through the library literature, going a long way back, to see what was on record about the condition of black people in our profession and to find out whether blacks had the same kind of difficulties in using libraries that they clearly had with other kinds of public institutions. The search was revealing: there was virtually nothing to indicate that any such problems had impinged on the serene world of libraryland. I said *virtually* nothing; there was one shining exception. Back in the thirties poet Stanley Kunitz, then editor of the *Wilson Library Bulletin*, wrote a marvelous editorial entitled "The Spectre at Richmond" which dealt with the shameful indignities that black librarians could expect to face at their own professional association meetings. Kunitz was years ahead of the profession in social consciousness, and if you have not read that historic editorial I commend it to your attention.

At any rate, here we were at the beginning of the sixties, and the library profession either didn't think that the most explosive issue on the national agenda had anything to do with us, or it didn't want to talk about it. *Library Journal,* I felt, had to make a dent in that stolid wall of silence because, as I saw it, libraries had a simple choice: to be a significant thread in the social fabric, an active participant in social change, or to face an inevitable passage toward irrelevance, possible extinction, or a grey existence as some kind of historical relic. The only question was how best to explode the bomb.

If I simply wrote another of those argumentative Moon editorials, which were already beginning to annoy a good many people in the profession, it might simply be written off as another of the excesses of that crazy limey, and what did he know about it anyway, having been in the country less than a year? A tactical sense is useful when you're going into battle, and I decided that what I needed was a statement by a person with impeccable credentials, a product of that white Southern magnolia world where segregation was practiced as a fine art. I found Rice Estes, then librarian of Pratt Institute in Brooklyn, a white Southern gentleman beyond all question, born and bred "down there" where it was all happening. Rice's article might not look that exciting to you today, but it took courage for him to write it and he became a pariah in some circles where he thought he had friends. When the full story of the civil rights battle in librarianship is written, I hope the author will recognize that the name of Estes deserves a place of honor in it.

The Estes article appeared in the Dec. 15, 1960 issue of *LJ*, one year after I came on deck as editor. Accompanying it was an editorial titled "The Silent Subject." That editorial, *LJ*'s opening volley in the conflict that would permeate the profession throughout the decade, was aimed directly at some of the barriers and attitudes that would have to be (and *would* be) cracked in the years ahead.

It questioned whether ALA was doing all that could be done to combat segregation. Somebody had claimed that ALA was as effective in this area "as its structure permits." In response to that claim we quoted ALA's own *Goals for Action,* which said: "The American Library Association recognizes its obligation as an organization devoted to the service of our society *to adapt its program of action* to the changing needs and problems with which our nation contends."

If the ALA structure didn't permit action, said *LJ*, then the structure had to be changed. "Here is one ALA goal that demands action."

Also challenged was the view of then ALA President Benjamin Powell that ALA "cannot and does not attempt to intrude upon local jurisdiction." What, we asked, constitutes "intrusion"? And how long does a situation that is a national scandal remain local?

The editorial also urged that the profession find some way to give legal as well as moral support to librarians—and indeed to others—who were fighting alone and at great risk to keep libraries open and free, and advised active collaboration with other groups involved in the struggle for civil liberties, such as the NAACP and ACLU.

And finally the editorial said: "The world is full of deterrents; don't we have any?" And the suggestion was made, I think for the first time, that Library Services Act funds be withheld from those libraries whose services were not equally available to all who wished to use them.

I have cited this editorial in such detail not just because I'm proud of it (I am), but to demonstrate a couple of perhaps obvious points. One is that we have come a fair distance, even if still not far enough, in the near quarter-century since it was written. That there is nothing revolutionary in it to today's reader is one evidence of that; at the time its reverberations echoed throughout the profession, and the fallout in the *LJ* and Bowker offices was dirty and heavy.

A second point I hope it demonstrates is what an important role the library press can play, if it will, in the never-ending struggle for principle and constructive change.

Now I do not mean to suggest that *LJ* was alone in this press effort to bring librarianship into the mainstream of social change. Up the road, in the Bronx before it became a modern Pompeii, was my old friend and former assistant in London's Finchley Public Library, John Wakeman, by then another limey editor of an American library periodical. He had much less support from the conservative bosses of the Wilson Company than I had from the directors at Bowker, but he too was opening up the same issues on the editorial page of the *Wilson Library Bulletin*. And within months other voices began to be heard in the library press in other parts of the country. Early and notable among them were Bill Eshelman in the *California Librarian* and John Berry in the *Bay State Librarian*. It is no accident that those two later took over the editorial chairs in the Bronx and Manhattan.

I do not mean either, with this long account, to give the library press too much credit, although I do believe that the achievements of the sixties might have come much harder without the public exposure the press gave the issues. Much of what I have said thus far is merely prologue to my main points: that all the efforts of the press would probably have yielded little without the daring and dedication of those individuals who fought the battle on the front lines—in their own libraries, in their own communities and states, and on the floor at ALA membership and Council meetings.

It was in that first year that I met the person who was to become, in the next few years, unquestionably the most important figure in that initially small band of freedom fighters. E.J. Josey at that time was the librarian of a black college library in Savannah, Georgia, and we became early—and permanent—allies. I am not much in favor of public display of one's honors and achievements; it always reminds me of the offices of doctors and lawyers, who have to rank among the most certificated and sometimes the most reprehensible professionals around. Of the few documents which honor something or other in my past, all but one are buried deep in a drawer of my desk at home. The exception—it has hung for nearly twenty years in my study—is a plaque recording my receipt of the Savannah State College Library Award back in 1966. That annual award, instituted by E.J. Josey, was not, as you might imagine, something you got for immaculate cataloging or some theoretical breakthrough in administration or for assiduous attendance at meetings. I was very proud to be among its earliest recipients.

During the early sixties E.J. helped me build a network of people, mostly black—librarians, community leaders and others—who would keep me reliably informed of what was happening: which libraries in the Southland really were being desegregated and which, like the Danville, Va. Public Library, were being reported as such while continuing subtle and silly forms of discrimination like "vertical integration." That, in case anyone here is not familiar with it, was achieved by removing all the chairs from the library, so that people of different color could not sit down together.

Meanwhile, twice a year, the floor at ALA meetings came more and more to resemble a gladiator's arena. The fight was no longer just over discrimination in library *services*; it had opened up to encompass discrimination in our own professional ranks, and particularly in our professional associations. E.J. Josey, soon the most readily recognized librarian from Georgia, could not belong to the Georgia Library Association, nor attend its meetings and conferences. E.J. and I, and a growing army of dissidents in search of decency—among the early ones were such persons as Annette

Phinazee, Dorothy Bendix, Virginia Lacy Jones and Eli Oboler—fought such issues against bitter opposition, notably from some of the tough white lady state librarians of the South, and kept fighting until they were won.

One of the first apparent victories was the expulsion from ALA chapter status of several southern state associations which did not operate in accord with ALA policies: that is, they did not admit black librarians as members or didn't permit them to attend conferences, at least under decent or human or equal conditions. It soon became apparent, however, that this expulsion was a paper victory, yielding no positive results. It was clear that more heat had to be applied.

The next move took the form of a resolution, presented by the old firm (Josey and Moon), which would prevent any ALA staff member, officer or committee representative from speaking at a meeting or conference of one of the offending associations. This was designed to attack the most sensitive area of the body politics: the pocketbook. That resolution, when passed, eliminated a large number of star speakers who would draw a good attendance at state association gatherings.

Well, enough of the nostalgia. By the end of the decade, despite a long and frustrating diversion created by something dubbed the Access Study (anyone remember that?), most of these battles had been won. The Southern associations had come to heel, they admitted black members, and they had returned, as some had vowed never to do, to the ALA fold.

All of this may suggest to you that I think there was only one issue in the turbulent decade of the sixties. There wasn't, of course. There was Vietnam. There was, as there always is, censorship. There was the emergence of library unions. And in ALA there was the beginning of the social responsibility movement. Nevertheless, it still seems to me that the over-riding, overwhelming issue was discrimination, and by the end of the decade blacks were no longer the sole focus of the struggle. There were the gays, the Spanish-speaking, and a number of other minorities. And for the first time at any serious level in our professional gatherings the cause of a non-minority group was being taken up. A new and powerful army was now involved: women.

Is there a point to this long excursion into the past? Yes, there is. I was told to discuss the issues that confront us *now,* and what you can do about them. That's a tall order, and I can only chop off and tackle one small piece of it. Before doing so I wanted to demonstrate that no matter how tough the opposition, you can win—if you put enough into it, as E.J. did. The other reason for the long prologue was that I don't believe the principal issue is substantially different today.

I have said that I believe discrimination was the primary issue of the sixties, and I believe it remains so today, though now the masks it wears are subtly different. What has to be fought now, and fought with much more conviction than the profession is exhibiting, is discrimination against certain classes of library users (most particularly the poor). A broader ramification of this issue is the sustained attack that is being made on the public sector, public services, certain professions, and just about all labor unions.

In a way this battle may be more difficult than the one we were engaged in twenty-some years ago. For one thing, our principal antagonist could scarcely be a more powerful one: it is the U.S. Government. Not just the current administration, although that's where the plays are called, but also a weak and vacillating Congress, which seems unable to resist the incursions this administration has made and continues to make upon democratic freedoms and rights and the public welfare.

The administration's most sustained attack has been upon access to and dissemination of information. Even the ALA Washington Office, which for years has made almost a fetish of "bipartisanship," has issued three chapters in a continuing chronology of government misdeeds in this area. The latest one I've seen is titled "Less Access to Less Information by and about the U.S. Government: III." If you haven't seen these revealing documents, write to the Washington Office and ask for copies.

Let me give you a few samples of what has been going on. During the past few years the Freedom of Information Act, in the words of Richard M. Schmidt, Jr. (Washington Counsel for the Association of American Publishers), has been "converted into more of a shield for government than a sword for the public." The federal Privacy Act has been developed as a new tool for government secrecy. Government authority to classify information has been greatly expanded, on the pretext of protecting national security. A National Security directive mandated pre-publication review of the writings of present and former government employees and lie detector tests to uncover information leaks. Use of public access laws has been made considerably more expensive to the public. Nuclear information which was previously in the public domain has now been restricted. Government attempts to manage the news saw their high point in the barring of press coverage of the Grenada invasion. Registration of films from other countries which deal with issues of U.S. public interest (such as acid rain) has been required. And the dimensions of the attacks on access to information can perhaps be indicated by this item from the third chronology from the ALA Washington Office:

On October 6, 1982, OMB released a list of more than 2,000 government publications—one out of every six—targeted for termination or consolidation into other publications. . . . According to OMB Circular 82-25, sixteen percent of all government publications will be discontinued. This amounts to 70 million copies, one-twelfth of the 850 million copies printed. . . . [And there is this nice sting in the tail of that story:] Each federal agency will be reviewing its publications for increased user fees.

A footnote to that brief review: the administration contends that the Freedom of Information Act is too expensive—it costs about $60 million a year. Lawyer Schmidt notes that "The Pentagon spends $100 million a year for marching bands."

Given all this, it is perhaps not surprising that the ALA Council passed a resolution, two summers ago, expressing concern that there is a "mounting threat to access to information needed for the fulfillment of the democratic process."

If some of the depredations I have listed seem a bit remote in terms of your own concerns, there are others that clearly affect us very directly. There are, for example, the standards proposed by the Office of Personnel Management, which would downgrade federal library and information positions, the ripple effect from which could be expected to reach out to all corners of the profession. And there is the heinous OMB Circular A-76, which lists library services and facility operation and cataloging as commercial activities, and which could result in many library services of the government being handed over to the private sector. Could result, hell—*has* resulted. Last August a contract was awarded to a private sector firm for the total library operations of the Department of Energy Library; another such contract followed in September for the Department of Housing and Urban Development. As Marilyn Gell Mason observes in her recent book, *The Federal Role in Library and Information Services*, "there is no doubt that the administration's actions have resulted in a deliberate shift of power from the public to the private sector."

If all this is bad news, it is not, at least for some of us, very surprising: we expected nothing better of this administration. What is more disturbing is the position of the National Commission on Libraries and Information Science, which we might reasonably expect to speak on our behalf. The establishing legislation for NCLIS, remember, says "The Commission shall have the *primary responsibility* for developing or recommending overall plans for, and advising the appropriate governments and agencies on, the provision of library and information services adequate to meet the needs of the people of the United States."

I spoke recently with both the Executive Director and the Chair of NCLIS, and both declare that the Commission has as yet taken no position on the issue of the respective roles of the public and private sectors. Those of us who managed to wade through and try to make some sense of the Commission's Public/Private Sector report find that claim a little hard to swallow. Marilyn Gell Mason, a former employee of the Commission as director of the White House Conference, is unequivocal on the subject. She says: "Even NCLIS, the agency responsible for the White House Conference, and thought to be sensitive to the public need for information, has issued a report that *recommends* the shifting of responsibility away from the public sector to private industry."

Now one reason why I think this trend is another aspect of discrimination is that it is based on an underlying principle, spelled out by OMB, that "information is not a free good but a resource of substantial economic value." ALA's response, that "To participate fully in a democratic society, citizens must be informed and aware, regardless of their individual ability to pay for information," is correct but does not spell out clearly enough the dangers of this move to transfer responsibility for information dissemination from the public to the private sector. There are two clear dangers: the first, obviously, is that in general the private sector can be expected to provide information only to those would-be users who can pay for it. The second, even more pernicious in its ramifications, is that the private sector is only likely to give broad access to that information which is most profitable, and is also likely to suppress information which it sees as not in its own interests.

The administration, of course, is not the lone enemy in this battle over whether access to information is a public good and a public right, or whether information should be treated simply as another major economic resource. There are also the enemies within our own ranks. And one of the issues on the agenda there is an alarming variation of the public sector/private sector fray. Given the rash of taxpayer revolts in recent years, the almost certain decline in federal aid, and the cutbacks by local authorities, we hear with growing frequency talk of "alternative sources of funding" for libraries. I suggest to you that this phrase, constantly reiterated, is one of the most insidious threats to the continuance of library services supported by public (i.e., tax) funds. I should perhaps make it clear that I am not referring just to public libraries but also to school and academic libraries supported in whole or in large part by public money.

Clearly, it would be stupid to oppose or reject funding from any legitimate source, providing such funding does not come with strings attached that may undermine the impartiality expected of a publicly-supported institution, or that create different levels of service and/or access for different user groups and individuals. But that word "alternative" is potentially misleading and offensive because it can too easily be understood to mean that such funds may or will *replace* public support, rather than complement or supplement it. We need to stress that the *primary* source of funding and the primary responsibility are both still public. If we do not, the goal of equal access to information will be submerged in a swelling tide of commercialism.

One of these "alternatives" that is being grasped with growing fervor by the expedient within our ranks is fee-based services. These are, in essence, an extension of the public sector/ private sector issue, since fee-based services are a sort of graft onto the body public of one of the most used and favorite organs of the private sector. And the government, which likes to have things both ways, has adopted the term "user fees" as a euphemism for additional taxes.

The White House Conference, which involved a considerable number of lay citizen delegates, had no doubts on this subject, affirming "that all persons should have free access, *without charge or fee* to the individual, to information in public and publicly supported libraries." In fact, the White House Conference went further, advocating the formation of a National Information Policy "to ensure this right of access without charge or fee."

ALA is equally clear on the issue. In a policy statement it "asserts that the charging of fees and levies for information services, including those services utilizing the latest information technology, is discriminatory in publicly supported institutions providing library and information services."

Nevertheless it is no secret that this kind of discriminatory practice, which we might call "the fees disease," is proliferating in library service, and is being promoted by some of our largest and most powerful libraries as a survival technique in hard economic times.

Once again the National Commission declares that it has taken no firm public position on this issue. And again there is evidence that would seem to refute this claim. A key piece of evidence is the recent report of the Task Force, chaired by E.J. Josey, on Library and Information Services to Cultural Minorities.

When NCLIS issued that report it took an action that I believe is unprecedented in the Commission's history: it rejected (or rather, to quote accurately, "declined to support") nearly 20 per cent of the recommendations made by the Task Force. Three key rejected recommendations dealt with financial barriers to information access, and two of these addressed the fees question directly. Said NCLIS: "The Commission supports, in general, the concept of 'free' basic library service. However, in order to take advantage of the enormous power of technology, it may be necessary to pass on certain related costs to users."

So okay, enough already. You get the picture. This is the new face of discrimination in library service: on one side, the handing over of public services to the self-interest of private industry; on the other, the use by the public sector itself of fees as a kind of means test for access to information. What can *you* do about it?

The first thing is to find out what the hell is going on. I'm still amazed at every ALA Conference by how little some of the members of our profession know about what's happening around them. So keep up with library literature, and get hold of (and read) some of the key documents that are issued from time to time which may have an impact on your professional lives and/or upon your library's services or potential for the future. That report from E.J.'s Task Force, for example, spells out many of the issues about which all of us should be concerned.

Second, get involved. Don't sit back and wait for someone else to do the job. There are issues to be dealt with at state and national levels, and if you want a real voice in these matters you have to be active, vocal participants in both your state and national organizations. Don't stand on the sidelines; find out where the power spots are, and work your way in. For this you will have to do your homework: learn about the organization's structure, how it works, how to get action.

Third, get organized. Very few issues have ever been won by one person fighting alone. One person, or a few, may lead, sure, but numbers count when you want to win an election, a cause, whatever. Organize a group of people with similar interests, but then go out and look for potentially supportive allies. That may involve trading support for each other's issues, but that's how alliances are built.

And lastly, as Larry Powell told a group of younger librarians at ALA last year, don't get too hung up worrying about your career. Raising hell is risky, and you have to recognize that occasionally you're going to get chopped down. I wouldn't claim there haven't been any casualties over the years (I know several), but in the main if you fight for what you believe in, honestly and without equivocation, there'll be others who will believe in you and support you—and your career, as Larry said, will take care of itself.

If you think all this is pious baloney, I suggest we have evidence here today that it is not. E.J. Josey is an outstanding example of what involvement, organization, hard work and courage can achieve. In the years I've known him there have been few times when his neck hasn't been way out on one issue or another, but I have never known him falter when something he believes in has to be raised, and then carried through. And nobody I know in the profession works harder for his beliefs, or makes his friends work harder (my own files of correspondence with E.J. testify to that). He has been hated and abused, but he is also much loved and admired for all he has done and continues to do. His election to the ALA Presidency is, in my book, one of the landmarks of American library history, and if you had predicted it twenty years ago you might well have been committed to another kind of institution.

As much as any single person can, he has given real meaning to that splendid, ringing final sentence of the Freedom to Read Statement, issued in the dark days of McCarthyism when too many Americans thought there was safety in silence: "Freedom is a dangerous way of life, but it is ours." If a few more EJs emerge, from groups like this one and others around the country, it will continue to be ours, whatever the odds.

A "Chapter" Chapter: E.J., ALA, and Civil Rights

Back somewhere in the early 1960s I was having a drink at a convention with my friends Ed and Rachel Castagna. Ed would shortly be elected as President of the American Library Association and we were probably discussing his chances. At some point during the conversation Rachel said, "One of these years, Eric, you're going to be President of ALA." Ed and I cracked up, each of us wondering how such a normally sensible woman could conjure up such a ludicrous idea.

Why was Rachel's comment so ludicrous? In December 1960, with an editorial entitled "The Silent Subject" and an accompanying article on "Segregated Libraries" by Rice Estes, I had launched a *Library Journal* campaign against segregation in libraryland that would continue through much of the sixties. As a result, among most of the ALA establishment and a good many other prominent members of the profession, I was during that time as much a public enemy as those gentlemen whose photographs adorn the walls of local post offices.

This incident with the Castagnas came to mind when I was asked to write this piece about E. J. Josey's journey from the front lines of the civil rights battles of the sixties to the Presidency of ALA. If Rachel's prognostication about me seemed hilarious, how then might any of us have reacted to the suggestion that "one of these days" E. J. Josey would be President of the American Library Association? After all, at the time he wasn't even allowed to be a *member* of his own state organization, the Georgia Library Association. Furthermore, like Moon, he was a persistent "trouble maker," marching to the microphone at ALA conferences and disturbing the calm of those semi-annual gatherings with inflammatory perorations on social

---

An edited version of an article in *E. J. Josey: An Activist Librarian,* ed. by Ismail Abdullahi (Scarecrow Press, 1992). Reprinted by permission.

issues—which, as the then current wisdom had it, were of no concern to ALA or librarians; we could properly debate only *professional* issues.

There were in these early years two targets in the civil rights struggle: *libraries* that discriminated against blacks, and *library associations* that did not permit black librarians to join or participate in their gatherings. And there were two principal arenas for this conflict: the library press (notably *LJ* and the *Wilson Library Bulletin*, though they were soon joined by the *California Librarian* and the *Bay State Librarian*), and the floor at ALA meetings (notably Membership meetings, since the Council seemed often to be little more than a docile rubber stamp for an entrenched and powerful Executive Board).

On the individual library front one of the major difficulties was obtaining reliable information about which institutions were desegregated and which were still practicing discrimination in one form or another. Given all else that was happening in race relations, the national press was paying little or no attention to library segregation, and the library press could not have done the reporting job it did without the continued active aid of a few people in the South, most notably by far, E. J. Josey. He it was who helped me build up a network of people, mostly black—librarians, community leaders and others—who kept us reliably informed about what was happening: which libraries in the Southland were *really* being desegregated....

Meanwhile, things were beginning to happen at ALA. A Special Committee on Civil Liberties recommended the addition of a new article to the Library Bill of Rights, stating that "the rights of an individual to the use of a library should not be denied or abridged because of his race, religion, national origins, or political views," and with the ALA Council's concurrence at the Midwinter 1961 meeting this became Article 5 of the Library Bill of Rights. It remains so today, though in amended form—and without mentioning "race."

That summer (1961), at the Cleveland Conference, the Intellectual Freedom Committee brought forward two recommendations: 1) "That every appropriate action be taken to determine whether or not certain chapters meet the requirements for chapter status," and 2) "That no library may become an institutional member which discriminates" (on grounds of race, religion or personal beliefs). At the following Midwinter Meeting (1962) the ALA Executive Board responded to these proposals with what Lawrence Clark Powell described as "a monstrously cynical statement, a confession of moral bankruptcy." The Board expressed its belief that drastic action, now "or within such a time limit as might be set by the

Council, would be neither wise, helpful, nor possible of implementation at this time." It was clear that the Board's major concern was over the possible loss of ALA membership were any action to be taken. Even the Council couldn't go along with this barren refusal to recognize the basic issues involved, and for once withheld its rubber stamp.

By Summer (1962) a new statement, spelling out the basic rights and privileges of membership in ALA chapters and insisting that they be met, was presented to Council and carried overwhelmingly. War had thus been officially declared on the library association front. By the following Midwinter (1963) Louisiana had withdrawn from chapter membership. Mississippi stalled for a while but finally reported, a year later, that it could not "comply with the requirements for chapter status." These two state associations, together with those of Alabama and Georgia, which were not chapters in the first place, thus became the focus of the battle to combat discrimination in our own professional ranks, and in the next year or so the floor at ALA meetings came more and more to resemble a gladiator's arena. At the summer '64 convention in St. Louis it became apparent that the lead gladiator, soon to be the most readily recognized librarian from Georgia, was E. J. Josey.

It was a suitably historic occasion. ALA Conference week that year was the week during which President Lyndon Johnson signed the Civil Rights Act. E.J., aware that the removal of chapter status had not yet had the desired effect of desegregating the four Southern state associations, decided to turn up the heat. During the Membership Meeting he rose and read a memorandum he had sent to the Executive Board:

> I vigorously protest the award . . . being bestowed upon the Mississippi Library Association for its National Library Week efforts, for two reasons. Firstly, Mississippi has withdrawn from ALA affiliation. Secondly, no state association should enjoy the benefits of membership and at the same time repudiate the ideals and bylaws of ALA. Therefore, I request that the award be withdrawn. Bestowing this honor upon the Mississippi Library Association makes a mockery of the words "freedom and economic opportunity" used by [the chair of the NLW Steering Committee] when he made reference to National Library Week.

For good measure E.J. asked that the Louisiana Library Association be added to his memo in the same terms.

But that was just for openers, or background. The real heat on the Southern associations was yet to come. E.J. followed up by presenting a motion, which I seconded, that ALA officers and staff members not be allowed, in their official capacity, to attend or speak at meetings of those state associations which were not chapters of ALA. E.J. noted that the principal speaker at a recent meeting of the Georgia Library Association—a meeting which he and other (black) ALA members in Georgia were not allowed to attend—was a prominent member of the ALA staff.

In the subsequent debate Virginia Lacy Jones, dean of the Atlanta Library School, and also not accepted as a member of the Georgia Library Association, pointed out that the Georgia chapter of Special Libraries Association had been integrated for five years, and voiced her dismay at seeing SLA so far in advance of the American Library Association. But the most significant, and unexpected, support for E.J.'s motion came from another Georgian, Ruth Walling, a white librarian from Emory University and the distinguished recipient earlier in the week of the Mudge Award. The motion subsequently passed with overwhelming support, and *LJ*, reporting on the conference in its August issue, carried on its cover the headline "Two Stars from Georgia" and the photographs of E.J. and Ruth Walling.

The fallout from this motion was dirty, noisy, and immediate. One friend of mine from one of the four affected state associations came over and cursed E.J. and me royally. "You guys have just screwed up my entire Fall program," she said. "But that was the idea," I replied. The remainder of the conversation is unprintable. Less than a week after the ALA Conference, however, as *LJ* pointed out, the White House espoused a position remarkably similar to that adopted by the ALA membership. The *New York Times* reported: "The White House made it clear that the Administration would not expect government officials to speak before segregated audiences."

Nevertheless, the ALA Executive Board and Council were not through with playing chicken. At Midwinter 1965 the Board said an interpretation of E.J.'s motion was needed to facilitate its implementation. The word "facilitate" must have been used with heavy irony. What the Board came up with was the narrowest possible "interpretation": that "all ALA officers" meant *only* the President, President Elect, Second Vice President, Executive Director and Treasurer of the Association. That list wouldn't have put much of a dent in the programming potential of the Southern associations. What had been clear to the ALA membership the previous summer—that we didn't want any ALA officers (including division heads, committee chairs, etc.) to speak to the four offending associations—was apparently not at all clear to the Board. The ALA Council, with its then customary independence and courage, unanimously adopted the new, "narrow" interpretation by the Board. *LJ* commented: "The membership of ALA should mark down the date, January 27, 1965, as a gray day for democracy. This was the day on which its elected representatives, the ALA Council, refused (or to put it mildly, failed) to implement the declared wishes of the membership on a basic matter of principle."

The Midwinter '65 discussion did, however, have a couple of more encouraging and even humorous moments. Bob Severance, president of the Alabama Library Association, reported that his association had desegregated, but did not wish to apply for chapter status "until we can prove to you that all members can attend and participate in one of our state meetings." He thought such proof would be forthcoming at the May 1965 meeting of the Alabama association.

Since Severance, a non-councillor, had been allowed by Council to speak, E.J. rose to demand equal time. He applauded the Alabama Library Association for "this historic step" but reminded Council that there were still other associations which were not allowing blacks to join. He said he was still not allowed to be a member of the Georgia Library Association, and had been so informed by the President of that organization.

Came then to the microphone a Ms. Sarah Jones, Council member from Georgia, to announce: "Mr. Josey *has* been accepted as a member of the Georgia Library Association. Apparently, communication has broken down." Indeed it had: the announcement was news to the person most concerned. There was thunderous applause anyway.

At the end of the year *LJ* devoted its editorial page to a number of "awards" for "unusual accomplishment" in the library year of 1965. One was the Salinger-Moyers Managed News Award, "to the Georgia Library Association for announcing publicly that E. J. Josey had been accepted as a member of GLA before telling Mr. Josey."

With these reports from two of the Deep South associations it was fairly clear that the writing was on the wall. By June of 1965 I was able to report in *LJ* on the first integrated meeting of the Alabama Library Association, which I attended. In the same issue was the news that the Louisiana Library Association had applied for chapter status. And *LJ* had received a letter reporting that the Mississippi Library Association had integrated.

A "Chapter" Chapter: E.J., ALA, and Civil Rights

The final chapter in the chapter story was a letter from E.J. in the December 15, 1965 issue of *LJ*, reporting on the first integrated meeting of the Georgia Library Association (November 4-6), which he had attended. At that meeting Georgia voted to apply for chapter status. Thus, within a very few years, this critical conflict had been resolved. That we had been able to clean our professional house so rapidly was due primarily, I believe, to the moral force which E. J. Josey brought to the endeavor. Without his forceful, passionate presence it is quite probable that the ALA Council and Executive Board would have dickered for several more years, as they did indeed do with the *library* desegregation issue, which got side-tracked for a few years by an ill-conceived "Access Study" which appeared to convey the message that our worst racial problems existed in northern libraries like Detroit and Washington, D.C.

All of the foregoing may appear to suggest that there was only one important social issue before librarians in the turbulent decade of the sixties. Not so, of course: there was Vietnam. There was, as there always is, censorship. There was the emergence of library unions. But the overriding, consuming issue was discrimination, and out of the victory in this area, and the inspiring example of E. J. Josey, came a reluctant, final acceptance by ALA that social issues were indeed a legitimate and unavoidable part of the professional agenda. And with this recognition came the beginning of the social responsibility movement. Others may have proposed the formation of SRRT but its real foundations were built upon those racial struggles of the early sixties, and E.J. became an example, an inspiration for the several other movements that began to form as the decade drew to a close—the gays, the Spanish-speaking, and other minorities—and one non-minority, a new and powerful army: women.

As the new decade began E.J. was still bringing black librarians together as a more formidable force within ALA and the profession, providing a unified voice with his founding of the ALA Black Caucus in 1970, of which he was the first chair, and a new focus of concern with his founding of the ALA Black Task Force on Librarians for Africa in 1972. To this day he remains *the* leader in our professional ranks of the opposition to apartheid in South Africa.

When I was elected President of ALA in the late 1970s I appointed E.J. as chair of ALA's International Relations Committee. The appointment surprised a number of people who were not aware of E.J.'s international interests, but in the years since he has become as significant a figure on the international scene as he was previously on the domestic front, and as great an inspiration to many Third World librarians as he remains to minority librarians at home.

There is of course much more to the career of this remarkable man, but much of that will be told in other chapters of this volume. My purpose here has been to demonstrate some of what it took to change the climate in the library profession to the degree that a man who was "unacceptable" for membership in the Georgia Library Association could, in just under twenty years, become so acceptable to the members of the American Library Association that they elected him as their President for 1984-85. If in the early sixties you had predicted that election, one of the landmarks of American library history, you might well have been committed to another kind of institution than library....

PART III

CENSORSHIP

Introduction

This section, again, is only as brief as it is because all of my writing on censorship which appeared in *Library Journal* (with one small exception) has been omitted from this selection. This is because much of that material has already been collected in *Book Selection and Censorship in the Sixties*.

The one exception is an early *LJ* editorial dealing with a problem which I believe to be still among us: restrictions placed on the right of librarians to write and publish, these restrictions most commonly being imposed by library directors, library boards and other authoritarians. This is also the topic of "A Priori Censorship," written in the eighties, which appears later in this section.

"Courage and Cowardice" was the first of a series of "New York Letters" I was invited to contribute to *The Library World* in England. I found rather appealing this opportunity to follow in the footsteps of Alistair Cooke, interpreting things American for a British audience. But I don't think the series lasted long (one other New York Letter appears as chapter 37 in Part VII of this volume). Whether this was a result of my natural laziness or because the publisher had had enough of it after the first few I don't recall.

"The Benefit of the Doubt," originally a speech to the Westchester Library Association and, strangely, published by *LJ*'s rival up in the Bronx, was yet another exploration of that hazy territory between book selection and censorship that Lester Asheim had mapped out so well years before in his classic essay, "Not Censorship, But Selection."

"To Disagree Is Not to Destroy" (title credit goes to Dorothy Broderick), heretofore unpublished, was a speech I was invited to deliver at the University of Alabama, which, I discovered, is impossible to reach by air at the same time as one's luggage. Dorothy Broderick, with whom I have shared an alliance in censorship matters which is as strong as my alliance with E.J. Josey in civil rights matters, had organized a symposium entitled "Freedom Is Dangerous: The First Amendment in Perspective" as part of a celebration of the University's Sesquicentennial. True to her principles, Dorothy had invited representatives of all shades of opinion to this gathering, and I remember, following my speech, a representative of the Eagle Forum rising and telling the audience they had just heard the voice of secular humanism, communism, godlessness and a variety of other evils. Later in the day, he said, when he would be speaking, he promised that we would hear what God and the people thought of it all. I remember responding "Sir, I can only admire your range."

Finally, "Living the Library Bill of Rights," one of the most recent inclusions in this volume, is a speech I was invited to give at the 1990 ALA Conference by the Intellectual Freedom Round Table. Even though it is one of the most effective documents ALA has produced, a number of librarians still want to tinker with the *Library Bill of Rights* for one reason or another. Count me among them. I believe this document should—no, must—say something about economic barriers to library access. Some claim this topic is covered by the word "background" in Section 5: "A person's right to use a library should not be denied or abridged because of origin, age, background or views." I can only respond that those who are victims of poverty find it pretty much a foreground matter. To suggest that those who are denied access because of inability to pay are protected or covered by a word like background is devious hogwash.

The Right to Write

The Fiske Report is a disturbing piece of evidence that there are librarians who do not in practice defend "the right to read" as rigorously as the profession preaches it. This is bad enough but we have been growing increasingly aware that many librarians are tolerating restrictions upon an even more basic right. "The right to read" remains an empty slogan, a pious pronouncement, unless authors are free to write, and to publish what they have written.

Three hundred and sixteen years ago the defense of this liberty was memorably laid down by a great poet with failing sight but no lack of vision: "What can be more fair, than when a man ... publish to the world what his opinion is ... Christ urged it as wherewith to justify himself, that he preached in public; yet writing is more public than preaching; and more easy to refutation if need be." Three centuries after Milton, many librarians are denied the basic liberty to publish, and too many accept this violation of their rights as individuals in a free world. If librarians are not prepared to fight against censorship of their own words, it is difficult to suppose that they will stand firm as defenders of intellectual freedom when censorship places its grubby paw on the works of others.

One who stood firm against this more personal form of censorship was a library school professor, Dorothy Broderick, who recently submitted an article to *LJ*. She was informed in writing by her university: "Your article entitled 'Librarians as Literature Experts' is disapproved for use under the name of St. John's University *and even under your own name while you are a member of St. John's University faculty.*" Since the latter part of this dictum is no longer in effect, and that others may judge the pernicious quality of this censored article, it is published in this issue, together with comments from a number of librarians.

Reprinted by permission from *Library Journal*, August 1960. Copyright © 1960, Reed Publishing, USA.

We know of numerous examples where less courage has been displayed in resisting such impositions from above. An ironic instance involved a review of the Fiske Report which appeared in the May 16 issue of the *New Republic*. A footnote said of the author of this review: "Raymond Stringer is an administrator in a large library system; he writes under a pseudonym because his employers insist on clearance before publication." A letter in the following issue of the *New Republic*, signed I. M. Gemel, Washington, D.C., carried a note explaining: "The pseudonym above is used to avoid the complications of clearance with my employer, the Library of Congress."

The irony is underscored in the comment by the pseudonymous Stringer in his review: "Librarians, as a group, are more than usually liberal in their general outlook. But they tend to be timid." The brave Stringer should fear for his glass house: his stone may boomerang.

Anyone who writes or speaks must be willing to accept any consequences arising from the exercise of his freedom, but "prior restraint" is contrary to our concept of individual liberties or legal rights in a free society.

The employers who impose such restrictions upon librarians would do well to heed Milton's advice: "We should be wary ... what persecution we raise against the labours of public men." But the librarians who accept such restrictions are more to blame, for no man who lives and works in the world of books should need reminding of *Areopagitica*'s message: "Give me the liberty to know, to utter, and to argue freely according to conscience, above all liberties." Nor should they have forgotten so soon that the *Library Bill of Rights* advocates "resisting all abridgement of the free access to ideas and *full freedom of expression* that are the tradition and heritage of Americans."

Courage and Cowardice

The *New Yorker,* which is really only *Punch* with a bow-tie, took a look at the subject of censorship last August. It was moved to do so by a Glasgow spinster, Miss Katherine McCardle, who so disapproved of a bookseller's window display of *Lady Chatterley's Lover* that she painted the window black—and was promptly jailed for her efforts.

In a Shavian tongue-in-cheek performance that *Punch* might just have equalled during its perverse Muggeridge days, the *New Yorker* declared, apropos of Miss McCardle's vigilante action:

> This strikes us as eminently correct and worthy behavior. If books have the right to paint people black, people should have the right to paint books black... Writers need censors; otherwise they will begin to censor themselves, with far more damaging results... Censorship, whether in the form of banning, burning or blacking, pays books the high compliment of taking them seriously... More anti-intellectual than censorship is its apathetic absence. So paint on, Miss McC. You are on the wrong side, but of the right fence.

If one accepts the *New Yorker's* ironical premise, there has been ample evidence in recent times that Americans take books seriously. Censorship has campaigned under a forest of banners and has aimed, shotgun fashion, at anything real or fantasy-born which might conceivably be considered a target. Norman Mailer, one of a prominent panel discussing "Sex and Censorship in Literature and the Arts," in *Playboy* magazine, July 1961, caught something of the atmosphere with this comment: "The authority of this country is like one vast, frozen, nervous, petrified mother who's trying to keep her favorite son—this utterly mad hoodlum—under control." But, bemused perhaps by his adjectives, Mailer missed a crucial

---

Reprinted by permission of McB University Press Limited from *The Library World* LXIII, No. 743: 293-296, May 1962.

point: it isn't authority alone that has been acting out of panic. Much of the wildest action and hysteria has been promoted by individual private citizens or maniac groups which have no authority and no literary pretensions, but which make a lot of noise (like other empty kettles). At times, censorship seems to have become almost as popular a citizen activity as membership in the P.T.A's (Parent Teacher Associations) which twitch so tiresomely at the domestic skirts of education.

Virulent Intolerance

Author, bookseller and publisher, all have taken heavy punishment, and rare is the library (public or school) that has not at some time felt the grimy touch of the censor's glove. Some librarians, like British heavyweights, have buckled at the first glancing blow; others have avoided this indignity only by throwing in the towel before the fight begins and using the mask of "book selection" to disguise their own subversive operation of pre-censorship. I do not, however, want to give the impression that the library profession in the United States is peopled entirely by cowardly intellectual pygmies. A great many American librarians, surrounded by a more virulent intolerance than most of their British counterparts have ever known, have faced it with the courage (and perhaps more intelligence) of some of the famous "thin red lines" of British history. "Freedom to Read," for them, has been something more than a slogan: American librarians have often been prominent among the most active and public freedom fighters.

The events of recent months have presented an array of opportunities for librarians to align themselves with the forces of courage and conviction on the one hand, or cowardice and conformity on the other, for the country has been engulfed in a maelstrom of censorship activity ever since the publication last year of the first American edition of Henry Miller's *Tropic of Cancer*.

Grove Press, encouraged by a publishing victory in 1959, when the courts finally approved the virtue of *Lady Chatterley* (or was it her lover's?), brought out the Miller book last June. Banned here since its Paris publication in 1934, *Tropic of Cancer* had hitherto infiltrated seldom beyond the book acquisition processes of the customs houses in the nation's major ports of entry. For several months in the summer of 1961 the Miller novels became the subject of "probably the strangest case of on-again off-again book banning on record," according to the American Library Association's *Newsletter on Intellectual Freedom*.

The tangled tale began in April, when a New York woman brought a court case against customs officials who had confiscated three Henry Millers she was trying to bring back from Paris. At just about the same time Grove announced that they had printed 30,000 copies of *Tropic* and that its publication date would be June 24. Somehow advance copies were on sale in the bookstores early in May.

On June 9, still before the "official" publication date, the Post Office Department of the Federal Government ordered the Grove Press book banned from the mails. Only four days later came the "switcheroo": the department's legal counsel rescinded the ban. Reason? The department said they were awaiting a decision in the New York case mentioned above. The *New York Times* said that the Justice Department had advised dropping the ban because so many literary critics supported the book on the grounds of literary merit that a court case would probably go against the Post Office.

The *Times* seemed not so wide of the mark when the United States Justice Department announced in August that *Tropic of Cancer* and two other Miller novels—*Tropic of Capricorn* and *Plexus*—were not obscene and that the Customs ban against the books would be lifted.

Two weeks *before* this decision, however, a Superior Court Judge in Boston, that Irish city which has always proudly shared the banning vanguard with Eire, decided that *Tropic of Cancer* was obscene and prohibited, statewide, the "selling, distributing, importing and loaning" of the book. And a few days *after* the Justice Department's decision, police in Dallas, Texas, ordered city booksellers to quit selling the book or expect prosecutions under a new Texas anti-obscenity law. Scorecard at this stage: a federal agency says *Tropic* is not obscene, a state government and a municipal government say it is. The last legal decision: a San Francisco court ruling in 1953 which pronounced the book obscene.

Limited Warfare

Compared with what was to follow, however, things were pretty quiet for a while. It was only what militarists call "limited warfare," and there was no very widespread effort to suppress the book generally. What really took the lid off was the publication of a paperback edition only a few months after the hard cover edition came out. When this reached the news stands and the drug store counters it also reached, for the first time, many people who would not be found dead in a library or a bookstore. Much maternal wrath erupted at the thought of such dangerous material within easy and economic reach of inquisitive teenage hands. The explosion at this point was sensational—and the fallout dreadful. By the end of November, Grove Press was able to report that in at least (and I think it was a conservative estimate) 57 cities and two states, Nebraska and Massachusetts, the book could not be sold because of actual arrests or threats of same.

If Grove and some unfortunate booksellers took the brunt of the attack, librarians were certainly not immune from it. In my review of *Tropic of Cancer* in the June 15 issue of *Library Journal*, I had said: "This book will present many librarians—public librarians particularly—with a test of conscience and courage in book selection," and forecast, accurately it seems, that the book would "become the No. 1 target for those bands of self-appointed censors who roam the country in search of four-letter words and in defense of adolescent morals." How did librarians stand up to the blistering fire that surrounded them? It must be said that the reactions were various, very various.

The A.L.A. *Bulletin* reported: "There was evidence that many public librarians were moving cautiously, not wanting to be in a position of having purchased a book that might be declared obscene in the courts." There were, of course, those librarians who avoided trouble before it began by refusing to buy the book, often on the untenable basis that it might get into the hands of young readers. There were others who did buy but who submitted meekly to the first demands that they withdraw it. Some, like Emerson Greenaway, a past-president of A.L.A., withdrew their copies under protest but were forced to do so by some local ordinance or regulation. Greenaway had bought some 84 copies for the Free Library of Philadelphia, but he was forced to take them out again. And finally, there were those librarians who refused absolutely to bend principle's knee, even before the powerful ministers of the law who frequently bent the law itself.

Iron Stand

A notable example of this latter group of librarians is Stuart Sherman, director of the Providence, Rhode Island, Public Library, whose full story is told in the February 1, 1962 issue of *Library Journal*. The pattern of developments in Rhode Island was a common one. The State's attorney general announced, at the end of October, that *Tropic of Cancer* was the "foulest, most obscene work" he had ever read, duly ignored the proper legal procedure, and promptly put pressure on all booksellers and libraries in the state to take it out of circulation. Sherman refused and took it to his Board of Trustees (library committee) who "voted unanimously that *Tropic of Cancer* would be circulated by the library until restrained or enjoined by competent authority (that 'competent' I like) or until there is a final judicial determination that the book is obscene."

Support for Sherman's iron stand came not only from his Board but also from the press, the general public, and encouragingly, from the library's staff association. The attorney general's next move was a threat to arrest the librarian who issued the book and any borrower who took it out. He said, through the press, that he was willing to cooperate with the library if it wanted to set up a test case. Sherman was immediately besieged by dozens of offers from members of the public to "borrow" the book in such a test case. Among the volunteers were a priest, a pregnant mother of four children, a lady over 70 who had, in her own words, "never ridden in a paddy-wagon," and a fiery gentleman who said he would take the sword his grandfather had used in the Dorr Rebellion and run it through anyone who stopped him.

Sherman reassured his staff about the arrest threat: if anyone was going to be arrested, he said, he would be the one. His Board wouldn't go along with this. They told the attorney general he would have to arrest the lot of them: they as a corporation were finally responsible.

The end of the story (at this writing anyway) is that no librarian or committee member rots in a Rhode Island jail, and *Tropic of Cancer* continues to be issued freely by the library. Courage seems to have paid off, as it usually does. If there is a point to Sherman's story it is that, in adhering firmly to principle, "even if we lose in the end, we will have won," in public respect—and self respect.

I have chosen to accentuate a positive example here, knowing full well that there are many cases where librarians have acted less commendably, because it seems to me that it is the negative aspects (i.e., the weakness of librarians in similar situations) that have received the widest publicity.

Much of this in the last year or two has stemmed, unfortunately, from Marjorie Fiske's classic study, *Book Selection and Censorship: A Study of School and Public Libraries in California,* a brilliant book which should be required reading for all librarians. Many of the Fiske Report findings are pretty dismal, however. For example: "nearly two thirds of all librarians who have a say in book selection reported instances where the controversiality of a book or author resulted in a decision not to buy"; and she tells also of librarians who even avoid buying any book "which they believe *might become* controversial."

When such devastating facts are given the benefit of press ballyhoo, there is a danger that all librarians may be condemned for the cringing sins of the few (well, perhaps not so few). So it is well to be reminded that there are librarians, not altogether an unrepresentative or exceptional minority, who have staked their very professional careers in a defence of principle against unreason.

That Warm Little Girl

Library Journal did a nationwide study recently checking on public library book selection in this area of controversial fiction. Part of my objective was to find out whether the national situation in any way mirrored the Fiske facts for California. I regret to say that on the whole I think they did. But I am also glad to say that *some* of the evidence I collected was vastly encouraging. Certainly it does not speak badly for American libraries that 82.3% of those I surveyed had *Lady Chatterley's Lover* in stock, and 77.9% of them dared to hold that warm little girl *Lolita*. Even *Tropic of Cancer* was available in more than half of the libraries that answered my questionnaire. How many British libraries, I wonder, would go so far out on a limb with a wolf-pack of censors howling below?

If one feels a twinge of shame occasionally at the actions of individual librarians, one can feel nothing but pride for the record of the profession as a body, at least as represented by the American Library Association. Its position on the subject of censorship has been unassailable over the years.

A.L.A. established a Committee on Intellectual Freedom as long ago as 1940, after a special committee on censorship, in its report to the A.L.A. Conference in Cincinnati that year, recommended the establishment of a standing committee "to throw the force and influence of A.L.A. behind any individual librarian or any library board confronted with any demands for censorship of books or other material upon a library's shelves."

Then too, in the darkness days of the McCarthy madness, A.L.A. was one of the few national organizations to go on record against the mass witch-hunt. In 1953 it produced its famous statement, "The Freedom to Read" (known often as the Westchester Statement), which was endorsed also by the American Book Publishers Council, and later by the American Booksellers Association, the Book Manufacturers Institute and the National Education Association. This is the statement that ends with the classic remark: "Freedom itself is a dangerous way of life, but it is ours."

Among other basic policy statements of A.L.A. in this area are the "Library Bill of Rights," adopted in 1948 and amended in 1961 to cover the segregationist or other discriminatory practices of some libraries; a similar "School Library Bill of Rights"; and a statement on "Labeling Library Materials," in which it is stated unequivocally that "Labeling is an attempt to prejudice the reader, and as such, it is a censor's tool."

Now, at its most recent Midwinter meeting in Chicago, the A.L.A. Council has approved a short statement designed to help combat the current rash of censorship activities. Entitled "How Libraries and Schools Can Resist Censorship," it also is likely (perhaps before this article is published) to be endorsed by a number of other concerned national bodies.

I find many faults with A.L.A., but in this area it has exercised consistent leadership, moral and otherwise, to the point where a librarian can stand erect in the middle of any censorship fracas, produce his documents, and say "This is what we stand for."

Can the Library Association in England offer similar pride and solace to its members? I do not remember the L.A. ever producing a policy statement which might support an individual librarian under censorship pressure (though I hope I am wrong). Perhaps indeed, there is no need of it. Though again, I do not remember the situation in British libraries as being *that* lily-white.

The Benefit of the Doubt

Whenever censorship is discussed in library circles, some acquisition room lawyer will point out smugly that librarians may be good or bad selectors, but they cannot be censors. Censorship, the argument goes, is a legal process. The word can only be properly applied when the law, through one or more of its agencies, clamps down upon all avenues of book provision, thus denying the citizen the right to buy, borrow, possess or read the book in question. I'll concede the technical accuracy of this point, but dismiss it nonetheless as a piece of semantic poppycock which is far removed from the realities of the day.

When Max Lerner, taking a peek behind the Iron Curtain, was asked in Warsaw what single word or concept he would use to describe the crux of American civilization, the word he produced was *access*. I must say I felt a little proud of Mr. Lerner. It's difficult enough to produce off the top of your head one word to sum up such a rangy, nebulous idea as "American civilization," but to produce one which so aptly illustrates the edge of real freedom that a man in a true democracy enjoys, or should enjoy, over the man under totalitarianism, is a master stroke.

Access lies not only at the heart of democracy. It is also the crux of librarianship—or rather, of library *service*. And it is in relation to access that censorship should be considered and defined. Censorship, then, becomes a matter of intent, the intention being to restrict unnecessarily access to a book, or a movie, or a magazine, or any of the other communication media.

When a band of good citizens in Atlanta, for example, previewed *Never on Sunday* and then refused to allow the other more susceptible citizens of that city to see it, one could say that this was not censorship. After all the people of Atlanta who desperately desired to see the delec-

---

Reprinted by permission from the *Wilson Library Bulletin* 39: 663-667, 704, April 1965, this was originally a talk to the Westchester Library Association, May 2, 1963.

table Miss Mercouri could travel to Chicago or New York, if their desperation would take them so far. In this sense, they still retained some degree of access to the movie.

But this view seems a little divorced from reality. In much the same vein, we know that if a book is not made available in a public library a good many citizens do not have effective access to it. If we do not accept this much, we should be hard put to defend the existence and support of public libraries. We know, too, that there are subtle (and some not so subtle) variations in ease of access to some of the books that are "available" in libraries. And finally, we know that there are some book selection decisions made, via the same thought processes, and if you like, with the same intent, as those of the would-be censor. So let us speak about censorship as a motivating force rather than as a tightly defined legal process.

Just for once, I wish that we could shake off the obsession permeating the American public library's concern with the child reader and consider our problem in relation to that neglected patron, the adult. But I suspect we can't, so I will merely quote Mr. Justice Stable, who asked, in the course of his summation of a 1954 obscenity case in Britain: "Are we to take our literary standards as being the level of something that is suitable for a 14-year old schoolgirl? Or do we go even further back than that, and are to be reduced to the sort of books one reads as a child in the nursery? The answer is of course not. . . . "

Too often we are guilty of underestimating the intellectual capacity and toughness of today's teenager, and some of our cloyingly protective parents are criminally guilty of this fault. Sometimes I begin to wonder whether we should not be better off in libraries if we reversed the situation, permitting some youngsters to roam freely among our book collections but restricting their parents to those antiseptic pastures we call young adult collections.

There are three kinds of censorship which concern me. The first kind is closest to the original definition of the word—that is, censorship emanating from legal or government sources (police, judges, legislators). All of us are aware of the growing role of the police and local district attorneys in these matters. One of the most disturbing factors is that these agents of the law are often the first to discard the proper legal processes in taking censorial action. Here is Hoke Norris, the *Chicago Sun-Times* book columnist, writing in the *Saturday Review* on the *Tropic* controversy in Chicago:

At one point... we seemed dangerously close to the police state. Without warrants, without consulting legal or literary authority, even without a law to operate upon, some police in Chicago and its suburbs took the paperback *Tropic of Cancer* off shelves, "persuaded" or "advised" merchants not to sell it, and generally, without proper procedure, attempted to impose their literary tastes upon their communities. One cop who was active in this subversive campaign admitted later that he was not operating upon an ordinance or upon statutory law—he was directed, he said, by moral law.

Let me add to this one example of what can happen when official government censorship prevails. In 1946 Ireland passed a Censorship of Publications Act. The government *Register of Prohibited Publications* is now a document of horror to anyone who believes in freedom. Here are just a few of the authors, one or more of whose works still are forbidden in the land of the Shamrock: André Gide, Sinclair Lewis, Pearl Buck, Hemingway, Faulkner, Pär Lagerkvist (all those are Nobel Prize winners for literature), Orwell, Steinbeck, Mailer, Farrell, Capote, Salinger, Tennessee Williams, Kingsley Amis, James Jones, Françoise Sagan, Lin Yutang, Somerset Maugham, Iris Murdoch, Aldous Huxley, Joyce Cary, Dos Passos, Robert Penn Warren, Margaret Mead, Angus Wilson, James Gould Cozzens, Bernard de Voto, Scott Fitzgerald, Zola, Remarque, Maurois, Sartre, Erskine Caldwell, Moravia, Edmund Wilson, etc.

Can you imagine a library without the works of *any* of these authors? Oh, but that can't happen here. When Sinclair Lewis wrote that, he was being ironical, and if you believe it, your faith is based on shaky foundations. Because the fact remains that each and every one of these authors has been attacked in this country, and the works of many of them have been banned or excluded from one library or another. Lists just as terrible as this one *are* produced here by various groups who desire to dictate the community's reading.

The second kind of censorship stems from the individual citizen, or more often from a group of people who frequently represent some kind of extremism and who wish either to limit the access of others to materials with which they do not agree, or to force their own opinions and materials to the forefront at the expense of others. Much of the wildest action has been promoted by these maniacal groups having no authority and few literary pretensions but which, like other empty kettles, make a lot of noise.

The more sanctimonious aspects were nicely captured by Dorothy Broderick in a talk to the Iowa Library Association. She said:

> Some years back the *New Yorker* had a cartoon parodying the "Man of Distinction" ads then so popular. I would like to see one in the same vein about reading and its effects. It would show a man in jail, dictating his memoirs and he would be saying: "I was a pillar of the community, an elder in the church, a successful businessman. I had a wife and children I loved. Then they asked me to serve on the Clean Literature Committee. I read one book, then another, and another...."

But the upright citizen-restricter would not think this funny, because he knows he is inviolate. He seeks only to protect the less tenacious morals and susceptibilities of the fellow next door. By his efforts he is doing much to produce a society which is frightened, suspicious and sometimes hysterical, and an atmosphere where the other man's "different" opinion tends to be regarded not merely as wrong (or even healthily eccentric) but as unAmerican, treasonous, sinful or criminal. In this atmosphere, the librarian who does a conscientious job of book selection *must* displease many of the people much of the time. And he must not only know that he will do so, but be prepared for the consequences.

As things are, pressure and controversy may fairly be regarded as "natural" and expected outcomes of a good, strong, "free" book selection policy. Conversely, if there is *no* protest and *no* pressure, it is a fair bet that the library in question is another which is following a safe, unimaginative, uncourageous middle road to cultural perdition and eventual extinction.

The librarian who buys or accepts the gift of the publications of the Birch Society or other "right"-thinking groups will never be a halo-girl in the eyes of those liberals who are ardent in name only. Askance looks may be expected from some Negro groups if you buy Carleton Putnam's mistitled book, *Race and Reason*. Buy James Baldwin and there are some who will accuse you of promoting miscegenation. Give space to books on the United Nations and you will have gone over to the Communists (this is perhaps the best example of the twisted reasoning of these fanatics). Exhibit a few Catholic magazines and ergo you are an agent of the Vatican and an opponent of the "traditional American view on Church and State." Worst of all, purchase Henry Miller's books and the ladies of the DAR or the PTA will tell the local police chief that you are corrupting the morals of their children. The police chief, afraid like all men of women on the rampage, and aware like all good fathers of the tenderness of teenage souls, will nevertheless make like a literary critic, and read to page five before concurring and then bringing the legions of other courtroom critics into play against you.

Is this exaggeration? No, only a concentration of realities. But the awful thing for the librarian is that he is not much better off if he refuses to buy all or any of these inflammatory materials—he succeeds only in reversing the mirror, changing sides. Reject books about the UN, you are an isolationist. Reject Baldwin, you are a segregationist. Reject Miller and the ACLU replaces the DAR rampaging at your door. Reject the Birch Society, and there you are again, back with the Communists.

So, librarians, universal love is not for us. Perhaps we should try instead to settle for respect—if we can get that much. Strength, conviction, honest neutrality, all can and are likely to be unpopular, but it is possible to be unpopular and respected too. In book selection we dare not sacrifice principle to the love cult we call public relations. And history presents few lessons of respect accorded to the weak and vacillating.

Yet there are libraries, more than most of us like to admit, where the book selection policy is one of fear and timidity, of deliberate avoidance of those books which dare to challenge the accepted or which hint of the possibility of repercussions. So here we are at our third kind of censorship—perhaps the worst kind—self-censorship, censorship by librarians.

I suppose it was Marjorie Fiske who first really threw wide the doors of the closet in which this skeleton of the library family had been hidden for years. Even when the doors were open there was still a good deal of covering up. Oh well, everyone said, that's California—anything can happen there. Miss Fiske did not claim her special sample as representative of all librarians, but Lester Asheim, in a very good article in the *Bay State Librarian* a while ago, said that he thought it was. So, on the evidence I have seen, do I.

Since the evidence, however, is still spotty, I would like to see a Fiske study undertaken in every state. It's difficult to suggest cures until we know just how sick we are, but certainly there are enough symptoms of ill-health to warrant a thorough checkup. Some of the funds of the Council on Library Resources and other foundations which ALA manages to acquire to build better newspaper sticks and the like might be diverted to such a purpose.

Instead of such action, I'm afraid that many people believe most of our book selection deficiencies will be cured if only more and more individual libraries produce printed book selection policy statements. After examining many of these statements, I am sure of one thing: any investigation of book selection practices should also take note of these "policies" which supposedly govern the practice.

Many libraries still have no policies, or have not had the temerity to commit them to print and public examination. And it may be that these are the wise ones. For many of the statements which have appeared look too much like crutches, and these have a dangerous tendency to develop boomerang characteristics. In the hands of an astute reader who is prepared and knowledgeable enough to compare the written pronouncement with the evidence of the shelves, the crutch can too easily be grabbed and used against you.

If we were to examine, in turn, the more common phrases which appear in book selection statements, we could show that each and every one of these "criteria" is a generalization, an evasion, or something so open to interpretation that it doesn't help one bit when you get down to the ultimate question, "to buy or not to buy."

Almost every book selection policy states somewhere that a major objective is to cater to the interests or needs existing in the community, either organized or individual. Now I suggest that the *organized* needs or interests may be fairly easily ascertained. But I still like to think, as does Ray Smith, the librarian of Mason City, Iowa, that the public library is "one of the last great resources of the individual as a private and original being, rather than a unit in a mass audience." I suggest that we actually know very little about *individual* reading interests and needs, and very little about those many individuals who make up what we like to call the community. Like the censors, we are prone to think in terms of the "average" man.

The phrase that walks hand in hand with the "average man" is the "standards of the community." Judge Bryan, in his ruling on *Lady Chatterley's Lover*, commented: "The contemporary standards of the community and its limits of tolerance cannot be measured or ascertained accurately. There is no poll available to determine such questions. . . ."

Yet when I have conducted book selection surveys I have found a depressing, and irritating, number of librarians who tell me that theirs is a very unsophisticated public, or that their readers are not mature enough for some of this controversial material. There is a built-in protectiveness and condescension here that is a long way from our ideal image of the library as the place where one may find the best that is thought and known in the world.

Ingredients of Opinion

Nearly everyone seems to assume that his own community is quite unlike any other. But in an age of mass communications, when everyone is open to the same influences by the same TV networks, the same magazines, the same propaganda from the same platforms, isn't it possible that *all* communities possess the same individual ingredients of opinion, prejudice, belief, sophistication, maturity? The ingredients may vary in quantity in different communities, but they are likely to be there in some quantity nevertheless. And despite our confusion over the concept of "demand" I am not ready to accept the fact that librarians really believe they should cater only to *majority* interests. If we abandon the rights of minorities, then we truly toss out the window freedom, democracy and all those words which are supposed to represent our beliefs. We also abandon recognition that minorities tend to change into majorities, that most great ideas in our civilization have started out being believed or accepted by a minority, sometimes a minority of one.

Our book selection statements seem to help least when we are faced with that curious chemical reaction which takes place between such factors as "demand," "controversial content," and our literary or other "standards." How much demand is demand, we ask ourselves? Do you need more demand for a poor book than a good one? Doesn't controversy stimulate demand? Then how come even some of those who kneel before the god of demand shy away from controversial books more than from others? Do the same literary standards (whatever *they* are) apply equally to controversial and "harmless" books? Are we guilty of applying a "double" book selection standard?

One Wisconsin librarian admitted as much when he said to me: "In effect, our practice is this: a book with a harmless theme designed principally to entertain and characterized by a style ranging from trite to mediocre to fair, is judged less vigorously than a book addressed to a serious, challenging or controversial theme."

I feel that, if we can't apply consistent standards (and in book selection I believe this is impossible), it would be better to reverse the double standard just described. That is, apply more rigorous judgment to the trite and mediocre and harmless than to the book which deals with a challenging idea or subject. I agree with the late President Kennedy's plea for "more controversial authors." I agree with Leo Rosten that "wisdom is not much more than the capacity to confront dangerous ideas with equanimity" and that "there is no freedom when controversy has been abolished." And I agree with Harold Tucker, librarian of Queens, who answered one complaint about the presence of *Tropic of Cancer* in his library with the comment that it was precisely because the book was controversial that the library should have it.

In the last analysis we admit that there *are* no easy dogmas we can apply to the imprecise process of book selection. Whoever does it, and whatever theory or policy is used, we are going to be right some of the time and wrong some of the time. We should be knowledgeable enough to back most of our choices with confidence, but this is not the same as certainty. This we should avoid in ourselves, bearing in mind the fearful certainty of idiots and tyrants. If we can accept this, might not our book selection practices follow the same basic concept which governs our system of law and justice—that of allowing ten guilty men to go free rather than convict one innocent man. Or, if you like, in all cases where responsible opinions differ, it is the book which should be given the benefit of every possible doubt.

To Disagree Is Not to Destroy

The present always seems to me to make more sense if you stand back a bit from it, so I'll give it a generous chance and begin back about a quarter of a century ago.

Picture the scene. It's the middle 1950's. The place is the Marlborough, a London drinking establishment, otherwise known as a pub, one block from the headquarters of The Library Association. (Note that the British, with the arrogance of tradition, see no need for nationalistic qualifiers. It is not the British Library Association, simply *The* Library Association, and it does no good to remind them that the founding of the American Library Association preceded theirs by a solid twelve months.)

It is late afternoon, perhaps ten minutes after opening time. I am sitting in the lounge bar, enjoying a pint of best bitter with my close friend Bill Smith (who is not a pseudonym). We are known in those days as the two terrible young turks of the library profession over there, but at that moment we are simply rehashing our perpetual argument about which of the London football teams is the best in the country.

The door to the bar opens and a young woman enters. She looks around and when she spots us her face registers shock and indignation. She marches across to our table, stands over us like a judgment and pronounces, "You two are frauds." Surprised and mildly amused, we invite her to sit down, have a beer, and present her evidence for the charge.

The explanation is that she has been present that afternoon at a meeting in Chaucer House, the L.A. headquarters, during which Bill and I had for a couple of hours been on opposite sides (not for the first time) of a fiery political debate, laced with what we both then thought of as the customary ingredients of invective and vituperation. At least they were

---

A speech given at a Symposium commemorating the University of Alabama's Sesquicentennial Anniversary. Titled "Freedom Is Dangerous: The First Amendment in Perspective," the symposium, held on November 9, 1981, was organized and chaired by Dorothy Broderick.

common in Parliament, especially when such luminaries as Aneurin Bevan and Winston Churchill faced each other without gloves.

The young woman had difficulty accepting that two people who only a short time before had been hurling insults at each other could possibly have been serious in their differences, since here they were, drinking together, obviously warm friends. The afternoon's events, clearly, had been no more than a cynical performance. Most people we knew then had no such problem in understanding that one could have fundamental disagreements, and express them strongly, without the inevitable consequence of enmity.

We put the incident down to the youth and naiveté of the young woman, and I probably would never even have remembered the occasion had I not come to the United States just a few years later. I arrived, ominously it now seems, on November 5, 1959, to take over the editorship of *Library Journal*. November 5 is a day the British, with the quirkiness that has branded them a nation of eccentrics, celebrate each year as Guy Fawkes Day, the anniversary of an unsuccessful attempt by Guy Fawkes and his cronies to blow up the Houses of Parliament.

Coincidentally, in another part of New York, the Bronx, my long-time friend and former assistant in England, John Wakeman, was simultaneously assuming the editorship of the rival *Wilson Library Bulletin*. When we went to our first Midwinter meeting of the American Library Association in Chicago, just a couple of months later, we did so with some trepidation, feeling that we might be exposed to a good deal of American resentment (justifiable, we thought) of this takeover of a substantial segment of the American library press by the Limeys.

Much to our surprise, we were feted and dined and royally welcomed by an impressive array of the leaders of the establishment. Clearly, we had underestimated the legendary hospitality and open friendship of the Americans. I intend no devaluation of that assessment when I add that, in the light of subsequent events, some of the warmth of that welcome may have been based on a fundamental miscalculation. Some of those people, I think, expected us to occupy our editors' chairs like reserved, polite young Englishmen, not very knowledgeable about the American library or social scenes, and therefore not likely to attempt to release with their press keys any skeletons which might be hidden in the establishment's closet.

Those subsequent events soon began to materialize. Wakeman and I plunged early into the civil rights and censorship arenas, raising unpopular questions about the library profession's and ALA's response to the social revolution that was so clearly gathering momentum in other spheres of activity. Within one year, at our next Midwinter meeting, some of those same people who had welcomed and entertained us no longer even recognized us when we met them in corridors or meeting rooms. We had become social lepers. And in the months to come, some of those leaders—and others—began to call or write to the President and the Chairman of the Board of my company, urging them to fire me because I was a disruptive influence and was likely to destroy all relationships between the Bowker Company and the profession.

Here was my first disturbing discovery about my new country: that there were Americans, some of them well educated and powerful, who, despite the noble pronouncements of Lincoln and Jefferson and the Bill of Rights—and in the case of the library profession, *its* ringing Freedom to Read Statement, issued in the dark days of McCarthyism—could not tolerate a challenge to their own orthodoxy, did not appear to understand that this nation's historic sheltering of the oppressed from many other parts of the world is an express acknowledgment that tolerance of dissent and disagreement is the very foundation stone of democracy, what distinguishes it from totalitarianism and repression, whether from the left or right. Suddenly, I found, I could not challenge or disagree without being hated.

I apologize for starting on such a personal note. I do it not for ego gratification but because it was the best way I could find to steer this paper toward the splendid title with which Dorothy Broderick presented me: To Disagree Is Not to Destroy. I was also prompted in this direction by an examination of the printed program for this occasion. A couple of lines in it intrigued me. The first, in the paragraph on the purpose of the meeting, was: "The symposium will focus on *current* First Amendment issues as they affect... schools and libraries." The second was the title of the paper to be delivered by Dr. Vick: "Censorship: A *New* National Pastime."

Both of these items seem to imply that something is happening today that is at least different in kind or degree from what has occurred in the past. It is not difficult to see how one could reach such a conclusion. Certainly there have been more stories in the media about censorship activities involving schools and libraries than at any time I remember (although I was not here in McCarthy's heyday). But does this media frenzy mean that new or different First Amendment issues have emerged? Or that censorship has reached some new and frightening level, to the point where it can be described as a national pastime? Let us take a look at each of these implications.

Are the issues related to the First Amendment current or constant? Certainly one major issue is a traditional one; it arises from that opening phrase of the Amendment: "Congress shall make *no* law . . ." Is this an absolute guarantee of free expression, as Justices Black and Douglas so resolutely affirmed over years on the Supreme Court, or does it admit of exceptions? The practical answer, of course, is that the Amendment means what the Court says it means, and the Court, being composed of fallible humans, and politically appointed ones at that, is likely to be responsive to some degree both to popular attitudes and to political influence and change. Some exceptions have, of course, been long accepted—from the too often quoted example of the man shouting "Fire!" in a crowded theater to the cloudier areas of libel and slander and even cloudier ones such as national security and copyright infringements. But any discussion of limitations upon the freedoms guaranteed by the First Amendment inevitably focusses sooner or later upon the most controversial exception: obscenity, a limitation confirmed by the Court in 1957 but never accepted by Black and Douglas, or by those who share their view of the intent of the Amendment. One problem with the intensity of concentration on the obscenity issue is that it tends to distract attention from the broader danger—that *every* exception to its guarantees that is granted takes the First Amendment nearer to meaninglessness and, thus, extinction.

There are those, in any case, who claim that the First Amendment is no longer valid in a society that has been so dramatically changed by social and technological revolution, by television and the computer, and by the increasingly complex ramifications of national security. Some even claim that for the first time in our history, the majority of the people, given a vote on the matter, would reject the first Amendment, or even the whole Bill of Rights. Although I doubt this cynical view of society, I am nervous enough not to want to see it put to the test, because I know all too many people who do not understand that where First Amendment freedoms are concerned, the majority does not rule. Here is a law specifically designed to protect the dissident and unpopular. It is rooted in the same concept of intellectual freedom as that expressed by John Stuart Mill more than a century ago: "If all mankind minus one were of one opinion, and only one person were of contrary opinion, mankind would be no more justified in silencing that one person than he, if he had the power, would be justified in silencing mankind." Freedom-for-me is an idea which has always had unanimous acceptance, but freedom for the person whose ideas I detest remains a hard sell.

There is another issue related to that opening phrase of the Amendment, and it requires only moving the emphasis to another word: "*Congress* shall make no law . . . " Many have seen this as a loophole, or the most profound limitation of all upon the intent of the First Amendment, notably those who hold to the belief that states' rights are sacrosanct. And the Court, vacillating in its view of the meaning of the phrase "contemporary community standards" as used in its test for obscenity, and eventually narrowing its interpretation from national to local, has lent credence to the view that if Congress can make no law restricting freedom of expression, then legislatures at state or lower levels certainly may. The manifest absurdity of this view seems to escape its proponents (all of whom I am sure would describe themselves as good Americans), but if a person be not free to express his or her opinion in Florida or Alabama, is he or she not less than other Americans, having lost a basic American, or even human, freedom.

Nevertheless, whatever the frailty of its logic, the Court's parochial view of community standards and other elements of the decisions it handed down on June 21, 1973, amounting in effect to a conclusion that a work accused of obscenity is guilty until proven innocent, represent the most serious incursion upon the First Amendment in many years and an ominous danger at a time when we have a national administration which seems not just ready but eager to hand back broad powers to local levels of government which in the past have been most directly responsible for many of the most severe restrictions upon civil liberties. At the time, in his separate minority opinion, Justice Douglas warned:

> What we do today is rather ominous as respects librarians. The net now designed by the Court is so finely meshed that taken literally it could result in raids on libraries. Libraries, I have always assumed, were sacrosanct, representing every part of the spectrum. If what is offensive to the most influential person or group in a community can be purged from a library, the library system would be destroyed.

Finally, another issue related to the Amendment—and here, I think, or at least I hope, we do see a current change, if only in the degree of interest in the matter—is whether the First Amendment relates solely to adults, or whether it guarantees those same freedoms to young people.

Among current Supreme Court Justices only Brennan, so far as I know, has declared flatly that all citizens of the United States, regardless of age, are entitled to equal rights and protection under the Constitution and the Bill of Rights. The courts, however, while generally recognizing the rights of parents to control what their children may read or see, have also on occasion ruled in favor of teachers' rights over parental protest and have also challenged the right of school boards to remove books from the library. In 1976, for example, the Sixth Circuit Court, in *Minarcini v. Strongsville City School District,* ordered the school board to return Vonnegut's *Cat's Cradle* and Heller's *Catch-22* to the school library. The court noted that it was concerned with the "rights of students to receive information that they and their teachers desired them to have," and added the comment that recent Supreme Court opinions firmly establish "both the First Amendment right to know involved in this case and the standing of the students to raise the issue."

In another recent case, Judge Joseph Tauro of the U.S. District Court in Massachusetts denied a school committee the right to remove from the library an anthology of prose and poetry which contained a poem by a 15-year-old girl to which one parent had objected. In ordering the book returned to the library, Judge Tauro said:

> The library is "a mighty resource in the marketplace of ideas" [a quote from the Minarcini decision]. There a student can literally explore the unknown, and discover areas of interest and thought not covered by the prescribed curriculum. The student who discovers the magic of the library is on the way to a life-long experience of self-education and enrichment. The student learns that a library is a place to test or expand upon ideas presented to him, in or out of the classroom. The most effective antidote to the poison of mindless orthodoxy is ready access to a broad sweep of ideas and philosophies. There is no danger in such exposure. The danger is in mind control.

Despite such splendid affirmations, the right of young people to full access to information remains a very cloudy issue in the courts, and this fuzziness, combined with the greater frankness of today's literature for young people, encourages the continuation of challenges in this area. The American Library Association has just revised its statement on "Free Access to Libraries for Minors" in an attempt to help librarians cope with the current pressures from parents and others. The statement says:

The American Library Association opposes libraries restricting access to library materials and services for minors and holds that it is the parents—and only parents—who may restrict their children—and only their children—from access to library materials and services. Parents who would rather their children did not have access to certain materials should so advise their children. The library and its staff are responsible for providing equal access to library materials and services for *all* library users.

In short, do your own censoring; don't expect librarians to do it for you.

Now what about the current rash of censorship? Has it really reached epidemic proportions? John Chancellor reported in an NBC News broadcast last March (1981), that there had been 53 attempts at censorship from November 1980 through February 1981. L. B. Woods, in his book *A Decade of Censorship in America,* reported that there had been 912 censorship attempts in educational institutions during the years 1966 through 1975, with only 27 recorded in 1966 and a high of 130 in 1971. Chancellor's figure, though I don't know that it is confined to educational institutions, would multiply out to an annual total of 159—certainly an increase over the 130 recorded ten years ago, though whether an increase of frightening proportions is hard to assess.

Other factors may well enter such calculations. The reporting may well be more thorough today than it was in the past. Woods' figures, for example, are based on information from ALA's Office of Intellectual Freedom, which was only founded in the middle 1960s and certainly has a much more comprehensive information network now than it had then. Another factor which may account for so much media attention lately is that some of the pro-censorship groups have not only grown richer and better organized in networks, but have become much more astute in sophisticated lobbying and aggressive promotion techniques. It is, I think, in part their pizzazz and skillful manipulation of controversy that has enabled Jerry Falwell and the Moral Majority, for example, to become with the media's help virtual household words in such a short time.

But if we leave unresolved the question of whether or not there is a volume increase in censorship, is there a discernible change in the nature of censorship activity? I think there is. Not a new development, by any means, but a current reversion to some very old dangers.

If you examine the categories of materials which are most often the targets of censors—and Woods' book provides some very useful quantitative information of this kind—the most common occurrences involve obscenity, politics, sex and nudity, morality, religion, language, and race. If you consider these carefully, as a good cataloger might, these problem areas really fall into two broad groupings: 1) Morality and religion (within which I would place all the objections about sex, nudity, obscenity and language), and 2) Politics, within which, for want of a clearer choice, I group racially-based protests. It's not very easy, of course, to bring logic to bear upon such an exercise because the expressed, surface reasons for a censorship attempt are often not the real reasons. For example, some of the attacks on Baldwin's *Another Country* or Richard Wright's *Black Boy* because of their sexual content have clearly been motivated more by racial than sexual fears.

However, the point I am leading toward is that censorship becomes most virulent and dangerous when those two broad categories I mentioned—morality and religion on the one hand, politics on the other—begin to merge and become virtually indistinguishable. And this, I think, is what is happening, to a scary degree, right now. The Moral Majority, it is very clear from the thrust of its activities, is a *political* organization, and religious extremism and fear are the weapons it carries behind its banner of morality.

I don't mean to suggest that this is a new development either, but there are alarming signs that we are facing a resurgent force, and we need to remind ourselves that censorship and the denial of civil liberties have enjoyed their finest hours when politics and religious extremism have joined forces. For a contemporary illustration one need look no further than Iran. And if you want a longer perspective on the matter you can go all the way back to the ancient Greeks forcing Sophocles to drink the hemlock "for not worshipping the gods whom the city worships, for introducing religious innovations and for corrupting the young men." My God (to coin a phrase), how that quotation rings yet today, when humanists are seen as evil, God-hating perverts, when an eminent theologian like Hans Küng is disciplined by the Catholic Church for introducing religious innovations and Sonya Johnson is excommunicated by the Mormon Church for her vocal support of the Equal Rights Amendment, and when authors from Steinbeck and Hemingway and even old Nat Hawthorne to Judy Blume and Maurice Sendak are accused of corrupting our young men—or worse, in some eyes, our young women.

Back in 1814, when Thomas Jefferson was concerned about a censorship case involving a book on religion, he wrote the following to a bookseller friend in Philadelphia:

I am really mortified to be told that, *in the United States of America,* a fact like this can become a subject of enquiry, and of criminal enquiry too, as an offence against religion; that a question about the sale of a book can be carried before the civil magistrate. Is this then our freedom of religion? And are we to have a censor whose imprimatur shall say what books may be sold, and what we may buy? And who is thus to dogmatize religious opinions for our citizens? Whose foot is to be the measure to which ours are all to be cut or stretched? Is a priest to be our inquisitor, or shall a layman, simple as ourselves, set up his reason as the rule for what we are to read, and what we must believe? It is an insult to our citizens to question whether they are rational beings or not, and blasphemy again religion to suppose it cannot stand the test of truth and reason. If . . . false in its facts, disprove them; if false in its reasoning, refute it. But for God's sake, let us freely hear both sides, if we choose.

I don't mean to dump the responsibility for all censorship at the door of religion, though it is not difficult to demonstrate that through the centuries religious men and organizations have been among the most persistent and vigorous proponents of censorship. Dr. Harold Fey, a former editor of *The Christian Century* and then Professor Emeritus of Christian Ethics at Christian Theological Seminary in Indianapolis, certainly concurs with that evaluation. In an article of his I published in *Library Journal* in 1965, he said: "Religious groups must bear a good deal of responsibility for the rebellion against cultural and political freedom which results so easily in censorship shading into tyranny."

My friend Stanley Fleishman is an eminent California lawyer who has defended in more censorship cases than almost anyone else. Over the years he has given much consideration to the relationship between religion and obscenity, and his contention is that obscenity has become a crime because of religious insistence that it is a sin. He maintains that the U.S. Government which, because of the First Amendment, may not establish a religion or interfere with religion, may not therefore maintain a morality rooted in religion. Obscenity laws, says Fleishman, are aimed at saving the reader or viewer from his own moral weakness, however private and discreet, rather than from acts which may transgress the law. And legislation whose sole or chief purpose is the preservation of religious morality, he says, is not consistent with the separation of Church and State. It is the separation of Church and State, the very substance of the First Amendment, that should most concern us in today's censorious climate.

If the most recent political morality drive masquerading under the banner of religion were all, we might perhaps not have too much to worry about. After all, when even such a senior conservative statesman as Barry Goldwater declares that the Moral Majority needs "a good kick in the ass," and right-wing columnist James Jackson Kilpatrick refers to the group as "the moral mob," we are clearly not dealing with any massive consensus, even on the right. Groups of this kind also demonstrate an amazing facility for hoisting themselves by their own petards. When the Moral Majority attacks a bastion of family respectability like *Readers' Digest* for a "hellish" plan to censor the word of God, it is not just funny, or another ironical illustration of Carey McWilliams' claim that "the paradox of censorship is that everyone is opposed to it—absolutely everyone." An attack on a target like *Readers' Digest,* one dares hope, may even awaken some people who have hitherto seen no great danger in some kid somewhere being denied the opportunity to read, and learn from, a marvelous book like *Catcher in the Rye.*

No, if the Moral Majority were all, the attack on intellectual freedom might be easily containable. What is more dangerous is that the current surge of group censorship attempts coincides with a pronounced move in the direction of secrecy and censorship by the government itself. Let me cite just a few examples. The best known may be the sustained effort, spearheaded by Attorney General William French Smith, to gut the Freedom of Information Act. A great example of bookburning is the recent order issued by Thomas G. Auchter, assistant secretary of labor for occupational safety and health, instructing OSHA to destroy 50,000 copies of a government booklet and to recall three films and three slide presentations prepared by the agency. What were these subversive publications? They dealt with the hazards posed to workers by cotton dust. A spokesman said Auchter was upset that the booklet portrayed on the cover a worker who was obviously ill. The inside cover noted that the worker died of brown lung disease. Auchter's quoted concern was—and it's a beauty—"that the cover itself makes a statement that takes a side." To disagree is not to destroy?

And a third recent example from our government: Energy Secretary James B. Edwards ordered 12,000 copies of his department's *Energy Consumer* magazine confiscated and locked in a storage room because, he claimed, it was biased against nuclear power. Even if this claim is valid, here is the censor's typical negative response. With all the government's ability to issue pro-nuclear power information—an ability it has shown no reluctance to employ—it is not willing to allow differing views to compete in the marketplace of public opinion.

Here is a good demonstration of what Donald Thompson says in his history of literary censorship in England: "Political censorship is necessarily based on fear of what will happen if those whose work is censored get their way, or if they are effective in persuading a large number of readers to share their point of view. The nature of political censorship at any given time depends on the censor's answer to the simple question, 'What are you afraid of?'" The same question can, of course, be asked of all censors; for the most part, fear is their principal motivation, though few would admit it.

In a time of earlier national crisis one of our wiser presidents assured the people that they had nothing to fear except fear itself. He well understood one of the great undermining dangers to a society—that fear is contagious. And among fear's greatest allies are secrecy, ignorance, indifference. The last of those three, indifference, may be the greatest danger of all, because it allows the spread of the others unchecked.

We cannot afford indifference in the face of an insidiously swelling assault on the people's right to know. The efforts of extremist groups to control what others, and notably others' children, may see or read or hear, are only the most visible element of this assault. It can be seen also in increasingly narrower interpretations of the First Amendment by the Supreme Court, which may be most obvious in some of its recent decisions on the freedom of the press; in a regression towards secrecy and censorship by the government; and, more and more, at local government levels. In Tampa, Florida, to quote an example from my own area, the City Council (or some members of it) are currently demanding the power to decide what books shall be in the library, and even where they shall be placed in order to give maximum protection to the innocent from the harmful. The sad irony is that those who hold to these attitudes or applaud these actions, though good patriots all, I'm sure, fail to see the parallels with the beliefs and actions of those whom we have decried as the enemies of freedom: on the right, the Nazis of Germany, one of whose most symbolic early acts was a massive burning of books; and on the left, the Communists of today, among whose main weapons has been the total control of information.

If information is power, as many have claimed, the reverse of the coin is that the withholding or suppression of information can only make those who are denied access to it more power*less*, a process which portends the demise of democracy, a basic principle of which is that power rests ultimately with the people. Viewing this danger, Chicago's resident philosopher, Studs Terkel, has coined an appropriate up-to-date revision of Lord Acton's overquoted adage. Says Studs; "Powerlessness corrupts. Absolute powerlessness corrupts absolutely."

Only by maintaining full and open and free access to information can we hope to counter the basic error underlying censorship, whether attempted by government or by voluntary groups. That basic error is that there is, or should be, a consensus, a basis of national agreement on what constitutes national orthodoxy. At no time is the pressure to establish such a national orthodoxy stronger and more vociferous than in times of crisis, and most particularly in times of war. It is significant, then, that at such a time, in the middle of World War II, the Supreme Court ruled against compulsory flag salutes in these memorable words:

> As government pressure toward unity becomes greater, so strife becomes more bitter as to whose unity it shall be. Probably no greater division of our people could proceed from any provocation than from finding it necessary to choose what doctrine and whose program public officials shall compel youth to unite in embracing. Ultimate futility of such attempts to compel coherence is the lesson of every such effort. Those who begin coercive elimination of dissent soon find themselves exterminating dissenters. Compulsory unification of opinion achieves only the unity of the graveyard. If there is any fixed star in our constitutional constellation, it is that no official, high or petty, can prescribe what shall be orthodox in politics, nationalism, religion, or other matters of opinion, or force citizens to confess by word or act their faith therein. If there are any circumstances which permit an exception they do not now occur to us.

In other words, our American national orthodoxy repudiates orthodoxy. Or, as another great First Amendment lawyer puts it: "The First Amendment does not exist to protect expression that is beneficial; it exists to protect expression. Indeed, if all it guarded was what we think is salutary, the Amendment would be surplusage." Charles Rembar continues:

> There is no need of a guaranty of freedom for what the majority wants. What is needed is a guaranty of freedom for what the majority does not want, or believes will do some harm, or even

hates with a quivering hate. The damage that may be done by (certain kinds of) expression . . . is damage we must risk—must risk unless we are willing to abandon a fundamental principle of our political system. The question is not whether the uses of the new liberty are all to the good, or even whether they are good at all. The question is whether we are to have the freedom of speech and of the press, with all the perils, jeopardy and fright that it entails.

The greatest danger, in my view, is not the censor himself but those who disagree with the censor and do not come forward and say so. I began with an account of the animosities stirred up by my editorial policies at *Library Journal* in the early sixties. Appalled as I was by the behind-the-scenes attempts to have me silenced, they worried me less than the apparent apathy or timorousness of the majority of our readers. For a while the lack of response to my clear invitation to argument and debate in the pages of the *Journal* so depressed me that I was tempted to quit. In time I learned that it wasn't quite apathy I was facing, so much as a widespread reluctance to put one's views on record, a feeling that it wasn't somehow polite to express open disagreement with someone, and certainly not in print. I have tried hard ever since to convey the message to this reluctant majority that to remain silent while others force down the drain principles you believe in may indeed be polite, but it is the sure and stupid road to the loss of the very liberties that make a polite society possible.

If there is one sure thing, it is that the censors and their certainties about what is right and good for all of us will never disappear from our midst. Our best defense against them is to exercise those liberties that the First Amendment guarantees. Without exercise, the mind and the body can atrophy; and so it is with those freedoms given to us by the First Amendment. If more people who want to retain an open society do not stand up and exercise their right to speak, to write, to think, to disagree, those who would limit or abolish those freedoms will win by default.

Sometimes I think what we need is someone on the anti-censorship side like that wonderfully mad television personality in the movie *Network*—someone who will urge and inspire people to stand up and tell the censors and the moral caretakers "We're mad as hell and we're not going to take it any more." Leave our minds alone.

A Priori Censorship

To what degree does a priori censorship by library directors and other supervisors exist? The difficulty of uncovering hard evidence, I would assume, is one of the reasons for the existence of this program. Few library directors or supervisors seem likely to jump into a public confessional box and confess to being censors. And few librarians who have been threatened or cowed by restrictions upon their freedom of speech are likely suddenly to emerge from the closet and expose the practice. I am therefore not sanguine that this ambitiously titled "Speak Out" will get us much nearer a solution to one of the most shameful practices in our profession. And even if we do, through this meeting, uncover a smattering of facts and evidence, I remain skeptical about the kind of clout ALA can, or will, exercise in dealing with the problem.

The fact that this meeting is presented under the auspices of the Committee on Professional Ethics is perhaps an advance clue to our probable helplessness. Some of us have watched for a quarter-century or more the Association's efforts to produce a Code of Ethics that was more than an assembly of pieties, and I think it fair to say that any visible impact of any of the respective versions of a Code over all those years is extremely hard to discern. And even if we had a tough, strong code, what teeth or force can be put behind it? Has anyone in ALA or the profession ever been successfully charged with a breach of professional ethics? I don't know of any. But if it has occurred, what has resulted from it? Again, I don't know. Which shows you what a big public issue this has been.

If the practice of a priori censorship has survived and flourished largely underground, anyone who has edited one of our professional journals is well aware of the problem, and that the practice is more

---

Originally a contribution to a "Speak Out on A Priori Censorship" at the ALA 1985 Conference in Chicago, this is reprinted by permission of the American Library Association from the *Newsletter on Intellectual Freedom,* Vol. 34, No. 5: 169-171, September 1985.

prevalent than is generally believed. The most notable example in my experience occurred when I was editor of *LJ* and Dorothy Broderick sent me an article for publication. It was, as I had come to expect from her, a wonderful, spirited piece of writing, but it expressed views directly antithetical to some strong opinions expressed by the president of her university which had just been reported in the national press. I liked the article but I didn't want to put Dorothy at risk by publishing it. When I called her she simply told me to get on with it in no uncertain "publish and be damned" terms. She knew she'd be fired (and she was) but she valued her freedom of speech beyond her job security.

The uninhibited courage of Dorothy Broderick, if not unique, proved to be very rare. I can remember, from my days at *LJ*, many occasions when I asked someone on the inside of a particular situation in a library to write about it for publication, only to receive answers like "Oh, I'd have to get clearance on that," or "I couldn't write it under my own name." It was partly because of this kind of response, and because I deplore both anonymous contributions and the kind of PR statements that directors (often) write about their own operations (the kind of writing that Ralph Shaw christened "how I run my library good" articles), that I began *LJ*'s "Day At" series in the sixties. John Berry and I, or other *LJ* reporters, would go out and spend a whole day (sometimes more) at different kinds of institutions and report, without fear or favor, what we had seen or learned, and what we thought of it all. But I always thought how much more valuable such reporting would be—not only for *LJ* and its readers but ultimately, given good will, for the institution itself—if it could be done by (or with the help of) someone on the inside, who in most cases would be likely to have a deeper understanding than we, as outsiders, could possibly achieve in 24 or 48 hours plus some background research.

One reason why the practice of a priori censorship remains largely underground is that there is a pervasive nervousness in our profession about hanging one's views and opinions out on the line, either in the professional press or on the meeting room floor. For every letter that the editor of a journal may receive in response to a published article, for example, the author of that article may receive ten, or twenty, from people who have something to say, laudatory or otherwise, but don't want it seen in cold print by thousands of others. You can see the same thing in our meeting halls; just check, for example, how many people elected to Council sit there for four years and never utter a word. When I was active on the speech circuit I used to insist on ample time being left for audience involvement; while there was usually some audience response, however, it was always over-shadowed by the number of people who wanted to talk or argue with me after the meeting was officially over. And when I went to talk at library schools I usually stayed overnight because I had found that students who wouldn't say much in the classroom in the presence of faculty members would rap for hours in a late night party atmosphere. (Besides, I liked the parties!)

I suspect that this same general nervousness about print or public statement may be among the motivations for a priori screening or censorship by directors and others. But what, really, are they afraid of? Can the director, or his/her institution, be seriously damaged by the public expression of a staff member's views? If the public statement is malicious or libelous, there are legal ways of responding. If an article is inaccurate, it can be answered with facts and evidence. But such arguments do not persuade the potential censor. One common trait among censors is their lack of faith in the ability of others to reach sound or reasoned conclusions when faced with conflicting evidence. Only one viewpoint will do: theirs.

That there are censors in our ranks was made abundantly clear by the landmark Fiske Report (*Book Selection and Censorship*) as long ago as 1959, and I have seen nothing that convinces me that things have changed substantially since. What is sad is that this problem should exist in a profession which for so long has been among the nation's most prominent defenders of the First Amendment. In the murky days of McCarthyism, when fear kept so many others silent, ALA—to use a favorite Reagan expression—"stood tall," producing what I still regard as its most memorable public declaration, The Freedom to Read Statement, with its ringing final sentence: "Freedom is a dangerous way of life, but it is ours."

In the years since then we have done battle with censors of all stripes, from left wing to right wing, from governments to the lunatic fringe, from the self-proclaimed moral majority to the sometimes overzealous minority. We have defended the First Amendment rights of porno movie stars, the editors of student newspapers, booksellers, publishers and many more. And, yes, we have defended librarians too, usually against school boards or other institutional bodies that have infringed their rights.

But, like many other professions, we have been less willing or able to do something about the transgressors within our own ranks. We may publicly decry the Reagan administration's efforts to silence federal employees, not just currently but for their lifetimes, but we see no such outcry about librarians silencing other librarians.

The answers to the questions posed at this meeting are simple and self-evident. Is it a violation of intellectual freedom principles? How could it be otherwise? It is also a violation of the basic civil liberties of librarians as individuals and citizens. And, just as surely, it is a denial of professionalism, and of the principles and beliefs which this profession has espoused throughout its maturity.

What is less simple is what to do about the situation. But one thing is clear, I think: no potential solution is likely to emerge without exposure of specific instances of the practice. We need concrete examples, real evidence, and we need to name names. Perhaps more meetings like this one can help us open some doors. Certainly the library press could be of some assistance in pinpointing occurrences. But, ultimately, successful exposure will only be possible if some of the victims of a priori censorship are willing to come forward and testify. I realize that is dangerous, and that it's a lot to ask. But I see no alternative. Freedom of speech survives only so long as it is exercised. If it is not, it is impossible to defend against its suppression.

I do not, however, believe we shall see a parade of testifiers until and unless the profession and the American Library Association show the same willingness and ability to deal with the censors in our own ranks that we have exhibited in battling those outside the profession who attack the principles that are our proudest expression. That is the challenge that faces the Committee on Professional Ethics, the Intellectual Freedom Committee and, eventually, the ALA Council. Unless they answer it we can expect the problem to continue on its insidious, undermining way.

Living the Library Bill of Rights

Living the *Library Bill of Rights*. Has a nice ring to it. But I have found that assigned titles, when you start examining them and consider how you can squeeze what you want to say under their narrow umbrella, are often a bit simplistic or annoyingly restrictive. Just as a person who lives by bread alone, never indulging in the joyous sin of whipped cream and chocolate cake, is unlikely to develop a taste for the *enjoyment* of food, the librarian whose life is devoted simply to the *Library Bill of Rights* seems to me likely to descend into dullness and pedantry.

Even if we consider the *Library Bill of Rights* as a set of principles by which librarians should live their *professional* lives, the title hangs on to its straitjacket qualities. I would argue, for example, that there is a larger, more encompassing Bill of Rights that librarians, as other Americans, should not only live by but strenuously promote and defend. And further, in this increasingly interdependent and chaotic world, that we need to think in less parochial terms and consider more universal sets of principles as being relevant to our lives, our thinking, our behavior.

ALA has adopted as policy, for example, "the principle of Article 19 of the Universal Declaration of Human Rights adopted by the United Nations General Assembly." Had our policies not been assembled in Topsy fashion to meet individual crises as they occur, we might well have considered adopting other sections of that splendid document. Could ALA possibly disagree with the second paragraph of Article 21 of the Universal Declaration, for example, which reads: "Everyone has the right of equal access to public service in his country."

If we peer over the *Library Bill of Rights* to these broader horizons of principle we may avoid, as recent administrations in Washington have not, falling prey either to the folly that our domestic laws and documents

---

This article, originally a speech delivered at the ALA 1990 Conference in Chicago, is reprinted by permission of the American Library Association from the *Newsletter on Intellectual Freedom*, Vol. 39, No. 5: 181-185, September 1990.

are applicable to and enforceable upon all the peoples of the world, or to the hypocrisy inherent in the belief that while law must govern our behavior at home we may as a nation flout international laws or principles whenever it suits our purpose to do so.

The intended purpose of this program is to focus on the provision of equality of service and I hear there are librarians who are not happy with Section 5 of the *Library Bill of Rights,* who see it as restrictive rather than expansive in its wording. For those among you who do not have the words of Section 5 engraved upon your memory, it reads: "A person's right to use a library should not be denied or abridged because of origin, age, background, or views." By specifying particular groups of users whose rights should not be abridged, the argument goes, those not named are, by omission, excluded from protection. There are those who would like to see Article 5 abbreviated as follows: "The rights of an individual to the use of a library should not be denied or abridged (period)." In this form, the statement certainly has the virtues of concision and of being all-encompassing. Why, then, the need for what some have called a "laundry list of protected groups" in the *Library Bill of Rights?*

About the time I was pondering this matter, I was charged, as a member of ALA's new Coordinating Committee on Freedom and Equality of Access to Information, with analyzing the ALA Policy Manual to see where we stand in regard to policies governing access. Apart from the simple finding that our policies are uncoordinated and fractionated, not to say chaotic, I discovered that the *Library Bill of Rights* does not have an exclusive on laundry lists. In the set of policies under Section 59, Minority Concerns, another laundry list appears in Policy 59.2 which opposes discrimination because of "race, sex, creed, color, or national origin." Note that race, sex and color are not mentioned specifically in the *Library Bill of Rights,* nor is age mentioned in the Minority Rights policy.

That isn't the end of it. Yet another laundry list appears in Section 3, on intellectual freedom, in ALA's Federal Legislative Policy. This one, the most inclusive, lists "age, sex, race, religion, national origin, disability, economic condition, individual life-style, or political or social views."

Wondering whether laundry lists were a particular obsession of ALA'S, I took a fresh look at that other Bill of Rights, the Amendments to the U.S. Constitution.

Lo and behold, similar specificities crop up in that venerable document. For example, Article XV, Section I reads; "The right of citizens ... to vote shall not be denied or abridged ... on account of race, color, or previous condition of servitude." And Article XIX adds: "The right of citizens... to vote shall not be denied or abridged... on account of sex."

But the U.S. Bill of Rights also suggests, perhaps, a solution to the objections of those who see the laundry list in the *Library Bill of Rights* as restrictive. Article IX of the Bill of Rights says: "The enumeration in the Constitution, of certain rights, shall not be construed to deny or disparage others retained by the people." A similar amendment to ALA policy might read: "The enumeration in the *Library Bill of Rights* and in other ALA policies, of certain persons or groups whose right to use a library should not be denied or abridged, shall not be construed to exclude other persons or groups not so specified."

The question remains, why do these laundry lists occur in our *Library Bill of Rights* and other ALA policies, and in the U.S. Bill of Rights? Why are they necessary? The answer, of course, lies in our history, in George Orwell's observation that some human beings have been regarded and treated as less equal than others. It lies also in the way that most policies are formulated. In the main they are reactive, responding to a sudden or a gradual realization that there is a wrong that needs righting. As we have come to understand, usually much too slowly, that certain groups or individuals have been dealt with less equally than others, we have felt it necessary, in amending both the US. Constitution and our own ALA documents, to give special emphasis to those individuals and groups whose rights have been most flagrantly denied, as a first step in beginning to remedy the wrongs that have been committed against them. There may also be a third element among the reasons for the existence of these laundry lists. Without the specifics, some of the less conscious among those whose rights have *never* been restrained may well wonder why such policies are needed at all.

Living the *Library Bill of Rights* requires a commitment from each of us on several levels, levels so integrally linked that we cannot hope to achieve our goals without involvement in all of them. As individual librarians, it is our responsibility within our own institutions to do all we can to promote equality of service, maximum access to information, resistance to censorship pressures, etc. But our policies and practices at local levels, and our thinking in these areas, are shaped to a significant degree by what evolves among us as a community of librarians, a profession, via our various associations and organizations.

As a community of librarians, we live the *Library Bill of Rights* by constantly refining and promoting policies that lead to more informed, more humane practices in libraries and among librarians. We also find in our associations the strength, the numbers, to do battle with the larger enemies of our goals, such as repressive and regressive government policies or unrestricted commercial control of the sources of information. Here, too, we see that bidirectional linkage between individual action and professional policy. ALA's Policy on Governmental Intimidation, for example, which we have cause to refer to in the light of recent FBI incursions upon libraries and library users, had its origin in a 1971 resolution presented by Zoia Horn and Pat Rom after Zoia had gone to jail rather than bow to government intimidation.

At a third level we need to recognize that we are members of the information and cultural and educational communities and that our defense of the rights of libraries and library users rings hollow unless we are prepared to defend intellectual freedom in this larger arena. If we are prepared to accept Sen. Helms, wielding federal funding as his axe in his recently adopted role as art critic, judging what is fit for us to view, can it be long before we face the prospect of Jesse as literary critic, deciding what is fit for exposure on the shelves of libraries receiving federal funds? When the First Amendment rights of an author, a publisher, a bookseller, a filmmaker, a scientist, an educator are attacked, we are all in danger. When the press is not free, freedom of information and access to much of what we need to know is gone.

There is ample recognition in ALA policy statements of this broader responsibility to intellectual freedom, notably in the *Federal Legislative Policy* and the *Freedom to Read Statement,* and many of the actions of the Freedom to Read Foundation in recent years have involved the defense of intellectual freedom beyond library boundaries. But there have been occasions in the past when we have been willing to sacrifice the rights of others in the book community in order to retain exemptions for libraries and librarians in legislation otherwise restricting intellectual freedom.

At the local level, the front line, the library profession has produced an array of heroes, willing—no determined—to wage the battle for intellectual freedom even at great personal risk. Examples include Joan Bodger, fired from the Missouri State Library in 1969 for protesting the suppression of an underground newspaper, and a decade later, Jeanne Layton, a Utah librarian dismissed for refusal to remove a Don DeLillo novel from library shelves. One could cite many more such examples, but the changing tenor of our problems is exemplified by the latest cadre of library heroes on the front line: the many librarians who resisted and publicly opposed the flagrant invasions of libraries and the rights of library users by the FBI under the mantle of the so-called Library Awareness

Program—librarians who, as a result, now find *themselves* subjects for investigation by the FBI.

The necessary change in our focus was noted by Gordon Conable, current chair of the Intellectual Freedom Committee, in his excellent report to Council last January. IFC's agenda, he said, "is no longer focused as much on specific censorship incidents." This is not, I'm sure, because Gordon or the IFC believes, any more than I do, that censorship pressures from individuals or vocal self-righteous groups are likely to disappear, but because, as Conable put it, "an explosion is occurring in the complexity and diversity of intellectual freedom issues which directly involve librarians," many of which "are being defined in the legal, political, and social environment in ways which tend to submerge their First Amendment implications."

It is not altogether new that the defense of intellectual freedom involves more than battling against a stream of what we have come to call "censorship incidents." Back in the fifties and early sixties, when ALA had already established a proud record as a leading defender of intellectual freedom, we had done virtually nothing to oppose and eradicate the most vicious censorship of all—the racist barriers erected between black people and libraries in many sections of the country. We had black people barred from using what were properly *their* libraries, or limited to use of "separate but equal" (i.e., inferior) facilities, or treated to such indignities in their use of libraries (anyone remember "vertical integration" in Danville, Va.?) that to talk of intellectual freedom was a mockery. It was only through the courageous and prolonged efforts of a few librarians like E. J. Josey and, I am proud to say, an increasingly activist library press—including editors such as John Wakeman at the *Wilson Library Bulletin*, Bill Eshelman in California and John Berry in Massachusetts—that the consciousness of the profession and of ALA was sufficiently aroused to recognize that here was an intellectual freedom problem (not to mention a human rights problem) of immense dimension, and one which, if our traditional stance as a defender of intellectual freedom were to have any credibility, had to be addressed and overcome.

Our credibility will always be suspect as long as there exist wide gaps between the policies and principles we espouse as a community of librarians and the practices that exist at the individual institution level. Conable referred to "the major threat to our credibility that is inherent in the widespread failure to apply our basic principles to new technologies." He cited a number of issues that "threaten to undermine our core values if we do not confront them directly with courage and with honesty," including, he said, "the widespread willingness of public libraries to modify or abandon their traditional commitment to providing fee-free service, if the services are based upon new technologies such as videotape or electronic storage."

This is another example of why the title of this program is too narrow. There is not one word in the *Library Bill of Rights* about economic barriers to intellectual freedom. That is not to say that the American Library Association does not have a policy or set of principles which address this issue. Indeed Policy 50.4, "Free Access to Information," may be the single strongest and most unequivocal statement in the entire Policy Manual. It reads, in part: "The American Library Association asserts that the charging of fees and levies for information services, including those services utilizing the latest information technology, is discriminatory in publicly supported institutions providing library and information services."

Despite the ringing conviction of this statement it is clear that many members of our profession are not convinced that this is a principle they can live by. Indeed, a couple of years ago, ALA's Planning Committee, I believe, urged us to reconsider this policy because so much of library practice was not in accord with it. Now there's a constructive attitude! If we had all along shaped our policies and principles to match the worst of library practices, there never would have been a *Library Bill of Rights* or a set of Minority Concerns among our policy documents. We could have concluded, as indeed some among us seem to have done, that we have *no* principles, other perhaps than "expediency is the best policy."

In my view, the economic barriers that have been and are being erected in libraries and library service are the nearest 1980s and 1990s equivalent of the racial barriers of the 1950s, '60s and before. The people who most desperately need certain kinds of information to survive and progress in our society and civilization—the poor and oppressed, including many members of minorities—are those most likely to be excluded from the enhancement of information opportunity made possible by expanding technology. This situation is exacerbated by the government's handing over of much of this kind of information to commercial brokers who are unlikely to find it either profitable or enticing to distribute, given the economic base of the potential market.

One can have some considerable sympathy for librarians and institutions faced with the dilemma of vastly increased costs and declining tax support. And we cannot zero in on technology as the lone culprit. Some of the abandonment of our traditional principles and beliefs is the result of a climate set by regressive national administrations and a corporate world seeking new territories, both of which have sought to foster the idea of information solely as a commercial commodity, a product, and to abandon public responsibility in favor of private gain. We must not, however, change our suit of clothes to match the tailoring requirements of this breed, but must turn more of our efforts toward working assiduously for changes in national policy, for recognition that equality of access to information is an essential ingredient of democracy, of government not just *of* the people, but by and for the people.

If librarians are to lay claim to a leadership role in defense of people's right of access to information, though, we must make every effort to ensure that our performance in terms of service matches pretty closely the words we utter as a profession, through our Association policies and public position statements. The fees question is by no means the only area in which there is a serious credibility gap between pronouncement and performance.

Listen, for example, to our words in "Free Access to Libraries for Minors," one of the interpretations of the *Library Bill of Rights*: "The American Library Association opposes libraries restricting access to library materials and services for minors. . ." and "the word 'age' was incorporated into Article 5 of the Library Bill of Rights because young people are entitled to the same access to libraries and to the materials in libraries as are adults."

Now how many public libraries do you know where the services to minors come close to equating with those policy interpretations? In how many libraries do children have unrestricted access to adult shelves? In how many libraries are youngsters permitted use of interlibrary loan?

Yet, 23 years ago almost to this day, a preconference in San Francisco on Intellectual Freedom and the Teenager, cosponsored by IFC, YASD and AASL, decided that not teenagers alone but all young people should be the focus of its discussions, and recommended that "free access to *all* books in a library collection be granted to young people."

Summarizing that three-day event, Ervin Gaines, then chair of IFC, dealt at some length with the comments of Edgar Friedenberg, author of *Coming of Age in America* and the most outspoken of the panelists on the program. Friedenberg said, among other things, "the library is just one more place where the kids are taught they are second-class citizens." Gaines reported that Friedenberg "made the assumption that intellectual freedom was an inalienable right, that age is not a morally relevant factor and that adults have themselves no right to determine for youth access to ideas." Sounding somewhat surprised himself, Gaines added: "This assumption echoed and re-echoed throughout the conference. There was surprising unanimity of opinion on this particular point."

Nearly a quarter-century later, I think it fair to say that our performance is far from reflecting that unanimity of opinion—*or* Article 5 of the *Library Bill of Rights*. Is it also fair to conclude that our fear of parents has weighed more heavily upon us than our belief in the rights of access of young people?

Public libraries, of course, are not alone in discriminating among their users. In how many academic libraries do undergraduates have access to materials and services equal to that of faculty, or even graduate students? In his article in the latest edition of the *Intellectual Freedom Manual*, Paul Cors, himself an academic librarian, says: "It is in the area of services, not collections, that academic libraries are more likely to fall short in their devotion to intellectual freedom," and he attributes this to the fact that "the academic community is a socially stratified one, and this stratification will affect the library." So here we see discrimination not so much on the basis of age as upon the basis of status—another item not covered by the laundry list in Article 5 of the *Library Bill of Rights*.

If the practices of some of our libraries tend to undermine the intellectual freedom principles we espouse, attacks on the freedom of speech and thought in the temple of purity itself, ALA, can only leave us subject to ridicule and charges of hypocrisy. In recent months, at least two librarian members of ALA have resigned from the editorship of division journals under pressures that we would probably abhor if they occurred elsewhere. In one case, the editor refused reappointment at least partly because the division president insisted on screening her editorials before publication. In the other, the editor was instructed, just prior to publication, to pull an article from the forthcoming issue because it was written by a candidate for the ALA Presidency. I asked at Midwinter whether this policy—referred to in some of the correspondence as an unwritten policy, which is an oxymoron—applied to candidates for all offices in ALA, and whether ALA was prepared to tell its members that in order to run for office they must be prepared to forego their First Amendment rights. One comment during the debate on this matter caught the ridiculous heart of the issue. A councillor said, "Of course we don't want our members to read what our candidates think while they are running for office. Better to wait until after the election. Right?"

Can we really expect individual librarians and libraries to adopt and adhere to ALA intellectual freedom policies when even units of the Association act as though the policies of the Association do not apply to them? The latest tactic of those whose desire to control information is stronger than their belief in freedom of expression is apparently to have these divisional journals edited by staff rather than members, on the theory, I suppose, that the freedom of speech of staff can be more easily curtailed. Such practices do great damage to the reputation of both the Association and the profession, and those involved need to be reminded of Ben Franklin's words: "We should all hang together lest we all hang separately."

I cannot close without a word or two about collections, which is where the spirit of the *Library Bill of Rights* lives, or should live. One of the things that concerns me here is that we seem to have focused much more of our attention and effort on defending what is *in* library collections than we have devoted to what is missing from them. This may be because those who want something *out* make more noise than those who want something *in*. But that is not the whole story.

Take the Salman Rushdie incident, for example. When Khomeini "called for international censorship, book burning and murder," to quote Pat Berger's splendid letter to the Chair of NCLIS, ALA and other library associations and many librarians throughout the country responded promptly and admirably, denouncing Khomeini's actions and demonstrating publicly their support of Rushdie's right to write and publish whatever he chose without being threatened with murder. Given how some other groups gave in to fear of reprisals or simply failed to act or express themselves, it was a moment to be proud of the library profession.

But what about the other side of the coin? There is no doubt that *Satanic Verses* upset many followers of Islam in addition to extremists like Khomeini. Could we say to them, your side of the story, the achievements of Islamic civilization, the tenets of the Islamic faith, are well represented on our shelves for those who want to understand *why* Rushdie's novel caused such uproar? I doubt it. Yet there can be no excuse for a failure to exhibit such balance in library collections. For decades now one of the most powerful forces impacting upon world affairs has been the Islamic revolution, an impact comparable perhaps to the incredible collapse of Communist power.

But so it goes with issues. In a recent *Library Journal* editorial, John Berry wrote:

> Libraries have never spent even a small part of the resources needed to dig out full information on issues like drug addiction, health care, the federal budget, housing, transportation, the sav-

ings and loan scam, or U.S. competition in foreign markets. Libraries have never adequately publicized the availability of that kind of information to the citizens who need it.

Most library service would collapse after the first two dozen serious citizen inquirers grabbed what they needed to understand, in depth, on any of these issues.

Berry's editorial comment is an exact echo of a comment made by Dan Lacy nearly thirty years ago: he was talking then of the Berlin problem.

In terms of living the *Library Bill of Rights,* I continue to wonder how far we have come since the classic Fiske Report of 1959. For those of you too young to remember, Marjorie Fiske, reporting on book selection in California school and public libraries, found that nearly two-thirds of all librarians who had a say in book selection reported instances where the controversiality of a book or author resulted in a decision not to buy. Worse, nearly 20 per cent habitually avoided buying *any* material known to be controversial or "which they believe[d] *might become* controversial."

For such librarians, if they still exist—and I am sure they do—there may be small hope, but library schools could do much to improve the attitude of future librarians if they would urge upon their students the advice of Dorothy Broderick, holder of the Robert B. Downs Award and one of the profession's most ardent defenders of intellectual freedom. Arguing that libraries must present an image of fairness, she says:

> We would have to be sure that we are not imposing our personal values on the collection. My rule of thumb for that is that at least 25% of everything you buy ought to be personally offensive to you. I believe every library ought to have two big posters at the doorway. The first would read, "This library has something offensive to everyone." The second would read, "If you are not offended by something we own, please complain!"

I am sure that Dorothy does not underestimate, any more than I do, the difficulties faced by the librarian on the front line, but we both know that principle cannot be defended by quiet acquiescence. Men like Nelson Mandela and Vaclav Havel understood that, and understood too the cost of defending freedom, but freedom and principle emerged incredibly the stronger for their refusal to capitulate.

We, too, have an obligation to resist attempts to limit freedom of expression in our country. Tom Wicker nailed that obligation with precision in a column a couple of weeks ago. What really threatens freedom of expression in America, now only more visibly than usual, is the persisting fear of difference, and the willingness to be different, even to be despised.

"Political dissent, provocative or outrageous art and expression, social protest, an insistence on the rights of the individual—all at some point," said Wicker, "strike fear into the hearts of many who loudly extol the land of the free. But that land cannot exist if it is not also the home of the brave."

Those who produced *The Freedom to Read* statement in the dark days of McCarthyism understood that when they wrote: "Freedom itself is a dangerous way of life, but it is ours."

Living the *Library Bill of Rights* can be dangerous, too, but if we fail to do it, the role of libraries and the library profession in society will, over time, crumble into insignificance. And the people will be the poorer for it. We must not allow that to happen.

PART IV

COLLECTION BUILDING

Introduction

This section is unlike any other in this book, in that the bulk of it is from the 1950s, when I was still quite a young librarian working in public libraries in England. If nothing else this indicates how long Collection Building (or Book Selection as we called it then) has been one of my major interests.

The first article, the earliest included in this collection, was inspired by the great Ernest Savage, in my view one of the two outstanding public librarians in Britain in this century (Lionel McColvin was the other). The youthful enthusiasm and naiveté are a bit overpowering today, but the message is sound. Very few libraries, still today I think, make sufficient organized use of the pool of knowledge which is present among their staff.

"The Assistant and the Bookish Habit" (the title is adapted from that of a very popular book—*The Reader and the Bookish Manner*—written by S. C. Holliday and published by the Association of Assistant Librarians in 1953) was my first speech at a national level, delivered at the annual conference of The Library Association. It continues and expands upon the earlier article's enthusiasm for the "bookman" librarian and inveighs against the growing obsession with administration and gadgetry. Little did I know then how far that obsession would go in subsequent years!

The third English piece, a speech I was invited to deliver at the North-Western Polytechnic School of Librarianship, was the result of my appointment to what was then virtually a "new" job in libraries: stock editor (though that was not yet the title given the job). I was, I think, only the second stock editor appointed during that period, the first being Ken McColvin at the Lambeth Public Library. The interesting aspect of all this is that it took a team of efficiency experts (not librarians) to realize that one of the most important functions in a library was the care and feeding of the collections, and that the person responsible for this should be a very senior staff member not burdened by other administrative duties. It was that organization and methods team's recommendation that led to the creation of the stock editor job to which I was subsequently appointed.

"Confusion and Conviction" is a brief, early *LJ* editorial, and "The Blue and the Grey" is the only substantial article on book selection included here from my American period. This piece was written especially as an Introduction to my collection of *LJ* material on *Book Selection and Censorship in the Sixties* (Bowker, 1969). It is, as the first couple of paragraphs indicate, a further discussion of the issues raised in Lester Asheim's "Not Censorship, But Selection" and of some other issues raised by societal changes since Asheim's essay was written. Those who get as far as the concluding paragraphs will see here the same convictions about the care of the collection as were expressed well over a decade earlier in "Stock Control in Public Libraries." *Plus ça change* . . .

Critics, Awake!

It is nearly eighteen months since Dr. Savage declared that the librarian as critic is a reasonable conception, "not even an ideal: an ordinary business aptitude." These terse shock-phrases were words of wisdom from a great librarian, curiously young in his love of books and people, and his conception of librarianship as something integrally connected with both; a rare librarian who, with the advancing years, has not wandered from these lush pastures into the dry (but more commonly respected) wastelands of administration and technique. Has anybody listened to him?

I read Dr. Savage's article and re-read it—with pleasure, with excitement, with hope. I felt, as perhaps many other young and still hopeful librarians felt, "Here for almost the first time since I have been receiving *The Library Association Record* is a man pleading for influence for librarians, not on committees, but in the world of books." Incredible! But did we do anything? Not us. Not me. And it wasn't until the other day that I realized that I hadn't digested one word of Dr. Savage's trumpeting-in of the renaissance! So I'd say, "Shout louder, Dr. Savage. One voice doesn't carry far. And it takes a lot to wake the dead."

The failure? I was approached by a reader in my Branch Library. "Can you tell me anything about Sally Hurrall, please?" A copy of *Plain Doctor* was held under my nose. [The author's name and the title cited are both fictitious.] My knowledge of this estimable author was as near nil as to make no difference, so murmuring vaguely a sentence of which only the two words "historical novelist" emerged, I eased gently away from further awkward questions.

Not much in that, you may say. Plenty of librarians probably share your abysmal ignorance about S.H., poor thing. Quite so. I derived further consolation from the thought that there are hundreds of novelists writing

---

Reprinted by permission of Library Association Publishing and the Association of Assistant Librarians from *The Library Assistant* 44: 66-68, May 1951.

today about whom I know practically nothing. And though I am still young, I told myself, if I live to be a hundred and twenty the position won't improve much. A satisfying line of reasoning this, followed by a sound and guiltless sleep that night.

Next day in the staff room, by way of humorous and light conversation, I threw out to my staff, "Any of you know anything about Sally Hurrall?", convinced already that the response would be the raised eyebrow, the "not a clue" or "never 'eard of her." Came the blow! For ten minutes I sat back while one of my assistants told me everything about the author in question. She had been at college with the rather plump girl who, with her mother, is known to the literary world as Sally Hurrall. She knew that the novels were backed by plentiful research and were written in a competent style, but were regarded by their author (the younger half) merely as "pot-boilers."

This is the crux of the matter. My own ignorance about S.H. is excusable and of no importance whatsoever. But that there should exist in my library a source such as I have just described—a personal contact with the author, with a knowledge of her work, intentions and methods—that this should exist without my knowledge shocked me out of my self-satisfaction.

This had been a wonderful opportunity to enhance, in the eyes of one ordinary reader, the reputation of the librarian as an able and knowledgeable critic, and I had missed it. Is this happening anywhere else? I am sure it is. "Are we not playing critic already, perfunctorily, even with some timidity?" asks Dr. Savage. Yes indeed, but with *such* a heavy accent on the perfunctory quality of our efforts.

Some suggestions for improvement then? All right. Let us begin by talking among ourselves a little more about books, and a little less about the design of the latest Mobile Library or the near-human achievements of Powers-Samas. I challenge you to sit around in Chaucer House (the Library Association's headquarters) during a lunch-hour and listen to the elite of the profession. If once in the course of the whole hour you hear a book discussed, described or criticized, you will be a very lucky man or woman. If we cannot sacrifice to this arduous task of talking about books some small part of the time we spend daily in tea-swilling, then why not allocate a fixed period on the weekly timetable for a staff discussion on the week's output (or intake, to bring the thing within more practical bounds) of books. Some more progressive systems have a regular weekly meeting of Branch Librarians and Departmental Heads to discuss book selection. But few, if any, find out the reading interests of *all* the members of the staff, from the newest junior upwards, and use the knowledge gained thereby. This can only be achieved by a similar meeting at each branch library, but the usefulness of these will be strictly in proportion to the amount of enthusiasm the Branch Librarian can infuse into his staff. Until junior assistants are treated as intelligent human beings this enthusiasm will usually be lacking. Junior assistants are not mechanical robots fit only for dealing with the intricacies of the Browne Charging System or the writing of overdue postcards. Some of them read, and some of them have worthwhile opinions. Their critical faculties may not always be too well-developed, but you don't teach a baby to talk by confining it to solitary.

Perhaps we can even canalize or direct some of the reading interests of our staffs, so that we thereby effect a greater coverage of the intake of the books to our libraries. Subject specialization in another of its aspects. But the point is that in this way we can build up at each service-point, within each system, a "team" of critics, each member of which complements the knowledge of his fellow-assistants. If the B.B.C. can use a team of critics why can't we? I realize that teamwork. like gallantry and other notions of the 19th century and before, is almost an obsolescent conception, but two heads are still better than one provided the heads are coordinated. And this final welding is obviously the librarian's job. Far better this than for him to remain aloof, knowing it all and never encouraging his assistants to widen or give tongue to their opinions and knowledge. Knowledge unshared is a barren thing, as somebody at some time or other is sure to have told us in more glowing phrases.

Where else can we improve as librarian-critics? Most noticeably, I should say, in our booklists. The bleak passages which, for want of a less pretentious word, we call annotations, strip us naked to the seeing eye and reveal us for the fakes and phonies we really are. How many of them are based upon actual reading by the librarian or members of his staff? Be honest—very few! Rather are snippets conned from the *Times Literary Supplement*, the *New Statesman*, the introduction, or worst of all, the blurb. And worse yet, we don't even acknowledge the source most of the time. Even the snippets used by Mr. Gollancz are more honest than that!

Think back for a while upon your Assistance to Readers [Reference] course. Remember all those useful indexes the good Readers' Adviser or Reference Assistant keeps handy. An index of readers' interests, classified under subjects. An index of local specialists or specialist sources, arranged ditto. Has anybody yet suggested a detailed classified index of staff reading, past and current? If not, why not? Have we such a poor opinion of ourselves? In a staff the size of Manchester's, for example, this would provide not only a handy reference tool but a fertile background for your librarian-critic. Even in the small library it would provide a firmer basis than four or five un-tapped, un-guided or un-encouraged assistants.

These are offered not as the whole solution of the problem of raising our public status as critics and bookmen, but simply as thoughts provoked by my own inadequacies, which it is hoped will evoke similar thoughts in other minds. While we think at least, we are alive. Some day we may even take action.

The Assistant and the Bookish Habit

Last year, Mr. James Carter introduced his brilliant examination of the sub-literature problem with the assertion that it had been the topic of the year 1951, at least in the pages of the *Assistant Librarian*. I would claim that another matter, the education of the librarian, has been one of the major topics of *several* years now, and in more pages than are encompassed by the *Assistant*. This revival in examining the warts on our own noses is, I think, due to one factor more than any other—the increasing status, influence and vocal power of the full-time library schools. But even before the advent of the library schools one aspect of education for librarianship, though perhaps not regarded strictly as such, was causing concern in a few minds. This was the increasing preoccupation with techniques and administration, and the decline of that figure of library mythology, the bookman.

Over the years of development in the public library service, and particularly since 1919, when the worst financial restrictions were abolished, the three basic essentials of librarianship—bookstock, staff and readers—have each maintained an impressive and constant expansion. Quantity however is not everything, and I think we should ask ourselves whether the service, so far as these three basic factors are concerned, has shown any qualitative improvement.

Our bookstocks are certainly still far from ideal, but book funds have increased to such a degree that, sometimes by accident, sometimes by design, more books which should be there are appearing on our shelves. Slowly also such progressive ideas as subject specialization and regional coverage are percolating through the profession, and it is probably no longer completely Utopian to consider that sometime in the distant future we shall be able to offer our public something like a comprehensive representation of British books at least.

Reprinted by permission of Library Association Publishing from The Library Association, *Proceedings of the Annual Conference,* Hastings, 1954, pp. 69-75.

Assessing the quality of the readers who use these books is a more difficult and intangible problem, but the increasing demands made upon our interloan services for technical, specialist and learned books may be taken not only, as it is viewed by the sour-minded, as an indication of poor book selection "in some quarters," but as an indication also of contact with a wider public. One group of readers is certainly transferring its affections to our libraries. It largely consists of refugees from the circulating libraries, whose soaring subscriptions and increasing limitations upon books available (mainly determined by price ceilings) have done more to encourage this situation than any studied effort or new concepts about publicity on the part of public librarians. Many of them tend to think of this new influx only as a fresh administrative embarrassment, but for all their obsession for the gleaming dust-jacket, many of these readers are intelligent people we should be happy to serve.

It is when we reach the third of our essentials—staff—that any qualitative improvement becomes difficult to trace or defend. I have benefited too much personally to wish the representatives of the full-time library schools to rise against me on this score, and I regard the establishment of these schools as the one major development in British librarianship since the war. They represent the youngest and least-diseased limb of a not very healthy body. The schools, nevertheless, cannot alone make us the respected specialists and professionals we always hope the public will take us for. What is required is a complete change of heart throughout the profession, or as G. R. Davies, the Cambridge Deputy City Librarian, called it in a *Bookseller* article last February, "a social revolution in public librarianship." We have reached the stage where the big names in librarianship are men known for their prowess in planning buildings (though all but the most determined of these have been severely frustrated for a number of years), or as experts on the problems of home binderies, authorities on punched cards or mechanical cataloging, or as capable administrators. Meanwhile the valid question remains: "Where are the bookmen?"

The equipment the average librarian and his assistant need today more than anything else is a sound knowledge of modern and contemporary literature; and particularly fiction. I must stress and repeat the word "sound," because such a knowledge cannot exist in a vacuum. It demands an acquaintance with the classics of literature of all periods and cultures. To fully appreciate Thomas Wolfe you need to have read Whitman; the influence of Dostoievsky on the motives and direction of the contemporary novel, and the debt Eugene O'Neill owed to the Greek dramatists serve to further illustrate what is perhaps an obvious point. It must be equally apparent that literature itself cannot and does not exist in a vacuum, and that some reasonable background knowledge of history, particularly social history, of the major philosophies and religions, and of the main political movements of our own and other countries should be acquired.

This is perhaps the moment when I should signify that I am aware that public libraries have moved on a little since the days when they considered the humanities their main, if not their sole, terrain. Technical and scientific books demand an ever-increasing amount of space in our libraries, and we are developing all kinds of subject specialists within our staffs, but there are limits, I think, to which we can extend subject departmentalization and subject specialization. These are, in the main, projects for the big library, like Manchester, Sheffield, Birmingham, Liverpool, or in the smaller systems, for the Central Library. As against some 600 central libraries, there are over 16,000 public library service points in this country. It is not feasible that every one of these service points, regardless of size, should be broken down into subject divisions, or that it should carry its own staff of subject specialists. Some libraries (in London, I believe, Wandsworth is an example) have carried subject specialization into the branch libraries, each branch housing a special collection on a particular subject, but this is not a very satisfactory arrangement. If a reader requires a specialist book or specialized information he cannot reasonably be expected to travel always to the other side of a large borough, or perhaps a large county, to obtain it. It seems far more logical to assemble all specialist collections, and the staff to exploit them, at the central library, which if it is a central library geographically as well as in name, should be most accessible to the majority.

No matter how departmentalized or specialized our services become, there will always be a need for branch libraries fulfilling their real function as natural centers for the general reader, whose needs may be informational, cultural or purely recreational. All doctors do not work in Harley Street; there is a need for G.P.'s as well. And branch libraries should not attempt to cater, in what can only be a half-hearted way, for the specialist or advanced student. Nor, I think, does the average reader of this kind expect it. For every question an assistant in a small branch library will receive on thermodynamics or genetics he will be asked fifty on some aspect of contemporary literature. What does he know about a novel reviewed in last Sunday's *Observer?* I wonder how often the assistant has even seen the review, or whether he could defend the library's policy if a decision had been taken not to buy it? Can the assistant recommend another author like Joyce Cary, or Arthur Koestler? How many branch librarians could assess fairly and adequately for an intelligent reader the qualities as novelists of the four Green(e)s, Julien, F. L., Graham and Henry—all of them important writers?

I do not wish to labor this point, but if these are the demands we can expect in our branch libraries, this is the direction the training of our branch staffs must take. Our branch librarians and assistants, and many small-town librarians, must become the general practitioners of the library profession. A considerable percentage of our bookstocks, and an even larger percentage of our circulation is represented by contemporary fiction, and no librarian who regards himself as a book selector can consider himself competent to spend his book fund wisely unless he has a sound knowledge in this field. Mr. J. F. W. Bryon, whose persistent probing must cause him to be regarded in some quarters as the Walter Winchell of British library journalism, underlined this point in his "Off the Record" column in January, 1952. In support of his disbelief that the librarian acting as book-selector is "a professional, coping with a task for which he is adequately trained," J.F.W.B. set a specimen paper in the contemporary novel, which he modestly and honestly admitted he would not like to have to answer himself, and which he suggested would provide *almost* as many pitfalls for colleagues. The qualification "almost" is probably the only false note in this claim. I cannot, for reasons of time, quote the whole of the test paper now, though it is certainly worth it. Here are three of the ten questions, which, though not the most difficult, may be taken as representative.

"The Oriental mind is best understood in its writers." Which modern novels would you recommend to a student of Asiatic life?

Compare and contrast the best novels of 1919-25 with the best 1945-51 fiction.

Which French novelists writing today are best deserving of representation on public library shelves, either in the original or in translation?

Is it an unjustified lack of faith in our own profession which prompts both Mr. Bryon and myself to feel that most honest public librarians would not feel altogether happy about answering spontaneously such questions as these? As book selectors, and as professional people spending thousands of pounds of public money each year on fiction, they should be able to do so, and the public who pay them have every right to expect them to be able to assess the worth of the books they purchase.

One of the solutions to this problem is so simple and obvious that it would hardly seem to require stating. It is that librarians generally do not read nearly enough. I heard this view expressed at a professional meeting in London some months ago by a librarian who spends £15,000 a year on books. His view of a librarian's weekly ration of reading was as follows: two books to be read thoroughly, six or eight others to be scanned, and some enormous number of periodicals (I think, about fifteen) to be read in addition. This verdict was greeted with a combination of horror and ridicule by an audience which consisted largely of younger members of the profession. The librarian in question did perhaps overstate his case, but his estimate is only astronomically high if you assume that all this reading is to be done in your own time. And it is unfortunately true that such an assumption is always made. Reading, even of reviews, is considered by very few librarians, and even fewer library committees, to be such an integral part of the librarian's or the library assistant's duties as to be an actual part of his working week. Recently I heard a well-known Borough Librarian announce at a meeting that he never read reviews because he didn't have time. What can he have to do which is so much more important? There should be room in every librarian's timetable for some part of each week to be spent with books and periodicals in order to gain more first-hand knowledge of the materials we are exploiting.

It is this change of emphasis from administrative to literary which Mr. Davies, in the *Bookseller* article I have already referred to, considered would need a social revolution in public librarianship, and I would like to quote two short passages from the picture he gives of the sort of prejudice and tradition which would have to be overcome. He says:

> One has only to imagine the reactions of a town council to the submission that the library staff should spend half of each day just reading new books to realize the first implications of the idea.

This is another example of a common fault among librarians; that of weakening a thesis by over-statement, but he continues:

It is the experience of library assistants of all times and places to hear from the public the envious comment on their good fortune in working among books all day "and being able to read them." It is a tragic observation that, within a matter of weeks, the library apprentice regards such a comment as a sadly misguided joke. And there are few librarians, if they have worked their way through libraries the hard way, who, even in seniority, do not momentarily struggle with a guilt-complex if they are apprehended during office hours, with an open book upon their desks.

Apart from objections such as these on traditional grounds—and how much of library practice is based on this bleak adherence to tradition ("we do it this way because we always have")—apart from such objections, the main bogey which is likely to be raised is Mr. Priestley's favorite preoccupation, time. This factor, I am afraid, necessitates consideration of another wide issue which has been troubling, but not activating, the British librarian's mind for a number of years. We cannot make time, we can only recover wasted time and use it to better purpose. And the surest way in which this can be achieved is the division of our library staffs into professional and non-professional categories. It is now 12 years since the McColvin Report, one of the major documents in librarianship in this country, was published. As long ago as that Mr. McColvin strongly recommended such a division, and the force of his belief was apparent in the wording of the first of his reasons:

> So long as there are duties which can be satisfactorily performed by non-professionals it is stupid, dishonest and prejudicial to the genuine professional man to suggest that *all* library work is professional.

I understand that Mr. McColvin has since changed his mind about the desirability of a division on these lines. This perhaps is indicative of the burden of 12 extra years on a busy librarian, or of the way in which practical difficulties loom ever larger with the passing years, but practical difficulties do not detract from the sheer necessity for this development in public libraries. This structural change could, and does, where it operates, make it possible for the professional librarian to spend more time with books, reading them, reviewing them, exploiting them and knowing what he is exploiting.

During the past twelve months I have been fortunate enough to have working with me an American librarian (Stanley Crane) who came over from Brooklyn Public Library on an exchange with my senior assistant (John Wakeman). From the two people involved in this exchange I have thus had two independent views of the way in which the professional/non-professional structure works in one American library. I would stress at this stage that I am not concerned with an over-all view of this problem—that is the subject for another paper. What is relevant to *this* paper is whether or not such a development in staffing would enable professionals to spend a reasonable time each week examining books and the periodical literature of their particular subjects.

The majority of the books added to the Brooklyn Library are first obtained on approval, and a review follows from a subject specialist on the staff before a decision is taken as to whether the book should be purchased or not. My American colleague informs me that on average throughout the year every professional librarian in each of the subject divisions of the Central Library reviews 3 or 4 books per week, while at the peak of the publishing season the figure may rise to 7 or 8. Some of this is done in personal time (which in itself is not a bad thing), but he estimates that usually enough time is allowed to adequately review at work about 3 books per week. Fiction is largely reviewed by professional staff at the branch libraries, a fact which supports the thesis that branch libraries are the general practitioners, and that fiction or general literature are their basic subjects. I consider also that the evidence from Brooklyn supports the theory that the division of our staffs on the professional/non-professional basis is the desirable first step towards a social revolution in librarianship which aims at converting librarians from administrators into bookmen.

So far I have been mainly concerned with a basic change in our internal organization which will free librarians from unnecessary routines in order that they may widen their book knowledge. There are other ways in which this change of emphasis can be assisted. The problem must be tackled at all levels, and one of the most vital places to begin is at the bottom, i.e., at the stage of recruitment.

Another burning topic of the hour, the graduate problem, demands attention at this point, but it has received and continues to receive so much attention in the professional press that I do not wish to discuss it at any length here. It is obvious that we should lure into the profession as many graduates as possible, but I do not think we can hope to obtain enough, at least for a very long time, for us to aim at this level of education as a prerequisite for entry to the professional side of librarianship. At this time, bearing in mind our meager inducements—poor salaries, awkward hours, limitations in opportunity for promotion—it would be suicide. Nor do I think it is necessary. The place where we shall most easily be able to find openings for graduates *as such* is in the large library, with departments able to exploit special subject knowledge. For the rest we should aim at the highest educational level we can get, but at the same time make a greater effort to recruit young people who show signs of a genuine interest in books, which could with care be developed into a real and lasting love of books. I do not maintain that this is the only quality we should look for, but it is one which is not sufficiently stressed at present. At the initial interview it must be soundly impressed upon the candidate that books and reading must form, if he is to be a librarian, a substantial part of his life, both within and outside the 38 hours a week for which he will be paid. If a heavy cloud passes over the nervous countenance of the candidate at such a prospect, the indications are that he is not the man for the job.

The librarian must realize, however, that he is committing himself quite as much as the new assistant when he takes this line. The formative years in a library assistant are probably the first five. If he works in a bad library or receives no encouragement during this period he is, unless exceptional, a "goner," a lost soul, another librarian-to-be in name only, forever without the bookish manner.

From the beginning the assistant must be treated as an intelligent person. If he isn't, why was he appointed? This implies that he must be given some intelligent work to carry out. Many of our routines could be performed by nimble-minded horses, not necessarily of the calibre of Swift's Houyhnhnms, and a work-sheet which offers the assistant stamping, labeling, overdues, issue checking for reserves, counter routine and nothing else is the antithesis of stimulus, encouragement or incentive to better things. It is not the slightest use dangling before him such a vision as the one of the Chief Librarian (which with a whole lot of luck, he might be in 20 years) who spends whole afternoons browsing in bookshops. Paradise is probably not visible from his present purgatory. Even without our ideal staff structure, more than this can be offered.

If the reading habit is to be encouraged, the assistant should be taught to examine and assess books at the earliest possible moment. Each junior should be given a couple of periodicals per week to read, with a view to improving his knowledge of the current literary scene. During the first few months, with the right sort of contact between senior and junior staff, personal interests and inclinations should become apparent, and the assistant can perhaps be given some sort of subject grading, and minor responsibilities for particular subject interests. Those whose interests are primarily literary, as opposed to subject, are the material to train into the general practitioners who will staff the branch libraries. In addition to the periodicals, the assistant could well be given a couple of books each week to review. Most libraries produce a booklist of some sort, even if it be no more than a simple typewritten list on a notice board. One of the most blatant and common faults in our booklists is the absence of annotation. The ideal should be something like the magnificent *Leeds Book Guide,* but this is not within the reach of every library. However, a simple booklist on a notice board may be almost as effective if well presented and well annotated. Annotation is perhaps even more difficult to do well than reviewing, if what you are aiming at is something brief which will whet the appetite of the reader while at the same time presenting the content of the book fairly and adequately. Apart from being helpful to the reader, such practice would be invaluable training for the assistant. All who have tutored or examined know how low is the general level of self-expression among library assistants when their views are committed to paper.

It is most important during these early stages to make some attempt to direct the reading of each assistant. I am aware that this will probably be a most unpopular suggestion, for most of us will have seen enough of controls and restrictions not to want any more of them than necessary. But it is a common fault in the majority of us to read somewhat in a rut. This is fine if we are reading purely for pleasure and recreation, and I would not dare suggest any intrusion upon an individual's personal interests. If reading is to be done in work time, however, this is reading with a view ultimately to improving the service offered by the library, and as such it should be as catholic as possible, taking in Ogden Nash as well as Dylan Thomas, P. G. Wodehouse as well as Robert Musil. Supervision over work-time reading will probably be necessary during the initial stages, but it should take the mildest and most intelligent form. I think a reasonable discussion between branch librarian and assistant about the periodical or book read will reveal clearly enough whether or not the reading privilege is being abused. The discussion itself could be valuable for another reason. The reviews or annotations by new assistants will not always be happy productions, worthy of presentation to the public, and guidance and vetting will have to be forthcoming from the branch librarian or departmental head. I hope I shall not be considered cynical if I suggest that discussion of this sort might be quite as beneficial to the senior staff as to the juniors, and might do something towards promoting a better understanding on both sides than is always apparent today.

In-service training is another aspect of library education, in the loosest sense, which is slowly becoming an accepted feature in public libraries, and nowhere is the lop-sided emphasis of modern librarianship better illustrated. So many assistants are taught how to deal with situations such as the one in which the reader approaches the counter with the announcement that his wife has typhoid fever and a mild enquiry as to whether we would like her books back, yet seldom are young assistants taught how to handle or examine books, either physically or textually. This becomes apparent if you sit in on a new Entrance class at any evening institute. The average student on commencing his studies has no idea how a book is put together, where the half-title is, where to look for a bibliography in a book, has never asked himself why some illustrations have to be printed on those odd sheets which are the first to fall out, or what the occasional letters at the bottom of certain pages are for. The main blame for this is not to be laid at the assistant's door, for he has, in the main, been concerned with books as nothing much more animate than grocery parcels, to be distributed over a counter to readers whose only problems are obscure diseases in the family and a penchant for slipping on polished floors. This latter problem in librarianship recently achieved the crowning importance of becoming an examination question.

It is scarcely hinting at revolution to suggest that some part of our in-service training should be directed towards developing an interest in books, from a physical as well as a literary point of view. Such training might eliminate or restrict the careless rapture with which some assistants, particularly on a busy Saturday afternoon, treat the books they handle. We have all seen the book needing a new label, flung from the in-counter to the repair bin (which is always on the other side of the counter) with such cheerful abandon that it is a binding job when it emerges from that same bin.

There are two other fields in which the young assistant may be helped to cultivate the bookish manner. These are the Staff Guild and the various Branches and Sections of the Library Association.

Staff magazines, where they exist, perform a useful job in stimulating young members to write, but while humor is obviously an essential element of such magazines, it should not be all. While Searle-ish or Fougassian portraits of readers, Louella Parsons-ish reports of staff activities, and facetious dissertations on the tonk abound, books are still all too frequently the missing element. Too often in their meetings Staff Guilds rely upon outside speakers and Brains Trusts, instead of organizing discussion groups or literary circles among themselves. Apart from its educational value this would assist the Guild towards another fundamental objective—that of breaking down barriers in the staff hierarchy and combating the isolation of branch staffs, for example. Guilds at present often do much to widen cultural and social interests, and the educational aspect is not always forgotten. But visits to binders, newspapers and libraries which use Adrema for cataloging, are not the end. How many staff guilds take parties to National Book League exhibitions, or even to a large bookshop?

Books still appear to be the missing link when we examine the activities of the various arms of our professional association, and the state of the professional press. The only English library periodical which displays any literary interest is the *Library Review,* a view which was supported this year by the April gushing of Clearwater in the *Assistant Librarian.* But even the *Library Review* is becoming more preoccupied with "practical" matters, and compares very unfavorably with the American *Library Quarterly.* Our professional meetings continue to display an unhealthy concern over internal politics, punched cards and charging systems, but much patience and persistence would appear to be necessary before bookish meetings can be made a success, if the response in London is any guide. At a recent meeting less than a dozen members of the Greater London Division's 2,400 turned up to hear a knowledgeable speaker on modern Welsh writers. To be fair, it should be mentioned also that Chaucer House was packed to the walls when Mr. Gillett spoke a few months later on pornography. Perhaps this is further proof of my point that librarians tend to read in a rut.

Finally, there is a clear need for a greater literary and bibliographical emphasis in library education proper, and the lead here *should* be given in the syllabus prepared by the Library Association. This is perhaps too large and tattyfeathered a duck at which to aim another salvo, but a lot still seems necessary if *this* ugly duckling is to be converted into a snow-white swan.

You will have seen in the July issue of the *L.A. Record* a revised syllabus for the Entrance Examination which is happily in the familiar state of suspended animation. Without doubt it is an improvement over the present syllabus, and it does do something towards preparing the student for the fiercer hurdle of Registration, but despite its more grandiose christening, it is a somewhat disappointing baby to be born of the union of such apparently young and virile parents as the Schools of

Librarianship and the A.A.L. Certainly it uses the phrase "library stock," but despite requiring a knowledge of the parts of books and periodicals, its main emphasis is upon the cataloging and classification of these objects, and the only category of books the student is expected to think of in terms of evaluation and use is the familiar undefined "reference books."

I should like to see the present banal Reference Books paper replaced by a general elementary paper on Bibliography and Assistance to Readers. As it stands, this part is a gift to those who possess the sort of minds which are at home with permutations and crossword puzzles, but it does not add much that is useful towards any preparation for librarianship. The sort of paper I visualize is one which would require of students some basic knowledge of the scope and purpose of bibliography; what and where the various parts of a book are, and what they are for; the general principles of reader assistance; how to examine and assess the qualities of books (and please, not just reference books). Surely principles should precede practice, and if the Registration Examination is to test the capabilities of a librarian to practice as a professional, I think the Entrance Examination should fulfil the function of instilling the underlying principles on which that practice rests. If the much-criticized essay is to go, and I agree that it should, I would like to see it replaced by a General Knowledge paper, which could be answered without too much trouble by any candidate alive enough to have read one good newspaper thoroughly each day throughout the preceding year. The gaping jaw behind the counter is an even sadder sight when the topic mentioned by the reader has been headline news for a week.

At the Registration level the major pruning should be at the expense of Group A. Only a minority of librarians ever become catalogers or have need of the amount of indigestible theory which must be swallowed to ensure a pass in the papers constituting this group. The place for so much detailed knowledge is in the Final paper, where the qualities of the specialist are tested. I would like to see this group cut to one paper, and Administration moved in as bedfellow, so that all the more sordid techniques are confined within the one group. This would leave room for expansion of the Literature group to two papers. The present paper (even after the recent bifurcation) is little more than a general knowledge test in literature, and it could be given a little solidity by the addition of a paper on a special period or the literature of a special subject. Group B is far from perfect, but such criticisms as I have do not come within the scope of this paper. This applies also to the Final Examination, which should be, and is already to some degree, the place for testing specialist knowledge in all fields of librarianship.

The second main field in which changes are possible or likely in library education is in the fertile one of the full-time library schools. Once the awkward hurdle of financial assistance for students has been satisfactorily cleared, I consider the vital first step to be an extension of the study period at library schools to two years for Registration, and at least that for Final. The schools would then have some opportunity to escape the shackles of the syllabus, and given that freedom, I am sure they would provide the sort of courses which are needed. We have been fortunate in the original minds which have gravitated to most of our full-time schools, and fortunate also that they have not created any aloof academic ivory towers. Like Wendy Hiller, they know where they are going, and say so with refreshing candor and frequency. The torrential, if sometimes fluctuating, ideas of Roy Stokes are perpetually whistling through the doldrums of our professional pages. Equally well-known are the views of that J.C.H. (J.C. Harrison) who creates such coy editorial confusion in the *Library World*.

Most of our professional teachers will, I think, agree that we have much to learn from America in the field of professional education. Dr. George Leyh, in an article in *College and Research Libraries* this year, summed up the American attitude in this way:

> The Americans believed for a long time that they had surpassed the European libraries because of their interest in purely administrative and technical matters. Since then they have realized that administrative technique must itself be based on sound scholarship if it is to serve a useful purpose. Many library schools . . . there are attempting to bridge the gap between the daily task of the librarian and scholarly activity.

This is the sort of approach which we should hope for our library schools to be free to pursue, bearing in mind also Dr. Leyh's warning that "the important thing is to train librarians for libraries, not for a romantic cultural policy." I think we can feel confident that in their present hands the library schools will proceed in the right direction. Some of the greyer minds in L.A. education circles may retard their development, but they will not halt it.

In conclusion, I should be disappointed if nobody disagrees with some of the things I have said, but I hope that I have not left a false impression. I do not want reading to become a dull technique like cataloging, nor a daily chore like overdues, nor a routine preparation for examinations. But I am certain that librarians should be book addicts, and if we are to achieve this, a much sharper emphasis must be placed on reading from the first moment of each assistant's career, so that a love of books and a desire for knowledge for their own sakes become natural aspects of the librarian's outlook. In the introduction to his *English Social History*, Trevelyan says: "Disinterested intellectual curiosity is the lifeblood of real civilization." I think this is equally true of real librarianship.

References

"Literary" or "Admin," by G. R. Davies. *Bookseller*, 20th February, 1954.
"The Education of the Librarian," by Dr. G. Leyh. *College and Research Libraries*, Vol. XV, No. 2.
"Off the Record," by J. F. W. Bryon. *Librarian*, January, 1952.

Stock Control in Public Libraries

The term "stock control" is a relatively new one which did not impinge on my vocabulary until a few years ago. It could be taken for another of those variations upon a theme, a new word replacing an obsolescent one, like "rock 'n roll" for "jive" or "swing" for "jazz"—but I take it to be a wider and more inclusive term than some of the old favorites among library jargon like book selection, stock revision, stock-taking, weeding etc.

According to my definition stock control is the coordination of a number of processes which include the selection, acquisition, recording, exploitation, preservation and manipulation of bookstock within a library system. If that definition were to appear in an examination paper I would hope for the word "coordination" to be italicized or otherwise stressed as the most important feature.

In these terms stock control is an enormous and, in a sense, specialized, function.

Staffing for Stock Control

The first consideration in determining how any specialized function is to be carried out is to decide upon the areas of responsibility. Who then should be responsible for stock control, and how far should his powers extend? Most librarians today, when they want a specialist job done, take the logical step of recommending the appointment of a specialist to do it. An archivist is appointed to deal with archives, a music librarian to cater for the needs of the less than tone-deaf public, a children's librarian to attend the requirements of an even more specialized public, a readers' adviser to meet the demand of the information seeker. These jobs are not

---

Reprinted by permission from North-Western Polytechnic, School of Librarianship, *Occasional Papers* No. 10, October 1957, pp. 1-9.

specialized merely in that they require special knowledge but also in their clearly defined fields of responsibility.

In public libraries of the thirties and before there was a generally held belief that the librarian was essentially a jack-of-all-trades, that he should not only be *able* to do everything which required doing within the four or more walls of the library, but that he should in fact do them. The specialist was not really born, even as an idea. This attitude of mind has largely disappeared so far as many library functions are concerned, and it is therefore all the more surprising that it should linger most persistently in this important field of stock control.

Few librarians, even today, seem to regard stock control as a fulltime occupation. In some libraries the Chief Librarian likes to retain a firm hand on the reins, in others the responsibility is delegated to the Deputy Librarian or Chief Assistant. In yet others the Branch Librarians and Heads of Central Departments have more or less final responsibility for their own bookstocks. In some libraries there is a loose coordination between a number of officers. The over-riding weakness of all these arrangements is that the areas of responsibility are often ill-defined (and when that is so, something inevitably gets left undone), and that where there *is* some definition the librarians at all stages of the hierarchy are playing their parts in the work of stock control only part-time. They all have other considerable and essential responsibilities and stock control becomes something to be done when or if there is time.

I am not suggesting that the Chief, Deputy, and Branch Librarians should not play an active role in building and maintaining a good bookstock in any library. I believe it is essential that the professional and specialized knowledge of *every* member of the staff should be utilized to the full in this field as in every other. But my contention is that the final cohesion and coordination can be undertaken only by a member of the staff who has no other departmental or administrative responsibility.

Cataloging is another specialist function where the same arguments apply. We have generally come to agree that it is better (i.e. more economical, more efficient) to have one Chief Cataloger responsible for the cataloging and classification adopted throughout a library system, rather than having each Branch and Department doing its own in its own way, however great the advantages of the latter system may be for training. Yet it is still the case that the highest members of the staff hierarchy determine general cataloging policy, and should be the case that Branch Librarians play their part by advising the cataloger of weaknesses revealed by *use* of the catalogs and classification at the points of service to the public. Only they can prevent the cataloging and classification from becoming as academic and theoretical as that of the *British National Bibliography.*

This is the sort of pattern which should apply when we consider how the function of stock control may best be carried out. That some librarians are thinking along these lines has become clear in recent years. A few years ago Mr. Callender created at Lambeth the post of stock editor—to my knowledge the first such post in the country. There are still very few, and one of the reasons why I have been asked to address this subject is that I was appointed about a year ago to a similar post at Kensington, though my title (Head of Technical Processes) would seem to suggest that I am responsible for anything *but* stock control. This post was created after an Organization and Methods investigation at Kensington, and the O & M team, as efficiency experts, with some encouragement from an enlightened senior staff, recognized the fact which many librarians will not accept, that a senior officer burdened with administrative, committee and other professional work cannot possibly control the bookstock and its organization in a library of any size.

The Stock Editor

Where should the position of stock editor fit into the staff hierarchy? I think it can be generally agreed that he should be relatively senior, have a wide background of general library experience, be fully qualified professionally and be or have the mental outlook of a bookman of one kind or another. This is not to suggest that he needs no administrative sense or experience. All librarians of a certain seniority need that, but the stock editor's responsibility for administration should be quite limited and basically he should be more concerned with liaison than administration proper.

My own feeling is that he should fit into the hierarchy at what we usually recognize as about the Chief Assistant level. This is the case at Lambeth, and more or less so at Kensington. This degree of seniority is desirable for diplomatic reasons. If he is to have overall responsibility for bookstock he must be able to move, withdraw, or add books at any service point, if necessary against the wishes of a Branch or Departmental Librarian, if it seems desirable from the viewpoint of the bookstock as a whole. I am not advocating power politics within the library, and hinted as much with the word "liaison," but the authority of a final decision must rest somewhere, and Branch Librarians are justifiably jealous of their own stocks.

I said earlier that stock control is a vast and never-ending job. From this it follows that no one person, even if he be stripped of all departmental responsibility and other administrative duties can carry out this function alone in a library system of any size. When, therefore, I talk of the work of a stock editor I mean, so far as the larger library is concerned, not one person but a stock-editing team. This need has already been realized at Kensington, and in a system of that size it probably requires a staff of about three professional librarians to do the job properly.

Policy for Stock Control

Being a pervasive and endless job, stock control often becomes a function which never gets started in any systematic way. How should it start? I believe that, like almost every other function in libraries or other complex organization, if it is to succeed it must start with a definite policy.

In my own library system recently the Deputy Librarian wanted (a) a book on plastering and (b) a copy of *The Forsyte Saga*. The Chief Librarian wanted a novel by C. P. Snow. The Chief Librarian of another large London library informed me some months ago that he went to his central library shelves for a book on Austria. All three of these librarians found that their shelves were literally a desert when they started to look for a particular water-hole. I am not seeking to condemn these two libraries—they are both central lending libraries of systems possessing pretty adequate book-funds compared with most other authorities in the country, and they are both libraries with high standards. But the situation revealed by these particular episodes is one which I believe to be true of almost every public library in this country, and if librarians had to use their libraries under the conditions imposed on the general reader they would perhaps be more aware that the situation exists.

The situation is one which can be easily cured. If it is agreed that these libraries should stock books on plastering and Austria, and novels by Galsworthy and Snow, obviously they must buy more copies, and more copies again until these subjects and authors are adequately represented on the shelves. These gaps are not just an indication of insufficient stock control but are the direct result of building a bookstock without a policy.

We all realize that the cure is *not* as simple as all that. If a man says to his wife: "I want more bacon for breakfast," he will very promptly be told that either he must increase her housekeeping allowance or give up his cheese and biscuits after dinner. Science has not yet made the quart out of the pint pot a possibility.

So in our libraries, if we are to provide the best books on all subjects and the best books by all authors in sufficient quantity to give the public a reasonable choice when they are looking for a specific subject or author, one of two things must happen. Either our bookfunds must soar astronomically, or we must each work to a policy. The policy must be an individual one for the particular library, related to the area served and the demands made upon the services, but it must state *standards* within which it will supply books to the full. There is, of course, no reason why, if the policies are worked out cooperatively, other books should not be obtained from other sources.

I see nothing in the crystal ball which indicates the possibility of the upward flight of bookfunds in public libraries. If anything, the indication is that our bookfunds are losing altitude all the time, when you relate them to rising book prices. A policy of restriction seems the only logical alternative, and I prefer it to no policy because I prefer a good service within reasonable limits to a bad service without limits. In most public libraries some restrictions already operate, however much it may be denied. For example, in the fields of medicine and law great reliance is placed upon the subscription services of Lewis's Medical Library and Law Notes Library. These two subjects have been singled out for economic reasons, and we should admit restrictions on no other grounds, or restriction shades off into censorship.

Saturation buying

One of the most important aspects of a bookstock policy is the degree of saturation to which particular books or subjects will be stocked. It is the first essential step towards a controlled and balanced shelf stock. In almost every subject field there are the landmarks, the books which have stood the test of time and the books in constant demand. These should be stocked to absolute saturation, i.e. to a point where the *normal* demand can adequately be met. An artificial demand may be created from time to time by a broadcast serial, a film version (musical or otherwise), or a television adaptation, but it is no more reasonable to expect libraries—unless they are forewarned—to meet such demands than it was to expect tailors to have ample stocks of gold-threaded tweed suits when Liberace landed. But in times of normal demand no self-respecting library should often have to ask readers to wait for a Shakespeare or Shaw, a Dostoevsky or Dryden, a Rilke or Racine. I do not mean to place an undue emphasis on literature or the humanities—I have been accused of that failing before—but I offer it as an obvious example.

It is equally important to stock in all fields within the library's policy the important books and those most in demand, and stock them in sufficient quantity to give the average reader the opportunity of finding them on the shelves. We all know hundreds of examples in all fields of books which are important, which are being continually asked for, and which rarely appear on our shelves—books like Benham's *Economics*, Innes's *Tropical Fish*, Lewitt's *Hydraulics*, Grantly Dick Read's *Natural Childbirth* (see the recent condemnation of public library service in the *News Chronicle* on this one), Morley's *Strength of Materials*, Mitchell's *Building Construction*, Mrs. Beeton, Old Uncle Tom Cobley an'all. Just recently I looked at a book we have at Kensington on protozoology. It is the only copy in the London Union Catalogue area and no copy exists in the S. E. region. This book has been in constant demand both by our own readers and those of several other libraries. Such books never appear on the shelves because the supply is not related to the demand, because we lean too heavily on the reservation service, because we often relate supply and demand only in the case of current best-sellers, and because we spread our bookfunds too thinly.

The main point is that the number of copies recorded in the catalog or stock register is quite irrelevant. If we are aiming at decent coverage of an author, subject or title the shelves are the only true guide, and this being so the stock editor's job becomes an enormous one. He *must* check the shelves continuously, thoroughly and systematically. There are many readers who want a particular book at a particular time, and for them the catalog has never made very fascinating or satisfying reading when the shelves are full of books they *don't* want.

Saturation buying is often most difficult in the field of fiction, and on our present incomes it can be achieved only over a limited range. The first priority, I think everyone will agree, should be—in this field as in all others—the classics, the books which have stood the test of time. If we stop at dead authors (physically dead, that is) the area of disagreement is not likely to be wide, though some librarians will be surprised to find that saturation buying will reveal a much heavier demand than they had hitherto thought existed. I believe that Bristol carried out some experiments of this kind some years ago and found that they needed a staggering number of Hardy's and Austen's before an adequate representation showed on the shelves at all times.

Beyond this point we ride into the country where borders, if they exist, are grey and shadowy and perpetually submerged in argumentative warfare. These arguments are a waste of time. One way in which this problem can be tackled is for the librarian to draw up a list of authors whose books will be stocked as fully as possible within a certain annual budget. Outside this list books would be stocked only in single, double, or such number of copies as the remainder of the budget would allow. Something of this kind operates at Westminster.

Clearly the list must be elastic and allow of infinite amendment, addition or deletion, rather like the non-existent ideal classification scheme, otherwise a farcical situation can arise. I heard recently of a list which used to operate in a London library which illustrates the need for sanity and a sense of proportion in the compiler. This list included all novelists with more than six novels to their credit. It therefore excluded irrevocably all the Brontës, Laurence Sterne and James Joyce, while leaving ample accommodation for Denise Robins, Colt Macdonald and James Hadley Chase. This list obviously set out to follow a possibly defensible course of stocking only established novelists, but it lacked even common sense elasticity and defined no standards.

I do not want to belabor the subject of saturation buying because it is a simple and familiar concept, but it is worth underlining that the degree of saturation should be governed by three factors only—local demand, the standards determined in the bookstock policy, and the size of the bookfund. And finally, once a desirable level is attained it must be maintained. It is not enough to leave that subject or author, and pass on. This is rather like setting up a good display and then leaving it to decay through lack of attention.

Stock revision

One of the most important aspects of stock control is the work of stock revision. This is clearly a continuous function, but it seems to me that it should operate on three levels. The first of these is the kind of systematic stock revision which entails working systematically through the shelves, compiling lists of books to be stocked at varying levels within each subject, checking holdings and shelf-stock, withdrawing out-of-date editions and tired stock, relegating to reserve or transferring to other service points, etc. This is straightforward routine stock revision understood by all. Is it cynical to suggest that it is not often done?

I cannot wrap up my second kind of stock revision in a neat term like "systematic," but perhaps "spontaneous" will do. This is revision not carried out continuously as a routine, but performed suddenly and activated by circumstances. These circumstances may simply be a demand by a reader for a list of books in a particular subject. Such a demand often reveals gaps, particularly in relation to shelf-stock, and should result in an immediate revision of that section of the bookstock.

The impetus may come in the other direction, i.e. from the subject rather than the reader. From time to time subjects assume a fresh importance, or new subjects suddenly create a spate of books in a short period. These too are cases for spontaneous stock revision. Examples of old subjects which have taken on a new lease of life in this way are South Africa, jazz, theatre techniques (Brecht, Stanislawski, and the current vogue for "method" schools of acting), Antarctica (through the geophysical year) and biblical history (because of the Dead Sea Scrolls). Newer subjects which have made a splash in the ocean of book output include automation, digital computers, transistors, radio control and the smaller-gauge model railways. How many librarians have looked carefully at their stocks in such subjects, new or old, with a view to obtaining a satisfactory over-all coverage?

Many will not consider my third category as stock revision at all since there is nothing about it which is deliberate or planned. This kind is the constant search for and acquisition of older standard books which may be out-of-print or scarce but which are still essential in a good bookstock. I regard this as revision because the absence of these books leaves gaps which all the 19,000 new books each year cannot fill. This job cannot be done entirely by sitting at a desk and checking the numerous lists which pour in from publishers and booksellers. It can only be done satisfactorily if the stock editor or book-buyer has the time and freedom to get out often and without restriction, so that he can discover resources for himself, and so that he can buy any book worth having wherever he may find it, without being hampered by petty rules about petty cash, booksellers on or off the licence, or the shadow of the audit department.

Other aspects of stock control

There are many of these, but I have time only to deal very briefly with three which seem to be particularly in need of attention in many public libraries today.

1. The first is the way in which the book-fund is allocated or distributed. In my view nearly every public library spends too great a proportion of its money on *new* books. Elaborate and intricate systems are devised and set up for what is essentially a very simple job: the selection (or rejection) and the ordering of new books. Apart from a couple of dozen outstanding books each year (and that is a generous estimate) we should duplicate far less than at present. Many of the books we buy in half-dozens, or perhaps more, are worthless or become so in a very short time and many more lose what is to some librarians their main virtue—temporary circulation value. We should grow thicker skins to protect us against transient pressures, retain longer memories for the books of lasting worth, and duplicate far more heavily the books which we think are going to last.

2. The second feature which needs improvement is the integration of the bookstocks at the various service points within a library system. The relationship between the stocks of the lending and reference libraries, between the central and branch libraries, and the relationship between each of them and the bookstock of the system as a whole needs in most libraries to be clarified. Binding and withdrawal should certainly be considered in this way if wastage in one form or another is not to be the result. For this reason I believe that central control of both these processes is desirable.

A library system too, in most boroughs at least, needs only one reserve stock, not half a dozen, with each branch hoarding many of the same books, and others which might have a new lease of life on the open shelves of another library. I am referring here to permanent reserve stock, not seasonal overflow or books removed from the open shelves for moral or other doubtful reasons. In the first place the retention of only one reserve stock saves space, and there are few libraries which do not need that. In the second place it allows the system to retain more of those books which may not be in heavy daily demand but which a library should have in its own stock, and for which it should not have to lean upon one of the subject specialization schemes. I prefer to see this main reserve stock kept at the central library or at any other point in the system where the heaviest demands may be made. It may be necessary (because of space limitations) to do as we have done at Kensington—distribute the reserve stock among the central and branch libraries, with each branch holding the reserve stock for the whole system within a particular section of the classification.

3. The third needed improvement in the field of stock control is greater mobility of bookstock, and having worked in both types of library I feel that municipal librarians have a great deal to learn from their county colleagues in this respect. The first step towards mobility is a greater flexibility in our book records, which are often encumbered by Victoriana like separate accession sequences and elaborate procedures of other kinds which often make it more expensive to transfer a book from one service point to another than to buy an extra copy.

Whether by accident or design I do not know, but the O & M team at Kensington seems to have tumbled to the connection between stock control and book records, and it was their recommendation that the officer appointed to control the stock should also be in charge of the production of book records. Hence the unusual name given to the post. Although this conflicts to some degree with my thesis that the stock editor should have no other departmental duties it does have the advantage that the stock records can be designed to meet the needs of the stock and its movement rather than vice-versa.

Conclusion

In conclusion I should like to put one thing in perspective. I have tried to build a case for stock control as an individual process but it has not been my intention to make the stock editor a little tin god, or to build empires new for him. I recognize that a good Chief Librarian is the most important factor in any library's progress. Without his efforts we can never start with a sound policy on which to base our stock control or enough money to implement it.

Confusion and Conviction

We have written before of Mr. John Ciardi, poet and controversial columnist of the *Saturday Review*. He is an anger-making man—in a sense like a beautiful woman, not easy to live with but hard to ignore—and sometimes we have taken the bait he has offered, and have bitten with fury. But we do now urge librarians to read his "Manner of Speaking" column in the June 2, 1962 issue of *SR*.

"May it not be," says Ciardi there, "that we have made too much of conviction as an ultimate goal? Show me a man who is not confused and I will show you a man who has not been thinking. He will be a man who has not asked enough questions.

"He will, in fact, incline to think that the reason for asking questions is to answer them. Is it? May it not be the greater merit of questions that they lead not to answers but to new questions, and the new questions to others, and they to others yet?"

Conviction, Ciardi argues, "is possible only in a world more primitive than ours can be perceived to be. A man can achieve a simple gnomic conviction only by ignoring the radical describers of his environment, or by hating them as convinced men have hated, say, Darwin and Freud as agents of some devil."

Leo Rosten touched on the same thought in our June 1 issue, when he referred to the men who have shaped our civilization, or most that is worth having in it, as those men "who resist the crippling effects of conventional education—who confront the known as if it is new."

One of the terrible dangers in our society, and in its educational processes, is that the *fact* too often seems to be elevated above the *idea*. People are being trained to look for answers rather than being taught how to ask questions. The speed reader lifts only the "pertinent facts" from the skimmed page. And the true limitation of the teaching machine is that it

---

Reprinted by permission from *Library Journal,* July 1962, pp. 161-2. Copyright © 1962, Reed Publishing, USA.

can only ask questions to which there are deliverable answers. (Suppose someone questions the question—what can the machine do about that?)

In our libraries, is the same trend not becoming dangerously apparent? The librarian experienced in book selection knows the perils of certainty. Back of him is the theory that he must or should provide alternatives. In front of him is the pressure of those certain men of the right and the left, and those with *convictions* about what is good and what is moral and what is right. But perhaps, after all, the areas of controversy are those that present the least danger, since here there is often an instinctive compensation, a provision of variety as the best defense against pressure from any direction.

May the greater danger not lie in the direction of the greater certainties? In our library services the accent falls ever heavier on words like "information," "source material," "reference." There is a growing and not always discerning preference for nonfiction over fiction. These are not *necessarily* nasty words or roads to perdition, but if we follow them too far or too devoutly we may well find ourselves running—and perhaps leading our readers, especially the young ones—always in the same direction toward the confirmable rather than the doubt-creating.

The telephone book, Mortimer Adler once said, is full of facts but it doesn't contain a single idea. It's a useful reference book, but is it essentially as useful a book as *Hamlet,* a play full of confusions, a play which poses more questions than it offers answers, a play which is endlessly fascinating because it is never the same?

Only the unreflective, says Ciardi, "always have their fast answers ready." And a better poet, Yeats, once said: "The best lack all conviction, while the worst/Are full of passionate intensity."

Libraries are not only places where fast answers may be found, and those who serve the young might perform their greatest service if only, to use Ciardi's words, they can "teach the sad young of this mealy generation the courage of their confusions."

The Blue and the Grey: Theory and Practice in Book Selection

When is a librarian's decision not to include a book in his library collection an act of book selection, and when is it censorship? Is there, in fact, any discernible difference in the two terms: book selection and censorship? This topic was discussed so lucidly and ably, long ago, by Lester Asheim in what has become a classic essay in the literature of librarianship, "Not Censorship, but Selection," that raising it again may appear to be an exercise in redundancy.

It needs to be discussed anew, however, because it remains a core question, a continuing problem, a point of vulnerability for the library, particularly the public library, because its objectives remain the least well defined among the institutions of the library world. In today's turbulent society one of the interesting confrontations is that between the individual and the institution—or the system. The decisions and motives of public institutions and the people who run them are coming, and will continue to come, under closer and more critical scrutiny, and individuals and groups can be expected to question, with increasing frequency, whether society's institutions are operated for their benefit or whether some of these institutions have simply become self-perpetuating entities, operated in accordance with some obscure, abstract set of principles which have little relevance for the individual the institution is supposed to serve.

Although most of the noisier pressures on public libraries are set off by group opposition to controversial publications which the library *has* selected and added to its collection, the defense of the positive book selection decision is not really the crux of the problem. This is not to suggest that defending such decisions is always easy or comfortable, but

---

Reprinted with permission of R. R. Bowker, a division of Reed Publishing (USA), Inc., from *Book Selection and Censorship in the Sixties* (Introduction, pp. 3-11). Copyright © 1969.

logically one *can* defend the inclusion of almost anything in a library collection under the broad umbrella of intellectual freedom, the Library Bill of Rights and other such pronouncements of the profession. The more difficult exercise, for the librarian, is the defense of the negative book selection decision; that is, book rejection, or the refusal to buy a book or periodical that an individual reader wants or needs. This is the point at which the reader may find it difficult to distinguish between library book selection and library censorship, since for him the end result is the same. When the library decides not to buy or supply the book he wants, the library, he may well conclude, has taken a decision against *his* interests.

In whose interest, then, is such a decision made? Failing the satisfaction of getting the book he wants, this reader, at the very least, wants a logical explanation of why this institutional decision should prevail over his need. And this is the point of vulnerability—because most of the policies and philosophies on which book selection practice rests are very shaky props. They appear to be—and the more so if you compare the policy pronouncements with the evidence of the library shelves—a series of prismatic evasions, of ad hoc excuses for whatever decision suits the book selector's whim of the moment.

One has only to examine some of the popular phrases from the lexicon of book selection policies to begin to sympathize with the reader's difficulties in distinguishing between book selection and censorship. There are other words and phrases which rarely get committed to print in such documents as book selection policies but which occur with some frequency when librarians discuss book selection among themselves. Every time I have asked a number of librarians why they failed to add a particular book to their collections, I have been surprised by the number who replied, simply, "Because it is trash." Several chapters in this book [*Book Selection and Censorship in the Sixties*], particularly those reporting on surveys of book selection practice, will document the frequency with which this value judgment is rendered, and the incredible range of its apparent applicability. It may be worth noting that "trash" and other equivalent terms are also rather large in the vocabulary of the pressure groups and censors who operate outside the library walls.

The librarian, of course, unless he lacks all public relations (and common) sense, does not tell the reader that the book he wants is trash. He wraps up the message in institutional verbiage, the language of the book selection policy. He may tell the reader that the book in question does not meet all the requirements of the library's book selection "standards." With this argument, particularly if he is faced with an acute or knowledgeable reader, the librarian is already walking in quicksand.

A learned Justice once said that trying to come to grips with a definition of obscenity was like trying to catch a greased pig. Applying consistent standards in book selection, as some librarians profess to be able to do, is considerably more difficult, perhaps like trying to lasso an eel. It ought to be obvious that book selection is not a measurable technique like circulation control or cost accounting. There is no slide rule which will cope with the complexities of calculation involved. This is why the written book selection policy is really of very little help when one gets down to the hard, specific case. What one then has to solve is a difficult equation which involves not just the individual book but also the library collection (and the judgments *it* reflects) and the individual reader who wants the particular book (and perhaps no other). At best, the policy will serve as a rough, rule-of-thumb guide, but at worst, it is used too often as a defense mechanism because there is no library which could defend all of its inclusions, or its exclusions either, on the basis of its written policy.

Again, other chapters of this book will document the quality and consistency of librarians' pronouncements on the "literary" or other standards they apply in the book selection process. These need not be repeated here, but way by of illustration it is worth noting that the librarian who declares that John Updike does not meet the literary standards of her library's collection, when the latter includes the works of the late author of *Peyton Place,* is doing one of three things: either she is saying that the library has *no* standards, or she is revealing that the general level of the collection is determined by standards which would not be considered remotely literary, or she is lying about the real reason for excluding Updike. Does the Updike reader see book selection principles at work here, or the hand of the censor?

Such clear value contrasts are not apparent in all cases, but a good many others illustrate the vulnerability of library pronouncements on book selection policy. In 1968, for example, the book selection policies of the St. Paul Public Library received a rather warm press after the revelation that the library had rejected *Myra Breckenridge* because "The book is well-written, but it has no literary merit." The same library defended its inclusion of *Valley of the Dolls,* even though the book had "no redeeming features," because the library felt it had an obligation "to show facets of our era such as the misuse of pills." Commenting on the St. Paul fracas with whimsical punch, the *Staff Bulletin* of Youngstown and Mahoning County Library, after noting that the St. Paul Public Library had no written book selection policy, suggested: "If they get one, it will probably be well-written but without literary merit."

Another recent example may illustrate a different point about standards in book selection. When Norman Mailer's *Why Are We in Vietnam?* was published I reviewed it for *Library Journal* and panned it as a bad book (Eliot Fremont-Smith in the *New York Times,* incidentally, said it was brilliant). Some time later, a librarian friend accosted me jubilantly at a convention. He had been glad to see my review, he said, because it supported his library's decision not to buy the Mailer book. My friend was somewhat perplexed when I told him I thought the library was wrong, that the Mailer book should have been added to the collection.

"But you said yourself the Mailer book was a bad one. Are you advocating that the library buy bad books?" he asked. It was a naive question which might have been answered with another question: "Are you so sure your library doesn't buy bad books?" Instead, I tried to explain that, had I been making the book selection decision in his library, I would have bought the book because: 1) Mailer is unquestionably a major figure in contemporary American literature; 2) Everything he writes is of immense public interest, and among the suburban public of this particular library there are surely many people who would want to read *any* book he produces; and 3) The implied topic of the book, and its rather obscure central theme, are closely related to important social and political concerns of the day—especially so in the Washington D.C. area where this library (and a good many others which did not buy the Mailer novel) was located. My friend could not buy book selection philosophies as elastic or elusive as these.

Standards as applied to book selection, nevertheless, must be elastic, and the message may be gradually becoming clearer to more librarians. This may, indeed, be the healthiest and most obvious impact that today's social upheavals are having upon the public library. As libraries, at long last, have begun to reach out for a public whom they and their book selection policies have ignored for years, they begin to discover that those policies which satisfied at least a large part of the known or predictable needs of a white middle class public which libraries, along with other social institutions, had made their own, are wildly irrelevant when applied to service to the new residents of the cities: the black, the foreign-speaking, the miscellaneous poor. Thus, Daniel Fader, advocating the use of books which could never have "passed" under old book selection policies, becomes a new prophet. And Marie Davis, president of ALA's Adult Services Division, warns that "book selection policies, based on 'balanced collections' and 'literary merit,' do not recognize the full thrust of [today's] modes of expression and all that they imply."

Not only the old, fixed ideas about content standards are being called into question; some of the rigid attitudes about form are also under fire. Resistance to the paperback wanes. Out in Venice, California, new-breed librarian Don Roberts declares that fifty percent of the library collection should be "electric." If you can get nine-track stereo on airplanes, he asks, why not in libraries? And Lowell Martin reminds the Enoch Pratt Free Library—and others who read his report, *Baltimore Reaches Out*—that "It is easy but not accurate to draw a sharp line with book readers on one side and the great unwashed on the other. This amounts to designating one kind of printed page as the real thing and excluding others." Martin, too, is arguing that libraries must get away from their obsession with the book.

The growing recognition that "the community" and the traditional library public are by no means the same thing has put a strain on book selection policies which may once have seemed secure in their generalities, and have exposed the hollowness of those various phrases that relate the library's book selection practice to "the needs of the community." Our individual reader, still in confrontation with the librarian who has rejected the book he wants, may well call up one of these phrases in his own cause. OK, he says, *I'm* part of the community. What about my needs?

What, indeed, do the policy statements mean when they talk about the needs of the community? In a very small town, perhaps, it may be possible for the librarian to sense the general tenor and tone of the community, and to have some knowledge of group interests. But even in such a community the possibility that the librarian will understand the inner beliefs and concerns of even a majority of individuals must be viewed skeptically. I would not even place any large bets on the certainty of my predictions on the reading tastes and desires of my own family; even less would I have the temerity to prejudge those of my neighbors. And in the large city, to talk in these terms about the community is ludicrous. When we begin to talk about the community in the mass, when we forget for one moment that the mass is made up of individuals, library book selection has already begun to operate on very suspect principles.

Among all the arguments raised when one questions book selection practice, the most unconvincing are those concerned with that amorphous body, "the public." Most alarming is the widespread, often unconscious, superciliousness of librarians who talk about the lack of "maturity" or "sophistication" of their reading public. In an age when mass communications reach into every corner of society, it is hard to understand the easy dismissal of the possibility (probability?) that the whole range of taste and all shades of opinion exist within *every* community. The quantity distribution varies, certainly, with each community, but few librarians would be prepared or able to defend the proposition that the library should serve only majority tastes and opinions.

Yet, forced to admit that our troublesome reader's needs are part of the community's needs, the librarian can fall into this box through reliance on another concept deeply embedded in the excuse vocabulary of book selection: the "demand" factor. As a defense for a policy decision, "demand" is a veritable Maginot Line. One might be forgiven for assuming, for example, that many controversial books would rank high among the books in demand. Yet it is amazing how often librarians have indicated "no demand" for such books, even when they were selling by the tens of thousands in bookstores. But even eliminating the element of controversiality, might not our reader, given the "demand" excuse, point to the shelves and ask the librarian how many times there has been active demand for, say, the poems of Wallace Stevens, or for Bacon's *Advancement of Learning?* How much demand is demand? And how is it measured? Does the library just listen to the vocal readers, or those who come in weekly with their batch of request cards after reading the *New York Times Book Review?* How much do libraries know of the unexpressed demands, of the disappointments of readers who never find what they want on the shelves?

Before we proceed to other matters one more concept from the book selection policies deserves mention: the muddled theory of "balance" in library collections. This is a sacred cow, propagated in all the most noble pronouncements of the profession (like the *Library Bill of Rights*), but every librarian knows that the theory is indefensible against the evidence of the library shelves. Rare is the library that gives as much weight to publications favorable to either communism or fascism as to democracy. And radical right pressures on libraries have gained some strength from the general truth of their argument that library collections tend to favor liberal over conservative points of view. And how often does one witness a balance between material on heterosexuality and homosexuality? Or between Christianity and atheism?

There is, nevertheless, one way in which libraries have managed to create and preserve an impression of balance. The seesaw analogy explains it best. Even if they are not evenly matched in weight, if you put two people as near as possible to the middle of a seesaw, the ends of the seesaw will not go up or down too much. The further out your people move, the harder it is to maintain a balance. Libraries—and who can say how consciously?—have preserved an appearance of balance in just this way, by staying generally as close as possible to the safe, respectable middle; by never placing too much emphasis on the outer edges, the fringe groups, the dissident or dissenting opinions, the impolite or abrasive voices. Here is one substantial reason why, in this time of social revolution, the relevance of libraries is called into question.

While librarians have talked of applying, or trying to apply, some vaguely consistent standards to book selection, what has been more evident has been the widespread adherence to a rather pernicious double standard. Thus, the polite or "harmless" or insipid book does not really have to be very good to reach the library shelves of most public libraries, is not subjected to the same rigorous interrogation as that book or magazine which treads ground that the conformists fear to approach. The book or magazine which is, or even may be controversial has, on the other hand, to be a near masterpiece, supported by almost unanimous critical opinion, before libraries will offer it the sanctity of the shelves—and certainly the open shelves.

If libraries *must* apply a flagrant double standard, one wonders whether the present one shouldn't be reversed in its emphases. Better, it seems to me, that the shelves be full of books which provoke thought and reaction in the mind and heart, and even perhaps a movement of the reader's juices, than that they be full of textual pap.

If this essay, thus far, appears to be thoroughly negative, defeatist, hopeless, it is not meant to be. It is intended to undermine the certainties of those who think book selection can be done by rote or formula, of those who believe themselves "safe" in their decisions if only they have a written policy, of those who ascribe fallibility or prejudice only to others. Daniel Melcher once told me that he'd asked a librarian what she did about burying her book selection mistakes. The librarian answered: "I don't make any." That librarian has not even learned the first mandatory lessons for the book selection practitioner: that we are all of us nearly as often wrong as right; that the only person who can be absolutely certain that a book is good is the reader for whom that book *is* good; that book selection, in short, is a fallible, human, prejudice-ridden technique.

Book selection, however, is not a *uniformly* difficult process. Some selection decisions, it would appear, are easy to the point of being automatic, others appear to be much more difficult. But it is interesting to examine whether the strengths and weaknesses of library collections coincide with the areas of comparative ease and difficulty in the selection process.

Most librarians, for example, would probably be prepared to accept that retrospective book selection is easier than current book selection. Time and society have rendered their withering judgments on the older books, have eliminated the transient, the ephemeral and have given a stamp of approval and permanence (sometimes an erratic permanence) to the survivors. There is no such perspective to help us in deciding upon the merits of current books. Society's hurried mass judgments, such as the best seller lists; the unpredictable irascibility or benignity, of critics and reviewers (they are human, too!); the imprecision of some of the criteria written into book selection policies, such as the reputation of the publisher—all of these factors, and others, may mislead the book selection in any one of several directions. If this proposition is basically correct, the conclusion one might draw from it is that the library shelves might be expected, in general, more adequately to represent the time-tested books than the more doubtful contemporary pretenders.

But it isn't so. I proved it to myself a number of times when I was a book selector, with carefully checked tests. I have had it sadly, and repeatedly, proven to me as a library user. And I checked it out again, in a small way, a few years ago, and reported the findings in an article called "A View from the Front." When one can find a Thomas Wolfe novel in only one quarter of the libraries one checks, or a collected Milton in less than half of them, and at the same time one does find the shelves crowded with the dross from the last several years' best seller lists, it does not appear that the greater ease of retrospective book selection leads to better shelf representation. I must stress that I am talking about books *on the shelves,* where readers want them, not entries for books in the catalog (though, frequently, they are missing also). I never knew an empty-handed reader who left the library deliriously happy with having found a catalog entry.

To take a second "degree of difficulty" proposition, most librarians would probably agree that it is generally easier to select "factual" books than to select what is sometimes called "creative literature." The factual books, those which assist the library in fulfilling its informational mission, can be measured against something, perhaps their predecessors. Does the new book add anything new? Does it provide later information? Does it have a special viewpoint? Is it addressed to a special audience? Is it accurate? Does the library need anything else in this subject area? These are *relatively* easy, practical decisions to make, even if one has to call occasionally upon subject specialists for assistance.

Where book selection gets much tougher (and this applies equally to reviewing) is when one is dealing with current creative writing—poetry, drama, fiction, perhaps some philosophy, history. Here every man's judgment is *not* as good as the next's, and no one's is certain. How, for example, do you assess the worth of a new play? Can you measure the new dramatist, with any accuracy, against Shakespeare or Shaw, or even Arthur Miller? What would you prove, if you could? Subject content is no help either. You cannot decide on the basis of whether or not the library needs another play about infidelity or doctors, miscegenation or religion. The play, the poem, the novel is only measurable against itself, and perhaps against what we know of ourselves and the world around us, today and through all the yesterdays.

So, if our proposition is correct this time, we should expect that the factual or informational representation in public libraries would be our strength, would be more supportable than the fiction or creative literature sections. But is it so? Let me illustrate by adapting and updating some remarks made by Dan Lacy in 1961:

> I wonder how many people have come to our libraries in the last month to borrow a book on the Vietnam problem [Lacy was talking about Berlin then]. What if a considerable number of the population *did* want to find out something about the Vietnam problem? In a community of 20,000 people, let's not be extravagant and say 50% or 30% or 20%, but suppose one percent of the 20,000 came into the library and said, "I want a book about the Vietnam problem." Your service, of course, would have collapsed after the first dozen arrived.

And so to a third proposition: that it is very much more difficult to select books for the small library than for the very large. There do not appear to be too many holes in this one. It is, of course, harder to select a very small number of representative titles from today's overwhelming publishing output than it is to buy most of them. Every housewife knows that the smaller the budget, the more difficult the shopping becomes; she has to be more certain about what the essentials are. But this is too simple a view of the responsibilities of selection, and this proposition falls in practice because it has the same glaring hole that the other two have. The "easier" selection problem *does* lead to better collections in the large libraries, in the sense that those collections have more range; but it is by no means always easier to find on the shelves of a large library the book one wants, when one wants it, than it is in the smaller library—whether the book be fairly current or a classic.

The reason why all three of these apparently reasonable propositions begin to look dubious when measured against the evidence of the shelves is that most libraries have tended to sacrifice depth in favor of range. Most library collections would be considerably more *useful* if some of the obsessive concern about "quality" in book selection were matched with an equal concern about *quantity*. A library needs not just specific titles and adequate coverage of subject areas but varying quantities of specific titles related to the varying intensities of reader interest and need.

In general, the larger libraries have dealt no more satisfactorily with the quantity problem than have their smaller brethren. Also, the academic libraries have done no better with it than the public libraries. Some of the larger academic libraries, indeed, have been so concerned with the status of statistics and with the widest possible range of titles that their book selection practices tend to lead to a very curious result: the more esoteric the reader's need, the better able is the large research library to satisfy it; and conversely, the more predictable the need, the more dismal is the library's performance. The degree to which the academic libraries have ignored the quantity problem has, in fact, accentuated the problems and difficulties of the public library—difficulties which in recent years have been encapsulated, inaccurately, in the phrase, "the student problem."

There is some evidence that some of the newer academic institutions may have learned the vulnerability of the "range at the expense of depth" philosophy. A considerable swing in the other direction is apparent in the approach, for example, of the New Federal City College in Washington, D.C. The following is quoted from the college's information leaflet on its media center, which began operating in the fall of 1968:

> In its first year the basic book collection will include 18,000 titles. The Center also will have a section containing 200,000 *duplicate volumes,* seventy-five percent of which will be paperbacks. These will be available to students on loan for as long as they are enrolled at FCC.
>
> Books in the basic collection cannot be taken from the Center by either faculty or students. Circulating hardbound books will be subject to recall when the demand is great, but paperback books may be kept by any student for months or even years. A student may borrow up to 50 books on this basis.

This example is startling because it is so exceptional. Undoubtedly, many librarians will consider this duplication ratio as excessive. We would not be surprised if it proved, in time, to be still less than adequate.

Any storekeeper who devoted as little careful attention to the quantity factor as most libraries, even if his judgments about the quality of his products were impeccable, would very probably go bankrupt. The shopper who goes to a supermarket, for example, for something as basic as a bar of soap and several times doesn't find it because the management consistently miscalculates customer needs, would very quickly stop using that supermarket. If reader dissatisfaction in libraries had the same immediate economic consequences as customer dissatisfaction has upon the store, libraries also would quickly be in deep trouble.

The principal reason why shelf collections are so frequently inadequate in meeting reader needs is that the book selection process stops too early, operates too much in limbo. A tedious and often unnecessary amount of time can be spent on the decision to include or exclude a particular title, but beyond that not much happens. The statistics that are so laboriously compiled by libraries reveal little that is helpful about the usage of specific books. Many modern circulation systems have removed even the last remnant of elementary evidence about usage from the book: the old date label. And rare is the library where trained personnel are assigned fulltime to the care and study of the book collection *and its usage*. When libraries assign the same priority to the content of the collection as they do at present to the mechanics of the collection, for example in technical processes, library collections may take on a relevance many do not exhibit today.

PART V

THE LIBRARY PROFESSION

Introduction

Despite its simple title, "The Library Profession," Part V is more diverse than perhaps any other section of this volume. Certainly it is concerned as much with library *service* as it is with the profession—but in a way perhaps the two are indivisible.

"A Jungle Tale," originally a speech at the Albany Library School, is included as an example of something I was repeatedly asked to do in those early years at *LJ*: to compare and assess the strengths and weaknesses (and peculiarities) of librarianship in the U.S. and Great Britain. One interesting response to this piece came from Kathleen Molz, then editor of the *Wilson Library Bulletin*. Her speech, which spent some time disagreeing with mine, appeared originally in the *Ohio Library Association Bulletin* but we picked it up and reprinted it in *LJ* (June 15, 1965, pp. 183-187). Her essay on the interplay of space and time and the mark this has left on knowledge, customs and institutions—including the library—is a typically Molzian piece, stylish, scholarly and a bit remote, as if the author were looking down on us from a great height. Kathleen saw the library, not as "Mr. Moon's jungle, but rather a 'peaceable kingdom' where the lion lies down with the lamb, and does not devour him."

Actually the Molz "Peaceable Kingdom" and my "Jungle" seem not to differ so much if you consider the following quotations. Molz: "What reading has become for most Americans is a kind of gigantic table of contents, and our familiarity with the great names of letters and art and science derives from skimming and scanning." Moon: " . . . there is the American myth that a library is a sort of home hobby-shop, a how-to-do-it encyclopedia of surface culture, a many-tentacled readers' digest, an easy answer to the crossword puzzle of comfortable but confused lives."

"Fire from the Maddened Crowd" (the title reveals another of my favorite authors) was the result of one of my fairly frequent jaunts to UCLA to see Larry Powell and his library school at work. Henry Madden, then the lively editor of the *California Librarian,* had unearthed that old,, tired question, "Is librarianship a profession?" Powell had set his students upon Madden's editorial and my report is an account of what followed. As the article concludes, one useful lesson to be learned from this confrontation is that our meetings and our journals need, once in a while, to revisit the perennial questions, "if only for the benefit of that new audience which grows and emanates from the library schools each year."

When Paul Dunkin (he and Seymour Lubetzky were *the* great names of the cataloging world in my day) became President of the ALA division then known as RTSD he called me and reminded me of one of my constant complaints about ALA conferences: that those who planned programs seemed unable to exercise restraint, with the result that meetings were so over-programmed that there was rarely time for audience involvement. I have decided to have only one speaker, said Paul. Good, I said. You, he said. Oh! "RTSD and the Big Wide World" is the result. I was not awfully popular with the cataloging fraternity at that time (which Paul well knew, but the quiet man liked things a bit spicy), and I do not believe this paper created wild enthusiasm in their ranks either.

"High John" was the first extensive account of what I still regard as the most refreshing and original experiment in library education circles during the sixties. For those who have not read it, I would highly recommend Evelyn Geller's follow-up article, "Think Session at High John" (*LJ*, September 1, 1968, pp. 2963-71), her report on a three-day conference on library service to the disadvantaged sponsored by Maryland's High John project. While Paul Wasserman and Mary Lee Bundy of the Maryland faculty were concerned with helping the library schools adapt to cultural change, the degree of interest in this conference among the other accredited schools is evidenced by the fact that only seven of them were represented. The conclusion of Geller's article is telling: "The practitioners huddled together, talked to themselves, made the conference an underground success. But it was clear they would be paving their own roads in their own way, leaving research, education and theory to straggle behind."

The title of the next paper was borrowed, as many of my titles are, from George Bernard Shaw, who influenced my way of looking at things perhaps more profoundly than anyone else. Shaw's declaration, typically containing no qualifiers, was: "All professions are a conspiracy against the laity." I was talking here about how our profession might soon be viewed that way unless we altered the emphases of our concerns and priorities. There's been some change, and occasional improvement, since then—but the danger remains.

Introduction

"A Potpourri of P's" may have been the only paper I gave at a conference during the period when I was a candidate for President of ALA. E.J. Josey, who was working very hard to get me elected, made sure that I was invited to this conference and we appeared together on the same program. The P's referred to in the title were: Professionalism, Personnel, People, and the Payoff.

The final piece in this section was written as the Foreword to the second volume of autobiography by Lawrence Clark Powell, *Life Goes On* (Scarecrow, 1986). At Bowker in the sixties I had persuaded him to write the first autobiographical volume, *Fortune and Friendship* (Bowker 1968). And I had joined Bill Eshelman, my successor as President of Scarecrow Press, in badgering Larry into producing this second volume. Powell retaliated by insisting that I write the foreword. There is much here, not just about Powell, but about other luminaries of our profession, and about my own early meetings with this profession's "Best recruiter and ... most effective lobbyist."

A Jungle Tale

"Our life is dominated by myths," says Leo Rosten. And from these myths, "only the thinker, the writer, the philosopher, the scientist, the free man can truly liberate us" (see *LJ*, June 1, '62, pp. 2072-5). If he is right about our life generally, is *library* life—or librarianship—or library service—dominated by myths?

As I thought about this I began to feel sure that prevailing myths about libraries and their function in society are somewhat different in Europe and the United States. The contrasts may derive primarily from the differing aims and emphases in educational systems on either side of that vast insulator, the Atlantic.

America has become so obsessed with the concept of democracy and so frantic about the dangers that seem to threaten it, that it has confused—and nowhere more so than in education—equality of opportunity with equality of potential ability and achievement. Equality is no longer something to be offered and grasped, but to be thrust upon the recipient whether or not he wants it, whether or not he can use it. There must be no winners, no favorite sons. The danger of this philosophy, devotion to this kind of false equality, is that it may condemn us eventually to a pervasive mediocrity.

The Europeans have always—apart from moments of Aryan insanity—accepted that society will be guided, if not dominated, by an intellectual elite. Their educational systems have traditionally been geared to the belief that only a certain percentage of the population is able to benefit truly from an academic education. It is almost certain that they have underestimated this percentage with alarming consistency, but they have recognized that the organization of society depends upon the use and development of a variety of talents, and that perhaps *different kinds* of education are needed to develop each and every one of these to the full.

Reprinted by permission from *Library Journal* 88: 179-185, January 15, 1963. Copyright © 1963, Reed Publishing, USA.

Another factor which may have made a difference in how we view our libraries is that America has achieved in this century a *material* wealth and success undreamed of anywhere else in the world. And because the results of this progress have been measurable, concrete *things,* we have given the credit, wrongly and totally, to the "practical" man, and have scorned that unrealistic and pathetic person, the man of ideas, the "egghead," as though he were a pariah and a parasite.

We have failed to realize that—Mr. Rosten's words again—"the most practical things in this world of ours are not dynamos, nor mechanisms, nor computers, nor aircraft; the most practical things are *ideas.* It is always from some curious, abstract, 'daydreaming' egghead that our marvelous gadgets come."

Let us examine some of the myths about the library and what it has to offer.

There is the still-prevalent European myth (dying in Scandinavia and most of Britain) that a library is a morgue-like place, shrouded in dignity and the undisturbed dust of time, a home for the preservation of a gentle, but never urgent, wisdom. This biblio-temple, says the myth, has about it an aura of gloomy grandeur, a church-like sanctity, a buckram-bound uprightness. Its dedicated users are those who have abandoned the sordid reality of capitalized LIFE for the cloister of lower-case learning. Its keepers, sometimes called that instead of librarians, are men with a profound sense of history, but men who see history only as the past, whose eyes are blinkered against the present and the future, who preserve but do not *perpetuate* wisdom.

In almost shoddy contrast, there is the American myth that a library is a sort of home hobby-shop, a how-to-do-it encyclopedia of surface culture, a many-tentacled readers' digest, an easy answer to the crossword puzzle of comfortable but confused lives. One searches here for *information,* never for wisdom or understanding. This is a house of facts, which being more material are therefore more valuable than ideas. Judicious use of this workshop will lead to better jobs, effortless term papers, more money, Spock-marked children, fewer ulcers, and always, *answers*—answers without questions, answers without the drudgery of thought and contemplation, activities not even implied in the current debased overusage of the word "research."

A plague on both these houses—on the American, which is a tinseled supermarket of quotation-marked and footnoted culture; and on the European, which is no more than a plushy Victorian mental brothel.

What then is a library? What is it *for?* Do we know—as librarians, as trustees, as students, as readers?

The real, or ideal library—and I use the words interchangeably, because I believe the real reality is not what *is* but what must or will or can be—is a hotbed, a dangerous, exciting, challenging jungle. No soporific place, no place for easy equanimity or myopic self-delusion.

You almost *have* to pass through this jungle to reach the ease and the peace that this tragic world of ours wants so desperately but has lost the trick of recognizing. Perhaps it's so difficult because there is only one pathway—that of unfettered freedom and unafraid imagination. And you can't find, or even recognize, this pathway without *living* in the jungle and learning to survive among the warring tigers that fight there—with ideas—for supremacy. Here are the bared claws of ideologies, the bared teeth of conflicting beliefs. Behind this tree, Marx. Behind that, Jefferson. In a huddle over there, Adam Smith and Robespierre and Tom Paine. Cavorting in a glade, Lawrence, Whitman, Miller, Rabelais and Chaucer—and watching them with analytic curiosity, Darwin and Freud. And off yonder, in the most tangled place of all, a figure with many masks and many names—God, Jehovah, Allah, Buddha, Mammon.

The principle of survival of the fittest operates in this as in all jungles. The permanent inhabitants, like Shakespeare and Rousseau, Cervantes and Melville, Plato and Goethe and Dante, are those who have most to contribute. There are youngsters here too, by the score, struggling for permanent citizenship—those like Frost and Hemingway, and even such babes in time's arms as Salinger and Malamud.

A place of dangerous peace

Despite the dangers, the visitor need have no fear. For this jungle is not only the most exciting but also the safest place on earth, just so long as the visitor will recognize that all deserve a place in it who *can* survive there. For as long as they can live there, even such vulnerable mortals as Vance Packard, Michener, Goldwater, Ayn Rand and Colin Wilson must be granted sanctuary. Once try to cage those whose appearance frightens you, whose fanged ideas you don't like, and you will transform this place of dangerous peace into a totalitarian prison. Then, sooner or later, you will have an uprising on your hands, because the majority of these inmates, though they may disagree about everything else, will always unite solidly behind the concept that each one of them has a right to hold, and propagate his own different ideas.

The password to safety in this dangerous place is simple wisdom, simple at least as Rosten defines it: "Wisdom is not much more than the capacity to confront dangerous ideas with equanimity."

Most visitors to the jungle of ideas will not be able to find their own way at first. Its growth is too rich after all the centuries of civilization, its paths too complex. There is need of a guide. And this is the true role of the librarian. He must, at least collectively, know the inhabitants and their habits well. He must, in exhibiting them to the visitor, be not negative, nor even neutral, but unprejudiced. He must see that all are known to be equally available. And he should strive constantly to see that the library fulfills the purpose which is captured in one sentence of the *Unesco Public Library Manifesto:* "It (the library) should not tell people what to think, but it should help them to decide what to think about."

We, as librarians, have too great a tendency to become engrossed in means at the expense of ends. We worry more about the methods of producing the catalog cards to record the books we own, more about the charging systems which will circulate these books faster and more efficiently, than we do about the books we don't own but should, the readers we *should* serve but don't.

Breadth and freedom—of content and use—these should be always our first concerns. But they are not. There are still too many millions of readers in this, the richest country on earth, who are not served at all or are disgracefully served by librarians because of apathy, discrimination, parish-pump politics, an introverted concern by librarian-administrators with piddling internal detail, and a variety of other sordid reasons.

If I am critical it is because I believe all of us *must* be more critical, particularly of ourselves and what we do and why we do it. Only after that can we afford to be absorbed with *how* we do it.

Roy Stokes, the head of my old library school in England, (and *LJ*'s new "Grindstone" columnist) answered the charge recently "that in the Schools of Librarianship we concentrate too much on what is wrong with the present day and look too little at the achievements." How can you look too much or too long at what is wrong? Said Stokes: The achievements "are not inconsiderable but there is something unhealthy in the self-praise which our profession too often lavishes upon itself. Our business is to prepare you [he's talking to his students] to create something new wherever anything is wrong, not to induce you simply to glory in what is good in your inheritance."

Examine our literature over the past 20 years and see if you do not find ample evidence of the "unhealthy self-praise" Stokes decries. Every little triumph is tiresomely trumpeted in half a dozen places, most solid defeats glossed over, or not reported at all. This is changing, but there are still not enough of our professional journals which have accepted that there is as much, if not more, to be learned from our mistakes and disasters as from our little victories.

You will still see more in print about how we ran a nice story hour, in French yet, than you will about the criminal barriers erected by some children's librarians between children who want to explore and stretch their minds, and the adult shelves where they might find something "harmful." You will still see more gentle theorizing about the benefits of cooperation than you will find good concrete and creative examples of cooperation in practice.

And while the President of the United States can say: "Let us welcome controversial books and controversial authors," while Rosten can declare "there is no freedom when controversy has been abolished," Marjorie Fiske finds California public and school librarians cowering in fear of those who wield the illegal big stick of censorship—and not only yielding to it but anticipating it to the degree that they become pre-censors themselves rather than have censorship imposed upon them. And let us not forget the irony of Sinclair Lewis's title, *It Can't Happen Here.* California librarians are not the only ones who have taken this easy and cowardly road to professional perdition.

Nevertheless, the critics of today are few and far between in library literature. You must go back to the early years, to the Deweys and Danas, and in England, to the Panizzis and the Edwards, to find the raging and courageous critics who revolutionized and built librarianship as we know it. There are a few who still distribute a rock or two to jolt the dwellers in over-cultivated beds of roses, but most of the rock-heavers are bent of back, thin of hair and will in very little time find the banner of progress too heavy to carry.

Those who will take our profession and its practice into the future and across the barrier into a new century and perhaps a new civilization are the students and the very youngest librarians practicing today. Do you sense there the driving imagination, the power of youthful revolt and individuality, the fearless opposition to accepted ideas that will be necessary to do the job?

My own visits to library schools leave me most of the time with a depressing memory of young people with old, gray-flannelled minds, unhealthily obsessed with visions of security, concerned clinically with status, without knowing that stature is vastly more important and must come first.

The library schools ought, above all, to be places, as Ralph Shaw says, where a fire is lit in the bellies of the students. Are they? How many of them teach the sort of philosophy and attitude expressed in the following remarks by Roy Stokes to his students:

> At no stage do I want you to think in terms of the world of 1961. This is not primarily your concern. The shaping of events in 1961 is, for the most part, being done by people who entered librarianship a quarter of a century ago and some of their minds are still irretrievably conditioned by the thoughts and policies of those years. This is not to suggest that everyone over the age of 40 is mentally fossilized. We can always produce magnificent examples to the contrary...

But, Stokes continues,

> all too often, ideas which the younger members of the profession put forward are judged by the seceding generation with regard to their immediate practicability. You are liable to be faced with objections that something which you propose is just not possible as libraries are now organized. To this your reply (even if respectfully muted) must be that, if what you propose is desirable, then the organization must be changed. Institutions are intended to be reshaped by gentle persuasion if possible, but it is better that they should be changed violently than that they should continue to be inefficient and out of date... Heaven only knows that our profession offers you an infinite array of things which need transformation. It has become bogged down in so many ways and it needs the fresh outlook which only those whose purpose it is to shape a career stretching into the next century can hope to bring to it...

Young words

Despite the uniform grayness of my words thus far, I am not a pessimist. While I am rarely guilty of the fragile idiocy of over-optimism, I do believe that librarianship offers potential, challenge and hope. These are young words, however, and they mean most when they are grasped by the young with a determination to translate them from words into reality. It is usually only to the young that the great leap forward seems not much more than a normal rate of human progression.

We can all help, however, if we will start by going back to examine everything we believe about our profession and our function to see what is reality and what myth. We can start with the humility of recognition and acknowledgment that our best libraries are not nearly good enough and our worst are often a disgrace.

In all this preoccupation with the present and the future, we must not, certainly, make the mistake of ignoring the past or failing to build on some of the solid foundations with which it has supplied us. At the same time, we must remember that the past is only useful if we learn something from it. Perhaps one of the most vital lessons we can learn is that there have been a succession of moments in history when nothing short of a revolution could bring about the desired result. Out of such a moment came the United States of America. Out of such a moment came the USSR. And perhaps it will take another revolution, of still another kind, before these two products of revolution will stop snarling at each other and come to the ultimate sanity of recognizing that "*a* way" of doing something and "*the* way" are not quite the same thing.

There have been such revolutionary moments in library history. The birth of the *public* library was one of them. The introduction of open access was another. And I think one of the most recent might have been the passing of the Library Services Act, which, if followed properly with vision as well as vigor, might not only open up bookless deserts (as it has been doing) and break down the old myth that total library service is only a city-centered possibility, but might also encourage adventurous new patterns in cooperation in the very areas where cooperation has been most an outcast.

Most of the librarians I know are progressive people up to a point. That is, the majority do not *impede* progress, at least knowingly. They can envisage, accept, even welcome the small and gradual change that comes almost daily to the library world. But most of us sag and stumble, perhaps even turn back, at the point where a revolutionary leap into a whole new way of thinking is demanded. We go along happily with the thought that change is gradual, inevitable, perpetual—but the vast changes appear to us always as way off in the future, certainly not in our time. Thus we miss our moment of history; it passes us by before we know it is here.

I believe we may be in, or coming up to one of those moments in library history right now. Whether librarianship emerges as an important profession or is replaced by other and newer disciplines depends first upon our recognition of the challenge, and second upon our ability to answer it. The two major elements of the challenge which is upon us are not hard to recognize. Indeed only the deliberately blind could fail to see them. One is a tidal wave of readers, the other a locust plague of materials.

One element—the largest—of the first area of challenge faces public libraries most noticeably, but also school and college libraries to a great degree, and perhaps they can only tackle it successfully if they work together much more than has been their wont. It is what has come to be known by the revealing and condemning phrase, "the student problem." What *problem?* Students have *discovered* libraries. For the first time in history they are invading our public libraries in swarms. They want books, they want information, they want to read, they want help.

You would think that librarians would welcome these youngsters with open beckoning arms. For years, circulation from American public libraries has been dismally low compared with circulation in Britain and Scandinavia, for example. The American public, we have been told or have told ourselves, is not a reading public. So we have worked hard on the kids, spending more money and time and energy on promoting children's library services than anywhere else in the world. Now at last comes the change, blown in by a late awakening, to the *necessity,* not just the pleasant desirability, of education. We no longer have to fight for a library public: it is lining up outside our front doors.

Bickering and barriers

How do we react? School librarians and children's librarians bicker about whose responsibility it is to serve these hungry children instead of getting down to the job of doing it jointly. School boards and library boards continue their mutually desired isolation; the one apparently still thinking that education is only something that happens in a school or a classroom, the other convinced that if a book is wanted in connection with any school project it is not their concern but the school's or the school library's. Larger libraries close their doors to the student, or erect barriers of restrictive regulations that make library use arduous if not discouraging. And the child goes on, unserved and unsatisfied, growing every day less and less a potential future supporter of library service because he finds it gives him precious little at a time when he needs it most.

These kids make a noise. They make it impossible for us to serve the adults. They want so much help. We don't have any books left. The adults are complaining. And so the chorus sounds. *Let* the adults complain. It's far better that they should at least become aware of the deficiencies of our library services than that they should continue to accept apathetically nothing more than a delayed best-seller service, which is what they get in many libraries. Let them become aware, through discomfort if necessary, that they must contribute *much more* if libraries are to serve children and adults, or either group adequately. They have had to learn the hard way that education is expensive. Well, so are libraries. You can't have a good one cheaply. And if libraries continue trying to be all things to all men, it is time the community realized that the job is impossible without a little more help. Let the kids come. Encourage, if necessary, a state of emergency. Even Congress sometimes reacts to a real emergency.

The other challenge which throws a spotlight on our tendency to hide from the future is the relentless pressure of materials which multiply like rabbits in an information saturated world. This swelling tide of books and reports and periodicals and filmstrips and indexes, and indexes to indexes, and bibliographies of bibliographies, and microfilm and Microcards and microfiche is driving us mad, but is it driving us forward? How many of us know what documentation is? We conjure up pictures of intricate machines and dehumanized services, we associate with a cloudy mental image of something called information retrieval. And abstractly, we worry about it all, but not too much. We still have our catalogs. But, let's ask ourselves again: what is documentation? And does it concern us? Jesse Shera, at the ALA conference in Cleveland, said:

> Documentation is not a mythical line of demarcation for separating the sheep from the goats, and certainly it is not, as some would have it, a synonym for the mechanization of library or bibliographic operation. Documentation, if it is anything other than a semantic differentiation, may be regarded as a theory of librarianship that is dedicated to the exploration of new ways for improving the utility of recorded knowledge, *for whatever purpose and at whatever level of use,* by developing new means for the analysis, organization and retrieval of graphic records . . . *a children's librarian* can be as much of a documentalist as the most highly trained literature scientist serving the most esoteric

requirements of a theoretical physicist. Documentation, then, is not is a matter or degree, or even of intensity of effort, it is a credo—a professional philosophy. If the line between the documentalist and librarian is difficult to draw, it is so because it is not a very important line except as it has been used as a whip to urge librarians into new areas of investigation and innovation.

It was, added Shera, "in the attempt to escape from the dilemma of poverty in the midst of intellectual abundance that the much maligned discipline of librarianship known as 'documentation' was devised."

Does documentation, as outlined by Shera, sound like anything other than really basic librarianship, in a slightly higher gear perhaps to deal with a faster world?

Should a whip be necessary to urge librarians into new areas of investigation and innovation? And if it is necessary, is it not so because we have for too long had our ostrich heads buried in the shifting sands of irrelevancies and trivialities, worrying more about overdues than about the progress which is desperately overdue?

Do we ask ourselves why special librarians in America and in Britain have broken away from the mainstream and formed their own powerful tributaries—SLA here, ASLIB in England? Do we worry when we hear men like Dr. Urquhart in England declaring, in effect, that librarians are unnecessary in the National Lending Library for Science and Technology? Or when we see whole new professions of documentalists, information officers and the like growing up all around the self-imposed boundaries of librarianship? Do we ask what these "specialists" are doing that we are not?

Most of the time we do not ask because the answer is humiliating. They are *thinking,* and they are trying to find ways to cope with this new ocean of readers and materials and with a demand for *library service* that should be a joy to us, but which most of us have not yet begun to believe conceivable.

The moral then, if there be one, is that the real—or ideal—library is not anything we now have. It is what we must create, or perish as an important and effective instrument of society and as a profession.

Fire from the Maddened Crowd

In the beginning (of this story, at least) there was Henry Madden, editor of the *California Librarian*. All editors' lives are punctuated by deadlines, their days plagued by the recurring yawning emptiness of the editorial page, their pride irritated by the perennial lack of response from the professional periodical readership. Perhaps provoked by these pressures, Madden, last July (1964), exhumed the oldest, most disturbed corpse of all, and tried again to breathe some life into that tired old question, "Is Librarianship a Profession?"

In the next issue, October, Madden continued along a familiar editorial path, with this note, apropos his July editorial:

> The Editor had some fears that his mailbox would be unable to hold the flood of letters protesting his derogation of his fellows. Phantom fear! Only three or four letters burdened the box . . . For people who deal with words imbedded in books and periodicals, who are presumably guardians of the written record of mankind's achievements, librarians are remarkably shy of using pen or pencil to defend the status which they assume to be theirs.

Madden, clearly, was still digging a little, but a terribly familiar story—it *seemed*—had ended with total predictability. All, however, was not as quiet on the Western front as the printed page suggested.

We visited the library school at UCLA last November, and there discovered that Dean Lawrence Clark Powell had given his students Madden's editorial to cut their teeth on. Powell then sent the "blue books" (a phrase descriptive of more than the covers of these class exercise books) to Madden and asked him to come to the school and discuss the matter with the students after reading their views.

Reprinted by permission from *Library Journal* 90: 578-581, February 1, 1965. Copyright © 1965, Reed Publishing, USA.

Well (as Jack Benny says with heavy emphasis), here was one editor who got more response than he might have wished for. As an ex-teacher he did not react with wild enthusiasm to blue books, having marked too many in his time. He came along but admitted—claiming the time-immunity of a busy man with two jobs, librarian and editor—that he had not read many of the papers.

We asked Dean Powell whether we might take the blue books—for possible *LJ* "treatment." He was pleased, the students were pleased, but we had other than public relations motives. Henry Madden's question has littered the pages of so many library periodicals that we are as tired of it as the next man. But to this group it was a question of some importance. Madden was really questioning the values to which were about to dedicate their future. How they responded to his probing, it seemed to us, should be a matter of interest and concern to all librarians, because not just the future of those students but the future of librarianship depends to some extent on what these embryo librarians believe and how much they care.

What did Madden say in his "provocative" July editorial? He adopted the editorial technique and began with the definition of "profession" given by *Webster's Third New International Dictionary,* then he commented on the significant parts of the perhaps less than significant whole.

The crucial word in the definition, he said, was "calling." On this his comment was that "It probably applies more to the healing arts than to the teaching arts. 'Calling' applies, I would venture to say, to a relatively small number of librarians; others simply have not had a call." "Specialized knowledge" he denied to librarians, granting them only "some generalized knowledge and a scattering of useful trade tricks." "Long and intensive preparation," he said, "hardly describes an undergraduate sojourn of four years in any subject of the student's choice, to be capped by a year in a school of library science."

"Skills and methods" were, he admitted, taught in library schools, but were the scientific, historical, or scholarly principles underlying such skills and methods? Librarianship appears to have, in Madden's view, "a lamentably small body of scientific or scholarly principles."

The "key element" in the Webster definition, said Madden, was that a profession "maintains 'by force of organization or concerted opinion,' the standards which it expects its members to achieve." He pointed to the power of such organizations as the American Institute of Architects, the medical associations, the bar associations, the presbyteries and synods. By contrast, he declared, "librarians are merely joined in a sham association which has some elements of uplift. Collectively, librarians still have no force of organization, no concerted opinion." Webster also declares that the members of a profession are committed to "continued study." "How many librarians," asked Madden, "patronize a physician who has only as much continuing study of medicine as they have of librarianship since leaving the university." Librarians' continuous study consisted of not much more than "a thumbing of lightweight current library periodicals."

Madden conceded, in one short sentence, one other element of the Webster definition, that librarianship is "a kind of work which has for its prime purpose the rendering of a public service."

Finally, editor Madden ventured to suggest one slight improvement in the Webster definition, the insertion of a clause stating that members of a profession "generally establish their own scale of remuneration." This, he said, was a "critical identifying factor. The physician determines his own honorarium; the architect tells his client what his charge will be; the engineer sets his own remuneration; the lawyer charges fees in accordance with a scale customary among other members of his profession."

So how did the students react? In general, with healthy, uninhibited fire and youthful idealism. Dr. Madden was described as pessimistic, cynical, contemptuous, smug, infuriating, without sympathy ("no empathy even"), superficial, as a "prosecuting attorney," and as "a fundamentalist" interpreting Webster in "the narrowest sense." "I wonder if he reads," pondered one student. Another questioned his education.

But scattered among the angry horde, Madden uncovered a few tentative supporters, and one or two who were prepared to go all the way with his disparaging view. One qualified supporter said, "I agree with him, but his is a static view." Librarianship, this student declared, "is in process of *becoming* a profession." Another suspected "that it is among the semi-professions (like editors) that librarians generally belong." One solid supporter found Madden's editorial "a commonsense, concise, and direct appraisal—very just."

And then there was the young lady who was "afraid" she agreed with Madden. In fact, she said,

> The very same epithet, "ludicrous," has occurred to me in considering the question of librarianship as a profession, or, more exactly, in considering librarians considering the matter. If librarianship were truly a profession the question would not have to be asked in the first place.... I am reminded of a girl who looks constantly at herself in a mirror trying to discover whether or not

she is beautiful. It is doubtful that she will ever know what she really looks like until she can stop worrying about her image and try instead to see what she is like inside.

On the whole, however, Madden's editorial received a popular vote which made Goldwater's look like a landslide victory. The reason was not hard to discern. There was Powell, of course, and a faculty of "believers," but one student put it in a nutshell: "My readings to date have been heavily weighted in opposition to this opinion."

On the question of "calling," most students were prepared to acknowledge the rarity of divine influence. But a great many also insisted that some of the professions which Madden exhibited as models were riddled with people who had not heard any "call." Only the ministry appeared to get any kind of vote of confidence, and lawyers and doctors in particular were hit hard. Among those who leaped to the defence of librarians was the student who said: "The general public considers librarianship an 'odd-ball' type of activity. Since most of us are hesitant about being unconventional ... we would not enter this 'weird' profession unless we had a strong dedication or calling." Another declared, "there are those [librarians] who are dedicated ... and enthusiastic to the point of genteel fanaticism." Yet another found hope in youth: "Many older people in librarianship have never considered it a profession, but younger people now coming in are motivated by the ideals and philosophy behind librarianship—they have the calling and will carry on the fight for professional maturity."

Against Madden's charges of lack of specialized knowledge and long and intensive preparation there was little convincing defense, but there were some interesting observations. Most interesting was that the knowledge and preparation of reference librarians, special librarians, and information officers was most often offered by way of refutation of Madden's arguments. Said one student: "The rise of the information specialist will erase doubts about the professional status of librarians." Many found comfort in the thought that the librarian was a "specialist in general knowledge." One Madden supporter described as "a sad sight" those practicing librarians "who drag their feet against new ideas, who are satisfied to follow rules of procedure, with never more than a scattering of knowledge and no curiosity to explore the reasons behind the rules." And an emotional opponent said, "It's true that the 'outside world' seems to have (in certain cases, e.g. USIS) the impression that anyone can run a library with just a push in the right direction. But that doesn't make it so."

On the question of long and intensive preparation, our two favorite rejoinders were: "Qualitative factors are much more meaningful than quantitative," and "One is always preparing to be a librarian through the very process of attempting to live an informed and committed life." Such sincerity can fail to impress only the jaded.

On skills and methods, and the lack of principles or a philosophy, charged by Madden, many were the students who fell back upon Pierce Butler, obviously first and essential reading at UCLA. But the defenses were mostly local. "Madden's criticism of ways of teaching 'skills and methods' in most schools," said one student, "is probably valid—but not at UCLA." And Seymour Lubetzky's teaching was often cited as emphasizing the critical approach and principles in, as one student put it, "an area of library work where it might be very easy to fall into merely the 'skills and methods' approach."

A variety of observations on professional organizations, particularly the American Library Association, were brought forth by that part of the Webster definition dealing with "force of organization or concerned opinion." There were stout supporters of ALA. "ALA has done a tremendous job for years to raise the standards of librarians and libraries. They have not done all they could do, but to say that they have no 'force of organization,' 'no concerted opinion,' is a gross misstatement." "The ALA," declared another, "speaks with a powerful voice and has risen many times to defend freedom of action and thought of librarians." We learned too that "the ALA *exists* to voice concerted opinion, on intellectual freedom or on political issues." (We did blink a little at the last part of that sentence.) On the other side of the fence was the student who said: "Librarians do have an organization—the ALA—but it does not enforce standards. Both professionals and nonprofessionals are members and there is no strong professional unity." There were several who echoed this last cry, one of whom declared, a bit intolerantly, "Non-professional members of library associations should not be tolerated."

One student expounded on professional associations generally: "Sometimes, alas, they seem to protect their incompetent members from loss of esteem caused by public exposure, acting as conspiracies or defense groupings against the layman, rather than as protectors of the public against unprofessional conduct." But, she added, "library associations do not exert this kind of pressure."

Another believed that salvation did not rest with organizations or associations. "Our image," she declared, "is *local*. If it is good enough, national and state organizations may bask in *our* glory. We will earn the title of profession through our deeds, attitudes, *and personal service*. Not any amount of legislation will give us prestige, status, title, and a place in the sun." Amen, we say.

Nobody really went to bat for the library periodicals or for librarians' penchant for continued study. Here the defenses were really weak, possibly because there are none. "How can you possibly be a librarian and not be learning something new every day?" one student paper plaintively asked. The only defense, it seemed, was attack. Said another student: "Madden is naive if he thinks this (i.e. continued study) is going on diligently in all other professions."

Even on his concession, that librarians do render a public service, poor Madden was attacked. "Madden gave least space to the most important thought—this is 'the heart of the matter,'" said one student, quoting Patricia Paylore. "Librarians give more and better, courteous service than does any other profession," said another unreserved type.

And so we got to the heart of Madden's editorial—money—embodied in his addition to the Webster definition, "members of a profession generally establish their own scale of remuneration." How did these students feel about money?

In truth, most of them seemed to like it and feel it a useful necessity, but certainly the majority at least *said* they didn't believe it to be a paramount factor in determining professionalism. The banner of principle waved firmly, and Mammon was given a back seat. One student found the Madden addition "completely irrelevant to the definition—professionalism is determined by the spirit and the intellect." "Remuneration," said another, "is not so significant a fact as service." One man admitted that we must eat, that we want the status of success, but asked, "does money mean so much that we must trade our dedication to a fixed set of principles for it?" One said her "ideal" librarian "would not sacrifice her values for the dollar." And one challenged the very foundations of Madden's argument. "What about the clergy, the theatrical profession, artists, musicians, and the technical professions—engineers, physicists, chemists, agronomists? They are mostly salaried. They do not set their own standards of remuneration."

Well, there it is—a lot boiled down to very little. What's the point? Our point, at least, is that Henry Madden's question may be old and tired, but it is still a valid one to put early to someone who is thinking of, or is about to enter librarianship. Whatever their feeling about the theory of what makes a profession, the question, put to students, reveals a good deal about what they believe and how they see librarianship from the worm's-eye view—at the bottom or beginning end.

If one can sit back far enough from one's experience and disregard the calluses of cynicism or age, it is difficult not to admire (and envy a little) the faith, the enthusiasm, even the naiveté of this new and future generation of librarians. We, at any rate, liked these UCLA students and were even a little inspired to take a less jaded view of things. With the thought that perhaps we all need such refreshment in more of our meetings and periodicals, we may have learned a lesson worth the attention of all the journal editors. It is that we need to discuss the perennial questions every so often, if only for the benefit of that new audience which grows and emanates from the library schools each year. There are so many questions to which we haven't found answers, or to which we have adopted easy or false answers just because we are tired of the questions, that each new generation should be given the opportunity, or should be prodded into producing its own.

RTSD and the Big Wide World

The title, as anyone with a feel for style may already have detected, is a Dunkin creation, not a Moon-shot. Mine tend to be gaudier, more blatant, without the impish Machiavellianism of *LRTS*'s cataloging king. I have it from an unimpeachable source that one member of the RTSD Program Committee felt that the topic sounded like "a TV sunrise program for children."

Titles of scientific papers these days are rather like bikinis—they are designed to fit all the curves and connotations of the subject very tightly. Titles of conference papers, on the other hand, are designed more like kimonos—they are very loose and have only occasional contact with what lies beneath. Whenever I pick my own title, I tend to choose something rather waspish from Shaw or Wilde or John Cotton Dana, and then forget about it. But when I am handed a title, as in this case, then the editor in me rises to the surface and I must needs examine it, like a manuscript, for motivations and meanings.

After examining this one in its awful entirety for some time I was left with no gleeful feeling that it was laden with potential. The classic technique in such circumstances is to break down the whole into its separate clauses, in the hope that the pieces will reveal meanings that the whole conceals. I proceeded with bifurcation.

RTSD, I discovered—after assiduous research—was an acronym for Resources and Technical Services Division, an aggregation of librarians (plus perhaps a Philistine or two masquerading under the name of documentalist or information scientist) within the American Library Association. Like other groups which are brought together in presumed

---

Reprinted by permission of the American Library Association from *Library Resources & Technical Services* 10: 5-12, Winter 1966. RTSD (Resources and Technical Services Division) is now ALCTS (Association for Library Collections and Technical Services). Dunkin (referred to in first paragraph) was then RTSD President Paul Dunkin.

professional harmony within a division (a term which always reminds me of battalions or regiments), this one is supposed to share a unity of interest or purpose or function.

Since RTSD is what is known as a "type of work" division rather than the more mundane species called "type of library"—whose relevance becomes foggier if we are to believe all those high-level speeches about a nationwide system in which all the old barriers and boundaries between types of libraries will disappear—our principle suddenly becomes sunray clear. *Obviously,* those whose lives are spent in contemplating the philosophical niceties of cataloging and classification theory are professional blood brothers of those whose minds and hearts are made of microfilm and whose thoughts are reproduced by Xerox. *Clearly,* the man whose life is devoted to acquiring, let's say materials (avoiding such an old-fashioned and loose word as books), will have more in common with the explorers of the library machine and the compilers of codens than he will have with the librarian who is a member of the Rare Books Section of ACRL.

My microscopic examination of the first part of Mr. Dunkin's title was, as you can see, leading me only toward that uncomfortable old armchair called doubt. I could not honestly persuade myself that a cataloger has less community of interest with a reference librarian (who occupies a more exclusive division), or an acquisitions librarian with a children's librarian, or the copying methods expert with a documents librarian, than do two green peas from two separate but nearly identical pods. What I was faced with, I decided, was one of those quite illogical anachronisms of professional organization. There seemed to be no demarcation or definition other than the same kind of fuzzy negative-positive shadow that separates book selection and censorship, or even eating and drinking., You see, in all of these activities something always crops up eventually like soup. It may be such a thin consomme that drinking is the only possible activity to connect with it; but it may be a vegetable soup so thick that drinking would be a ridiculous word to use for the process of consumption.

But all my probing of those four vowel-less letters did get me somewhere in the end. I did discover a sort of line. Divisions like ASD and RSD and CSD (I will not insult you be translating these into their full terminological glory) seem mostly concerned with the problems of service to the public. This is true of RTSD only by remote control. If indeed it is true that the RTSD man, in general, only makes contact with the reader (whose satisfaction is the end objective of all we do, whatever kind of librarian we call ourselves) *via* the public service type of librarian, isn't the greatest professional need for the RTSD type for contact with the RSD or CSD man (or preferably, woman), rather than with his fellow absorbed techno-theoreticians? At the end of my pondering, it seemed an open and valid question—and that's the way I like to leave questions.

The first half of the title being so unproductive, to save my time and your patience, I decided to switch rather than fight with it longer. The second part of the title was simpler and therefore more profitable. I could—and I will—start here with a categorical denial, unclouded by doubt, and enjoy the rare experience of proving Mr. Dunkin rhetorically wrong. There is, twentieth century friends, no "Big Wide World."

In a day when a man, should he have the urge and qualifications, can pass around the earth in less time than it takes some of us to get from bedroom to office; in a day when the President of the United States, at the drop of a ten-gallon hat, can, via communication satellite, take over the BBC and, if General de Gaulle would let him, the French TV network too; in a day when an atomic or natural tremor in deepest Siberia can be reported within minutes or hours (depending on the state of government security consciousness that day) by Chet Huntley to the American public from Miami to Ketchikan—in such a time we clearly no longer have "a big wide world."

Nor is the world of librarianship any longer so wide or so big—not even the world of American librarianship (if that is not in itself a misnomer or another anachronism). I bumped into Ralph Shaw recently at a hurried midpoint in one of his frequent commuting trips, which take in administering a university library and a nascent library school in Hawaii, doing a little talking, teaching, or research at Rutgers, visiting his own pet Scarecrow, and sitting on two or three committees in Washington—all, as he says with a breezy *c'est la vie* acceptance, in a day's work. Well, perhaps allowing for Shavian exuberance, two days anyway. I had a drink with Louis Shores in New York the night before he took off on a recent trip which took him a distance equivalent to three journeys around the earth. With encyclopedic help, he took in libraries and librarians and library meetings on a global scale, and when I saw him on his return he seemed only to have been away for the weekend. Nor have the ladies been left, as of old, to watch the hearth and home. Witness those charming RTSD ladies, Sarah Vann and Pauline Seely, who, modern missionaries, carried Melvil's message to the farthest parts of once-darkest Africa and Asia. Marco Polo himself was an old homebody compared to the more peripatetic of our librarians today.

Patently, it wouldn't be either desirable or practicable to have even a moderate proportion of our professional librarians continually wandering the globe in this manner. But our problem is not so much a lack of mobile bodies as it is a deficiency in mental mobility. Too many of our professional minds are stationary and local—parochial, if you will. Many of us still do think of the big wide world, and see it as a collection of remote places and events "out there somewhere" which have little relevance to "our own" condition. I tend to react to such old-fashioned souls very much as Mary Gaver does to those of her students who raise minute, "practical" objections like "where is the money coming from" when she is trying to get them to dream and plan and think big. I heard Mary charge one such student with being guilty of "depression thinking." The condition I am talking about might better be described as "isolationist thinking."

I had just written this when someone delivered into my hands an advance copy of the Presidential Address to the (British) Library Association of Sir Frank Francis, the Director and Principal Librarian of the British Museum. His speech appears in the June issue of the *Library Association Record*. In it he too talks of "the tendency we all have, to look at the library situation . . . [from] a parochial point of view. We each of us have our own drums to beat, and we are sometimes prone to beat them so hard that we can't hear the drums of our colleagues in the next group of libraries."

Let us take, as an appropriate example of isolationist or too-small thinking, the world of bibliographical control or, to use a smaller-world term, of cataloging. I understand this to be a subject of some concern to RTSD, although I cannot refrain from observing that the Association of Research Libraries seems to be backing *its* concern with more immediate and insistent action than does RTSD. If one is to judge by the wordage (I will not use the popular term, "the literature," because it seems singularly inappropriate to describe most library periodicals and monographs), the topics which have been at the top of the collective RTSD mind in recent years are centralized cataloging and processing centers, book catalogs, catalog code revision, and the potential (for good or ill) of automation.

Like everything else in our new, small, muddled world, these are not separate but inextricably related subjects. Automation and the new technology have taken us back to the once archaic book catalog which, with all its faults as well as its virtues, is now, because the production problems are easier to solve than they were fifty years ago, the apparent St. George which will save us from the space-devouring card catalog dragon. It has become as mandatory for a library to announce its progressiveness by declaring that it has converted to a book catalog as it is for an unknown starlet seeking publicity to appear in a *Playboy* centerfold or in a topless bathing suit in Cannes or Los Angeles.

In turn, the computer and the book catalog have given rise to doubts that the new code, when it finally emerges from its inhuman period of gestation, will really be a child of paradise. It will, in any case, be a very old child, of whatever variety. Mr. Dunkin asks, in the most recent of his sparkling annual reviews of the cataloging scene: "Will the new code be a dinosaur on the freeway?"

If book catalogs and computers are multiplying in the library field, the real rabbit of fertility is the centralized cataloging and processing center. Not alone among the reasons for the growth of this species, but certainly the prime motivating reason, has been the theory that these centers would help solve one of our most excruciating staff problems. They would help us get by with fewer catalogers. They would, to quote a favorite phrase, "free professional librarians for better things." But one observer noted, after studying processing centers for school libraries in New York State: "It is ironic that the problem of inadequate staffing—which caused many of the school systems in this study to adopt central processing—still remains, though now transferred to the center itself." We have, and have had for many years, to understate the obvious, a critical shortage of catalogers. The situation may be getting worse, if that is possible. A recruiter for one of the major research libraries told me that he recently visited 22 library schools and interviewed 263 potential candidates. He was most interested in finding catalogers, but only five or six of those he spoke to were interested in even discussing the possibility of a cataloging job.

The cataloging centers appear to me to be accentuating rather than relieving the situation. They are being set up by the dozen; all require some cataloging staff. Of course, if each center needed two professional librarians for cataloging, and served a group of libraries formerly employing a dozen catalogers between them; and if that group of libraries was thereby enabled to dispose of half its "local" catalogers (or direct them to other functions), we should certainly be ahead of the game. But the mathematics seem not to work this way. I have seen little evidence that libraries served by these centers have relinquished or discarded their own catalogers. They must, it seems, remain on the establishment in order to foster, maintain, and attend to those local peculiarities which have wreaked such havoc with what was once called, ironically, library economy, and which have been a potent force in undermining the potential of cooperation throughout the years.

Nor have those wonder boys of the world of automation done anything so far which promises much relief from the cataloger crisis. Indeed, they keep talking about the much greater depth of subject analysis that the computer will make possible. What they are saying, in simple terms, is that the card catalog's bulk and the flooding book output have brought libraries to the point where they make do with two or three subject headings per title. The computer will easily store 20 or 30 or 100, if necessary, and can produce them easily on demand (though not cheaply). But all this begs the crucial question. As the head of one of the nation's largest cataloging operations said to me recently, "It's not the hardware costs or problems that worry me; it's the software." The software he had in mind was people—catalogers. To produce ten times as much subject cataloging you may not need ten times as many catalogers, but you surely need a lot more than we have. While we talk so much about which machine is best for what purpose, or what kind of printout is desirable for any particular purpose, there is, it seems to me, a deliberate cloudiness, a smoke-screen over the whole major problem of input. Here, cost is a big problem, but it is as nothing compared to the problem of the availability of people able to prepare that input. Whatever we call them in the machine age, if we are dealing with bibliographical control, they are essentially catalogers, and their language capabilities, collectively, must now encompass the world.

If these sketchy comments appear to be running off wildly in all directions at once, they are. But in doing so, they are following closely in the tracks of most of our contemporary wayward searchers for solutions to our cataloging crisis. Now I'm not saying that none of these developments has been worth anything. All that I'm trying to suggest is that we might entertain the thought that our remedies thus far may all have been too piecemeal—and too small. Perhaps our problem has grown so large while we have fiddled that only the really revolutionary, big idea offers hope of any solutions.

Our theories, our philosophies, our goals are described in such colossal, magnificent phrases as "making all knowledge available to all men." Our major research libraries, in fact, are doing more than talk like this. They are now collecting, as never before, vast quantities of material in every language and from every country in the world—notably via the Farmington Plan and the P.L. 480 program, not to mention the auction rooms or the marauding expeditions of representatives of the University of Texas among others. Clearly, this kind of large-scale, universal collecting is accelerating the cataloging crisis, and I'm not sure that the $5 million the ARL requested of Congress, to include a centralized cataloging program under the Higher Education Act of 1965, is anything like ambitious enough.

The first and most basic step toward a solution of our vast problem is, of course, a profession-wide realization that "rugged individualism" in cataloging practices is now only rugged stupidity. If we could ever afford it, the day when we could do so has long gone.

Beyond this pious hope, however, don't we perhaps need to look for a wider (perhaps a "big wide world") approach. I started contemplating this when I read recently the (British) Library Association's report, *Access to Information,* which very briefly sets out a national plan under which a national bibliographic center would be established. Among the many functions of this proposed national center would be the establishment and control of a *full* national bibliography, both current and retrospective. The *British National Bibliography,* one of the best in the world, is not enough for these newly ambitious bibliographic planners in Britain. The *BNB,* says the Library Association report, "covers only books and pamphlets since 1950, and music since 1957. It needs to expand to cover fully government and other official publications, maps, charts, and other sorts of published material. The only serious approach to a retrospective national bibliography for the eighteenth and nineteenth centuries is the *British Museum Catalogue.* The provision of a full apparatus of indexes to periodical and report literature is also an essential part of a national bibliography."

I ask you now to dream along with me for a while and suppose that we could really make international cooperation work in the library field. Suppose that each of the major publishing and/or library countries (at least) could set up a national bibliographic council such as the one the British report suggests. Suppose further that these national bodies could form an agency in each country—staffed internationally to cope with language and other problems—to provide full bibliographic coverage for the total publishing for that country. Where this leads is to the formulation of, in effect, say 120 centralized cataloging operations to cover the world. All publications emanating from France, for example, would then be cataloged once, and once only, for dissemination in whatever form required to any library in any country in the world. They would not need to be done again, countless times, in the US, the USSR, Great Britain, Pakistan, Australia, Tanzania, Greece, you name it. I don't have any idea how many catalogers such an operation would require, but it certainly would be fewer than we are now using in libraries around the globe, all reworking the same material endlessly. Cost? Well, the relatively few members of the Association of Research Libraries are already spending $18 million a year on cataloging. I shudder to think what the full national figure might be.

The predictable reaction to this kind of proposal would be hysterical laughter or horror. Think of the problems. Think of the endless squabbles about cataloging rules or form of entry. Think of the endless varieties of physical forms in which libraries would want the catalog copy to be delivered. Florida Atlantic University, obviously, would want computer tape or punched cards or something edible by its machines. The school library down the road would want cards or nothing. The state library would surely demand the book catalog that its new-found, federally-aided prestige demands.

Perhaps we should consider physical form for a moment. Let's entertain the dastardly thought that none of these libraries needs a catalog at all. Walter Brahm, Connecticut State Librarian, dared to do just that in a recent *LJ* column. Why, he asks, if we can cope, without card catalogs, with the many thousands of publications per year which are issued in periodical, pamphlet, or report form, should we give "special treatment to a paltry 40,000 book titles?" Why not, he said, compile and print "an author, title, and subject index" with cumulations every quarter, annually, and every three, five, and ten years? "We are," said Brahm, "slaves to the form in which material is issued rather than to its content, which is the same in any form."

Why, indeed, do we need any longer to accept the albatross of a catalog for every library, or every system of libraries? At the very least, we might try to reduce this absurd exercise in duplication to the point where we have one catalog per state. Fifty catalogs would certainly be preferable to 50,000.

We have made an idol of information and its retrieval. We know that the researcher—at all levels, from high school or below to the most esoteric laboratory—needs a much broader range of material than he did ten years ago. We can comfortably predict that the range will go on expanding. If we believe that the reader should, if he wants it, have at hand a key to the whole of his particular subject universe, we have to accept that the individual library catalog, whose boundaries are determined by the budget and the book selection capabilities and prejudices of that library, will not do the job. To be sure, the catalog will be reinforced by a motley collection of subject bibliographies and other libraries' catalogs, courtesy of G. K. Hall and others. But bibliography, we all know, has had a fragmentary history, and we know that, however bulging the bibliographical shelves, we shall be offering any reader a very imperfect universe of information—and a not very accessible one at that.

If we are prepared also to accept that the new technology and vastly improved communications systems will make it possible for any material, wherever it is housed, to be consulted where it is needed, this takes us further toward the desirability of comprehensive bibliographic planning and further away from the efficacy of the local library catalog—whether it be Harvard's or Podunk's.

Given some sort of sophisticated bibliographical apparatus, what real purpose would the individual library catalog then serve? It would, I think, be reduced to its proper role—that of a finding or inventory list for a particular institution or system of institutions. Relatively few seem to be much more than that now. If we could emphasize that simple function sufficiently, we might perhaps finally be able to persuade more librarians that full cataloging at this level and for this purpose is grossly wasteful. The full description and indexing should appear in national bibliographies, quickly, currently, and efficiently produced and distributed.

The cost and complexity of a solution to our bibliographic dilemma are frightening, but I don't believe they are insurmountable if only we will get our social priorities in some decent sequence. Education in this country, really for the first time in history, is beginning to be dealt the kind of financial cards that formerly were only passed across the table for roads, industrial development, power projects, and the like. The space program is a very prominent current example of what we can achieve when we put enough of our resolution and resources behind what we set out to do. Perhaps, at this point, it is appropriate to quote the opening paragraph of a *Times Literary Supplement* editorial entitled "How Much Jam?" (March 11, 1965):

> Recently we have had a minor debate in the motoring press about whether a man's wife or his car should matter most to him. Put the car against such lesser things as knowledge, culture, ideas, and it is only too clear which lies closer to the modern British heart. [You may read American for British there.] It is not just that cars rank higher as individual status symbols and objects of Sunday morning devotion; traffic in cars has come (quite rightly) to be seen as a problem for urgent study by experts, while our

traffic in ideas and knowledge has not. Yet the two types of traffic are in a similarly confused state, and in both cases the confusion seems like a useless and perpetually irritating brake on our progress. Intellectual traffic with the help of a somewhat primitive system of libraries and information centers gets along somehow, as does road traffic; in time everyone gets near enough to his destination to shrug his shoulders yet once again ("We can walk the last bit").

That could, I think, as easily have been written here. But all of this, you will be saying by now, is very far out on some philosophical and terribly impractical plane. Indeed it is, but I believe we are in such deep trouble, with a vastly increased publishing output all over the world, with greatly increased library funds for books, and with vastly increased acquisitions by libraries of all types of material, allied with a static or declining intake of cataloging personnel, that only far-out proposals are likely to get within reach of a remedy.

In any case, if you had wanted a good, hard, practical paper, I guess you would have invited a good, hard, practical cataloger, an information retrieval expert, or a solid representative of some other canyon of RTSD respectability. If you ask a generalist and a dreamer, you get generalities and dreams. I only hope they don't give you nightmares.

High John

High John was about a month old when we got there in November. Conception had taken place maybe 18 months before, but the gestation period wasn't any too long. Difficult kid, old HJ. Unusual. Might almost say unique. Finally came into this world, real noisy, night of October 23, 1967. Birthplace: Fairmount Heights, Maryland, known as a "deprived area," alias an urban slum. Birth like a Hollywood premiere: lights, music, general hoop-de-doo. Wanted people to know HJ was something special.

High John is a library. Also a laboratory, an experience, a project, an educational experiment, perhaps a pioneer. If you want to be pedantic about it. the name really belongs just to the library (or the laboratory), but it's begun to pervade and be used for the whole bit. And no wonder. What are you to do with a project title like "A New Approach to Education Preparation for Public Library Service: an Experimental Program in Library Education for Work with a Specialized Clientele"? Throw that around a couple of times, you can kiss your readers goodbye.

There was movement—turmoil might be a better description—when we arrived on the High John scene late in November. But before we can tell it the way it is (or *was*), there's background, genealogy, to be filled in. Stay with us; we'll get back to the action soon.

High John is not really a poverty program, nor yet really a public library operation. It looks and feels like both, and in some degree, it is.

But what it is primarily, and in its motivation, is an experiment in library education and research. The program is operated, not by a public library, but by a library school, the School of Library and Information Services at the University of Maryland. And most of the money comes not from the Office of Economic Opportunity or out of the Library Services and Construction Act, but is awarded under Title II-B, the research section of the Higher Education Act.

Reprinted by permission from *Library Journal* 93: 147-155, January 15, 1968. Copyright © 1968, Reed Publishing, USA.

> **The Name**
> High John? Actually High John, the Conqueror, that is to say, High John de Conquer. A mythical morale officer for ante bellum slaves; an omnipresent dispenser of hope and humor; a sly fox of a man who with folksy wit and cool cunning could outwit Massa hands down—well, usually. "Ol' High John," they'd say, "wouldn't let this get him down, why I recall the time when Big John . . . " And the stories passed themselves around—and then were lost. A few yet, but most gone. Gone with the memory of High John de Conquer. Well, High John is still around.—*from "Jottings from High John," by Richard Moses,* D. C. Libraries, December 1967.

The project is the brainchild of Paul Wasserman, dean of the library school, and Mary Lee Bundy, associate professor on the school's faculty. On the project application Wasserman is listed as "initiator" and Bundy as one of the principal investigators (we'll get to the other one), but on this, as on many another Maryland idea or project, the two work as a nearly inseparable team.

If they have one principal mission, it is to find ways to initiate change in the library field. Service to deprived sectors of the community stood out like a sore thumb—an obvious example of the imperative need for change. Maryland's project application repeats the charge that library schools and library practice have been and continue to be middle class in their orientation and claims that "the profession simply does not have sufficient background and experience to reach other than traditional library users."

The public library is not likely to be able to break out of this mold, Wasserman and Bundy assert, "without the support of its educational programs. Yet, while the schools have stressed the community service commitment, this credit has not been backed by the prerequisite sociological and other disciplinary approaches."

Academic knowledge, however, is not enough, according to the Maryland duo. "If library education is effectively to bridge the gap between theory and practice, it must be prepared to experiment in the field and so provide its students with a laboratory in which to observe, to participate, to study, and to learn. Where no appropriate laboratory exists, it [the school] must create the laboratory in order to advance its educational purposes."

That is the nub of the High John idea, though Maryland points out that "the need is not confined to library service to the disadvantaged: it is a neglected ingredient essential to the advancement and reinvigoration of ever facet of library activity . . . In the main, library education has lagged [behind] rather than led practice. The present program, therefore, is viewed as an experiment in advancing education and research through the use of a field laboratory approach."

After the idea came the search for money, and the selling job wasn't easy. Wasserman waxes strong on this subject: "The Office of Education and OEO have gone around screaming for innovation, but just try to sell 'em a new idea . . . " Agency after agency he contacted lauded the idea but said, "It doesn't quite fit into our pattern." Try someone else was always the final advice. It gradually became clear that the project had to be sold under the umbrella either of professional training or research, or the university couldn't get into the poverty act. Wasserman bombed out on training funds but finally came up with research money under HEA Title 11-B. He asked for something over $176,000, actually got slightly less than half that—$88,000—for the first 18 months of the proposed three-year project.

Concurrently with the search for money, Maryland had to look for the talent capable of carrying through the laboratory, or practical, part of the project. For the research end, they already had Mary Lee Bundy, well equipped with relevant experience in research of public library problems. But it was clear that the project's chances of success rested heavily on finding someone with proven experience in library service in poverty areas and a proven willingness to experiment and initiate. The talent pool in this area was thinly stocked (which was one reason for the program), but Maryland got off to a marvelous start by landing Richard Moses of the Enoch Pratt Free Library and persuading him to leave his work in Baltimore's Community Action Program for the still nebulous High John experiment. Moses was to supervise the library work in the field and also join the school's faculty to teach a seminar in library service to the disadvantaged. He arrived on the scene when the federal money came through, in June 1967.

Hard on the heels of Dick Moses came R. Geraldine Hall, also from Pratt. Children's librarian, former teacher, an actress and singer, and full of bounce and talent, Gerry Hall was to be High John's librarian. The HJ arsenal began to look very strong.

Cooperation at local and state levels provided more financial strength. Prince George's County Memorial Library chipped in with about $20,000 for the first year. Half of this was LSCA money, approved by the State Division of Library Extension to cover Gerry Hall's salary. Another $7300 was for books, this money coming out of Maryland's Metropolitan Cooperating Libraries project. In addition, Prince George's County provided other "material" aid—maintenance staff, supplies, processing materials.

Finding a building in the Fairmount Heights community in which to locate the library/laboratory proved to be less difficult than might have been expected. There isn't too much terribly desirable property around in that area, but this fact had led an apparently socially-conscious builder, a year or two earlier, to attempt to upgrade the physical environment. He had built two new houses, but, failing to find investors for the project, had gone broke in the process. One house had been sold; the other, almost finished, had remained empty for some eight months. The university snapped up the latter on an 18-month lease, with an option to renew for another similar period. All Dick Moses then had to do was turn this nearly finished house into a library. All!

The only major missing element at this stage was the students who, along with the Fairmount Heights community, were to be the guinea-pigs for this social and educational experiment. There wasn't much time to round them up—a bare two months, in fact. This time pressure may account, in part, for what seemed to us like a serious lack of balance in the experimental student corps. There are 12 students in the project, only one of whom is male, and all of whom are lily-white.

Of the doughty dozen, eight are enrolled in the school's normal master's program, and one of their chosen courses is the class in Library Service to Unserved Communities, which also involves them in working four hours a week at the High John library. The other four students are appointed as research assistants. They get paid $2700 a year and their tuition is waived. In effect, this is for them a work-study program; they work 20 hours a week at High John, spend the other half of their time studying in the master's program.

The educational program for the project consists of three main elements: 1) the seminar in Library Service to the Disadvantaged, conducted by Moses; 2) a Research Methods Seminar, conducted by Mary Lee Bundy, as part of which each student has to design an independent research project closely related to the program and objectives of the demonstration project: and 3) an Independent Study seminar in which each student will pursue her research topic and develop it into "a fully drawn research report under faculty supervision." Dr. Bundy will also direct this seminar, together with senior faculty in the library school and other social science departments of the university.

Finally, evaluation is an important part of the Maryland project. A committee will review the work of the individual students and periodic reports on the laboratory program by Moses. It will also review critically a final report by the principal investigators (Bundy and Moses), "assessing the soundness and implications of the experiment for library education, research, and public library practice." This committee, which also acts as a general advisory group, includes the members of the library school's research committee (Wasserman, Bundy, and Laurence Heilprin, late of the Council on Library Resources), plus three others: Dr. Jennie McIntyre of the university's Department of Sociology and Anthropology; Jane Mathieu, director of Echo House in Baltimore, a social work center in a ghetto area; and William Lawrence, chief of evaluation and research in the Office of Economic Opportunity's Community Action Program. One item of interest here: Mr. Lawrence's wife is one of the students enrolled in the program!

Visit to High John

That's maybe enough background for openers. How was High John in the flesh? We visited the library on a beautiful Fall Monday afternoon, driving out there from the library school with Dick Moses in the High John van—new, painted a pale blue that matched the Fall sky, and with a bird chirping somewhere back in the brake linings. The van will be used not just for trucking staff back and forth between the university and High John, but also as a mobile film unit—something Moses experimented with in the Baltimore Community Action Project.

It wasn't hard to tell when we reached Fairmount Heights. We were near the city limits of Washington, D.C. Behind us were the pleasant suburbs, the open country, the jungle of parkways and interchanges. Just ahead was what passed for a main street and the local shopping center: decaying buildings on both sides of the street, broken windows, stores closed down and boarded up. A deprived neighborhood seemed an inadequate description.

We began to spot signs on telegraph poles on nearly every corner. Just "High John Library" and an arrow. The signs were the work, Moses told us, of Persis Darling, one of the students in the program and the wife of Richard Darling, supervisor of school library services in neighboring

Montgomery County, Maryland. When the signs were put on trees, they disappeared overnight. On telegraph poles they seemed to be invulnerable. Don't ask about the psychology.

The signs are needed. The library, a single-story house, is in a tree-shaded area up along one of the typical unpaved back streets. It stands there on its rather unkempt lot, clean and white, in a little better shape than some of the neighboring houses, but plain and unpretentious and friendly—far removed from one of the those institutional monsters of the Carnegie era. It *looks,* at least, an integral part of the community.

Up a couple of steps, open the front door, and you're in the living room, now the children's world of High John. Presiding over the scene, from his cage atop the pint-sized high shelves, is Chico, the half-moon parrot—a gift snagged by one of the students. Chico is colorful, lends a touch of the exotic to the room, and the hard-eyed stare of his beady eyes hints at the need for a touch of decorum, too.

A central feature of the room is the Book Box, an idea imported from the library rooms in Baltimore's neighborhood centers. It's a way of dealing with those big thin books that are the slithery bane of the bottom shelves in most children's libraries. Like a sandbox on dumpy legs, the Book Box is geared to the fun of untidiness, the books just dumped in, any old way, so that the kids can rumple through them as though it were a treasure dip. Like much else at High John, it's *supposed* to be casual, even vaguely messy. But kids are unpredictable; they keep straightening things up, putting the books into neat piles.

Next to the front room is what was probably intended by the builder to be a dining alcove. Room is too large a word for it. It's almost filled by a huge round table and four chairs. Deliberately crowded, cozy. The shelves around the table include a small reference collection and a miscellany of other things including all the "sex books" (Moses's term)—the books on dating, contraception, and all that. This, if anything, is the unorthodox equivalent of a young adult room in more formal library establishments. But there aren't any labels on the High John rooms. Nor any doors or barriers. Wander where you like—it's one library. The afternoon of our visit, the alcove filled up as soon as school was out. Kids jammed in, sitting, standing, doing homework, talking, just passing time—hats and books and the ever-present transistor radio, all over the table.

Beyond the alcove, what was probably the master bedroom, now the adult section of the library. Over in one corner, the magazines: *Sports Illustrated* and *Science News, Ebony,* but *Look* and *Life,* too; *Down Beat* and *Consumer's Reports; Ingenue* and *Jazz & Pop; Model Airplane News* and *McCall's; Ellery Queen's Mystery Magazine* and *U.S. News & World Report.* A kid got fascinated with something in *Model Airplane News,* thought he'd like to try his hand at making it. Take it home, the staff member said. "You *mean* it?" We remembered Lowell Martin's recent Deiches report on the Enoch Pratt's efforts to reach the disadvantaged, his warning that librarians stress books too much, tend to divide people into *book* readers and the great unwashed.

What about the books? Well, maybe it's time to reveal the great, unprofessional secret: there is no order, no rigid sequence to the High John shelves. No cataloging, no classification, no alphabetical-by-author bit. Perhaps what you might call a "reader-interest" arrangement. Shelves labeled "Around the House" (how-to-do-its, motor manuals, cook books); "Your Money's Worth" (*The Great Discount Delusion,* several Vance Packards, *The Intelligent Buyer and the Telltale Seller*); "Family Life" (Dr. Spock, Gesell & Ilg, smoking, alcoholism, first aid); "Science" (computer programming, electricity, heavy accent on biology). And over on the "Great People" shelves, Madame Curie and Dick Gregory, Gandhi, Eleanor Roosevelt and Lena Horne, Koufax and Willie Mays—integrated biography.

Much of the shelving looks as though it were intended for periodicals. But the tilted, bracket shelves hold books—face out, just like periodicals, so that the pictures and the color show, rather than spine out, with rows of type standing on its side. You don't get so many books on the shelves this way, but it may be a good way of getting them *off* the shelves—which *ought* to be the objective.

Paperbacks are everywhere, in every room, on wire revolving racks, on the shelves of former and now doorless closets. Book niches, Moses calls them. Arrangement? Again, indiscriminate, informal. Just like a popular bookstore.

We talked with Moses about the collection. It consists of about 4000 books and "probably won't get much larger than that," he says. "We send someone over to the Prince George's book selection room weekly," he said, and added that High John was already over its allotment. Most of the newer fiction is obtained from McNaughton and comes out of the materials budget under the federal grant.

We were impressed by the uniformly high quality of the adult fiction, and commented that it was probably of a better overall standard than some collections we had seen in more affluent areas. Moses agreed: "Even though the library's in a depressed area, you don't have to underestimate people's interest or capacity. Also, a library is a library is a library. Without Camus or Sartre, for example, it's not a library. We just tried to pick a fair cross-section of the fiction world."

Moses was to underline this philosophy in the seminar at the library school next day, saying to the students, "The library has no mission, no moral imperative, it is not on a literary crusade. We buy a sampling, as much as the budget will allow." He was highly critical of the decision, made by nearly every public library in the area, not to buy Norman Mailer's *Why Are We in Vietnam?*

"Fader's my boy," said Moses apropos the collection; he was referring to Daniel Fader's *Hooked on Books*. "I don't care what people read—books, magazines, comics, what all. The stuff we've tried to push in libraries is not related to some of these situations. Magazines, newspapers, are more immediate."

But isn't the magazine collection at High John a bit thin, we asked. The library had ordered about 55 subscriptions to magazines before opening, Moses said, "but this was the only major hold-up we had. The subscription agency just didn't come through. We had to go out and buy them off the newsstands the first couple of weeks."

But why just single-copy subscriptions, we asked. Isn't this another example of orthodox library thinking, going for range rather than depth? If the library is willing to circulate current magazines (and it is), why not more magazines and perhaps fewer books? Or even more copies of fewer magazines? Moses, acknowledging the point, said: "You know, it's hard to overcome orthodoxy. You're trained that way. Maybe we will have to up the magazine subs."

Next to the "adult" room is the messiest, most casual room of all. It serves as office-cum-workroom. Just a couple of desks, back-to-back, some more shelving, housing overflow and duplicate copies of books (here, as elsewhere, *Manchild* is *the* book), unpacked cartons on the floor. There is nothing to indicate that this is A Separate Place, a place for staff only. Kids wander in and out here, too. It's all part of the library scene.

Along the passage is the circulation area, just before you go out the back door. One small desk and a chair. Opposite, the paraphernalia that reveals the room's kitchen heritage: a stove, a sink, cupboards. It's the barest room in the building. But it's just where people go out; the place where the only mandatory bit of formal business (the charge-out) has to be done. High John uses a quaint circulation system, a kind of marriage of the Detroit and England's token charging systems. It seems to work—and nobody asks more than that of it.

Just to the right of the kitchen (and library) exit is the only imposing barrier in the whole building: a very solid-looking wooden door, intriguingly lettered, a foot or so from the floor—WOMEN. Moses explained that he'd had to find something solid for this spot—the entrance to the basement—to prevent break-ins to the library via the basement route. The source of the door was obvious from the lettering, but Moses didn't reveal which ladies' john had sacrificed its privacy for High John's security.

The basement is a story in itself. It still looks sort of bleak—and feels it. The heat's on but you wouldn't know it. Sinkage has opened up minor canyons in the walls; windows get kicked in with some frequency (one window had been replaced six or seven times in half as many weeks). But the basement is better than it was, thanks to the home-handyman, budget-saving efforts of Moses and Tim Huston (the sole male among the students and therefore the natural recruit as laborer). At the insistence of the fire marshal, they bought sheet rock, lugged it across town in the High John van, and set about lining the basement and enclosing the furnace with it. They worked with tin cans strapped to their feet, so they could reach the ceiling. There are nails galore in some pieces of that sheet rock—the parts they put up before they found how to locate joists they couldn't see. Shirtsleeves librarianship. But it saved money—and time.

Part of the basement story, too, is the saga of the missing hammers. Nine went astray—lost, stolen, or broken—before the project was completed. Hammers seem to circulate at High John almost as well as books.

The basement will be used for a variety of purposes, not all of them perhaps thought of yet. One idea is a teen canteen in the afternoons, but the kids have to persuade some of the community's adults to get together and run it. There may be more tables down there for homework. Perhaps music, or movies, or games. All are possible ... but not rolling yet.

The principal factor about High John is its looseness, its sense of ease. It tries hard to be as much home as library. Wall-to-wall carpeting helps—dark blue-green, in nearly every room. (The library school librarian commented ruefully on the absence of this feature in her library at the university.) A campy Danish lampshade lends warmth to the kids' room. And there are other nice touches, like a couple of attractive Cézanne and Manet prints in the passage (they can he borrowed, too, just like the books), donated by two of the students in the program. And then there are the signs. "No Escalation," says one, as succinct a disciplinary notice as we've seen in any institution. "Read a Hundred Books, Get an Alligator Free," says another. This was Tim's idea, and he means it. A *live* alligator. One kid is racing for it; he's read nine books in the last couple of weeks.

The looseness, the ease, extends beyond the physical facilities—to the routines and regulations. The circulation system is part of it; the tokens each reader holds give him a sense of ownership—each one's worth a book, any time. And there are no fines, the element that has brought some other promising outreach efforts to a near standstill. "Fines don't get the books back anyway," says Moses, "but they can keep the kids away." High John circulates books for two weeks, but doesn't send overdues. Of 250 books circulated on opening night in October, about 40 were not back four weeks later. Gerry Hall seemed pleased with the percentage. No one had checked until we asked. "If they don't come back soon," Moses said, "we'll go around door-to-door and get 'em. Not demanding, but simply asking people why *they* haven't come back."

It's as easy to join High John as to use it. Anyone can join. Yes, *anyone*. No geographical barriers. And no identification required. A new borrower can take out a book immediately. His borrower's card is mailed to his home. "If he gets it, that's enough identification for us," Moses says.

Is it true, we asked, that the library has been used to date almost exclusively by children and teenagers? Was this expected? Was this the reason that a children's librarian (Gerry Hall) had been chosen as High John's librarian? Moses looked surprised at the latter question. "We asked several people before Gerry," he said. "and not one of them was a children's librarian. It was only after Gerry accepted that it occurred to me that she *was* a children's librarian—and that this was just what we needed." He confessed to his own weakness in this area, for example in the selection of children's books. "Gerry filled that gap beautifully," he said.

The answers to our questions on use of the library by adults, or about circulation of adult versus children's books, were typical of High John's "looseness." There were estimates—"a few" adults used the library, "two or three" regularly came in during the evening—but loose estimates they were. During the several hours we were at the library (in the afternoon) we saw only one woman, a mother who had brought her children to the library. Most of the "few" adults who have begun to use the library are women.

Again, on circulation, the library could only estimate how many of the books borrowed were adult books. The estimate was ten to 15 percent, "maybe 20 percent." But the circulation records produce no figures of this kind, no breakdown. All the bookcards are the same, for both adult and children's books. "Our clericals can't tell," said Moses. "We'll have to change this in order to produce some facts instead of feelings."

The Classroom Scene

The operation of the High John library, is, of course, only part of the Maryland project. Let us flash over, for a change of pace, to the other—library school—side of things.

We spent our second day at the university, knowing that Moses held his seminar regularly on Tuesday afternoons. The morning was taken up with interviews—with Moses, Wasserman, Bundy. We wanted also to interview some of the students in the program, but with one exception (more a corridor captive than a volunteer) the students refused to talk to us. We were to discover why as the day went on.

At the seminar, after a few opening announcements, Moses took up the issue which had been discussed the previous week and which continued to bother, confuse, and worry the students: the matter of discipline and the keeping of order at High John.

"How do we operate the premises?" said Moses. "Democratically. That means freedom with responsibility. Anyone can do anything he wants in the library, as long as he doesn't interfere with anyone else's freedom. That's about as close to a rule as we can get. From here we have to play it ear."

It clearly wasn't anywhere near enough of a rule to satisfy some of the students. Things had been pretty rough on occasion during High John's first few weeks. Windows had been broken repeatedly; there had been looting, purses stolen, and equipment of various kinds taken (but not books); and youngsters now and then had cut up a bit, probably to test the atmosphere and the capability of the people controlling it. Some of the girls had already refused to work nights, or had asked for more people to be on duty at night for the sake of security. The one student we did interview said: "I *was* scared at first. We were robbed at the beginning. But I think it's all right now—as long as people are prepared and protected." This, plus some dire warnings from a local detective about the fantastic dangers of the area at night, had led to a cutback in the evening hours. High John now closes at 8 P.M. instead of nine.

One of the students in the seminar said: "We were there the other night. Some of the kids kept turning out the lights on us. All we could do all evening was guard the switches. That isn't librarianship." She complained also that the relaxed tone and absence of rules established by Moses and Gerry Hall didn't always work for the students. "What you do," she said to Moses. "is not what I'd do. I can't react the way you do

... If I start reading a story, it doesn't work. And I can't throw a kid out of the library the way you or Gerry do. I just can't do it." It had already become a matter of legend among the students that the week before, slim Gerry Hall had taken an unruly and very large six-foot teenager by the scruff of the neck and had thrown him out the door. Few of the students could picture themselves in the role of bouncer.

"Discipline," said Moses, "is a form of love. You have to see it that way. You must. It means caring. This is part of the problem. Nobody has cared about some of these kids enough to discipline them. And remember, these children have not led our sheltered lives. They're older than us, some of them, and they've been talked to or shouted at, harshly as often as not, all of their lives. You have to be firm without being harsh, establish some sort of tone. If you do, nobody's going to go off and sulk."

Gerry Hall acknowledged that it was harder to maintain order with relaxed rules. "You're always near the edge, close to an explosive situation. But it has to be done."

Another student complained that "We confront them with the usual library attitudes—Read or get out," and started another useful discussion. Moses summed up: "We can't allow the library to become a recreation center. We're a library. We don't need silence, but we have to have a certain degree of quiet. But nor does everyone have to be reading all the time."

It was evident that one of the greatest problems the students were facing was adjustment, both to the flexibility initiated by Moses and to a community that wasn't just dying to take books off the shelves. The slow, frustrating period in which the important task was merely making contact and building confidence didn't seem at all like librarianship to many of them. Some were clearly suffering from cultural shock.

We began to realize why the students had earlier refused to talk to us. On the one hand, they were fantastically loyal to the project, to Moses and Gerry Hall; on the other, they were full of doubts, fears, and frustrations. And they were afraid that we would open them up on the latter without understanding their hopes and real desires that the project would succeed.

It was not the discipline problem alone that made them uneasy, but also the fact that they had been thrown so early into the deep end of the pool and left to swim alone. One of them asked Moses: "What are your roles in this project—you and Gerry? Are you librarians or administrators?"

The question wasn't as naive as it sounds on paper. Moses and Hall have increasingly become administrators and teachers; they spend less and less time at the service end. Moses admitted this; even indicated it had been, in some degree. deliberate: "Gerry and I have pulled out of this situation as soon as we could—some of you think, too soon. But until you have the load on you, you haven't begun to adjust to the situation." He admitted also: "We didn't adequately prepare you. But we weren't sure, either, what you were going to meet, or what you'd need to meet it."

If this left the students less than reassured, they may have derived some comfort and inspiration from the invited speaker of the afternoon, Jane Mathieu of the Echo House Program—"a coordinated human resources program working with low income families in West Baltimore." She talked, not just about the achievements since she started this program three years before, but also about the frustrations, chaos, dangers, and disappointments. It was Balzac-real, but every word glistened with dedication and genuine enthusiasm. For the students, perhaps, Jane Mathieu herself was the object lesson: here was a young woman, very attractive, who certainly didn't physically outweigh any of them, who had been through all they were worrying about (and much more) and had emerged, not merely unharmed, but obviously inspired by the worth of what she was doing.

Miss Mathieu began by criticizing much of the discussion which had preceded her talk. All this stuff, she said, about librarians and libraries, and what they should be, was beside the point. The same problems of the balance between progressive and traditional approaches, the same fears and uncertainties, faced anyone—be he lawyer or social worker or librarian—who set out to reach these traditionally neglected areas of society. "The only basic thing is your approach to people." Moses accepted the reprimand for the irrelevance of the discussion he had led, nodded silent agreement with his invited speaker.

"Some of your short-term goals," Miss Mathieu advised the students, "may be totally unrelated to your long-term goal. For a while, High John may not seem to be anything like a library. But you may have to do a great many nonlibrary things before you can *get* a library, or a response to it as a library. Echo House was nothing but an idea for six months. No one knew what it was, including me. But it worked to do things slowly." Four weeks (the time that High John had been in operation), she seemed to be saying to the students, is not forever. And frustrations will last longer yet.

Guinea-pigs?

We went to investigate this project equipped with some doubts and questions of our own. The major one concerned the community which is one of the integral elements of the program. Were the people of Fairmount Heights being used as guinea-pigs for an educational experiment? Did anyone have *their* long-term interests at heart? What happened to them, and to their expectations, at the end of High John's three-year federal support? Was this to be another example of hope offered, only to be abruptly withdrawn—the kind of build-up and let-down that Negro communities and individuals have suffered too often! We discussed this, first with Wasserman and Bundy, later with Moses.

The academic pair recognized the problem, but one really couldn't feel that they gave it much priority. Their primary interest is not in the community but in what relevance libraries have in such situations, in what they can find out about the preparation of future librarians for service to deprived areas. As Wasserman puts it: "What the hell are libraries doing out there? Can we do anything for people who need help? Or are we reaching only the white Negroes—the ones who are after the usual middle class values represented by schools and libraries? Is library service meaningful or irrelevant in terms of the real needs?"

Both Wasserman and Bundy clearly *hoped* that something permanent might emerge in Fairmount Heights as a result of the High John project. But they also seemed to feel that if it didn't—if library service just ended—the community would have had *something* for three years, and would be no worse off at the end than it had been at the beginning. We pointed to the theory that some of the worst riots maybe occurred in places where hope had been offered but not fulfilled (as in Detroit), rather than in places (like Alabama) where hope had hardly ever poked its head above ground.

Well, sure, was the response, but if you're going to try something completely new, if you're shooting for change, you've got to take risks. "We're taking risks with the careers of Dick Moses and Gerry Hall," said Wasserman, "and with the students we've plunged into this project." We allowed that he had a right to take risks with people who volunteered for or were employed by the project, but continued to question the ethics of taking risks with a community for which the university held no public responsibility.

Wasserman, of course, is himself taking some pretty gigantic risks. If the High John project were to explode in some public or personal disaster, the only body which could be held responsible would be the University of Maryland—and that presumably means Wasserman's personal head. But he is fervent about the idea that the universities "*ought* to assume more public responsibilities. Why shouldn't universities be worrying about this rat business? Too many of our best brains may be concentrating on the wrong problems, involved only in abstractions. The university has been too disengaged, too detached. It belongs in this kind of social effort. And certainly a professional school has a commitment."

The problem of the community's library future loomed somewhat larger in the mind and plans of Dick Moses. He told us that Gardner Soule, recently appointed assistant director of the Prince George's County Library, had already submitted a proposal for a model Neighborhood Library Center in the Fairmount Heights area and the county was seeking funds to finance it. But this might take two or three years, and in the meantime Moses was exploring other possibilities.

First, he said, he was trying to build a Library Council in the area, made up solely of residents. Its first meeting was expected to take place in December. "I want to involve them," said Moses, "to the extent that they know their way around the library business, to give them potential power, so that they know how to go about *demanding* that Prince George's continue or give them better service."

Another possibility, he said, is that High John might be continued as an experimental library, run cooperatively by the county and the library school, in as independent a manner as now. In other words, Moses said, it might continue as a workbench, rather than a standard library operation.

We had questions, too, about High John's relationships—with other libraries, for example. High John operates so loosely that we wondered whether any of its users who might sometime use other (even neighboring) libraries wouldn't run into conditions and regulations they hadn't been led to expect.

Moses didn't see this as much of a problem. Prince George's County Library, like High John, for example, doesn't have fines—which was a surprise to us. Its circulation system is also not much different in essence, Moses said, though photochargers are used. "We've tried to simplify everything, but to stay as close to Prince George's as possible." He indicated that he was going to use the High John van to take patrons on trips to other PG libraries, so that they could see that High John is not the only kind of library. Moses mentioned specifically the Oxon Hill branch of the county library, which has a Sojourner Truth Room (a small equivalent of the New York Public Library's Schomburg collection on the Negro), as one place to visit. "We're very conscious," he said, "of trying not to set up a *separate* library system."

What about community involvement in High John, relations with other community agencies? "We haven't solicited community involvement much yet," Moses admitted, "but there's been a good deal, nevertheless." He has talked, for example, with local community action workers, and about a dozen of them have volunteered to help out with anything the library needs. The library also employs three teenagers from the community as clerical workers, to run the circulation desk, etc., and pays them at the same rate as the student assistants. Moses has also been to see the Mayor of Fairmount Heights—"a good way to make contact is to go and ask for favors"—and has already visited all the elementary schools in the area and met the principals.

One of the projects at High John, also, is to start a community information clearinghouse. Moses talked about a directory of local information sources compiled by the Sun newspapers in Baltimore, based on questions asked by the public and the answers given by the papers. High John had taken this directory and adapted it to local use, adding to it by clipping local and county papers. "We try to keep up-to-date on what's going on in the whole county," he said.

But the thing doesn't begin and end with a card file. Moses added. "We contact the various agencies ourselves and strive to get positive answers. We try to establish a *person* in a particular agency who might have the answer needed by one of our patrons. If you just give someone an agency or an institution to call, they're liable to run into another bureaucratic dead-end—and then they never come back."

We asked about relations with the police. "We told them before we moved in," Moses said, "and they've been good. There are two lots of cops—county and local—and they stop by frequently. We had them over to investigate when we had the heavy looting. And we've called them in once or twice of an evening when things seemed to be getting out of hand ... but it was always better by the time they arrived."

"The fewer times you have to involve the cops on business, the better," Moses advised. "But they should be in on what's happening."

Publicity has been somewhat low-geared in the early weeks of the experiment. "We're still riding on pre-opening publicity," Moses said at the time of our visit. For that campaign the students produced 100 posters, put them up in every available open window in the area. And they got out

1000 hand bills and delivered them personally, door to door, to every house in the neighborhood. Press releases were sent to every newspaper, radio and TV station in the area. "The *Washington Post* did a story and ran a lousy picture. But the *Afro-American* didn't even run it," Moses said. The tone was one of faint disgust. One problem with the public relations and publicity is that two agencies are handling it—the county and the university—without much coordination. "I can't stress the importance of PR enough," Moses said, then added, almost as an afterthought: "There's a billboard near the library. I think we have to look into that."

The Students

Let's get back to the students, we suggested. Are they really getting any training in anything other than the public service aspects of librarianship in a deprived area? How much are they involved in the administrative or political problems of library service in a situation like this? The truth seems to be that most of what the students get in this area has to be derived from the standard course offerings of the library school. "But we do try to get them involved when decisions have to be made," Moses claims.

The students—or at least the 20-hour people (the research assistants)—do get involved in book selection. One of the four is given the responsibility each quarter, goes over to county headquarters regularly to select books, and then comes back to discuss the decisions with the other students and staff members. As far as paperbacks are concerned, said Moses, "we just shop for them. The students go out and pick them up at a local distributor's as needed."

Each of the students, of course, also is responsible for developing her own project within the overall High John framework. Moses told us about a few of these. "Don't come to me with ideas," he tells the students, "but with plans." Two students are working on a pre-school story hour program—one from the children's side, the other involving the mothers. Another is working on an extension program to clinics, shut-ins, etc. Yet another is responsible for developing the community information services program, together with a pamphlet file; two more are planning teenage film programs; one wants to start a girls' club. And Tim Huston, the lone male, is special events man. He's already written to Cassius Clay and to some of the Washington Redskins, inviting them to High John, and he wants to do a balloon ascension in the Spring as a promotional device. "He's crazy, man," says Moses, "but full of ideas."

Mary Lee Bundy, at this stage, is looking for information, both from the students and from Moses and Hall. She wants to know about the library's *impact* on the community, what kinds of people are making use of it, and for what purposes. "I want," she said, "to open up the 'why' question of research. My commitment is to the students, to see that they get a research experience out of all this." She has asked the students—and staff—to keep daily diaries. "Be factual, observe things," she tells them, "but have an attitude, an opinion, a reaction to what you see." When we were there, four weeks after High John's opening, Bundy had still not seen any of the diaries. And it must be said that, whatever other kind of experiences the students were having, research did not seem to be much of a part of it to that point.

If there is a central problem in the High John project, it may be in this area—the schism between the practical and the academic ends of the program. It is really not surprising that it should be so. The service end of the operation works as well as it does, is as alive and exciting as it is, because of the kind of people Wasserman hired for it. Dick Moses and Gerry Hall are people-oriented (to use an academic term). They work off-the-cuff, reacting to situations as they come up. And this is just what is needed. But it doesn't produce the kind of potential research information that Bundy wants and needs to give the other end of the educational program any real foundation.

The students, it seemed to us, may wind up in the middle, more than ever confused as they are tugged in opposite directions by these contrasting forces. The experiment's success will rest very heavily on the ability of Moses and Bundy to marry their objectives—something that may be much more difficult than it sounds. It did not seem to be happening while we were at High John.

This report, while lengthy, is undoubtedly far from complete. And if it is rambling, inconclusive, imperfect in its understanding of all that is happening in this Maryland program, it may, at least partly, be because the High John project is itself still groping, rambling, and inconclusive.

Nevertheless, the Maryland experiment is an inspiring try to do something that needs to be done: to find out more about the library's function in deprived areas, and to determine what the library school's role is in preparing librarians for this and other neglected areas of service. It occurred to us that one thing the Maryland team may discover is that the training is less fundamentally important than the initial selection of people for this kind of service.

In any event, we hope fervently that this project has some measure of success, certainly in changing the tenor and tone of library education. We shall go back and take another look at High John after the project has had more time to settle down and find a direction.

A Conspiracy Against the Laity?

Let's begin with a professional roll call. Sir Laurence Olivier and Rock Hudson—both professional actors. Saul Bellow and Irving Wallace—both professional novelists. Walter Lippmann and Walter Winchell—both professional columnists.

So? . . . What possible relevance can these apparently absurd variations on the odd-couple theme have for librarians gathered together to tackle that alliterative triangle: Preparation, Professionalism, Productivity? Just to preserve a modicum of suspense, I'll save the answer to my rhetorical question for a bit.

Six months ago, I received a small slip of paper bearing these three key words (a 3-P-slip, I suppose one might call it), plus a statement presumably intended to reveal their deeper significance. One thing about this small document (and perhaps the only one) could be discerned with immediate and absolute certainty: it was clearly the product of a committee. Now, if one has any inherent charity in his soul at all, one learns over the years to be charitable about committee products, and discards heady expectations of inspiration and creativity. In this case, faced with such a theme, all one could do was give the most serious consideration to formulating something which might conceivably be of interest and then see whether, by some devious device, it could be squeezed under such a weatherbeaten umbrella.

The trick with a theme is to find some part of it that speaks to one's own concerns, experience and understanding. And if one cannot see the trees for the wood, one resorts (like a good librarian should) either to the analytic process or to the more mundane operation of weeding. *Preparation*, I decided, was the easiest element to discard. All life, all experience, is preparation—for whatever it is that you are or are doing. And such a

---

Originally a paper delivered at the Texas Library Association Conference, Houston, March 29, 1969, this article is reprinted by permission from *Texas Library Journal* 45: 61-72, Summer 1969.

profoundly philosophic thought can only be treated at book length or proclaimed in that one simple, declarative sentence. The first of these alternatives is impractical and the masochism of conference-goers is such that, given a simple one-sentence speech, they would feel cheated rather than released.

Productivity also presented an easy decision; it went into the out basket one day when I took a look at my sons, towering over me now like the lean skyscrapers of New York over one of the old brownstones. Productivity, at least the best kind, was clearly something with which I had not had direct experience for quite some time. To talk on a subject where you have to rely more on memory than recent experience is risky; memory is a fragile tool, constructed more often of romanticism than hard fact.

But *Professionalism*—there was a fish of a distinctly different odor. No doubt about that one speaking directly to my own concerns, my own experience. I had been, or believed I had been, a professional librarian for a dozen or more years in Britain, but it took only five days at sea and a landing on the shores of North America for that professionalism to become apparently invisible. In Britain one can spot a man carrying home his fish and chips because they always come wrapped in recognizable newsprint—the *News of the World* preferably; it has a flavor all its own! So it was, I discovered in America, with professionalism. If it didn't come wrapped in precisely the right kind of paper, it had to be something other than the real thing, a counterfeit, a pretense.

In my case the outer wrapping was fairly solid; very few people questioned the validity of my library education and qualifications, or my library experience. What was missing was the regulation inner lining, that union ticket of the white collar class, the university degree. I was at first surprised and chagrined to find such total non-acceptance of the possibility of education by other than the formal route, particularly on the part of the faculty of the traditional "university of the people." But I was to learn, as time went by, that such inflexibility is born not so much out of a devout faith in the formal educational system as it is a symptom of insecurity and nervousness about status.

I was to learn also that it didn't much matter *which* part of the wrapping or trappings of professionalism was missing; it was as black and white as a chessboard, a case of all or nothing. Only last year I witnessed Canadian librarians working themselves into a lather over the appointment of Guy Sylvestre as their National Librarian. Now M. Sylvestre is a cultured, experienced man: a former Associate Parliamentary Librarian, an unquestioned scholar, a man of considerable education (*he* has several degrees), and a man with good experience and contacts at the federal level (which one might think would be useful for a national librarian). Nevertheless, Sylvestre became a whipping boy because he had committed a major sin of omission: at some point in his career he had neglected to spend the "required" one year of incarceration in a library school, even an unaccredited one.

These Canadian capers, of course, were a re-run, with unsubtle variations, of a farce played out thirty years earlier by American librarians when a fine scholar-poet, Archibald MacLeish, was appointed Librarian of Congress. Such asinine public spectacles as two national professional associations mounted in these instances seem to me to do little for our professional prestige. And conversely, I think it might be difficult to demonstrate that other holders of high office in the world of librarianship who have brought to such offices the outward trappings of professionalism have necessarily also brought more status and prestige to our profession than did the appointment of MacLeish as Librarian of Congress. It's worth noting that when he left LC, the staff expressed "their admiration for an inspiring administrator; their continuing loyalty to the sustained and penetrating vision which has given *new meaning* to librarianship, to the high purpose, to the relentless drive towards accomplishment, and to the integral humanism of his insistence upon the participation of libraries in the processes of democracy and civilization and the liberation of the human spirit."[1]

Interpretations of Professionalism

During the years of my editorship of *Library Journal* I discovered yet other curious interpretations of professionalism. I never too much minded the correspondents who suggested I was an idiot, or ignorant, or insane, or just plain wrong. In such cases I used that classic stopper devised by H. L. Mencken for dealing with the irate correspondent, a brief letter that read: "Dear Sir, or Madam, as the case may be: You may very well be right. Yours sincerely . . ." The ones who bothered me were the people who were constantly insisting that it wasn't *proper* for a professional magazine to do this thing or that. I am prepared to admit that my view of the boundaries of professional propriety and legitimacy may be fairly broad, but I cannot help regarding some of the prodigiously varied taboos erected by some *LJ* readers as little short of quaint.

To give you a few samples: It is not, apparently, even in the nudie sixties, permissible to publish, in a "professional" magazine, a picture of a librarian, male or female, in a bathing suit. Nor, to take a different kind of example, is it enough to review the substance and style of a book; one must include specifics about the word on page 213 or the sentence on page 164 so that the "professional" will, without reading or glancing at the book, be fully prepared to deal with the certain convulsions of the local Mrs. Grundy. Further, it is a severe breach of professional etiquette to tell the truth about an unpleasant or difficult situation, especially when such truth reveals a librarian or library in a poor light (leave that to the newspapers and scandal sheets, we only want to hear good of ourselves). Similarly, it is OK to report pure fiction in the form of rosy predictions for some yet untested and unlaunched library project, system, or development, but it is very bad form to report the often poor results, and sometimes the failures, from which, incidentally, we might learn much more than from those inspiring but unfounded advance trumpetings. And, worst crime of all, no decent professional publication ever discusses, let alone advocates (horrors!), a political position or a public stance on a major social issue. (My editorials on Goldwater and, later, Vietnam, incited more angry letters, I believe, than maybe all of our library periodicals have received about everything they have published in a decade.)

All this brings me to the sticky part—and I do not like having to say what I am going to say because it sounds ungracious to those who invited me (and I have had a wonderful time and great hospitality from many good friends, old and new). But I don't know how else to relate, without equivocation, to your conference theme. I have been talking thus far about limitations or distortions in our thinking about professionalism and what it is made up of. Limitations just as serious, if not quite of the same kind, are inherent in that question in the conference theme statement: "What are the hallmarks of the professional which can be quantified, data processed, and measured on the scale of productivity?" That, ladies and gentlemen, is an awful question—and in a way an insulting one. If we are really so far from understanding the important elements of professionalism that we believe we can find answers only by feeding raw data into a computer or by drawing complicated graphs and flow charts, we are in worse trouble than even some of the evidence suggests. If you haven't grasped the full ramifications of that question, let me refer you to an article in the January issue of *Special Libraries* entitled "Large Scale Data Banks: Will People Be Treated as Machines?" The author, Dr. Maron, who is associate director of the Institute of Library Research at Berkeley, says:

> ... the basic notion of automatic selection; that is, of being able to write a computer program (no matter how carefully it is conceived) to select people by some general set of specifications, suggests that people will not be considered as individuals. ... the notion of selecting people for some nontrivial purpose according to any general rule, masks the notion of *relevant* individual differences. It implies that most individual differences are irrelevant. Thus it contradicts the basic notion that each person is an individual.[2]

And now, before we get deeper into more obviously "professional" matters, let's take that promised look back at our three odd couples. Remember who they are: Olivier and Rock Hudson; Bellow and Irving Wallace; Lippmann and Winchell. If we measure them on the scale of productivity, unless you slip some cute qualitative measures in with the quantitative, I think it is probable that the parties of the second part (Hudson, Wallace, and Winchell) would come out well ahead. Take another measure, financial reward (which, in some of the library field's manpower discussions, has been linked much too closely to recognition of status), and again I think it is likely that the second person in each pair will have the edge. And even on the basis of a third measure—public recognition—I believe it is possible that the parties of the second part will be better known to more people than their partners in these pairings.

Yet, asked which person in each of these pairs is the more professional, I doubt that many people in this room would give me other than the parties of the first part (Olivier, Bellow, Lippmann). Some of us might reach that judgment, however, for the wrong reasons; for example, the simple verdict that the first named person in each pair is better at his craft than the second. This is not only too easy an answer, it is too supercilious a conclusion. Better and more professional are by no means synonymous.

Personal Commitment

The essential difference, I feel, is not that Olivier is a *better* actor than Hudson, or Bellow a better novelist than Wallace, but that there is about each of the first parties in these pairings a sense of personal commitment which is clearly not present, at least in the same degree, in their partners. Olivier, for example, is clearly concerned with the potential of the theater to illuminate man's understanding of himself, with the theater's potential humanizing influence in a world which needs it desperately. Rock Hudson, on the other hand, exhibits in his work little concern for anything more worthwhile than pursuing Doris Day, movie after movie, in a vain effort to get that all-American, middle-aged virgin to bed. And while Bellow digs ever deeper into the soul and mind of man, Wallace merely continues his careful scrutiny of the genital area. Each of the first named individuals, in short, is concerned with the condition of man, and with using his talents, his discipline, his professionalism to better it if he can, or at least to explain it sufficiently so that man might try bettering it for himself.

Each of the first parties, too, grows and develops and changes over the years; the impact of continuous self-education is evident in their work. The others continue, year after year, to do their thing in an apparently routine manner—perhaps with great skill, but routinely nevertheless. Somehow you know that if Irving Wallace took a stab at a modern version of "The Song of Solomon" it would come out looking like a verse rendering of *The Chapman Report*. Each time Olivier does Shakespeare, on the other hand, he brings something new to it, something to add to the Bard's wisdom, and to our understanding of it. All six of these people know the "how" of their disciplines; what distinguishes the first-named in each pair, and makes him the more professional, is that at every stage of his development he asks—of himself and others—*why*, what is my purpose? It is in the why that creativity and growth lie; without it the skills atrophy, become meaningless, routine.

I have taken this apparent sidetrack because too often in these gatherings we tend to get too emotional when discussing ourselves and our own profession, particularly when someone waxes critical. Facts or theories we can easily accept about other people and professions have a habit of turning sour in the mouth when applied to ourselves. But we have to risk that, so let's turn to librarianship and professionalism, remembering the elements that separate our odd couples: commitment, dedication, a concern for the condition of man; personal growth and change through continuing education; the search for creativity through understanding of purpose.

All of these factors may be present in varying degree, but they are not exactly the first things we see when we examine professionalism in libraries. I remember the head of my library school, long ago, declaring that 70 percent of all the functions performed in a library could be carried out by fairly intelligent horses (he was, I think, a Swift fan—Jonathan, that is, not Tom!). We seem to have had a desperately hard time trying to distinguish which is the significant ("professional"?) 30 percent of the operation. Many have been the committee or other group assaults on the intellectual problem of separating professional and nonprofessional functions in libraries, but no one, witnessing the latest skirmishes over library technicians, could seriously suggest that this surgical operation has yet been satisfactorily performed.

Archibald MacLeish, as a recent article notes,

> deplored that some of those who had tried to put librarianship on a professional basis, "began not with the inward function of librarianship but with the outward furniture of professionalism— the professional schools, the professional terms, and the professional privileges." To arrive at a meaningful definition, he believed, called for a reconsideration "which cuts beneath all this to the essentials of our work and our lives."[3]

Philosophical Uncertainties

Even when we descend from the lofty heights of over-all purpose to specific parts of the library operation, we find definition still toppling under the weight of philosophical uncertainty. Ask most librarians, for example, for a short list of clearly professional tasks and it is a certainty that some of the most devout and strenuous responses will rank book selection high among the Olympian functions of librarianship. Yet, in many academic institutions, the major responsibility for book selection has rested for years not in the hands of librarians but with the faculty.

And now that there is something of a swing away from this inefficient process, the librarians are again handing on much of the responsibility— this time to booksellers, jobbers, or other suppliers under blanket order programs. What is so professional about the librarian's role in either of these situations?

Reference librarianship is another area generally considered with due reverence as one of the havens of the higher professionalism. But how many reference librarians do you know who while away many of their hours in the mechanical processes of interlibrary loan? Isn't this, again, work that in general could be done by any intelligent, trained clerk?

High also among the professional holies is cataloging, that great inner mystique of the library trade which is really little more than a bastard child of a superior science, bibliography. (Certainly, the evidence is conclusive that admission to the ranks of the great bibliographers is not confined to those who come armed with a library degree.) The Library of Congress, the world's greatest cataloging operation, as it has enormously expanded this enterprise with the NPAC program and others, has found it totally impossible to fill its cataloging ranks from the "professional" pool. For one thing, fewer and fewer of today's entrants to librarianship want to be catalogers; for another, few of the libraries which join the common chorus celebrating cooperation are willing to relinquish part of their cataloging manpower in the interest of getting this job done once and for all and for everybody. LC's solution, in the circumstances, is interesting: it moves more and more toward a policy of hiring people with the language and subject competence to handle the great and complex variety of materials coming through its doors, and then teaches them to catalog. Doesn't this make sense? Which, after all, is the more valuable asset—and the more difficult to acquire: the language and subject knowledge, or the rules and skills of cataloging? And which, if we're honest about it, are the more professional of these attributes?

Rugged Stupidity

Technical services operations, nevertheless, remain the greatest single source of waste of professional manpower in libraries. I remember, a few years ago, analyzing some statistics and then writing an editorial which pointed out that 44.4 percent of all professional librarians in Canadian academic libraries were working in technical services and that 38.2 percent of the total wages and salaries bill in these libraries went into these operations.[4] Incidentally, I used Canadian figures not for the purpose of condemning my old friends north of the border but because I couldn't find relevant American statistics. Figures like these indicate the enormous price we continue to pay for what we like to call "rugged individualism." To any cost-conscious administrator it has to look more like rugged stupidity. No wonder that Neal Harlow, among others, talks about "wildly wasteful employment of professional staff."[5]

Narrow Points of View

Worse than these contradictions between our pieties and our practices, however, is another development which may have grown partly out of our increasing affluence and size, and partly from our greater concern about structure and resources (though the latter needs to be qualified) than about service. We seem to have had our eyes glued almost exclusively on the machinery of librarianship: the haphazard application of evolving technology to circulation and registration procedures; the evaluation of book truck casters and newspaper sticks; the nebulous theories of networks; and the building of systems on dubious and unresearched principles.

Convinced that "cooperation is the road to salvation," for example, we have spent much time and effort constructing cooperative systems whose shaky geographical and political underpinnings are already beginning to show signs of decay. A few of the structures which are beginning to come apart at the seams have been noted in *Library Journal*—in the interests of brevity I refer you only, for a few recent samples, to the news pages of a recent issue.[6] What is strange is that while we profess to find some mysterious virtue in a tenuous link between public libraries hundreds of miles apart or college libraries spread out around a state, we have done singularly little to break down those seemingly impenetrable barriers between libraries in the same community. As Emerson Greenaway says: "We are so compartmentalized in our thinking of problems by *types* of libraries that we forget library service as a whole and for the total population. The years of struggle to develop and improve the school library, the college library, the special library, and the public library have led to parochial and narrow points of view."[7]

Middle Class Services

Many of our city libraries, the oldest of our big library systems, have moved steadily for several decades in the direction of larger regional branches and toward a lessening of the number of local service points. Only now are they beginning to discover that they may have bought our own professional propaganda without sufficient evidence. And so we find Lowell Martin, in one of the Deiches Fund studies dealing with the problems of service to the disadvantaged, advising one of our most prestigious institutions, the Enoch Pratt Free Library, that it "should carefully reconsider its policy of moving toward a few large branch libraries in the inner city."[8]

While the city libraries have gradually become aware of that formerly invisible population which is now known by such slogan names as the underprivileged, the disadvantaged, the under-educated, much of what we offer to these people who may need service more than our traditional patrons still takes the form of special projects and experiments rather than basic, continuing service. We seem to have reached the doubtful logic that continuance of our old, traditional, essentially middle-class services is a "normal" library function, properly financed out of city funds, while service to the poor is something special, only to be undertaken if one can get a federal or state grant to do it. This, too, is a form of discrimination, and it is one reason why the kind of intense pressure now being exerted upon the cities to decentralize those monolithic school systems will in time move in on the public libraries. This pressure has already begun in a small way in some cities, though it hasn't worked up a full head of steam yet.

Publications Explosion

I mentioned resources as another of our hang-ups. We have been a bit bedazzled, I think, by all the talk of a publications explosion and have not examined nearly critically enough whether this explosion, like most I have ever seen, has produced mostly a lot of garbage. Our simple conclusion, rather, seems to have been that the library which doesn't make the million-volume club hasn't much of a chance in this publication-saturated world. A prime example of this thinking is the academic library. Many of them begin to look like costly pyramids built by pack-rats who worship so blindly at the altar of the status of numbers that they have lost sight of their main purpose: to improve access to knowledge. In some of these institutions there are now more books backlogged in the technical services departments than there are in the hands of students. And while their random collecting has led to a higher frequency success in satisfying the more esoteric demands, it has too often left service to the everyday needs of students at a dismally low level.

While we have gone along in this manner, building libraries which are ever larger and more complex and more difficult to use, we have not, I think, noticeably improved our services—at least those which are generally accessible to most users. It is interesting to note also that while much of our critical attention has been focussed on abolishing the smaller unit of service, or incorporating it into some larger whole, it is generally true, in my experience as a library user, that the larger the institution the worse the service.

One reason for this is that these gigantic institutions persist in presenting the blunt end of the arrow of service to the public, the sharp end being buried somewhere back in the administrative woodwork. In automobile racing I believe it takes about sixteen men in the pits to support one man in the driver's seat. In many libraries it appears to take some large but undefined number of professionals in administrative, technical, or consultative areas to maintain a part-time clerical assistant in direct touch with the reading public. The professional part of the staff thus becomes like the large part of the iceberg—out of sight, below the waterline, until the whole edifice begins to crumble!

Information Assistants

Somehow, as we have laboriously considered how to separate professional and nonprofessional functions, we appear to have moved toward the conclusion that subject competence, book knowledge, cultural experience, and their use in direct service to the public, are either nonprofessional or at best subsidiary, and that *real* professionalism means backroom privacy or a peripatetic role as advisor or consultant to those who *are* serving the public. An interesting item in this context is the recent announcement of a new staffing pattern at the New York Public Library.[9] Twenty-two professional librarian positions have been abolished and replaced by 26 Information Assistant positions. These latter will be people with bachelor's degrees who will work with collections related to their educational background. The move, we are told, is designed to bring to NYPL individuals who are interested in working in a specific subject area and in advancing through further study, rather than going on to formal study in librarianship. They will work, we are told, under the supervision of librarians. Once again, here, we see librarians being taken one further remove from the public. What, one wonders, will they be doing? And as the information assistants become specialists in their subject areas and know more than anyone else about the users of those collections, and go on with their further study, will they remain less professional than the professionals?

This is indicative of the process by which some of our administrative superstructures have burgeoned. And in this process we have so shaped our salary and career routes that it has become virtually impossible for a librarian to advance very far in his profession unless he is prepared to forsake the service aspects of the job for the administrative. If you were to take all your neighborhood doctors out of their practices and put them into research laboratories or into civil service offices where they could run, by remote control, a medical service manned by technicians, you might well achieve a comparable lunacy. It would, of course, be more apparent because there is so much more concern about physical well-being than intellectual.

This structuring, rather than achieving a separation of professional and nonprofessional functions, seems instead to have divided library staffs—indeed to some extent the profession itself—into administrative and nonadministrative classes. And I believe we are beginning to see reactions to this, both within libraries and in our professional organizations.

Library Union Growth

One such reaction is the blossoming and growth in the past couple of years of library unions, particularly in the larger libraries which, as I have suggested, are ripe targets. During a recent Midwinter ALA meeting I went to one function sponsored by some of those who are trying to propagate the union movement in librarianship, and I was intrigued to pick up a little flyer issued by the Librarians Guild at the Los Angeles Public Library, which is Local 1634 of the American Federation of State, County and Municipal Employees. The leaflet is entitled "Are You a Professional?" Some of the questions which follow the title question reflect, I think, the kinds of concerns I have been talking about, the concerns of many librarians who are unhappy about the role and the lot of the nonadministrative professional in librarianship today. The leaflet begins with these questions:

> Do you participate in shaping library policy and setting goals for public service?
>
> Do you attend professional meetings and workshops to discuss new tools and modes of service with other librarians?
>
> Is your obligation to continuing education and professional involvement recognized and rewarded?

Can you advance within a valued specialty—as a children's librarian, young adult librarian, reader's advisor, subject specialist?

Now I ask you to note very carefully the words and the emphases in these questions: public service; participation in policy and planning; continuing education; professional involvement; the value of service specializations. Is this not the language of professionalism? Yet the immediate emotional reaction of many librarians is that there is something basically unprofessional about joining a union or becoming involved in collective bargaining. Unions, the argument goes, are interested only in better salaries and working conditions—to the exclusion and at the expense of all else if necessary.

I think this is a canard. The objectives of the library unions are much broader than this, as the Los Angeles pamphlet indicates, but even if the main emphasis *is* on salaries, fringe benefits and the like, is this so unprofessional? Administrators, for example, as in a public library system or a college library consortium, see nothing wrong with getting together to bargain collectively for better binding contract prices or bigger discounts on books. Why does the collective bargaining process suddenly become distasteful when applied to salaries? Which, if we're talking about professionalism, in the long run aids the profession and library service most—cheaper bindings and more books, or salaries which will bring us a caliber of people we're too often unable to attract in competition with other professions today?

"The Image"

Before closing I want to say just a few words on one other subject, that most hackneyed topic of all, the image of the librarian and of librarianship. Much of the debate in this area—all the stuff about old ladies with buns, and "shush" signs in libraries—is futile nonsense and ignores the essential problem, which is one of identity rather than image. It is not that people think of librarians as this or that; the problem is that in the main they don't think of librarians at all. The great mass of the general public does not know what librarians are—or are for—and has not much of a concept of what a library can or should do. The turmoil which has hit other social institutions—the schools, the college campus, even the church—has mostly bypassed libraries (so far), and the reason, I think, is that libraries do not appear to many of the revolutionaries to be a very significant or relevant force either for or in opposition to social change. Very few people wax passionately either in favor of, or against, libraries in general—they're just *there*. And this is the core of our problem, this pervasive social anonymity.

It stems in some degree, I believe, from the fact that most of us, from the outset of our training and our library career, have been fed the doctrine of neutrality. The typical wording of this doctrine, as deeply etched in our minds as the Lord's Prayer or the Ten Commandments (perhaps deeper than these), is there to be seen in many of our most pious and sincere statements of policy, such as the *Library Bill of Rights*. I accept the principle that libraries, like other educational institutions, should seek to expose all the alternatives rather than indoctrinate in any one of them, but I do not believe that institutional neutrality rescues us from individual responsibility! What disturbs me is that the institutional neutrality principle has been extended in many librarians' minds to encompass the individual. The library should not take a position on public issues—*ergo* the librarian shouldn't, either individually or collectively. A sizeable percentage of the objections to *LJ*'s several forays into the political arena seem to derive from this cockeyed attitude. Those who think this way neither remember John F. Kennedy's charge to teachers that "Every citizen holds office," nor understand that it is equally valid for librarians.

Nor do they see some of the damaging side-effects which arise from our apparent neutrality. Some librarians today are trying sincerely to find paths of change and innovation which will bring libraries more into tune with the turbulent changes in society around us. But they are finding that the very people they most need to work with, and many of those they should be serving, in many cases reject the library and the librarian's help as unimportant or irrelevant to their needs and concerns. Some of those front-line librarians know that it is only through a larger and more sustained demonstration of individual concern and involvement that the institution's efforts are likely to be found acceptable. Another danger and problem is that the new people we need desperately if we are to break the traditional mold of library service, to help us to reach areas of society which we have ignored and about which we remain frighteningly ignorant, are unlikely to come clamoring as eager recruits at the doors of our profession while they see it as so neutral and uninvolved.

The Conspiracy

Now I do not see our library world as quite so negative and depressing as this paper may suggest. In the past couple of years, indeed, I think I see hopeful signs that the rumbling revolution which is rocking our society at its foundations has begun to reach into librarianship. The unions, the social responsibility movement, the growing aggressiveness of younger librarians, some of the more experimental programs in both public and college libraries—all are indications of a new realization that society and its needs have changed so much faster than our institutions, services and philosophies that we must run and reach out or be superseded as other institutions have been throughout history when their relevance has declined below the horizon of general visibility.

The title of this paper comes from Bernard Shaw, who, despite his warning that "People should not be forced to adopt me as their favorite author, even for their own good," I did adopt long ago, and have retained ever since, as my favorite author. The full quotation is: "All professions are a conspiracy against the laity."

I put a question mark after the title of this paper because I do not believe that librarianship *is* a conspiracy, only that it is in danger of being seen as one by the growing population which is suspicious of society's institutions because of their apparent inability to respond to the tenor of the times. If only to safeguard ourselves against such a conclusion, we must alter the emphases of our concerns and priorities, spend less time worrying about and redesigning the furniture of professionalism and more in a dedicated search for relevance and purpose. In the process we must, both individually and collectively as a profession, exhibit a greater sense of involvement and participation in the social and moral issues which beset our society. If librarianship does not become, as MacLeish suggested, "the affirmative and advocating profession of the attorney for a cause,"[10] we shall have little further need to worry about our domesticities and the solutions to them that lie in quantifying and data-processing them. We *shall* be condemned as a conspiracy—a conspiracy of silence and irrelevance—and the recent events at Newark, New Jersey, may be revealed, not as an isolated quirk of a backward and unscrupulous local government, but as the early *sinister* writing on the wall of our future.

References

1. *Annual Report of the Librarian of Congress for ... 1945*, pp. 11-12.
2. M. E. Maron, "Large Scale Data Banks: Will People Be Treated as Machines?" *Special Libraries,* January 1969, p. 8.
3. Eva Goldschmidt, "Archibald MacLeish, Librarian of Congress," *College & Research Libraries,* January 1969, p. 21.
4. "Rugged Stupidity," Editorial, *Library Journal,* September 1, 1965, p. 3406.
5. Neil Harlow, "Misused Librarians," *Library Journal,* April 1, 1965, p. 1597.
6. "Pendicton Public Library Secedes from System," news story, *Library Journal,* March 1, 1969, p. 936.
7. Emerson Greenaway, "The Library Faces the Future," in *The Public Library and the City,* ed. by Ralph W. Conant (M.I.T. Press: 1965), p. 171.
8. Lowell Martin, *Baltimore Reaches Out: Library Service to the Disadvantaged* (No. 3 in the Deiches Fund Studies of Public Library Service), Baltimore: Enoch Pratt Free Library, June 1967.
9. "New Staffing Pattern for NYPL," news story, *Library Journal,* March 1, 1969, p. 938.
10 Archibald MacLeish, "Of the Librarian's Profession," in *Books, Libraries, Librarians,* ed. by J. D. Marshall and others (Hamden, Conn.: Shoe String Press, 1955), pp. 264-71.

A Potpourri of P's

I'm going to lay out, very briefly, a number of broad issues which seem to me related to considerations of personnel. This is an institutional term for people. I've called this presentation A POTPOURRI OF P'S (which sounds like a vegetarian dish or perhaps one of those British bathroom jokes). The P's here, by no means mutually exclusive, include Professionalism, Personnel, and just Plain People—and The Payoff, what and where, if anywhere, it is.

What I'll be doing mostly is asking questions, of myself as much as of you. Never having worked in an academic library, how should I propose answers? I never cared much for answers anyway, other than very tentative or temporary and very flexible ones. Answers have a tendency to stop you in your tracks. Questions can open up interesting, if sometimes dangerous, paths for those who are willing to explore.

Let's adopt a good classification principle and work down (or up, depending on your viewpoint) from the general to the slightly more specific. And what could be broader than the most pervasive topic in our literature and our conference rooms for a century:

The Profession and Professionalism

The "question is whether or not the established model of professionalism is an ideal to which librarianship should aspire. Until recently, to ask such a question would have bordered on sacrilege. There was only one model of a profession, and it was based on the two venerable professions of medicine and law."

That's a quote from a fairly interesting article entitled "An Alternative Model of a Profession for Librarians," which appeared in *C & RL* in May 1975. The authorship was interesting, too; it was written jointly by a

---

An edited version of a paper delivered at the Rhode Island Library Association Conference, April 3, 1976.

library school student at Albany and the director of libraries at SUNY, Albany.

These two point out that these twin pinnacles toward which underprivileged occupations like librarianship have scrabbled in their quest for the societal accolade of profession, may themselves be a bit over the hill. In their words, "... our medical and legal systems are social disaster areas and ... in part, the professions charged with their upkeeping are responsible for their deterioration." Few of us, I hope, can forget the Dorian Gray portrait the legal profession painted of itself during the murk and grime of the Watergate and impeachment melodramas. And the medical profession demonstrates its dedication to the health of society at no time more luridly than whenever the prospect of a national health service peeks above even the farthest legislative horizon.

The *C & RL* article notes that this traditional model of a profession, fashioned on these tarnished godheads of medicine and law, is a strongly elitist one, in which the professional is autonomous, a member of some superior level of society whose judgment is not open to question by lay persons. It is this view that may have provoked Bernard Shaw's comment that "all professions are conspiracies against the laity."

What the Albany pair argue for, by way of an alternative, is a less conservative profession, more amenable to change; a more democratic model in which the professional is "an integral part of society, depending on it for strength and intelligence as it depends upon the professions." Nothing very new here, at least in the rhetoric; but in practice the client-commitment approach these two authors preach remains in the underdeveloped nation status, at best.

This article, like so many of its predecessor dissections of our profession's philosophies, left me with some very insidious questions, which I will now lay out for your delectation.

How can we effectively and persuasively argue what we are worth (monetarily and societally), and fight for it, when still after a century we seem not to have reached a common understanding of what we are *for*, still have not dedicated ourselves in unity to some central purpose, or set of purposes?

And a second, more dangerous question is: if there are already the first flickerings of societal disenchantment with the elitism and authoritarianism of the most powerful professions, can one not expect that society will first bring its displeasure to bear upon the weaker professions, the ones it can handle best? That the professions have generally lost status (in real terms) in recent years is written on the political hustings and in the changing balance of fire-power as between the professions and other occupations. Let us not even mention powerhouses like policemen and firemen; in New York's turmoil, for example, even gravediggers seem likely to have more clout than teachers or librarians.

The Search for Status in Librarianship

If one accepts the proposition that the position of the professions is weakening, and accepts further (which doesn't take much realism) that librarianship has always been among the weaker brethren (or sistren) of the professions, does it not seem logical that our profession would at least seek the strength that unity can bring? Gandhi (Mohandas, that is, not Indira) well understood that if you didn't have arms or economic power, you had better at least have numbers and unity. But do we?

If Gaul was divided in three parts, our profession seems to be disintegrating into ever more separate components. We have subdivided our organizations in myriad ways: by type of library, by library departments (reference, technical services, juvenile), by type of material (government documents, serials, av materials), by user groups (young adults, the disadvantaged, the institutionalized), by size or geography (ARL, the Urban Libraries Council), and there are even current attempts to fractionate by sex or religion.

And our apparent desire for disunity can be seen in other ways. However unconsciously, there appears to have emerged a curious kind of class structure in librarianship. Academic librarians believe (yes, I know I'm indulging in generalizations) they are different from public librarians (somewhere in the psyche "different from" translates into "better than"); public librarians tend to be scornful of school librarians, etc. And then there are the whiz kids of information technology, who are more "with it" (*it* being some future nirvana) than any of these groups.

Even within our institutions there are similar rifts and conceptions of "difference." Reference librarians are a breed apart from catalogers; circulation is a kind of nether region; administration either a plush inner sanctum or a murky Tammany Hall.

And so librarians, of all types, tend increasingly to look elsewhere than to their profession in their quest for status and recognition. Academic librarians tie their star to the coat-tails of faculty; public librarians, having nothing else, unionize or in some other way try to maintain parity with other community workers like police and firemen; school librarians lean toward NEA and teacher unions; and special librarians strive for—what?—perhaps product effectiveness and recognition as an integral part of the business world.

Now I do not for a moment suggest that all of these things are undesirable. Certainly our professional organizations should provide for special or particular interests. Certainly librarians should form alliances with other professionals with whom they work or whom they serve. But once again, I am left with a battery of nagging questions:

Unless librarians see themselves primarily *as* librarians, and only secondarily as some particular species of the genus—like college librarian or reference librarian or whatever—is there much hope that urgent profession-wide concerns will take precedence over parochial ones? Or shall we remain so firmly focused on a number of individual trees that we don't notice the whole wood disappearing? If librarianship generally loses professional status or social recognition, can we really expect that status can be accumulated by some individual segment of librarianship? Unless the profession gains recognition overall, will not librarians in their special alliances always be considered hangers-on, people without a true profession of their own and therefore struggling to be accepted in someone else's?

I'll come back and look at some of this from another angle later on. For the moment, a change of pace.

Impacts on Libraries and the Profession

I think it is self-evident that a number of forces already impinging upon us will come increasingly to bear upon libraries and/or the institutions they serve, and that the impact of these forces will inevitably create drastic change in libraries (which will certainly affect personnel as much as anything else). How well the profession emerges from this process of change depends, I think, on whether we are dragged along kicking and screaming in the wake of these forces, or whether we anticipate and help shape and direct the change.

What sort of forces am I talking about? The first can loosely be called political. Let me demonstrate with a few quotes from a speech by Dwight R. Ladd, a professor at the University of New Hampshire (*C & RL*, March 1955):

Perhaps the most dangerous of our myths is that governance is basically the function and prerogative of 'insiders'—faculty, academic administrators, students, professional staff, and so on....

In its 1973 report on governance, the Carnegie Commission observed that we are in the midst of a "transfer of authority from the campus to outside agencies." The outsiders are indeed making more of the decisions traditionally made on campus. Whether a particular institution will offer instruction in a particular subject is now often decided by a coordinating board and not by the institution itself. Legislatures regularly consider, and sometimes pass, regulations of faculty teaching loads and minimum class sizes. Nor are publicly controlled institutions the only ones experiencing this transfer of authority.

And here, Ladd goes on with some more examples, including "affirmative action," issues referred to courts, etc.

He comments: "To recognize this shift in the locus of governance is not to know what to say or to do about it. There really are no relevant experiences or parallels on which to draw. One thing can be said with a good deal of confidence: If the shift of authority to outsiders becomes very widespread we will be in a very new and different ball-game."

I believe there is every likelihood that the shift Professor Ladd is talking about will not only continue but will probably accelerate. And one sure result of this kind of impact is that with it will come a demand for much sterner and more detailed accountability than has been the traditional lot of academe or of academic libraries. And with that thought, we can merge uncomfortably here into the second of the forces impacting upon libraries and librarianship—the economic.

The sixties were fat, golden years for libraries, but I wonder how many of us would like to deal with a sort of retroactive accountability for some of the drains down which we poured so much of that gravy. As a sad example there were the libraries, a great many of them academic, that fell for the blandishments of a locust-horde of newborn reprinters who suddenly conjured up from deserved graves thousands of books and periodical sets that would have been reprinted long since had there been a true need for them. Suddenly, there they all were, these faded remnants of the past decked out in mod jackets, and like Everest, because they were there and there was money for the expedition, they had to be had. So now, instead of quietly gathering dust on the crowded shelves of perhaps half a dozen major research libraries, they lie dormant—expensive status additions to the volume-count—in the stacks of perhaps 600. We found other uses, too, for the loose cash of the sixties. There were our excursions into the Lilliput of media in an attempt to find the microform a reader could be comfortable with. There was that biggest drain of all—computerization. There were the off-with-the-old, on-with-the-new ventures into reclassifying whole libraries. There were buildings, of course, and of course, building consultants galore. And there were workshops . . . and workshops . . . and workshops.

But what sort of a case could we make for improved service as a result of all that? Did it come more richly flavored for all that gravy? Did all the growth in the collections, the new buildings, the classification games and the endless bull sessions send out into the world hundreds of users willing to testify to a fantastic improvement in library service—surely our one essential purpose?

If we did not produce that one centrally important result when the going was good—and certainly my sons and their friends, in or recently out of college, are not ecstatic about the library service they got—what can we expect during the lean years? The lean years are upon many of our institutions already, particularly in the crisis-stricken metropolitan centers, and we may see a good many more of them—particularly if the present incumbent gets a second lease on the White House.

To the possibilities of increasing outside control and more strident calls for accountability and the probability of leaner budgets we can add the certainty of escalating costs. Prices of books and other materials, I can assure you, will continue to soar in the next few years. One recent forecast by Random House's production director was that the cost of producing a book will rise by 50-60% by 1980. By then, he estimated, the average novel would cost $15 to $18, the average biography with a minimum of illustration, $20 to $25. You can project from those figures what scientific and technical and art books will cost. Nor will salaries decline—though staff numbers may.

If this not very cheerful forecasting is accurate in any degree we shall have to do some harder thinking about priorities than has usually been the case, at least for many years. We shall have to be concerned not just about the cost of operations, but about how and where our funds and our energies are apportioned. What is a reasonable ratio as between staff costs and collection costs? Where are the professional staff most needed in academic libraries? What kinds of collections do we most need, and for what purpose? Where are our *service* priorities?

And here we can do an Antonioni fade into the third of the forces impacting upon libraries—the forces of social change. American education at the college level has in some respects been more democratic in the past than the elitist models of Britain and certain European countries, but the system had its ramparts nevertheless, and until the past decade or so few members of minority groups were able to scale them, and proportionately a very small number of women were able to clamber into the graduate levels. Social and political pressures are changing all that, most evidently, again, in the urban areas, although this is certainly not exclusively an urban phenomenon.

At any rate, here is a problem that grows apace. I'm not just talking about minority groups here, either—when you use the term "educationally disadvantaged" you are encompassing one hell of a proportion of young people graduating from high school. Remember the terrifying fact that it only takes 8th grade reading ability to graduate from New York City high schools.

So we have an influx 1) of students from a broader stratum of society, and 2) of students who are sadly equipped for college work. This is not only a vast challenge for academe (some think only a vast headache) but it could be viewed as perhaps the greatest opportunity the academic library has ever had to prove itself an essential part of the educational apparatus. Thus far, with the exception of a few noble innovative attempts, according to Tom Shaughnessy in a recent *C & RL* article (Nov. 1975), it must be said that academic libraries have not exactly exulted in either the challenge or the opportunity.

As Shaughnessy points out, while our literature "abounds with articles describing *public* library services to the urban poor, minority groups and the educationally disadvantaged," one of the few "substantive articles to address the question of academic *library* services to disadvantaged students" is E. J. Josey's article on that topic in *Library Trends*—an article published *five years ago.*

If some among us have maintained a rather blank unawareness on the social front, the propaganda and public relations characters have kept us alert to the fourth major force that is already at work on the future of library service and the library profession—that is, technology. Nobody can be in doubt any longer that technology is going to change libraries. The only questions are *how,* and to what end, and for better or worse?

As I see it, among the major problems in this area—and I cite only an obvious few—are the following:

1. Much of the terrible waste of the sixties occurred because so many individual institutions each chose independently to chase their own technological rainbow. Result: tremendous duplication of cost and effort. But at the end of the rainbow—for some at least—was an unexpected result: the systems they had tested, experimented with, even put into operation, often proved to be so expensive that they couldn't afford to maintain them. Or, in some cases, the expensive hardware purchased only a few years earlier was already obsolete. This was expensive education, but if the lessons were learned it may have been worth it. What were they? First, beware the hardware salesman; check the track record. Second, nail down some realistic operating costs before you leap. Third, under no circumstances automate anything unless it can do the job not just faster but more effectively and *cheaper*. Certainly, don't adopt some system because it will produce a whole heap of data or information you have never before felt the need of.

2. Much of our technological future has been and is being shaped by the large research libraries and the information industry. What they come up with finally, if it is economically practicable at all, may serve the purposes (or some of them) of these giants, but it is highly debatable whether many of the benefits can be made transferable, at least economically, to, say, the average college library.

3. While all the other pressures I have mentioned are pushing us toward greater economy, greater control and accountability, technology—which always seems to come along with the promise of great savings, usually in manpower—on the record thus far, at least, appears only to make library service more complex (which users surely don't need) and at the same time grossly more expensive (which we surely can't afford). The evidence, meanwhile, that technology has made library service more effective for the majority of users is scanty and unconvincing.

Technology merges conveniently here with our fifth force: organizational change. That old impossible dream, pursued by many institutions in search of membership in the million-volume library club, of being able to manage one's own house and meet one's own clients' needs, is now well understood, even by the biggest of the giants, to be the real impossibility it always was. So we see the rapid growth of systems and consortia, and of—the magic abracadabra, pop word today—networking.

While much of this is undoubtedly inevitable, some of it even desirable, we see the merging of the technological and organizational forces perhaps most clearly and frighteningly in the growth of networks like OCLC and its several kin, and in the dreams of NCLIS of building a big grandaddy of a system that will supersede or combine all those that exist already.

What scares me most about OCLC is that its costs and ambitions are expanding to Brobdignagian proportions and at a rate which makes the inflationary rate throughout the rest of library service look like normalcy. These costs, both the real ones and those of the ambitions, inevitably are passed on to members and subscribers. And there is the specter in the background, which I mentioned a little while ago, that OCLC's hardware may soon be obsolete. And the cost of retooling will be enormous, if possible at all.

And here we get back to accountability. Can we really demonstrate that the OCLC's have saved us money, saved us staff or released staff from technical services to real reader services, or in any way improved our capacity for service at all? If there is such evidence in the literature, I confess I must have entirely overlooked it. Further, I believe one does not need an ear very close to the ground to hear the growing swell of disenchantment among libraries which looked with desperation in this direction for relief but are gradually discovering that they may only have found another gaping economic drain.

What's Ahead?

To follow up that fairly depressing picture of how things are all around us, of the pressures working upon us, let us take a look at some other trends—some changes which are already occurring, some that probably will, some that we must effect. Among the areas I want to touch on here are the following selected few:

a. Changes in management, policy- and decision-making
b. Changes in staffing patterns
c. Unionization

Some of the forces I've mentioned, plus some others—like increasing radicalization of library staffs and a growing disenchantment with autocracy—have already ushered in the first flickers of change in library management. Indeed, Kenneth Shaffer wrote a rather convincing obituary in *LJ* of the administrator as "boss."

For a while, I think, libraries are going to be plagued by incessant experimentation with a battery of management theories—some, like performance budgeting, perhaps imposed from outside; others, like participatory management, perhaps imposed from inside; and some just occurring because some librarians like to try anything "new," whether pertinent to the situation or not.

A lot of these theories, as Ellsworth Mason has pointed out, have been picked up by the library schools and other institutions from the world of industry. And, as Mason says: "It seems that we must repeatedly be reminded of the fact that industry is permeated with meretricious practices, and that industrial managers leap from one jazzy topic to another in an attempt to stay on top by convincing everyone that they really know what they are doing. The past few years have once again demonstrated what those of us who grew up in the Depression learned thoroughly—that industry seldom knows its ear from a hole in the ground about what it is doing."

That typical Mason salvo was Ellsworth's way of introducing his attack on the current enthusiasm for participatory management, a theory which did emerge from the business world but which doesn't appear to operate there. Says Mason: "My inquiries among friends in the commercial world have as yet turned up none who have had any contact with it," a judgment with which I would have to concur.

Now I do not share Ellsworth's totally sour view of this development, although I do have some distinct reservations on the subject. On the whole I am more inclined to Shaffer's view that, "However brutal and uncompromising the movement for participatory management may in some instances have been, the good which has resulted from it undoubtedly (I'd say probably—I like a little doubt) outweighs the hardships which accompanied it."

But much depends on how you define participatory management. I see it as little more than the common sense method the *good* manager has always employed; i.e. in formulating policy, one shares and utilizes all the knowledge, all the talent, all the ideas that exist in a total staff; and one keeps the communication channels wide open for at least two reasons: 1) to gather maximum information on which to base an intelligent decision, and 2) to keep everyone informed about the steps leading to that decision. The second is perhaps more important than the first, because a policy (like a law) isn't worth a damn if the people who have to translate it into practice don't understand it, don't believe in it, or at least accept it as tenable.

On the other hand, I do not share the view of those who see participatory management as a method of reaching decisions by committee vote. For one thing this leaves wide open the possibility that 49% of the people will disagree with the decision. But, more importantly, I do not know of a more inefficient or ineffective mode of management or *decision*-making than by committee. As someone once said: "A camel is a horse designed by a committee."

There are some other aspects of participatory management that evoke questions. How much do some of those who press this approach so vigorously believe in it if it is extended beyond their own involvement? In short, do they really believe in the principle or do they just want a piece of the action? Why, for example, limit participation, as is true in many cases, to professionals? Are they the only ones whose ideas are of any value, the only ones touched by the formulation of policies, the only ones who need to be communicated with?

And what of the most central group of all—library users? Libraries, after all, are for users, not for librarians. But, as Mason says,

> The users of a library can influence its actions only in minor ways. They are working unorganized outside of the organization and are helpless when confronted by the power of the organization. This fact can be verified by anyone who studies the so-called chain of command, who will find that decisions of a policy nature are constantly made by anyone of any level of authority on the line, where it actually affects library users.

Until participation becomes much broader than even some of its proponents advocate, until it involves in some manner those most affected (or afflicted) by policies and practices imposed from above, I don't think I can feel very enthusiastic about it. Extending the decision-making process from one top administrator to a corps of top professionals isn't, in my book, much of an improvement. I haven't noticed, in recent history, that a junta is very different or noticeably better than a dictator.

On staffing I want to say very little except mention briefly a few things I think are going to make a difference in the next few years. The most important influence, of course, will be affirmative action. The attitudes displayed in some corners of academe on this topic are reminiscent of Wallace's stand in the schoolhouse door in Alabama, and the adoption of "backlash" terms like "reverse discrimination" hardly does us much professional credit.

With broader application of affirmative action, I believe we may begin to see another trend, greater use made of part-time employment for those who want or need it. A rash of articles on this subject has appeared lately, one of the best of them by Laura Arksey, a part-time humanities bibliographer at Seattle Pacific College (see *PNLA Quarterly,* March 1975).

There has been much opposition to the concept of part-time work and a rather pervasive feeling that those who want to work part-time can't be truly professional. Ms. Arksey claims that one reason for this prejudice is the male domination of the administrative levels of our profession. She quotes Page Ackerman of UCLA, for example, as saying: "In my own library, at least one large public service unit has more half-time librarians than full-time librarians, primarily because, though many of them started out full-time, family responsibilities made it desirable for them to shift. Most of these staff members are women and these changes were made under a woman department head." Ms. Ackerman, however, does add a note that hints at the possibility of the social educability of the male. She says: "Now there is a male department head who argues enthusiastically for half-time assignments because it gives the unit flexibility and because each of the staff members is a superior performer."

I am inclined to think that Ms. Arksey is right in assigning some of the blame to male shortsightedness, and one can only hope that an increase in women administrators will bring with it an increase in consideration for and understanding of those in our work force with dual responsibilities. And I don't think the latter are necessarily only women. There are a great many librarians around today, for example, who would happily accept a half-time job rather than continue with none.

Allied with this development is the emergence and slow growth of what some have called alternative librarianship; i.e., people, professionally qualified in many cases, who don't want to tie themselves to one institution. In effect, they operate freelance, offering their services for special projects—a recataloging job, an indexing or bibliographic project, a survey—or perhaps for general employment for a limited, perhaps emergency, period. This, again, offers some real advantages in flexibility, freshness of viewpoint, varied experience, etc.

One other staffing development I must mention in passing is the growth of the subject bibliographer or area specialist, or whatever other name you put to the species. This can be a very healthy development, or it can be just another extension of our tendency to grow the bureaucracy of professionals behind the scene. If the impetus in the subject bibliographer's work is from the user *to* the collection, if he or she uses this position to find out much more about users' real needs and to translate that knowledge into both collection development and increased accessibility, then this will be a tremendous advance in service consciousness. But if this subject specialist is a behind-the-scenes operator only, building more theory-based collections, we shall have done nothing except extend the already wasteful technical services empire.

The most powerful influence on personnel matters in academic libraries in the years ahead will undoubtedly be unionization. If you doubt that, you have to overcome some impressive evidence, particularly the growth dimensions of academic unionization in this decade of the seventies.

For my data on this subject I am much indebted to my friend Jack Weatherford, the librarian of Central Michigan University, who has studied and experienced this phenomenon at least as much as any academic librarian in the country. He is also the author of the book *Collective Bargaining and the Academic Librarian*, published by Scarecrow Press.

The first formal collective bargaining involving faculty occurred in two-year colleges in 1965 (only just over a decade ago). Within five years 56 two-year colleges were involved. The process was slower in four-year institutions. In 1970 there were still only two which had bargained agreements: CUNY and Central Michigan (in 1968 and 1969 respectively). Five years later, by June 1975, faculty on 157 four-year campuses had adopted bargaining agents; 37 had rejected them. Now this is pretty rapid growth. Today there are about 60,000 faculty and others on campus who are unionized, including some 2000 academic librarians.

Both the impetus created by that rapid growth and current social and economic conditions seem to dictate that unionization on the campus will profilerate, probably at an increased pace.

The Payoff

This leads me nicely into my conclusion, which earlier I referred to as "the payoff" (mainly for alliterative reasons). What is the payoff? As I see it, it is these things:

1. The recognition by society—at all levels: politicians, faculty, other professionals, students, PEOPLE—of the real value, indeed the essentiality, of library service. And ergo, of the real value and essentiality of professional librarians.

2. The proper recompense of librarians as valued and essential professionals who have a key role, perhaps several key roles, to play in the betterment of our troubled society.

3. A restructuring of libraries involving more humanitarian personnel policies, the utilization of staff strengths where they are most needed instead of a hierarchical system leading to adequate rewards only in administration, and a reversal of emphasis from collection empire-building to user consciousness and truly user-oriented services.

4. A reordering of financial and political priorities, particularly at the national level but necessarily permeating all the way downward, so that libraries may acquire the means and the power to achieve their social and educational roles.

Now there are several diverse elements involved here, and these varied goals can not be achieved by any simple formula. There are three elements, however, which I believe will be enormously important in determining our future, i.e. how nearly our grasp can approach our reach. They are:

1. The strength, conviction and unity of our political effort.

2. The degree and kind of our union involvement.

3. Most importantly, the degree of our dedication to user-oriented librarianship, based on the sort of principles spelled out in Richard Kluger's devastating book, *Simple Justice*—which, at the very least, should dissuade us from any longer taking the legal profession as one of our models.

Let me add only that we shall not achieve much of what I have talked about through passivity or middle-of-the-road attitudes. What I'm trying to say was perhaps best expressed by F. Gerald Ham about 18 months ago in his presidential address to the Society of American Archivists, in which he was arguing throughout for a more enlightened social attitude and people-oriented view among the members of *his* profession. Just switch the word "librarians" in where Mr. Ham says "archivists." Ham's speech ended:

As archivists we must be in a more exposed position than we have been in the past, one that is more vulnerable. We might well heed the advice of one of Kurt Vonnegut's minor characters, Ed Finnerty, "a chronically malcontent boozer" and the real hero of the novel *Player Piano*. When someone suggested he should see a psychiatrist, Ed replied: "He'd pull me back into the center, and I want to stay as close to the edge as I can without going over. Out on the edge you see all kinds of things you can't see from the center.... Big, undreamed-of things—the people on the edge see them first."

Who's Larry Powell?

About a couple of years ago two young librarians (almost all librarians are "young" to me these days) were visiting us in Sarasota. We were sitting out on the porch, enjoying Bombay gin and watching that marvelous Florida sunshine subside gently into a pinkish dusk. The talk turned, as it inevitably does when librarians gather, to gossip about libraries and librarians. Somewhere during the conversation, inevitably, I mentioned Larry Powell.

Like an over-trained Greek chorus, in mystified unison they said: "Who's Larry Powell?" I remember only one other occasion when my eyebrows had been sent soaring so high by a question. It was shortly after my arrival in America, when my children were very young. Talking to them and some of their friends I had dropped another name. The answering chorus then was: "Who's Lindbergh?"

Had I mentioned Gandhi or Lloyd George or Smuts or even so recent a figure then as Aneurin Bevan, the vacuum behind that question would not have had the same power to surprise. One only needs to listen to the pronouncements of some of our political leaders, or to read the letters columns in any newspaper, to become aware that a knowledge of the history of other nations, other parts of the world, is not one of the strengths of most Americans. Too often, what is taught as history in our educational institutions is *American* history—and even that may be truncated to *U.S.* history.

But if the attachment of such blinders may be attributed to a certain parochial nationalism—by no means a uniquely American phenomenon—how does one explain the education for a profession that leaves its graduates ignorant of its *own* giants, those who have shaped or given character or inspiration to that profession? As I pondered such questions

---

Originally the Foreword to *Life Goes On*, by Lawrence Clark Powell (Scarecrow Press, 1986), pp. vii-xvi, this is reprinted by permission of Scarecrow Press. Copyright © 1986 by Lawrence Clark Powell.

in the wake of that response to Powell's name I thought back to my own days in library school in Britain and realized that one would have to have slept through almost every class to have emerged into the profession without an awareness of the achievements, not only of such figures of British library history as Panizzi or James Duff Brown but also of such more recent, then still practicing giants as Lionel McColvin, Ernest Savage and Frank Gardner. More importantly, in the context of our professional heritage, in our pantheon there were also many names from across the Atlantic. They included not just the obvious lions of the past—Dewey and Cutter and Winsor and Dana and Putnam—but more recent giants, like Joe Wheeler, or then emerging ones such as Powell, Shera, and Shaw.

Such thoughts may be attributed purely to (and perhaps a bit rosied by) nostalgia, a popular pursuit among those who have more years behind them than lie ahead. But if it is true—and I think it is—that without learning the lessons of the past we are ill-equipped to deal with the problems of the present, let alone the unpredictable future, there is more to it than nostalgia. A profession like librarianship, engulfed today in change of unprecedented rapidity, if it operates without the stabilizing forces, the values and thinking and creativity, that have brought it thus far, may well find itself rudderless, making decisions out of expediency rather than accumulated wisdom, accommodating to change without a foundation of purpose or belief

That innocent question from two librarians on a porch in Sarasota reinforced my belief in the project that Scarecrow Press began a few years ago. It may not be a significant contribution to publishing profits but it is, I believe, an important contribution to the profession to persuade such people as Robert Downs, Ronald Benge, Ralph Ellsworth, Guy Lyle, Will Ready and Johanna Tallman—and yes, Lawrence Clark Powell—to leave us some personal record of their lives and beliefs and achievements. Powell's Introduction to Librarianship course, incidentally, came about as a result of his teaching at UCLA for six years, one semester a year plus summer sessions. He always included a week on "library leaders." In a recent letter he told me: "I have always revered our giants and tell my students to."

"People, librarians no exception, are forgotten. Books remain." No need perhaps to tell you who said that, but what Larry Powell didn't add was that one of the supreme contributions of the books that remain is that they can remind generations to come of what those otherwise "forgotten" people (librarians no exception) did, what they contributed to bring us to where we are, and of how much less we and our institutions and services might be had they not been a part of our history and development.

The question that provoked all this serious contemplation also reminded me of how the tempo of change today seems to have telescoped time, to the point where you can go into Sam Goody's and find both The Beatles and The Rolling Stones in a bin labeled "Golden Oldies." Twenty years ago I had persuaded Larry to write his autobiography, *Fortune and Friendship,* which was published by Bowker in 1968. If twenty years ago seems to some members of the now generation like the Middle Ages, perhaps one should not be surprised that that volume, despite the wonders that technology has brought to bear upon bibliography and cataloging, is in a sense no longer accessible. It was with all this in mind that Bill Eshelman, Scarecrow's president, and I began our barrage of persistent persuasion that led to Larry's writing a second volume with its optimistic (or resigned?) title, *Life Goes On.* Larry is current, a "now" person again.

As I was writing this I read the news that Lee Iacocca's autobiography had just become the best-selling hardbound nonfiction book of all time. It's not an entirely new phenomenon: examine the best-seller lists over a period of time and you will find that half of the titles, or more, are autobiographies. What is it that makes this literary form so popular? The author, of course, his or her fame or notoriety, is a large factor. But I think an equally large part of the fascination may derive from curiosity about the author's connections—with events or, more importantly, with other people—and what he or she has to say about them. A person writing about himself tells an empty story if his pages do not record the links with those who have influenced his life and work and with some of those upon whom his ideas and personality have had an impact. That Larry is aware of this is evident in the title of his first autobiography, *Fortune and Friendship.* "Friendship"—one kind, an important one, of connection.

When you know the author, reading an autobiography can be even more fun, because you are reminded of your own connections. As I read the anecdotes in this volume about such library luminaries as Ralph Shaw, Jesse Shera, Luther Evans, and Sir Frank Francis, episodes from my own life and career, connections with each of them, danced into memory and I wanted to add my own anecdotes to LCP's. But it is not because of those shared acquaintances that I am writing this Foreword. Bill Eshelman assigned me this pleasurable task, I suspect, not just because I had persuaded Larry to write his first autobiography and had helped to dragoon him into this successor volume but because he knows of the many and interesting ways in which Larry and I have "connected" over the years. He knows, too, of my great (but far from uncritical) admiration for this man who, when he was awarded the American Library Association's highest honor, was described so aptly as "a magician."

Our first connection, Larry's and mine, was in 1957. I had just become one of the two founding editors of *Liaison,* the official news organ of the (British) Library Association, a weapon we had devised to counteract the determined dullness of *The Library Association Record.* My partner, Bill Smith (now a successful bookseller) and I were setting out to bring newspaper vitality and technique to library literature. I had heard that three famous figures of the American library world were to be present at the Library Association conference in Harrogate, Yorkshire that year, and was eager to pull off a scoop by interviewing all three for our fledgling publication.

Discovering them all together one evening, ensconced in armchairs around a large fireplace and sharing drinks and conversation with some of the greyer eminences of The Library Association, our enterprising but brash young reporter, armed with camera, pad, and pencil, charged upon the scene. The three Americans were LCP, Quincy Mumford, the Librarian of Congress, and Howard Haycraft, president of the H.W. Wilson Company and master analyst of detective fiction.

I have often wondered since what it was that made me choose Larry as my first target—perhaps blind luck, or fate, if one is inclined to believe in that. At any rate I planted myself in front of him and said something like: "So you're Larry Powell. Why don't you come outside with me for a few minutes and tell me what makes you so great?" Amid dark frowns all around—bad British form and all that—like a burst of sunshine through the clouds there emerged the famous twinkle in the Powell eyes. "Sure, young man," he said, getting up out of his chair, "You have almost as much gall as I had at your age."

That generous, spontaneous response to a young, unknown (and in this instance, certainly undeserving) individual, though I did not know it then, was typical of Powell. So too were the humor and humanity that warmed our corridor conversation in the following minutes. When I told him that I was going after Quincy and Howard during the week, he grinned and said: "I wouldn't advise the same approach." It was the first time, but not the last, that he would give me very sound advice.

The connections were renewed when I came to the U.S. in 1959 to assume the editorship of *Library Journal.* In our correspondence before my arrival Dan Melcher, Bowker's president and *LJ*'s publisher, suggested, since I had no experience of America or American librarianship (other than through extensive reading about both—a demurrer of which I'm sure Larry would approve), that we appoint a board of consultants, comprised of eminent American librarians upon whose advice and experience I could call during my first couple of years. The first person I told Dan I wanted was Lawrence Clark Powell. Another person featured in this book who was part of that impressive assembly was Luther Evans, who often broke up our gatherings with huge Texan belly-laughs over my accent and my "unAmerican" pronunciation of certain words.

Subsequently I asked Larry to become a columnist for *LJ*, and for a year (all he would agree to), among his myriad other activities he ground out his "On the Grindstone" column, always coming in—a real rarity among columnists—ahead of deadline. It was over this column, though, that we had our first major disagreements, though not confrontations, as you shall hear. I wanted Larry to bring to bear his power and influence upon some of the critical issues with which *LJ* and I were so deeply involved in the sixties, but I couldn't budge him from his "Passion for Books" message, although he claims to have been "magnificently diverse" and to have tackled what he saw as the issues: they just weren't *my* issues. One tough day when things had not been going well, another of those bibliographic sermons dropped onto my desk. I read it with impatient fury and promptly dashed off a long, angry letter accusing Larry of avoidance of responsibility . . . and then on up (or down) from there. My uninhibited language in that letter was somewhat similar to Ralph Shaw's response to Larry's famous ALA keynote speech, "The Alchemy of Books." Larry's delightfully unfazed and coy response came by return mail: "You didn't *like* my column?" How can you stay mad at a man like that? What is now clear, in any case, in the context of time, is that both Shaw and I were wrong. Larry had to be *his* man, not ours, and that speech and those columns are still read and cited by many today.

But enough of reminiscences (although they could go on for many more pages). What is it, to repeat that infamous question of mine on our first meeting in the fifties, that makes Larry Powell so great? Certainly his achievements are undeniable: his transformation of the UCLA library into one of the great libraries of the world; his fight for and establishment of a superb library school with a wondrous faculty including the likes of Seymour Lubetzky, Frances Clarke Sayers, Everett Moore, Betty Rosenberg, Andy Horn, Bob Hayes; and his writings, among the most enduring of any librarian's. Among his greatest contributions, too, were the bridges he built between the library world and the larger world of books—with authors, printers, booksellers, publishers. More than any of this, though, it is his personal qualities that elevate him above most others in our profession, qualities that have inspired and irritated, annoyed and exhilarated, and that have produced more converts and followers and friends, inside of librarianship and out, than most of us could ever dream of.

And that is the hardest thing to capture in writing about him. Like all complex persons he is full of contradictions: he can be ruthless or incredibly kind, caring or oblivious, sneaky or disarmingly open, phony or utterly convincing, sentimental or harshly realistic. All those contradictions, and more, carry over into the evaluations of him by others, including many of those who have known him best, admired and loved him. Consider some of those reactions and judgments.

Andrew Horn, perhaps Larry's closest friend in the library world, asked for his reactions, mentioned *first* Powell's strength as an administrator and manager. This comment is echoed by another lifelong friend, the great antiquarian bookseller Jake Zeitlin, who calls him "a thoroughgoing administrator." This is the same man who has been more often characterized as a bookish evangelist, even a "biblio-simpleton," the same man who will shrug off as unimportant or untrue any reference to his administrative skills (there's some of that phoniness for you). Horn, as usual, puts this particular contradiction into some perspective: "His management style was highly personalized. His definition of management could fit one I've heard, viz., 'Management is getting things done through people'." That indeed sounds like something Powell would say. People, and getting things done, are among his strengths. Just don't call it administration!

Andy Horn was as well aware of the Powell contradictions as anyone. In another note he said: "Sensitive and emotional on the one hand; practical, realistic, and nearly ruthless on the other. Often seems a paradox when analyzed." That word "ruthless" crops up surprisingly often in evaluations by his friends and colleagues, as in the comment by Betty Rosenberg: "Ruthless when the library is at stake. "

A passionate man himself, Powell evokes passionate reactions from those around him. A good example is Everett Moore's comment on "this unique man." Says Moore: "I've admired and hated, enjoyed and endured, turned hot and cold in turn, along with many of his associates. I owe him much. I'm grateful for my associations with him."

So how does one sum up this outrageous, contradictory, complex man? He himself, in *Fortune and Friendship,* talks of his "personal, autobiographical, egocentric, didactic, flamboyant, hyperbolic manner."

All true. On another occasion I added, if only indirectly, another adjective to that list. During a little celebration to mark the publication of *Fortune and Friendship* I gave a copy to Larry's wife and wrote in it: "To Fay, the most objective of the Powells." There is much more than objectivity to this wonderful woman whom Larry calls his "sail and anchor." He's undoubtedly needed both, though almost certainly the anchor more often than the sail. Whatever he is and has achieved, Fay has been an integral part of it. *Her* autobiography would be fascinating.

LCP's colleague of these later years, David Laird, librarian of the University of Arizona, comments:

> As impressive as Larry's careers are in things that show up on a résumé or an entry in *Who's Who,* it is an intangible thing that most impresses me: Larry has that magical spark that we call charisma, or once did before the word went out of fashion. Nearing 75 [David wrote this a few years ago] he still has more enthusiasm for life and love than most folks have at 25, and when he comes in contact with other minds the sparks fly, the wires hum and all systems are GO.

Laird comes close to the essence of Lawrence Clark Powell in that comment. Larry's personality is perhaps his greatest weapon, the ingredient that may best account, along with the passion of his beliefs, for his tremendous impact on so many people over so long a period of time. Important too is his energy, that "enthusiasm for life and love" that Laird mentions. That it continues was evident at the 1983 Los Angeles ALA Conference, at which Larry was the speaker at a Junior Members Round Table session.

To those who haven't known him a long time it appears, before he starts speaking, that this bowed, frail-looking man will just not make it through the program. But he's looked pretty much like that ever since I've known him, and we his fans who were sitting in the front row at Los Angeles knew the transformation that would occur the moment he got behind the microphone. Larry is more actor and performer than speaker, and a microphone and a platform will do more for him than a double martini. He just turns on, lights up and, as David Laird says, "All systems are GO."

On this occasion, in his late seventies, there he was in full histrionic form, urging on the younger librarians to fight for what they believed in and not to be too bothered about job security. The man in the grey flannel suit would not have approved at all. At one point he leaned over the lectern, grinned down at me and said: "We gave 'em hell, didn't we, Eric?" But the moment in the speech that was pure LCP was when he announced somberly: "This will be my last appearance before you at ALA." There followed a long pause, to allow us to absorb the sadness of the moment ... and then it was broken. Up came the head, the twinkle was back in the eyes, and Larry whispered: "Unless you ask me back." It was coy and corny and funny, but you knew that here was a man who *wanted* to return. He did not want to give up the limelight, the missionary spirit was still strong, the sermon wasn't over—and probably will never be while he is still on his feet.

The essential Powell is best captured, in my opinion, in the citation that Larry received when he was inducted as an Honorary Life Member of ALA. Since many readers of this volume will never have seen it, it seems appropriate to end this Foreword with just a small sample from that splendid statement:

> Author, bibliographer, bookman, essayist, librarian, teacher, dean, and adroit administrator, Lawrence Clark Powell is many things. But essentially he is a magician. He turns young people into readers, students into book owners, scholars into bibliographers, book dealers into colleagues, library workers into librarians, academic administrators into library defenders, university regents into buyers of book collections, and legislators into fighters for library funding . . . He is the profession's best recruiter and its most effective lobbyist. No one knows where his influence ends.

I hope there are a few answers here, and in the pages that follow, to the difficult question those two young librarians asked me a couple of years ago: "Who is Larry Powell?"

PART VI

LIBRARY ASSOCIATIONS

Introduction

Having spent so much of my life actively engaged in library associations (in Britain, Canada and the U.S.) I find it somewhat surprising that this section is so sparse. I suppose it may be that most of what I have written about associations has been in reports of their meetings, conferences and other activities, in such vehicles as *The Assistant Librarian* (when I was Honorary Secretary of the AAL) and *Library Journal* (when I was its editor and chief reporter). Even though Archie McNeal once described one of my conference reports as "one of the longest editorials in library periodical history," this particular kind of journalism, I felt, did not belong in this collection.

"Potential for Power" was an *LJ* editorial which attempted to rouse some slight fervor in what was then known as the Junior Members Round Table (it has recently been re-christened, with enviable inventiveness, the New Members Round Table). I compared its lack of influence and political clout with the power often exerted within The Library Association by the Association of Assistant Librarians. The editorial, it must be admitted, had no effect on JMRT. Even with its new name it is still a pretty tame outfit.

"Library Association Agonies" (first delivered at the Dalhousie Library School at the behest of Norman Horrocks—who has been known to create a few association agonies) is a fairly critical view of the state of library associations, particularly ALA, as of twenty years ago. If I were writing it today I believe the article would be much more critical than the version here. I said then: "But if it is all a mess, it is a healthy one, in my opinion." Today things are not nearly so healthy, though mess there is aplenty.

"The State of the Union, Jack" was delivered at the Centenary Conference of the Library Association in London, at a session sponsored by the Association of Assistant Librarians, who asked me before the LA got around to it. I was very fortunate to be serving as ALA President at this time and took great satisfaction in having the opportunity to lead the American delegation attending this auspicious occasion. My return in that role had one significant advantage: it was possible for me to say some things to a British audience for which another ALA President might have been branded an "ugly American." The speech stirred up things for a while, particularly vis-à-vis the LA's method of appointing its Presidents. But tradition and the establishment prevailed and democracy has yet to make a dent in the process—though my old friend Edward Dudley has recently raised the topic again in his "Libraryland" column in the *Library Association Record*.

The final item in this section was delivered as part of a panel discussion of what became known as "The Lacy Commission Report," after its chair, Dan Lacy. This report created much controversy at the time, mainly because so much of it was in opposition to existing ALA policy—despite the presence on the body of an all-star delegation of librarians. The principal defender of ALA policy, and of what many of us regarded as socially responsible positions, was, interestingly enough, none of these librarians but the distinguished journalist Ben Bagdikian, whose minority opinions remain a pleasure to read.

Potential for Power

An editorial in a midwestern newspaper some months ago welcomed the nation's Young Democrats to the city. In doing so the editorial commented: "We not only welcome you, Young Democrats, but we also extend to you our deepest sympathy. Why won't the Old Democrats let you grow up? Why are you discriminated against, segregated into a perpetually juvenile branch, kept in political short pants?"

One librarian who read this editorial said: "I've always felt this way about ALA's Junior Members Round Table and never joined, even when I was eligible. Nobody over 14 should want to belong to a group labeled Junior anything."

We do not go along altogether with these comments, but must admit to some grave misgivings about the Junior Members Round Table in its present state. As an organization it has been in existence nearly 30 years. What has it ever achieved?

Its declared purpose is "to help the individual member to orient himself in the library profession and in its organization . . . to promote a greater feeling of responsibility among younger members of the profession for the development of library service and librarianship; and to inform young people of the scope and potentialities of the library profession," the latter mainly through cooperation with recruiting agencies. These objectives may be laudable: to us they seem at once nebulous and dull. There is little in them to stimulate the imagination or excite the enthusiasm of the young, less that appeals for independence of thought and action, or makes demands upon the potential energy and vitality that should be the most valuable product our young librarians have to offer the library service and the profession.

We suspect that those who set up this organization and supported it in the beginning might have had an important and undeclared objective,

---

Reprinted by permission from *Library Journal,* September 1, 1960. Copyright © 1960, Reed Publishing, USA.

or at least a hope—that the Round Table might reveal so much earlier the "coming" young men and women in the profession, the future leaders. We know that a number of senior members of the profession are disappointed that the Round Table has not fulfilled this hope to any noticeable degree.

There is, in our view, a reason for this failure, and it is perhaps best revealed by a comparison of the Round Table with the English Association of Assistant Librarians. This latter group, an official section of the (British) Library Association since 1929, and before that an independent organization, has been variously described as "an anomaly," "a ginger group," and in other less savory terms. But you would be hard put to find more than a sour minority who would dismiss the AAL as irresponsible, and there are few who would advocate its abolition.

This group is represented on all the important committees and on the Council of the parent body, and it wields tremendous influence and power. It has on occasion wielded that power by bringing together its forces (about two-thirds of the total voting strength of the Library Association) to overthrow the dictates and decisions of the elder statesmen. Sometimes it has been wrong; more often than not, it has shown greater wisdom than has been apparent on higher levels.

The weakness of the Junior Members Round Table* is that it does not have the AAL's potential for power. It does not have a strong local or regional organization; it is not represented in the inner conclaves where it can have influence upon the more important activities of the association. There must be angry, or at least dissatisfied, young men (and women) in the library profession. A vital junior organization should provide avenues for the constructive use of the energy generated by that anger or dissatisfaction. It will not happen while younger librarians are herded into a "dolly" organization where they may play, but where guns are forbidden.

---

* The Junior Members Round Table has since been renamed the New Members Round Table.

Library Association Agonies: Or, Life with ALA and its Brothers and Sisters

I'm going to ramble a bit about library associations. But I'm not going to get hung up with definitions and altercations about what is or is not a *professional* association. That's library school lawyer rhetoric, academic garbage, a waste of time. The only substantive question is whether our associations are doing the job we them want to do—indeed, whether they can do it.

Forgive me if I talk mainly about American associations, and most particularly about the American Library Association (ALA). But a man (unless he be a consultant or a rogue) should talk about what he knows best. And I have been out of both Canada and Britain too long to have a very keen current perception of how things are with their associations. Although from across the border, CLA looks no more scintillating and forceful now than it did close-up a dozen years ago.

I'm going to start off with a medley of quotations to set the scene, the theme, the tenor of what is to follow:

Quote 1 (on Special Libraries Association): "If the 62nd Annual Conference of SLA is to have an overall meaning, it does not lie in its meaningless theme, 'Design for Service: Information Management,' but in the death of a concern—the merger (with ASIS)—that has already drained energy which might have been better used. For however well the merger might have served the association members themselves and reduced somewhat the schizophrenic anxieties of librarian/information

---

Originally a talk to the Dalhousie University School of Library Service, October 4, 1971, this article is reprinted by permission from *APLA Bulletin* 35, No. 4: 87-94, December 1971. It also appeared, slightly revised, in *American Libraries* 3: 395-400, April 1972; and in *The Best of Library Lit. 3* (Scarecrow Press, 1973), pp. 58-70.

scientists, it would have made little difference in service to the library user."

Quote II (on the Medical Library Association): "The 1,400 librarians who gathered in New York ... for the 70th Annual Meeting of the Medical Library Association may, collectively, have known more than any one doctor about the treatment of physical diseases, but the group still entered its septuagenarian era suffering from those afflictions common to all library associations: professional identity crisis and organizational obsolescence."

Quote III (on the Canadian Library Association): "The theme was 'Reorganization, Recruitment, and Results.' It had a ring of desperation to it: CLA must restructure and revitalize itself or it will lose both present and potential members. Some would have added 'Rehash' to these three Rs, because CLA has covered this ground many times before—without results."

Quote IV (on the American Library Association): "If more ALA members now realize that real power in the Association is beyond their grasp, Dallas also proved to them that you can still apply effective pressure, and in time, achieve rhetorical goals. This appeared to be especially true if all you wanted was an expression of ALA sentiment on a current issue, and it wouldn't cost any money."

Quote V: (also on ALA): "Dissent and disenchantment counterpointed the week's events, with school librarians seriously considering terminating their ALA ties while the college and university librarians set up August 31, 1972 as their *federation or forget it day.* Trustees, too, entertained independence, with the urban group making the loudest noise and then agreeing to stay on for a while to help the other trustees get the courage to strike off on their own."

Those five quotations come from the pens of four different writers, writing in the "big three" American library periodicals (*LJ, WLB, AL*) about the meetings this summer of four different library associations.

If, collectively, they seem to you to present a picture of confusion, desperation, chaos, you read them correctly. The library associations are, without exception, in a mess, trying to find a direction, a purpose; trying to understand what their members really want (and generally to find ways to tell them it's impossible); trying to find a role for themselves in a society which is changing faster than ever they knew how; trying to survive a battery of pressures they have never faced—perhaps never seen—before.

But if it is all a mess, it is a healthy one, in my opinion. At least the associations have been knocked off the dead center of the status quo. Some bullets of concern have riddled the armor of complacency and left it yawning with holes of doubt and uncertainty. The reason that words like restructuring and new directions pervade every meeting of every association is that there is, finally, an awareness that change is no longer desirable but mandatory—or the associations will die or be replaced. I also think the chaos is healthy because the library paste that has held the associations together—membership inertia—is finally coming unstuck.

While the realization is dawning, however, that the associations must change drastically, must gear themselves up to deal with a world and a membership which are both vastly different from those of 1876 (or even 1945), the big question which hangs over the association scene, as the bomb does over us all, is whether a structure and a purpose which will hold everything together can be found quickly enough, before the friction and the forces burn and blast the remnants of a century of dedicated, if not always inspired, effort into a cloud of ashes.

Let's look, then, at ALA, which is better and worse, in various respects, than most of the other library associations, to see if we can discern where some of the problems lie and what, if anything, can be done about them.

It may be almost a cliché, but I have to say that the most powerful force which is making the gothic pillars of the library associations tremble is morality. This is a problem that our associations share with many of the most basic and prestigious institutions in society: the schools and universities, government and the courts; science and the church; and many of the other professions, beginning with the most prestigious (hitherto) of them all, medicine. The gulf between word and deed in all these arenas seems not only to have become more apparent today but it is being challenged and questioned as rarely, perhaps never, before.

Now I do not mean to set up any simple, black and white dichotomy in which the establishment (i.e., the oldies) are all immoral, and the turks (i.e., the kids) are all snow-white and virtuous. I do mean to suggest, though, that many of those who grew up through the years of the Depression and World War II, the years when material comfort and prosperity were major, urgent and difficult goals, have an understandable survival complex, and thus an armament in which expediency and a deliberate (i.e. slow) rate of change are honored and well-used weapons. Many of the younger librarians, like other young people—and, let it be said, a goodly number of oldies, too—do not see materialism and survival as synonymous, and they can get so hung-up on principle that expediency can appear downright immoral.

What I'm talking about may make better sense if we examine a few prominent specifics, vis-à-vis ALA. Perhaps the most holy sacred cow in the ALA stable is the association's legislative program and its Washington Office. It is understandable that it should be so. Remember that prior to 1956 federal aid to libraries, for all intents and purposes, just didn't exist. From the first passage of the Library Services Act that year, literally hundreds of millions of federal money (and a few million more from other sources, stimulated by that flow) have poured into library coffers across the land. Libraries owe most of that manna to ALA, to a hard-working and exceptionally able lobbying staff, and to the number one priority which the association has given to that effort. There was no doubt of the need, and no doubt either that in this area ALA has produced, and produced big. Can there be room for criticism, then? Yes, there can.

It is a fact of life—still, but it was even more so in the late fifties and early sixties—that the real power in Congress lay in the cotton and tobacco stained palms of Southern committee chairmen. So, too, did the fate and continued health of library legislation. It was no coincidence, nor any real reflection of the concentration of need, that the early emphasis in the Library Services Act was on rural library development. Nor is it any coincidence that today, when the screamingly obvious crisis in libraries is in the big metropolitan cities, federal aid to city libraries is still, proportionately, pathetic.

That fact of life is also why pressure was brought to bear, heavily and rapidly, on me and on my friend John Wakeman at the *Wilson Library Bulletin* when, very early in the sixties, we decided to expose the racial situation in U.S. librarianship. Not only were discrimination and outright segregation rife in libraries—most evidently but not exclusively in the South—but ALA was nestling under its wing a number of state associations, several of them as chapters of the parent association, which were themselves segregated. Wakeman and I were urged to cool it because too much noise about all that racial stuff was calculated to upset our Southern sponsors in Congress and thus jeopardize all that lovely federal loot they were dealing out to libraries. In the racial climate of today that sounds not only immoral but pretty foolish. But then I remember asking, with youthful naiveté, "If you have no principles, what good is the money?" And the question made no sense to some of those of whom I asked it. Political expediency was obviously paying off for librarians. Now which could possibly be more important? Money or morality?

A more recent example of greater interest of ALA's legislative forces in matters fiscal than matters moral occurred at the Midwinter meeting last January (1971)—or, more precisely, began to occur there.

The ALA Council passed a fairly forthright resolution offered by the association's Intellectual Freedom Committee, which commended the Presidential Commission on Obscenity and Pornography for "amassing a significant body of empirical evidence in an area of great social concern . . . " The resolution also quoted President Nixon's statement: "I have evaluated that report and categorically reject its morally bankrupt conclusions and recommendations" and urged the President and Senate to reconsider this "categorical rejection."

The ALA Legislative Committee quickly mounted its opposition. Its chairman (ironically a former chairman of the Intellectual Freedom Committee) tried from the floor to water down the paragraphs which were clearly critical of the President and the Senate because of the effect these might have on the ALA's legislative programs.

Even after the Council passed the resolution, another attempt was made, just two days later, to water it down. Another long-time worker in the ALA legislative fields protested that it wasn't within ALA's field of expertise to take issue with the President's and the Senate's evaluation of the Commission Report, and that to do so would "detract from our credibility in Congress" and make "legislative work increasingly more difficult."

It was the first time in perhaps many years that anyone had suggested that opinions on intellectual freedom matters were not within ALA's province. To suddenly deny our special interest and involvement in this area, it seemed to me, and clearly to many others, might do more to damage our credibility than anything else. Council at any rate, stood firm, and the Executive Director was instructed to send the resolution, as an expression of association opinion, to the President and the Senate. The opposition from the legislative group was perhaps not too surprising, but they had been defeated, and that seemed the end of the story.

It wasn't. At the next conference we discovered that the resolution hadn't been sent out immediately, as everyone expected it would be, and as it clearly should have been for maximum effectiveness. It had been held up for something like six to eight weeks before being transmitted. The general suspicion, and I believe it was entirely correct, was that the legislative committee and/or the Washington Office had been responsible for these stalling tactics.

That may be enough to demonstrate, in that one area, the morality gap I referred to earlier. A second area—and another relatively holy one—in which ALA has been under pressure for the past several years is intellectual freedom itself. In the past, the association has made some notably fine and courageous statements—most particularly its Freedom to Read Statement, issued during the dark days of McCarthyism, when many another group was very carefully keeping quiet.

But as the pressures against dissent in the U.S. have mounted these past few years, librarians themselves (not just the books and magazines on their shelves) have fallen victim to repression and attack, and a steady stream of librarians have lost their jobs for supporting the very principles which ALA has long espoused. As the librarian casualty list has grown, the gap between ALA's promise and performance in the intellectual freedom arena has become more apparent. Impatience with the continued parade of noble statements has grown more vocal, and the demands for action, not just words, have grown more insistent.

Once again, however, in this area as in the legislative one, the dollar has been ALA's paramount interest. As each demand for concrete action has been made—notably the demand for a defense fund for librarians—the demand has been met early with the same argument: it cannot be done because it might injure ALA's tax exempt status. Gone, apparently, is the memory of that final resounding sentence of the Freedom to Read Statement: "Freedom itself is a dangerous way of life, but it is ours."

ALA's master ploy, at once preserving its precious tax-exempt status and at the same time giving the appearance of action, was to set up a separate organization, the Freedom to Read Foundation. The assumption was that the Foundation *could* do what ALA wouldn't because of its fear of being jilted by the Internal Revenue Service. Only a short time after, the Foundation told us that it couldn't take some of the actions for which it was set up, because it might lose *its* tax-exempt status. So the Foundation set up another fund under its wing, called the Leroy Merritt Fund, which was *not* tax-exempt, and which *could* be used for action purposes. It seemed only logical that if the Foundation could set up a separate fund, ALA could have done that too. But, no, the Foundation and ALA had different categories of tax-exempt status. It's a sad, funny, surrealist story—but it's clearly written on green paper.

Closely related to intellectual freedom is a third pressure point within ALA. The pressure in this area has come, not just from the radicals, the activists, the young, but also from some of the most conservative in the profession. A few years ago a President of ALA was unwise enough to indicate that ALA was more concerned with the welfare of libraries than with the welfare of librarians (though I couldn't find the actual quotation when I was looking for it). He was speaking the truth, even if it was dangerous. The ALA leaders do think, have thought, institutionally for most of the years of the association's existence. You need only to look at the ALA's Statement of Purpose to see the emphasis: "The promotion of library service of excellent quality, freely available to all." No one could quarrel with that statement, but it is possible to differ with the emphases in the implementation of that purpose. Listed under that statement are seven ways in which that purpose should be fulfilled; only one of them deals at all with librarians. It reads: "Improvement of professional library standards through better professional education, working conditions, salaries and certification."

The words, again, read better than the performance record, as the mounting cries for ALA to show its teeth in such matters as status, tenure, salaries, working conditions and the protection of librarians' rights have testified. ALA has begun to move in this area, and at its last conference it set up a new procedure and a new committee: the Committee on Mediation, Arbitration and Inquiry, which was given as its domain the broad sweep of "tenure, status, fair employment practices, due process, ethical practices, and the principles of intellectual freedom."

It is obviously too early to expect or pass any judgment about the prospects of this committee producing the kind of results the membership wants but, pessimist though I am, I believe this is one part of the machinery that may move into action. This is not pure optimism, but is based on the belief that ALA can, in this instance, see its dollar interests at stake. It has seen the steady growth of library unions the past five or more years, and must know that they have grown because the association left them room to grow. If the unions do what librarians want, and ALA doesn't, it obviously won't be long before much of the ALA membership income is translated into union dues. Self-satisfied as it often is, ALA is not stupid, and it has seen, for example, the rapid transformation recently of the National Education Association, which has become much more militant about matters like working conditions and teachers' rights because it was rapidly losing membership and influence to the booming United Federation of Teachers. If the unions can move ALA off the pot in such matters, they will have rendered a real service to the profession, because it will be a long time before the unions themselves can accumulate the prestige and influence that ALA undoubtedly has in certain quarters, even though it may be timid about exercising it.

A fourth area of pressure—and this is certainly one that just about every organization is experiencing—is the swelling demand for (to use a popular contemporary redundancy) "participatory democracy." (If democracy isn't participatory it isn't democracy.) The ALA membership has grown increasingly vociferous about the continued presence of the same select band of people on all the key committees of the association; increasingly frustrated over the continued rejection of membership proposals by the ALA Council and Executive Board; increasingly angry that priorities and programs are not funded while, at the same time, the huge headquarters grows more obese, eating away at larger and larger portions of the ALA budget, and less responsive every year. Indeed, at the last ALA conference, the membership vented its spleen on the ALA budget committee (COPES) for making no attempt in its 1971-72 budget to reflect the priorities of the Association which had been voted in by the membership and adopted by the Council, the supposed policy-making body of ALA. COPES was the first committee that most people could recall ever being roundly censured by the membership.

Nevertheless, despite the swelling volume of membership discontent, the ALA, like the other associations, continues to be dominated by administrators. The principal reason is not hard to discern: while the administrators have such a stranglehold on library policy at the local level, while they are so often the only members of the staff who are paid to attend meetings and conventions, they have an access edge that is terribly difficult to overcome. Until there is more participatory democracy at the local (library) level, it will be hard to achieve at the national level. This is one area, incidently, where staff unions may play a key role.

But a major part of the problem continues to be one of attitude, and this is most clearly illustrated by a little internal document circulated among members of the ALA Nominating Committee for 1972-73. This document spelled out some of the proposed criteria for candidates for the Council, for President-elect and Treasurer. The committee wanted "some evidence of having accomplished good for the association," or "evidence of cultural refinement"; the candidate "must have presence"; and worst of all, perhaps, the committee said "age bracket between 45 and 55 desirable." Other tired criteria listed included "experience," "knowledge of the ALA structure," and such vital elements as "physical stamina," or "international dimension," or "articulate." As *Library Journal* commented: "If you added 'strong baritone' and 'good looks' to the list, you might think we are about to elect the U.S. Ambassador to Monaco, or the MC for the Miss America pageant."

Despite this evidence of the intransigence and durability of 19th-century thinking, the noisy restlessness of the membership has had *some* effect, and a number of new faces and voices are infiltrating the committee rooms of ALA. The establishment, though, picks carefully, and it seems to know its own kind very well, even when they are in the embryo stage. It is interesting, even if not surprising, how like the establishment some of the young malcontents of only a year or two ago look and sound, after just a short period of close contact with the establishment bosom.

Faced with an attitude gap that will clearly take an intolerably long time to counteract, some of those who seek radical change in ALA have begun to learn the uncomfortable lesson that organization and knowledge are necessary weapons to overcome the fear, the inertia, the defensiveness, and so they are learning the machinery—the bylaws and the constitution, the election procedures, and how they can be used to advantage. In the past few years they have pressured for the liberalization of the nomination and election machinery: the one weapon that is not locked in the establishment's arsenal. And there is now a steady input of new names on election ballots, either put there by petition or—and this is important, too—put there by those who control the nomination procedure, as a means of quelling some of the protest.

The thing the change-seekers have not yet done—or certainly have not done effectively—is to go out and organize votes for those they have gotten on the ballot. It's a lot of work, but it can be done and it has to be. All current appearances and the Yippies to the contrary, successful revolutions have never been organized or won by people who want to play games, or who see chaos and turbulence as just another kind of fun. They are won by people who have a target and who go after it. If that makes me a structure freak, so be it.

I have saved the biggest and perhaps most important pressure point for last. The most overwhelming protest in ALA (and this again is true of other organizations, indeed of society itself) is on social issues: race, sex and war, to name only three potent elements.

ALA has been struggling with racial issues, as I indicated at the outset, for about a decade now, but the pressure has accelerated recently, primarily because of the emergence a couple of years ago of the Black Caucus. Adding to the pressure has been the Social Responsibilities Round Table of ALA, also formed just a couple of years ago. In the past twelve months these two groups have had the Executive Board, the Council and the Intellectual Freedom Committee of ALA in a turmoil over such matters as: 1) the Black Caucus's charges that southern schools have been providing library services, with public funds, to newly formed private schools which were set up to bypass the law of the land on integration of schools; 2) the same group's charges that the Library of Congress has been discriminating in employment and promotion against blacks; 3) SRRT's donation to the Angela Davis defense fund, without prior consultation with ALA.

Other groups which have been pushing hard are the Women's Liberation and Gay Liberation Task Forces of SRRT. Indeed, at the Dallas meeting this summer, the Gay Lib group stole most of the association's headlines in the press, on radio and television, with their "Hug a Homosexual" booth in the exhibit area, and a variety of other activities. They also got through the Council a resolution calling for the better protection of the rights of homosexuals in libraries and in librarianship.

Beyond these groups' pressures, however, there is a more pervasive insistence that ALA deal with and express itself on social issues. The most persistent topic, of course, has been the Vietnam war. This summer, a resolution against the War finally passed both the membership and the Council. One member, afterwards, commented that it had passed this time, after several abortive attempts, because the thrust of its argument on this occasion was on the "reallocation" of national resources, with greater emphasis on domestic needs (i.e. libraries, for example), rather than the issue of the war and its killing and devastation. Dollars, again, this member was saying, as I have said repeatedly, are a more persuasive argument around ALA than morality.

Two other points should be made about that Vietnam resolution, and another about the social pressure in general, because they may demonstrate why I thought this paper might be pertinent at a library school.

First the Vietnam resolution was drafted and presented by two library school students, part of the Students to Dallas group which was composed of delegates from every one of the accredited library schools in the U.S. and Canada. They proved, by their handling and presentation, that you don't need to be well into the sere and yellow before you can hope to have an impact, even on a mammoth, cumbersome, labyrinthine organization like ALA.

The second point about the Vietnam resolution was that it came too late to be very meaningful. Had it been made, even two or three years ago, ALA might reasonably have been considered as an organization working at the forefront of public opinion.

Now, opposition to the war is the accepted, majority position. Thus, ALA's statement is, as so many of its others have been, just another motherhood and flag parade.

The point I want to make about the social pressure generally is that it really began for ALA, at least on a heavy scale, at the Atlantic City Conference in 1969.

The group that opened up the big guns was called The Congress for Change. It, too, was very heavily a student group. Its real successor, the Social Responsibilities Round Table, though not a student organized or dominated group, has the youngest leadership in the ALA—unless one counts seriously the Junior Members Round Table, which very few people do. SRRT is the most volatile group in the association, and though it loses more often than it wins, it has done much to upset the equilibrium of the upper establishment and it has, far more than it knows, I think, changed the climate of ALA. There is nervousness, even fear, among those who were merely complacent before, and some of the inertia has been translated into an unwilling receptivity. . . .

I said earlier that I would suggest some of the things that ought or need to be done to rescue ALA and the other associations from the chaos in which they find themselves. I'm going to keep my remedies very brief but here are a few to wind up with:

1. A large step in the direction of democratization must be taken. No valid reason exists, for example, except the economic (and I think I've said enough about dollars dictating all our courses of action)—no valid reason why it should be made difficult for anyone who wants to run for any office whatsoever, to get on the ballot. Those who get nervous about this apparently see no difference between nomination and election. Nomination is only democratic if it is easily available. Election is only democratic if it is competitive.

More people must be brought into the key operating committees of the associations whose views differ radically from those of the traditional incumbents. If nothing else, the committee rooms might become less deadly places to pass a few hours if a modicum of dissident opinion were heard there. The club members, who have served endlessly and repeatedly, must be weeded out and replaced.

2. The associations must hammer out specific program and policy priorities, and must then proceed to budget them. Policies and programs mean nothing unless they are financed. Priorities which are not reflected in the budget are no more than pieties.

3. The associations, to mention further pieties, must desist from continually making public policy pronouncements unless they are prepared to follow them up, and particularly to defend their members who carry out those policies on the front lines. In short, we need not more words but more teeth behind the words.

4. Decisions must be made as to what activities can best be handled centrally, on behalf of the whole association, and which might better be decentralized and left to smaller, perhaps looser and faster-operating groups. On the really big issues, however, which demand the force of unity, of maximum numbers, the associations must vigorously resist the splintering which has been weakening the library profession throughout this century and must stamp heavily on parochialism—particularly type-of-library parochialism.

5. The associations must begin to regard themselves as a responsible and potentially powerful voice in society, as bodies with a responsibility and a right to speak out (as many other groups do)—not just on matters bibliographic but on major social concerns. They have only to remember the biggest, oldest cliché of them all to get the point. How many times have you heard: "I became a librarian because I love books and people"? It isn't as silly as it sounds, but the *people* interest isn't as clear from our words and actions as the devotion to books. If we don't talk about social ills, social needs, social concerns, do we really expect anyone to know or believe that we're interested or that we care about people? And if we seem not to care, can we be surprised when libraries get into trouble and no one else seems much to care about that?

6. Finally, the young, the dissident, the radical, the change-seekers must keep up the pressure and must resist despondency about the temporary losses. The climate can be changed, even by defeats. And the over-all war, which is worth winning, for sanity and responsibility, can be won. And must be.

The State of the Union, Jack

This is, I think, the second most difficult paper I've had to prepare in a very long time. The hardest was last year, when I was inaugurated as ALA's President. I have always been more comfortable, like Michael Foot perhaps, in opposition and the warm minority of the back bench, and I do not adjust easily to august occasions, the polite nothings of diplomacy, or the aura of history.

I remember how I struggled to get started on that inaugural speech. A certain amount of reverence is conjured up by events like inaugurations, but I didn't want to start off sounding like a pompous ass. The pathway through the dilemma was cleared by my favorite American columnist, Russell Baker of the *New York Times*. He's my breakfast diet three mornings a week and he's good for the soul and stomach both. He serves up perspective and a sense of proportion about the horrors and inequities and foolishness recorded daily in other pages of the paper, and he roundly and regularly deflates pretentiousness.

I had saved a column he had written in the autumn of 1976 entitled "Historic Occasion Fatigue." This is how it began:

> It is disappointing to hear that the Ford-Carter debates will be historic. One had hoped for more. Almost everything is historic these days, except for speeches, which all seem to be major.
> It's been years since anybody has given a minor speech or taken part in an unhistoric occasion . . .

And so on. And it got better from there. Well, that column was just the ticket for me. We had packed all our historic occasions into 1976: the

---

Originally a speech at The Library Association's Centenary Conference, London, October 5, 1977, this appeared in *The Assistant Librarian* 70, No. 11: 166-172, November 1977, and in The Library Association, *Centenary Conference Proceedings,* 1977, pp. 73-78. It is reprinted by permission of Library Association Publishing and the Association of Assistant Librarians.

nation's bicentennial, the ALA's and *Library Journal*'s 100th birthdays, and the inauguration of my friend and predecessor, Clara Jones, as ALA's first black president. I could feel secure, after all that, in the knowledge that 1977 could only be anticlimactic—certainly far from an historic occasion.

But here, Russell Baker is of little help. This *is* the LA's centenary; it *is* an historic occasion. So I had to grope for another handle to open the door. Well, librarians are supposed to have some training in logic (who can forget the library school hours spent poring over Jevons and Mill and Hulme, and even Howard Phillips' collection of multi-colored rags?), and it seemed logical to me that one might find some kind of entrée to an historic occasion in history itself.

At that Conference of Librarians a hundred years ago in London, at which the Library Association burst upon the scene (if that's not too explosive a term to describe such a seemingly sedate occasion), the American Library Association, a strapping one-year-old, was present in impressive force. The numbers aren't quite certain. *LJ* counted 21 or 22, though with Dewey doing the counting, I'm surprised he didn't come up with 21.5. Budd Gambee, ten years ago in the *Journal of Library History,* records a definite sixteen. Whatever, it was a creditable proportion of ALA's then membership—and certainly of its establishment. Included were such giants as Cutter and Dewey, Poole and Justin Winsor, and even Dewey's future bride, Miss Annie Godfrey of Wellesley.

Most of ALA's Executive Board being on that "junket," as Gambee calls it, it seems they tried to put things in a better light by having a couple of Board meetings on shipboard, one on the way over, another on the way back. The return fare for the "best accommodations," Gambee informs us heartrendingly, was $90.

I can assure you that our Executive Director this time came up with nothing so appealing as a long leisurely ocean voyage or a fare that even puts Freddie Laker in the shade.

Like Dewey, I don't seem to count very well and I'm not sure how many Yanks are here, but Bob Wedgeworth and I were most insistent that ALA recognize this occasion properly—as you did ours a year ago, with no less than eight British librarians present in Chicago, and many more from the Commonwealth. I know we have with us four of ALA's five top officers—all save the Treasurer, who is back home grimly holding on to the association's vulnerable purse strings. And I know we have a fair number of other American librarians here to do you honor and share this great week with you.

It's interesting to speculate about some of the differences between these two conferences, one hundred years apart. One thing's for sure: they had a lot more staying-power (for meetings, at least, if not for swinging boat trips). The first session of that 1877 Conference lasted four and a quarter hours, including announcements, the inaugural address and subsequent discussion, and two other major papers, discussion on the last of which had to be "deferred till the evening." Since the session started at 10 a.m. they had already gone right through lunch!

The interests of the American visitors have undoubtedly changed somewhat in the past century, too. Those doughty 19th-century American librarians were concerned over the fact that Englishmen wore their hats in the reading room; that few English women were employed as librarians (there are still some of us who like a lot of women around!); and that the bookcases in British libraries were so high that ladders were required (which brings back 30-year-old memories for me of the Birmingham Reference Library).

The fascinating papers at that founding conference included one on "An Evitandum in Index-Making, Principally Met with in French and German Periodical Scientific Literature." If that doesn't grab you, there was a scintillating thriller "On the Alphabetical Arrangement of the Titles of Anonymous Books."

But the most remarkable aspect of that conference, seen from today's perspective, was the press coverage. *LJ,* then the only library periodical around, was having its difficulties. The October 1877 issue began with an apology: "We had hoped to give in this number a letter from Mr. Dewey summarizing the results of the gathering in London, but have been disappointed in its arrival." It wouldn't be the last time that old Melvil proved to be something less than a hot-shot reporter. Waiting for Melvil, *LJ* meanwhile picked up snippets of news from the London papers and a source described as "elsewhere." *The Times* (of London) was a goldmine. Gambee says it "reported every sitting with a stenographic thoroughness second only to the official transactions." Would that librarianship—on either side of the Atlantic—could attract such national press attention today!

But there were, then as now, cynics among the press corps. One rather jaded journalist, writing for the *Globe,* declared that he was "not young and hopeful enough to imagine that much good will result from the conference." He saw the "meeting as a pleasant social incident . . . likely to produce a certain esprit de corps and sentiment of brotherly acquaintance" (he apparently also noticed the paucity of women!).

"The Conference," said the opinionated *Globe* reporter, "will doubtless be attended with some conflict of opinions and a good deal of useless talk; and when the discussions have closed with the usual interchanges of compliments and courtesies, the orators will return to their homes little wiser than they left them. . . . But it may safely be predicted that the conference will have no revolutionary consequences."

Here, it occurred to me, was the clue I had been searching for in the historical record. Though I have shared that *Globe* reporter's sentiments through some pretty deadly meetings and conferences, it seemed to me that a conference on an occasion like this is particularly vulnerable to sinking into the quicksand of platitudes and pleasantries, and that it *ought* to have some revolutionary consequences. And if the AAL [Association of Assistant Librarians] is still remotely like the AAL I used to know, this is the place to explore the possibilities, because the AAL, if anyone, ought to be a prominent instigator in ensuring that revolutionary consequences result. This, perhaps, was the hook I could hang this paper on.

Before I reached that point I had toyed with the idea of venturing some comparisons of libraryland, British and American subterritories, and to prepare for the exercise had launched into a fast survey of some of the British library literature I hadn't read these past twenty years. It was a dispiriting exercise. The more I read, the more apparent it became that I knew so little about British librarianship as it now is that it would be a gross arrogance for me to attempt to comment on it at other than surface depth. The landscape has been transformed so dramatically by the panorama of revolutionary developments that have taken place these last two decades that my view from the Finchley, Brentford & Chiswick, Kensington, and the Chaucer House of the fifties is comparable to what one sees through the wrong end of the telescope.

Two massive local government reorganizations—which have even created place-names I don't recognize (Tower Hamlets, indeed!)—the total reorganization of your national libraries, an endless parade of reports (Parry, Plowden, Maud, Mallaby, Dainton, the Library Advisory Councils, etc.), the wonder of your Open University, new national library legislation, library education transfigured with an academic face-lift, libraries nestled under the wing of the Department of Education and Science, my old colleagues Sewell and Jones as some kind of Gogol-like government inspectors of libraries—all this was a world created in my absence, a library world I didn't understand at all.

Clearly, the home wicket was likely to be a little less sticky and it would be wiser to dig in there. In the U.S., presidents always talk about the State of the Union, which was one reason for my title. Another was that when I was asked for a label I hadn't even envisioned the jacket to which it would be attached. But I could not resist that confluence of Union and Jack, and that little comma in the middle was there to represent my still mid-Atlantic leanings. At any rate, ALA is the union who's state I have to care for at present (though it surely wouldn't much like the word), and some of the revolutionary changes I've seen in it since I crossed the water are what I want to discuss. I may yet risk a few comparative points along the way, impressionistic as they must be—and if my impressions of this side of the Atlantic are, as we say, 'way off base, as they may well be, let me apologize in advance.

When I went to the States, as editor of *LJ*, on Guy Fawkes Day, 1959, two of the first things I noticed were the avoidance of controversy and the absence of anything like the AAL. I even thought there might be a connection somewhere between those facts. In one of my earliest *LJ* editorials I compared ALA's Junior Members Round Table (the only and nearest equivalent we then had) with the AAL (see chapter 33). The concluding paragraph of that editorial read:

> The weakness of the Junior Members Round Table is that it does not have the AAL's potential for power. It does not have a strong local or regional organization; it is not represented in the inner conclaves where it can have influence upon the more important activities of the association. There must be angry, or at least dissatisfied, young men (and women) in the library profession. A vital junior organization should provide avenues for the constructive energy generated by that anger or dissatisfaction. It will not happen while younger librarians are herded into a dolly organization where they may play, but where guns are forbidden.

Later, I came to understand that there was even more to our lack of an AAL than that. A little over a year ago, my wife and I were at a Canadian Library Association conference. We watched and listened as a comparatively young man handled a very thorny and potentially explosive meeting with complete aplomb, quiet skill and total authority. He clearly knew parliamentary procedure, and just as clearly had solid experience on the platform. His accent was unmistakable, even to an American, and my wife said: "How come all you British librarians are so good at this stuff?" I knew that British librarian, and knew where he had learned that "stuff." I said, simply, "He's an old AAL type."

I don't know how many hundred conferences, meetings, committees I've sat in on during my years in America, but I can tell you that I've seen dozens of meetings mangled, mired in confusion, suffused with boredom, flooded with anger, when that kind of competence in the chair, or even at the floor microphones, might have prevented any of these reactions. In general—and of course there are a good number of shining exceptions—American librarians do not handle such matters as well as you do, and I think the early training in the heat of the kitchen that younger librarians get through involvement in the AAL may really account for some of the difference.

The JMRT has improved somewhat, I think, but it still lacks clout and, though it does some useful things, it still in my view is more social than activist.

However, we did have something of a library revolution in the Sixties in America, and many other units and sub-units have emerged in ALA, some of which certainly cannot be described as tame or inactive. One is our Social Responsibilities Round Table (what we call SRRT), which for a time I hoped might emerge as our equivalent of the AAL. There is no doubt that, over the past six or seven years, it has been our "ginger group," as the AAL has so often been called. But it, too, lacks the AAL's organizational talent and established place in the power structure, and it has never developed into the cogent force some of us hoped it might become.

This is not to say that it has not had impact. SRRT came out of the cauldron of controversy and rebellion that *was* the United States in the Sixties—a cauldron kept boiling with ingredients like the Vietnam War, assassinations, Kent State, Martin Luther King, student activism, riots in our major cities, the Black Panthers, the CIA and FBI, and many other elements.

Many saw this as a terrible period in our history; others of us saw it as hopeful, as a reawakening of social consciousness. In any case, it had its impact on libraryland, and what there was of a revolution in librarianship reached its high point at the most incredible and exciting conference I've attended in nearly four decades in the profession: the 1969 ALA Conference in Atlantic City.

Leading the activism there was a new group called the Congress for Change, its membership heavily, though not exclusively, library school students. They kept the establishment (or some of them) on the brink of nervous hysteria and our membership meeting began to resemble one of those Congressional filibuster scenes they used to like to make movies about. I seemed to be one of the relatively few people both sides knew and felt they could talk to, and I remember both those on the platform and those jamming the front seats and the floor microphones, each asking me about the other, "What do they want?" That simple question seemed to me to say everything about our problem: the tremendous gulf of understanding that existed between the top and the bottom of the profession.

Let me backtrack for a moment to the early Sixties to record my own awakening to the fact that libraries had two choices: to be a significant thread in the social fabric, an active participant in social change, or to face a dodo-like slow passage toward extinction or existence as a historical relic. I did not have to be in the States very long to see that, in some library circles at least, there was a much greater awareness of social issues as they affected librarianship—of civil rights matters, of the need constantly to man the free speech barricades, of where libraries fitted into such governmental dreams as Johnson's War on Poverty—than I had ever known in nearly twenty years in British librarianship.

The consciousness was in some ways an old one. In the fifties, when much of America cowered before the indiscriminate fire of Tailgunner Joe McCarthy, the ALA, one of the few organizations not to remain silent, issued its ringing Freedom to Read Statement: it's still a document and a moment to make one proud to be a librarian. And back in the thirties, poet Stanley Kunitz, then editor of the *Wilson Library Bulletin,* wrote an editorial called "The Spectre at Richmond," which was years ahead of the profession generally in social consciousness and exposed the shameful treatment and indignities black librarians could expect at their own professional association meetings.

This is not to suggest that ALA was a model of social consciousness in the early sixties (or that it is now, as we shall see). Indeed, some of us battled right through that decade trying to prove to some of our colleagues that social issues were library issues. On the other side were those who wanted not to let us talk about Vietnam or poverty or whatever unless we could demonstrate a "library" connection.

Apart from the morality, where did they think the money was coming from to kill all those people so many thousands of miles away? Right out of the hides of our library services and of other *social* services, that's where.

Nevertheless, the U.S. Supreme Court's historic Brown decision calling for integration of schools throughout the United States was almost a decade old in the early sixties, and racial awareness and activism were growing fast. Both John Wakeman, my former assistant at Finchley, who was then editing the *Wilson Library Bulletin,* and I, over at *LJ,* quickly became embroiled in the raging debate over civil rights issues—and particularly over segregated libraries and segregated library associations in the South. Nothing either of us had ever experienced in British librarianship was preparation for such involvement; we had to learn the hard way. Meanwhile, the ALA acted, often reluctantly, usually under great pressure, sometimes too slowly and unconvincingly, but act it did, and some of the wrongs in our associations and our library services began to be alleviated, if by no means removed altogether.

We are still far from home or on safe ground on racial issues. If people, whatever their heritage or color, may now use most libraries without distinction or barriers; if any librarian may now join and attend the meetings of his or her association, we have still not achieved equal treatment in recruitment, training, hiring and promotion of librarians. White middle class people still mostly run libraries, and they naturally tend to gear their services to the needs they know. We don't have to be naive enough to believe that prejudice can be eradicated to insist that such visible and unjust *results* of prejudice be eliminated.

Worse, perhaps, after all these years of grappling with racial problems, is the degree to which otherwise intelligent people remain grossly insensitive in this area. We faced the results of such insensitivity again this year at our annual conference in Detroit, where a film called *The Speaker,* made we must assume with good intentions, and with the sponsorship of ALA's Intellectual Freedom Committee, managed to split our association wide open on racial lines, to a degree we have not experienced in more than a decade.

I am sure that some of you are feeling at this point that all of this is far removed in time and spirit from anything that has impact on you or on British librarianship, but, like Andrew Young, our U.N. ambassador, I don't believe racism is a national characteristic. It blooms, like weeds, in any overcrowded garden where the soil is not carefully tended. You have growing and already substantial racial minorities in this country, and even from across the Atlantic we see and hear familiar omens. The voice of Enoch Powell, accent apart, does not sound so terribly different from that of George Wallace.

With the appearance of Bob Usherwood in the columns of the *Assistant Librarian* some years ago there seemed to be signs of a budding social consciousness. I remember, for example, an article by Peter Jordan on "Social Class, Race Relations and the Public Library," and thinking, "here's a breakthrough." I remember reading elsewhere of a speaker at a one-day conference of the Library Association a couple of years ago who was concerned that British libraries were offering a very conservative and racist service. And I remember a comment in a recent chapter by Arnold and Usherwood, that "the harsh reality remains that few librarians or library authorities are really prepared for the challenges and opportunities which are provided by a multi-racial and multi-cultural society."

I hasten to add that I do not know from experience how accurate such comments are, but these rumblings in the British library literature seem to suggest that you are really just beginning to discern the potential dimensions of an issue under whose shadow the United States has lived throughout its history. Two things I can tell you. One is that inaction and delay—that abused Supreme Court phrase, "all deliberate speed"—will not make things easier, but much worse. And secondly, if you haven't done it already, you ought early to get some black and brown advice; whites alone cannot find the answers to problems of racism.

Now maybe you are already going out and actively recruiting Pakistani and Indian and West Indian and African librarians and getting them into library school so that you will have people in your libraries who understand the needs and problems of many readers (and probably many non-users of libraries) in this society who were not reared on Trollope or Agatha Christie. If you are doing these things, fine; if you are not, it may be growing awfully late to make a serious start.

I offer such advice humbly, not in the often arrogant manner of Americans abroad, who can be over-generous with their expertise. Their message is, Look how we've progressed, you can learn from us. It is not mine. But, please, there is a lesson in the *agony* of our experience. If you take note of that, and of the record of it in our literature, you may avoid duplicating the turmoil, the anger, the indignities that we had to go through on the road to whatever understanding we've yet achieved.

I hope the AAL, in its role as ginger group, will give high priority to convincing the LA and the profession that books and other media, the needs of the research community, the customary services to the white middle class, are not the whole library story. If libraries have a serious role in society, they must be aware of society's needs and problems, and must take an active role in attempting to solve them.

In a way, while I've said I'd like to see our SRRT take on some of the characteristics of the AAL, the AAL seems the natural body over here to undertake some parts of the role that SRRT plays in ALA. SRRT's charge, in the *ALA Handbook of Organization,* includes: "To provide a forum for discussion of the responsibilities of libraries in relation to the important problems of social change which face institutions and librarians . . . to act as a stimulus to the association and its various units in making libraries more responsive to current social needs. . . . "

The best job SRRT has done during its existence is to heighten awareness, increase the association's consciousness of needs and issues. It has done it in a variety of ways, but the usual first step has been to form what it calls a Task Force. One of these created an *Alternative Books in Print* to give recorded life to the publications of small and underground presses that didn't get into established bibliographic sources like *Books in Print*. Others deal with library service to minorities or to other groups which have been ill-served, such as migrant farm workers. Some task forces respond to the cause of those in our profession who lack influence or have suffered discrimination or lack of representation—two very different examples are Chicanos and gay people. But if SRRT (and other groups, like the Black Caucus in ALA) heightened our awareness of the needs and problems of minorities, SRRT also put up front and center another long-standing problem in our profession and in society: discrimination against the majority. That is, women.

You may remember that those American librarians who came to the 1877 Conference were concerned about the lack of women in British librarianship. That certainly is not the case today. On our side, the library profession is about 80% female. I don't know what it is here, but I'd guess no less than 70 to 75%. But where are the women in the leadership positions?

The sexual revolution lagged behind the racial one by a few years, but it is really with us now and a nationwide battle is going on to pass an Equal Rights Amendment to the United States Constitution. At this year's Detroit conference ALA joined in that battle, passing a resolution that after 1981, it would no longer hold any of its conferences or meetings in states that had not ratified the ERA. One of those states is Illinois, where our headquarters are located!

One new symbol of ALA's rising consciousness in this area is that we now have a new major Council committee on the Status of Women in Librarianship, part of whose charge is "to ensure that the Association considers the rights of the majority (women) in the library field."

Now this time I'm not just venturing an impression; there's no doubt in my mind that the LA and the AAL need some such mechanism. I could scarcely believe it when, a few months ago, my friend Norman Horrocks, another expatriate Englishman who serves on ALA's Executive Board, said to me: "Do you know the LA's only had one woman president in 100 years?" and asked, "Are you going to say anything about that?" "You're damn right, I am," I said.

Well, the AAL, I thought, with misplaced loyalty, will have done better than that. So I looked. My count may not be totally accurate, but it seems you have done better. Not much, however. I count less than half a dozen women presidents of the AAL in its history, which doesn't exactly reek with justice or equity either. And the Miss Book World beauty contests and the *Assistant Librarian*'s parade of pin-ups don't quite speak to any advanced level of consciousness of women as anything other than sex symbols. It's not that I have anything against sex symbols. In fact, I'd rather like to be one; but, like many women, I'd want someone, sometime, to notice that I might have something else, too.

I spoke of all this with a couple of visiting British librarians in the States recently, and while the male member of the duo admitted that one woman president of the LA in 100 years seemed "a bit off," he added, "but we wouldn't appoint someone president *just* because she's a woman."

The implications of that remark are devastating, if you think about it. If, given the mathematical proportions of membership, there has not been discrimination against women, it means that women are, generally, inferior to men and thus have only a very small chance of making it to the top of the heap. It's an attitude and a situation that is awfully familiar to blacks, and in recent years, in the U.S. at least, women have become increasingly aware of, and vocal about, the fact that they have been similarly and just as consciously discriminated against.

Talking of presidents and representation takes me on to another issue which was a major element of our internal ALA revolution in the sixties and early seventies, one aspect of which I saw raised a few years ago in an *Assistant Librarian* editorial on the "question of confidentiality and open meetings."

When I was active in the AAL many of us were concerned then that the upper echelons of the Library Association seemed to operate like one of those old-fashioned gentlemen's clubs. If you grew to be accepted, finally, after twenty or thirty years, you might be admitted to membership in the club. In the meantime, they weren't about to tell you what the hell was going on about anything. When Bill Smith and I took on the initial editorship of *Liaison* (which was the AAL's idea), we insisted on being able to attend any meeting we wanted to, and to call the shots in print the way we saw them. Sayers and Cashmore, I remember, were among the elders who were horrified at the thought, but Frank Gardner, a former

Assistant Librarian stalwart who by then had climbed the rungs of power, prevailed.

It wasn't too unlike that in ALA at the time of my arrival. As editor of *LJ* I wanted no strings on what I could report and I used to "crash" closed meetings regularly. I got very promptly marched out of quite a few. But the message got across and others began to understand the perils of privacy, and began to insist that the doors be opened. Today, it is a requirement that *all* ALA meetings be open to members, and to the press.

You have to have a very solid reason for an executive (that is, a private) session—for example, a meeting at which individuals may be being considered for some appointment—and even then, the results must be reported in open session. Our Council meetings are major public events in the Association and are heavily attended by members, since they take place during our annual conference and our Midwinter meeting.

With the doors open, the campaign to democratize the association took on a new head of steam. As a result of the revolutionary fervor of the late sixties we emerged with a succession of committees with exotic acronyms like ACONDA and ANACONDA, set up essentially with the purpose of bringing forward proposals for reorganization and democratization. I liked their unofficial name best. It derived from our then president, Bill Dix of Princeton, who appointed the original ACONDA (in short, the Committee on New Directions). The committee became known by a name that sounded like a *Variety* magazine headline, "the Dix Mix."

It's hard to nail down exactly what came out of all this, but one thing that certainly did was a larger awareness among members that they could use the system, the bylaws and regulations, to *their* purposes. They didn't have to sit back and accept dictates from above, even as to what candidates they could have and vote for in elections of their officers and their Council.

One mechanism that began to be heavily used by members and by activist groups in the association was the petition process. The usual procedure was (and still is) that a Nominating Committee, appointed by the President, puts forward a slate of candidates. You can see how self-perpetuating that process can be. Under this system you have some choice, but not much, and the limits of the choice are determined by what the Nominating Committee thought. What changed was that members began putting forward their own candidates. Under our bylaws now, all you have to have are twenty-five legitimate signatures on a petition to put a candidate of your choice on the ballot. Here was democracy in action, and though some people have tried to put a brake on it, it has prevailed. Clara Jones and I are here this week as living proof that it works: two ALA presidents in a row who were nominated by petition and beat the official slate, indicating that, at least in those two years, the Nominating Committee was apparently not in tune with what the membership wanted.

Here, I would have thought, is a reform that might appeal to the AAL, indeed to spirited members generally. I find it hard to believe that there is general acceptance and equanimity about a procedure by which a small group of senior citizens of the association retires to a small, closed room, like some medieval Star Chamber, later to emerge and tell you who your next president will be. Not only do you have no voice in the matter; you aren't even offered a choice between two. It doesn't sound like the democracy for which Britain is famous. Certainly, American librarians would not sit still for anything so authoritarian. Who knows, with a more democratic system, you might even get another woman president!

The big issue in ALA today, as I see it, the one that will occupy center stage perhaps for the next several years, is more obviously a library service problem than some of the others I've discussed. It was raised here, in an *Assistant Librarian* editorial as long ago as 1970, and it has been looming as an increasingly threatening spectre the past few years on our side of the Atlantic. I'm referring to the troublesome question of fees, which are more and more being charged for library service. This development, I believe, poses the most serious threat to the philosophical foundations of library service that we have yet seen.

Information is becoming (is!) big business. What has become known, loosely, as the information industry is, perhaps, if you consider its conglomerate whole, already the largest industry in America. My inaugural address, titled "Data Bank Is Two Four-Letter Words," which may establish my viewpoint, was largely concerned with the ramifications of this development. The combination of ever more costly information storage, location and delivery devices, and the probability of continued economic stringency makes the maintenance of what we have known as "free" library service even more difficult because it becomes such a vulnerable target. But now, while the temptations are so enticing for the commercial entrepreneurs, is no time for us to vacillate or equivocate. If this door is left ajar, commerce will invade and destroy principle as surely as Hitler's troops waltzed around the Maginot Line.

My whole presidential program in ALA this year is based on the belief that free access to information is the very foundation, not only of our profession and its services, but of individual liberty. My one big effort this year, through ALA, is to persuade President Carter that it is as important for us to have a National Information Policy as it is to have one concerned with energy problems. And a basic ingredient of any such policy has to be that simple, moral declaration contained in the *Unesco Public Library Manifesto,* that a public library "should be maintained wholly from public funds, and no direct charge should be made to *anyone* for its services."

I mention this here not because I expect you to be interested in the details of my presidential program, but because the problem, the threat, is undoubtedly a worldwide one, or will be if it is not yet. This problem is one that calls for a united international effort by the library community, and I hope this is one terribly important, creative area where we, and other library associations, can work together in united purpose. There have been too few such instances where we have done so, and agreement on a Cataloging Code will not save us.

I hope you are not disappointed that I chose mainly to discuss library associations rather than libraries. I did so because I believe our associations are the place where we can and should gather in force and unity. They are our political potential for change and influence. It is there that we must clarify our communal thinking and translate it into influence and action. What we say and do there has much to do with the kind and quality of our front-line services in libraries. If we do not, as organized bodies, understand today's world turmoil, or the reasons for it, that misunderstanding will be reflected in increasingly irrelevant services in our libraries. If we choose not to participate in the certain massive changes ahead in society—here, in the U.S. and elsewhere—not only we but our libraries will become relegated to the role of bystanders.

There was a nice poster going the rounds in the U.S. a few years ago, which picked up a line of Eldridge Cleaver's. It read: "If you are not part of the solution, you are part of the problem." That, it seems to me, is the clear choice for us all.

The Lacy Commission Report

Shortly after the Midwinter Meeting (1985), Dan Lacy wrote to me and invited me to comment on the draft of the Commission report we had received at that meeting. In replying I reminded Dan that when he had given us a progress report at last summer's conference I had asked what consideration the Commission was giving to existing ALA policies on some of the major issues under consideration by the Commission. I told him that I felt his response at that time had been vague and far from reassuring, and that after the appearance of the draft report a number of ALA members had commented to me that the report seemed intended to reverse, or at least undermine, existing ALA policies on some very important issues—an observation with which I concurred.

We were told repeatedly, by Bob Wedgeworth and Carol Nemeyer among others, to remember that this Commission report was a report *to* ALA, not one by ALA. But here was a Commission appointed by an ALA President (Carol Nemeyer), more than one-third of whose membership was a high-powered librarian delegation including three ALA Presidents and a former chair of the ALA Legislation Committee (not to mention the current and future executive directors of ALA). Given that representation and assuming the report was eventually published *by* ALA, would this fine distinction—about whether this is a report *to* or *by* ALA—be readily apparent to those outside the association who read the report? Will it not appear, I asked Dan Lacy, that ALA has in fact reversed itself on some earlier positions, or is now at best very confused about them?

In the past several months Dan and I have been in constant correspondence and I must express my admiration and gratitude for his calm

---

Remarks made at the Membership Meeting, ALA Conference, Chicago, July 1985. Also invited to comment at this meeting were Jeanne Isacco, Kenneth Dowlin and Gary Strong. The last two were members of the ALA Commission on Freedom and Equality of Access to Information, chaired by Dan Lacy and known as The Lacy Commission.

courtesy and receptiveness in the face of my often vigorous disagreement with some of his and the commission's views. Perhaps the crux of our differences may be seen in one exchange from this correspondence. In one of his letters Dan said: "I suspect that there is less difference in our views as to what would be sound policy in concrete cases than there is in the expressions of principle." My response was: "It is the principles underlying goals, and the emphasis given their expression, that seem to me to define the true meaning and spirit of the goals. Policy is only sound, I would think, if it is based on sound and clearly-stated principles."

I hope you will bear with me through a little more background. Several weeks before I received the version of the report which is before us, I obtained (through sources leading back, interestingly, to the Information Industry Association) a copy which lacked only the Preface, Appendix and Chapter VI. That version also lacked the minority opinions now included at various points because it was the one sent out in early May on which the Commission members were asked to vote.

Accompanying that copy was a cover memo from Dan Lacy to commission members which spelled out specifically what I believe are the main areas of concern to members of the American Library Association. The memo said: "In general, opinion within the Commission seems to have been relatively unanimous except with respect to three points." The three "points" were:

1. The treatment of the fairness doctrine and section 315 of the Federal Communications Act (the equal time provision).

2. The problem of private-sector versus government publication of information created or collected by the Government, particularly in electronic form.

3. The question of public library charges for on-line access to data bases.

What was also interesting about the memo was that Dan Lacy said he was sending Commission members contrary views on each of these three points. All of these contrary views, if I read the memo correctly, came from Ben Bagdikian, a member of the Commission, who disagreed with the majority on all three, and from Eric Moon, who expressed disagreement on two but had not commented on the third.

Given that these three points are among the major issues—if not *the* major issues—of the whole report, and that on each the Commission view is in conflict with expressed ALA policy or generally known ALA positions, could it be that there was no other dissent on the Commission? Where was that parade of top-level librarian-members of ALA? Could it be that none of them agrees with ALA's policies and positions on such important issues? And if so, by what curious method of selection were they chosen for this Presidential Commission?

It was with such disturbing thoughts in mind that I quickly scanned the current version of the report when it arrived, looking for evidence of some disagreement, other than Bagdikian's, with the majority view of the Commission on these three issues. I was able to find only one instance of disagreement with the majority by any of the librarians on the Commission. It appears as a footnote on page 31 of Chapter III. I was delighted to see Brooke Sheldon and Gary Strong joining Ben Bagdikian in upholding ALA policies in opposition to charges for electronic access to information through the library, and in opposition to distinctions between kinds of users and purposes of use. But if this was the only librarian departure from majority views, what impact did this relative unanimity among the professionals have upon the "outside" members of the Commission? Had more of them supported known ALA positions would there have been the same relative unanimity throughout the Commission that Lacy mentioned in his May 6 memo?

So what of the current version of the report? Is it an improvement over the alarming draft document we were presented at Midwinter? My answer is an unequivocal yes. In many places the discussion is well-rounded where before it was narrow or slanted. Some of the views have been tempered with a reasonableness that was absent six months ago. And in a few places the report is mushy where before it was unattractively clear. Most of all, the dissenting statements by Ben Bagdikian, which express with great clarity the principles that I find absent elsewhere, represent the greatest single improvement in the report. If they were officially endorsed by ALA, which I believe they ought to be, there would be little left to differ about.

Let me now comment briefly on each of the three major issues referred to earlier. I do not want to say much about the Fairness Doctrine and Equal Time provision because I have personally long been ambivalent on this subject. As a former journalist I am uneasy with the proposition that the protections of the First Amendment should be applicable to one medium but not to another. On the other hand I recognize the valuable social purpose of the Fairness Doctrine and Equal Time provisions. ALA's position on this issue is quite clear: the Council passed a resolution last

Midwinter opposing "deregulation of the broadcast media and the repeal of the Fairness Doctrine including the Equal Time provision."

Interestingly, the Commission report—and this is the only example I could find—does mention the ALA position, if only parenthetically. Unfortunately, the paragraph in which this mention occurs is one of the cloudier ones. The first sentence, beginning at the bottom of page 11 of Chapter III, begins: "Opponents of deregulation (such as the American Library Association) . . . " and is an accurate statement of ALA's position. The next sentence, which begins "They further suggest . . . ," may express a view held by some opponents of deregulation but it is not one I remember ever being expressed by ALA. That pronoun "They" with which the sentence opens, can easily be understood to refer back to "Opponents of deregulation (such as the American Library Association) . . . " If our positions are to be mentioned, which would be an improvement, let it be done with clarity so that they are not misunderstood.

I would like, if I had time, to comment at length on Chapter IV: Access to Government Information, but Jeanne Isacco is concentrating on that section of the report. This is one chapter which (while I still disagree with some of its conclusions) is much improved over the Midwinter version. My reaction to it then was expressed perfectly by another correspondent who wrote to me shortly after the meeting. He said: "I find it shocking in its unashamed adoption of the entire rationale of the knowledge industry."

I was particularly upset by the wholesale endorsement in the Midwinter version of those seven so-called "Principles" from the NCLIS Private Sector-Public Sector task force report. As I said in one letter to Dan Lacy: "When they were offered by one body which is supposedly supportive of library and public interests it was horror enough; to have had them endorsed by the Commission would have left some of us feeling that the public sector has few friends left anywhere."

You will see, on page 39 of Chapter IV, that the Commission report now tempers its earlier unequivocal endorsement of those seven "principles," and says: "We believe that they may be (What about *are*?) too much concerned with theoretical distinctions between appropriate spheres of public and private services and insufficiently concerned with practical questions as to what arrangement, in particular concrete cases, best serves the public interest in effective and equitable access to government information." Amen.

Despite such fine-tuning I remain at odds with the Commission on the question of access to government information. I believe the minority opinion of Ben Bagdikian (pages 41-42 of chapter IV) is an accurate reflection of ALA concerns and a laudable statement in the public interest. As that admirable little publication from ALA's Washington Office (*Less Access to Less Information By and About the U.S. Government*) reminds us:

> ALA reaffirmed its long-standing conviction that open government is vital to a democracy in a resolution passed by Council in January 1984 which stated that "there should be equal and ready access to data collected, compiled, produced, and published in any format by the government of the United States." In his inaugural speech, ALA President E.J. Josey asserted: "Again, nobody would deny the utility of many of the services provided by the private sector, but they are not available to all of the American people; their purpose is to yield a profit, and they are designed only for those who can pay for them. Nor do they have any obligation to provide access to all or any information; only that information which the suppliers deem profitable or potentially so. Only the preservation of *public* services, publicly supported, can assure that each individual has equal and ready access to information..."

Turning now to the question of fees for access to information in electronic form, the passage in the entire Commission report with which I disagree most profoundly, and which is most directly in conflict with ALA policy, appears under the heading "Cost of Access" on pages 29-31 of Chapter III. ALA Policy 50.4 is crystal clear: "The American Library Association asserts that the charging of fees and levies for information services, including those services utilizing the latest information technology, is discriminatory in publicly supported institutions providing library and information services." That policy statement goes on to promise that "ALA will actively promote its position on equal access to information." It certainly will not be carrying out that commitment if it allows Chapter III in of this Commission report to go unanswered.

There the Commission sets up a straw man (straw person?) in the form of a pair of polarized, and indefensible, alternatives in defense of its assertion that fees are necessary to control "abuse of the library's resources." I do not want to waste your time by giving you in great detail my objections to this section of the report because once again they are expressed with splendid conviction and clarity in the minority opinion of Ben Bagdikian on pages 38-39 of this chapter. As he points out, rather than raise the specter of "insurmountable" problems, the report ought to adopt a more positive stance and re-assert the principle of free access to library materials, of whatever kind. And instead of assuming the inevitable poverty of libraries, as the Commission appears to do in several places, it should stress the need for vastly increased support, not just to enable libraries to provide terminals and professional assistance (see recommendation 10 in the Appendix), but to enable them to preserve free and equitable access to all library materials in the more expensive electronic era. If the electronic era means that libraries, in order to remain adequate community resources, need added funds, then the right course is to urge the appropriation of those funds, rather than declare that this is both impossible and unmanageable.

It is in such matters of emphasis that the Commission report becomes curiouser and curiouser, as though it were the product of individuals who never talked to each other. Compare, for example, the section on libraries in Chapter III, about which I have been so critical, with the chapter specifically on libraries, Chapter VI, which I understand was written, or revised, by the executive director team of Wedgeworth and Galvin. While chapter III wails about insurmountable problems and apparently sees fees and discrimination against certain kinds of users and uses as the only available ladder with which to climb over such problems, here is the situation and remedy as expressed more positively in chapter VI:

First quotation (situation): "The combination of reduced public funding, diminished buying power, the necessity to incorporate information in an expanding range of formats and the adoption of user fees and access charges constitutes a growing barrier to access to community library and information services for an increasing segment of the population. "

Second quotation (remedy): "To maintain adequate levels of access to information in traditional formats, and to provide comparable access to resources in newer electronic formats, community library and information services simply must achieve substantially higher levels of *public* financial support."

If Messrs Wedgeworth and Galvin could achieve this clear and positive declaration of principle in Chapter VI, where were they when the Commission, with the exception of Sheldon, Strong and Bagdikian, went along with the nattering negativism of Chapter III?

Before concluding I'd like to touch very briefly on a few of the matters discussed in Chapter V. Each of the topics glanced at in this miscellaneous chapter could have been the subject of a report at least as long as the entire Commission report.

In his May 6 memo to the Commission Dan Lacy asked: "... Is the problem of library censorship adequately treated? Is the brief discussion of copyright adequate? Are the problems of national security in the control of information sufficiently recognized?" My answer to all three questions would be "No," although I think the slightness of treatment of these important topics is more likely a measure of the Commission's time and financial constraints than an indicator of its concern.

As chair of the Intellectual Freedom Committee, however, I must say that the section on censorship disturbs me because of what I feel is again a misleading emphasis. While in earlier chapters, perhaps in order to build its case for deregulation and for a greater role for the private sector, the Commission catalogs the ways in which Government (and notably the current Administration) increasingly seeks to limit and control access to information, in Chapter V the Commission appears no longer to see much danger from government sources or agencies but focuses almost exclusively on the censorship activities of individuals and private groups. On page 1 of this chapter there is the incontrovertible statement that "there will probably always be efforts on the part of some individuals and groups" to remove materials from libraries. And on page 3 the Commission declares that it "deplores individual attempts at closing off access to ideas because they are inimical to a specific world view."

One can have no quarrel with this view, except perhaps to note that individual and group attempts can only be ultimately successful if they are supported by action of government agencies of one kind or another, at federal, state or local levels. I would like to have some recognition here of the escalating pro-censorship stance of government at all these levels. At the present time, by way of illustration, the Freedom to Read Foundation is involved in cases stemming from the U.S. Information Agency, the National Security Agency, the State of Maryland, the city of Indianapolis, the Governor of South Dakota, the Evergreen School District, the city of Oklahoma City, etc., etc. And finally, although this is not mentioned in the Commission's otherwise good section on libel, the FTRF is also involved in an Illinois case that presents perhaps the most serious threat yet on the libel front, a case that if lost would disallow even truth as a defense to libel.

To conclude, apart from its conflicts with ALA policies on several important issues, among the other disturbing qualities of the Commission report are the inconsistencies of emphasis between some of its parts, and the occasional inconsistency between its often perceptive questions and statements of problems and the solutions and recommendations it eventually delivers. Some of these faults are undoubtedly the product of time limitations and of the way in which the Commission has had to work (mostly at long range) because of financial strictures. The current version of the report is such a pronounced improvement over the Midwinter version that it leads one to hope that if the Commission were given more time and some informed input from ALA, it might be possible to wind up with an impressively useful document for future policy consideration and action.

If, however, what we have is indeed the *final* statement of the Commission, and if ALA is to publish it, I believe any such publication must be contingent upon the inclusion of an Introduction which makes absolutely clear ALA's policy differences with certain Commission views and recommendations. Without this I see the clear danger that the Commission's views may be interpreted as ALA's, which could only lead to the conclusion that ALA has changed its positions on some major points of policy, or is now at best ambivalent about them. We cannot afford the possibility of such doubts.

PART VII

THE LIBRARY PRESS

Introduction

"Hello, Out There, or Let's Communicate" was the second in a series of "New York Letters" I was invited to write for *The Library World* in England when I was *LJ* editor (see Introduction to Part III concerning the first installment). The transatlantic dialogue I was hoping might emerge never, sadly, materialized.

"The Library Press" is, without question, the most often cited article among my many writings, perhaps because it said, with what many regarded as appalling frankness, what a number of others thought but did not dare to say publicly. This piece was prepared as the wrap-up of a week-long institute for regional and state association periodical editors which I helped set up at the Kentucky Library School. There were faint indications, for a few years, that the institute had had an impact, but still today too many state associations spend too large a percentage of their budgets producing journals that have insufficient quality material, when they could provide a better service to their members, and more economically, with a timely newsletter. They would also assist the image of our profession by reducing the volume of garbage in our literature.

"The Journalist and the Writer" was written as an Epilogue to Paul Dunkin's *Tales of Melvil's Mouser* (Bowker, 1970), a collection of essays that grew out of his column for *LJ*. (For more on Dunkin, see the Introduction to Part V in this volume). I tried here to do something I had never essayed before (and probably will never attempt again): to write something in someone else's style. Only those who are familiar with Paul's captivating and apparently simple style will be able to judge whether I was successful or not, but I can assure you that the printed page is a very difficult place to carry off an impersonation.

Dunkin's flair is featured again in the next item, "Hook, Line and Sinker," which originated as a paper for a program at Rutgers University (where Dunkin taught) on "Publishing—Not Perishing." Since my wife Ilse was the organizer of the program there was not a prayer that I could escape this assignment to tell people how to go about getting published.

The last item in this section is an interview which appeared in a volume entitled *Activism in American Librarianship, 1962-1973*. The interview came about after I had refused to write for that volume an article on the impact of the library press on the events of this period. Since Mary Lee Bundy and Fred Stielow (the editors of the volume) insisted that I ought to be a part of their book's story I agreed to be interviewed, though the results of this process are rarely very satisfactory—and this piece is no exception. I have included it nevertheless because it does touch on some things that are not mentioned elsewhere in this volume.

Hello, Out There, or Let's Communicate

A "one-worlder" is a current derogatory expression hurled by "right" thinking people (politically speaking) in America, and perhaps in Britain too, against anyone whose vision extends beyond the shores and the traditions of his own country. America's notorious isolationism has not disappeared, but it has declined. The more moderate majority now accepts the inevitability that what happens elsewhere will, sooner or later but with certainty, affect his own circumstances. It *is* an international world: communications, transportation and politics have made it irretrievably so, and dogmatic nationalism has become a fuse, horribly dangerous in its potential, always capable of releasing international idiocy and catastrophe.

Has librarianship internationalized its thinking, abandoned its customary domesticity? There are small signs that it might finally be moving in the right outward direction, although the proverbial snail's pace (a professional snail, of course) seems still to prevail.

The library periodicals, for once, seem to be leading instead of following, and exhibit an increasing awareness that libraries are building and booming in all corners of the globe. *Library World* recently devoted a whole issue to Indian libraries; the *Library Association Record* has started a "Letters from Abroad" column; *Library Journal* has had two international issues within the past few months, one each devoted to librarianship in Latin America and the Soviet Union, and also published in May the first article ever to appear in an English-language library periodical on the libraries of Ethiopia.

At the association level, while the Library Association has been accused of neglect by even its own "corresponding" members abroad, the American Library Association continues to empire-build its activities and the influence of American librarianship around the world.

Reprinted by permission of MCB University Press Limited from *The Library World* LXIV, No. 745: 22-24, July 1962.

Success breeds success, they say, and A.L.A. has recently received ample and very material recognition of the success of its international efforts.

Last autumn, the Rockefeller Foundation gave A.L.A. three tidy sums to be administered through the association's International Relations office. One grant, totalling $175,560, ensured the continuance of the activities of this office until at least 30 September, 1966. Another grant of $38,850 is to be used for the development of a library training program at the National Taiwan University, and a third nest-egg of $56,795 will help in the establishment of a graduate library school in the University of the Philippines.

Given this much gas, A.L.A. stepped on the accelerator. They immediately appointed a new director of the International Relations Office for a five-year term, and for the first time, expanded the I.R.O. by the appointment of an assistant director. The important thing is that they brought to these posts men of stature, or as the *Times* would have it, "top people." Lester Asheim, the new director, is the former head of the Graduate Library School at the University of Chicago and a man in whom the factors of talent, thought, knowledge and action are present in just about the right proportions. Joseph Shubert, the new assistant director, is the young and energetic former State Librarian of that gambling state, Nevada.

But A.L.A.'s activities abroad are concentrated heavily in the underdeveloped and newly emerging countries, and the L.A.'s seem not concentrated anywhere, except perhaps in a disintegrating commonwealth. Britain and America are, with Scandinavia, the most advanced library territories in the world. Why don't they talk to each other?

I remember a survey Roy Stokes did—back about 1956, I think—on the holdings of *Library Quarterly* and *Library Trends* in English libraries. I don't remember the actual figures, but I do know that the results were shameful. Nor do I know the actual American circulation of most of the British library periodicals, but I am sure that the picture is not any more encouraging.

I ran an article in *Library Journal* recently in which the author commented on what was happening to public library cataloging in Sweden and Denmark. "This is news," he said, "this is an astonishing trend." If it happened in America, the journals would have been full of it, but because it was happening in another country not a word was typographically breathed until this one young man got incensed at such myopia.

I can assert, without fear of contradiction, that most American librarians, including many of the faculties of library schools, have only the smoggiest idea of what goes on in British librarianship. In this respect, the situation in England, at least at the time I left, was somewhat better, thanks mainly to one or two library school heads there who vigorously—tiresomely, some thought—waved the American flag. But there is no doubt that, through these efforts, students were leaving British library schools with more knowledge of current developments in American librarianship than their counterparts are likely to acquire about British librarianship from those who teach here.

The library periodicals on the American side of the Atlantic have been full of talk in the past year or two of "the image" of the librarian or the library (this is Madison Avenue language for "what do they think of us?"—"they" being the public, or some segment of it). Let me play for a moment with a couple of trans-Atlantic images.

The American librarian with no transAtlantic background and little discernment looks at the British scene, and his generalized view might be something like this: British libraries are dingy, old-fashioned, on occasion, quaint. They are cruelly under-staffed, poorly administered, and heavily overcrowded and over-used because they issue nothing but fiction, popular biographies and travel books. They virtually ignore the child as a reader, do not believe in extension or community activities, think public relations and publicity are dirty words, and abhor aid from any government source other than the local. They put small faith in catalogs, none in machines, and are adamant in their refusal to admit any form of recorded knowledge other than the book (which is holy) within their walls. They exist on a shoestring, overwork their staffs, pay them abysmally, but by way of compensation, demand little of them so far as education is concerned.

Across the water, the equally blind (or at least, dim) British librarian retaliates with his hand-drawn picture (image) of the American library. Being British, he will concede a little more, his ego not being quite so well developed, and will admit that American libraries are like the little girl with the curl in the middle of her forehead: when they are good, they are very, very good; when they are bad, they are horrid. However, to get back to more solid generalizations—American libraries are over-staffed, over-administered, over-gadgeted, and very little used. They idolize the child reader but ignore the adult. They waste vast amounts of money, time and energy in public relations and inessential "fringe" activities. Cataloging and classification are obsessions, other techniques only slightly less so.

Films, slides, pictures, records, audio-visual materials, a *mardi gras* of microforms, and other bric-à-brac are rapidly driving books from their minds, if not from their shelves, and already books are mentioned rarely except under the general heading, "materials." Their staffs are lavishly paid, have little to do but read reviews, or sometimes, eccentrically, books, and would not soil their hands with menial routines if the future of America depended upon it (what are *pages* for?). They appear to be well educated in a general way, but are sadly theoretical and lacking in professional knowledge and experience. They know why, but never *how*, to do anything.

This is nonsense? You know, the interesting thing about nonsense is how much truth there often is buried in it (*see* Thurber, Lear, Carroll, or even Snaith, for that matter). The truth may be magnified, diminished, distorted perhaps, but it's there all the same. These monstrous capsule descriptions I have given are distorted alright, but they are made up entirely of comments made to me in conversation by librarians on both sides of the Atlantic. They are composites of idiocy and ignorance, and I say again, let's communicate. We need to.

One of the grimmer ironies of the situation is that, in a way, the British distortion of the American library scene may be worse than the distortion in the other direction. The Americans, in the main, just plain don't know, and since they have a habit of assuming "if it's American, it's best," they tend to let it go at that.

The library schools in England, however, in an effort to break down the barricades of ignorance, may have merely replaced ignorance with misunderstanding. They have on occasion, I think, gone overboard, so that there is a younger element in British librarianship which *also* tends to believe too easily, "if it's American it's best."

One result of this is that when some of them come to America they are shocked. Shocked to find that while cooperation is a living, breathing reality—and a substantial one—in England, it is often no more than a token word in America, reverently spoken, dutifully acknowledged, but thought of most of the time as one of those dreams of the future. Shocked to find that while England is now about 100 per cent blanketed with public libraries, there are huge cultural deserts in the U.S. where no public libraries exist, or where those that do are so bad that perhaps they shouldn't. Shocked to find that the majority of public libraries in America exist on leaner shoe strings than some of the most dismal in England. Shocked by the professional apathy of many staff members of even the plush libraries.

Hello, Out There, or Let's Communicate

Now I'm not trying to convey the impression that American libraries are no damn good. Many of them are superb (what a lesson the British university libraries could learn from their American counterparts), but some British librarians, dazzled by the propaganda, have put on critical blinders. When they get to the U.S., those blinders are torn off, and the innocent eyes are transfixed by the light shining through the holes in the propaganda. Because of the consequent blaze of disillusionment, some of these younger exchange librarians may well miss the many good things they could retrieve from American practice and which they should carry back for transplanting in British libraries.

One of the things I shall attempt to do with this regular "New York Letter" is to fill in the no-man's land between ignorance and the propaganda. I'll try to do what Alistair Cooke did (does still?) with his superb radio program, "Letter from America"—illustrate some of the major differences and the many similarities in American and British practice, conventions, habits, strengths and weaknesses. I hope that a few of my old British colleagues will get the message, and get down to the job of transmitting a little information in the other direction. Hello out there—have we lost contact again?

The Library Press

The deadliest disease afflicting the library press is proliferation. The kindest and most conservative estimate I am able to bring myself to make is that there are at least three times as many library periodicals in this country as we can afford or are necessary. Perhaps the most constructive single thing that could be accomplished would be to persuade at least one in three publishers of a library periodical to cease publication.

One might reasonably expect that librarians, who have done so much public wailing about the publications explosion, would be among the chief advocates and practitioners of birth control in the world of print. Instead we find them cavorting as uninhibitedly in the king-size bed of printed procreation as do the denizens of the Sodom and Gomorrah of science and technology. Just about every library of any consequence (and some of little consequence) and, almost without exception, every group or organization within the loose boundaries of our profession, decides, virtually at the moment of its birth, that it cannot survive without a publication of its own—a newsletter, a journal, some regular calling card to announce its presence to the world at large.

The incentive may be a genuine desire to communicate—in itself a healthy desire in a profession which *should* be a significant element in the machinery of communications. Or this massive outpouring may be just another symptom of man's most desperate struggle in today's enveloping society: the attempt to establish and maintain an identity. The trouble is that when one examines the content of much of this debris (and debris is the main result of most explosions), one is forced to ask:

Originally a paper given at the Institute on Upgrading the Knowledge and Skills of Editors of Regional and Statewide Library Journals, University of Kentucky, September 7-12, 1969, this article is reprinted by permission from *Library Journal* 94: 4104-09, November 15, 1969. Copyright © 1969, Reed Publishing, USA. The article also appeared in *Southeastern Librarian* 20: 34-43, Spring 1970.

1. Is it worth the cost and effort?
2. Is it communicating anything that anyone really needs to know?
3. Is the identity it establishes one that we really want to live with?

And the answer to all three questions, if we were honest, would be a resounding NO.

Proliferation has a very severe impact on the over-all quality of the library press. Among its specific evils are:

1. It spreads too thinly the limited amount of good material, so that *all* the periodicals (and I exempt not the big three) tend, in greater or lesser degree, to flesh out their pages with material about which they are less than enthusiastic.

2. It also spreads too thinly the advertising support which otherwise could help sustain a smaller number of stronger, well-staffed, economically and editorially independent magazines.

3. It occasionally diverts into an obscure publication a piece of writing that deserves to reach a wider audience. This problem is not irremediable, of course, if the big boys will keep their eyes skinned and perform the necessary rescue operation occasionally—though some of them are afraid to do this because they may leave themselves open to charges of unoriginality.

4. Worst of all, proliferation makes it possible for almost anything on the topic of librarianship, no matter how appalling, to find its way into print somewhere. Almost everything I rejected in nine years of editing *LJ* subsequently turned up in another library periodical—sometimes as many as four or five pieces in one issue of one periodical (I once counted that many in one issue of *College & Research Libraries!*). Now, some of this occurred, no doubt, because of poor judgment on my part, and some of it is attributable to the infinite variety of human taste. But much of it was the result of editorial desperation. There is—and everyone who has ever edited a library periodical for any length of time knows it—simply too little quality material to fill all the pages the library profession insists on producing.

The dearth, the paucity of quality, is most noticeable if you examine only one element among the features of the library press: the articles. Yet this is the element most of our editors are hung up on; they all want to publish articles. If I may again guess at some motives, I'd say that the most likely reason articles are so popular among editors is that they fill up a lot of space. And the lazy editor, who can close his eyes and conscience, can fill up space this way without much creative effort (or effort of any kind) on his own part. Another possible motive, and a slightly more laudable one, is that many people who become editors have, somewhere inside them, some small residue of literary ambition. If they can't be Truman Capote or John Updike or Norman Mailer, they secretly tell themselves, perhaps they have a chance of becoming a Harold Ross or a Norman Podhoretz. And about as near to a literary form as you can get in a library periodical is the article.

Whichever of these motives is operative the new editor quickly finds himself facing the same bleak landscape. There are articles a-plenty around in librarianship (are *all* librarians writers manqué?) but the majority of them say nothing, or say what it is no longer necessary to say because it has been said so often, and most of them say it so incredibly badly that the editor who accepts one of this breed is left with only two choices. If he is truly lazy, he may say: "This thing isn't worth any effort; the only thing to do is print it the way it is—it'll soon be forgotten, in any case." Or the more scrupulous editor will find that, even to make the article vaguely comprehensible entails more work than if he were to start from scratch and write something himself. To make his disenchantment more complete the editor quickly realizes that there are few oil wells to be discovered on this land he has chosen to explore, and that his chances of reflected glory through the discovery of a library Thurber or Baldwin are about as remote as Lyndon Johnson's chances of being remembered as the Peace President.

It's not easy to understand the reasons for this appalling lack of quality, particularly in a profession in such close physical proximity (if not necessarily intellectual proximity) to the printed word. The formal educational system must be held somewhat responsible for the widespread inability to string a few dozen words together in some sort of coherent sequence, and for the paucity of ideas and the cloudy thinking behind this word butchery. I cannot help noting that the library schools, though they certainly cannot hope to correct the ills generated by the educational system at earlier stages, appear to me to have added another awful dimension to the written output of our profession. They have been prominent instigators of what is best described as scissors-and-paste research. The procedure is well known: before you write anything you must first ferret around in the literature of the distant past, extract the thoughts and ideas of another time, then paste them together, using footnotes and references for glue. This grubby composite is then presented as your own work. Original thought, ideas advanced before they have fossilized, are not required—indeed, they may be frowned upon. The most concentrated example of this kind of library "literature" today is *Library Quarterly,* which is still thought of by some as a "scholarly" periodical but which looks to me more like a collection of rather antiquated gentlemen examining their navels, perhaps in the hope of finding a live appendix.

Most editors in our field, after their first month or two of exposure to this incredible stream of garbage, either go into shock or lapse into a prolonged period of deep despair. Those who recover and begin to look for remedies are likely to adopt various courses of action. For example, Kathleen Molz, after a few months of editing the *Wilson Library Bulletin,* apparently decided that there was little hope for the library profession and went outside thereafter for the great bulk of her material. I admire the skill and the style and the persuasive ability she brought to this endeavor and I think for a few years she gave us an interestingly different library periodical—but one of little relevance to the library scene today.

She once said at a meeting at which we were both speaking, that she was trying to make the *Bulletin* the *Harper's* or the *Atlantic* of librarianship and that I was trying to make *LJ* the librarian's *Time* magazine. If you discount the icepick lurking behind that remark (she knew that *Time* is my pet hate among all magazines), there was a measure of truth in it. My solution to the garbage explosion was to try to build up a top-level staff of writer-reporters who would look at the contemporary library scene and describe it and criticize it in relatively clear prose, without too many frills or too much equivocation. In that way, I felt, we could begin to reduce the number of public relations releases that librarians write about their own operations and hobby-horses and then try to peddle as articles. John Berry, I suspect, from the evidence I have seen during the few months of his editorship, wants to push further in this direction and to cut the number of contributed articles even more drastically. So, my second suggestion, and I assume the first (that library periodicals commit editorial hari-kiri) won't be accepted, is don't be afraid to publish a thinner periodical, be a lot tougher in acceptance decisions, and deliberately set out to publish fewer articles than last year. I believe *LJ,* for example, is now publishing not much more than half the number of articles it published per year a decade ago, and I think it is better for that. I know that in my first year as editor-in-chief I cut 1000 pages out of the magazine. Nobody (except the other editors) noticed or complained. Not only were our economics improved, so was the overall standard of what did appear.

So far, I must admit, this sounds like an exercise in weeding run amok. I've suggested that one-third of the library publishers might kill off their magazines, and the other two-thirds might cut out half the present content of the remainder. Another affliction of the library periodicals that has always been a particular concern of mine is the news gap. Few professions are as ill-served as ours in the area of current news and information. One must not, of course, blame the editors alone; the disease is spread and stimulated by the profession itself. The majority of librarians are completely lacking in news consciousness; they do not know what news is, why it is useful, or that timing is a major factor in its potential value.

This news blindness, this obliviousness to the value of recording and reporting what we do—and currently—has achieved for our profession a social anonymity almost unequalled among the professions. It has also, among other things, given us statistical services which are unbelievable in their incompleteness and inaccuracy. It leads our organizations and institutions to produce the reports of research projects or the proceedings of conferences or symposia as much as seven years after the event. And it allows us to duplicate research, experimentation, and other efforts, over and over again, without knowledge of what the other guy is doing or has already discovered. For a profession which is supposed to aid others in research and in keeping themselves up-to-date within their disciplines, we set a resounding example of near-total inefficiency.

Even taking into account that they can expect little help from their colleagues in the field, however, the library periodical editors must take much of the blame for our inadequate news and information services. Much real news has been suppressed or has deliberately not been pursued. And much of what *is* published is canned news, most of it supplied in release form by foundations (CLR), professional organizations (ALA), a few libraries, and a variety of other sources such as publishers, suppliers, and public relations firms. Rarely is any digging done by the editors of most of our periodicals to find out whether there is more to the story than the release reveals. Many of the releases, indeed, are not even edited before they are set in type by the library press. The supreme example is *The Indian Librarian,* which prints (verbatim) releases from Bowker as though they were either ads (which isn't so far from the truth) or reviews (which is a long way from the truth). But our own press isn't much better. Just check out a few of these release-generated stories in half a dozen periodicals (and you can include some of the national ones). Essentially, you'll find the same stuff, the same wording, in pretty well all of the periodicals. Total waste.

So, third suggestion: one thing to start filling up with after having emptied out some of the tons of garbage is some useful hard news and current information, which our profession needs desperately. I think, indeed, that the library press might be much improved overall if a substantial number of the present journals at state and regional levels were to become newsletters. Too much membership money is spent on printing and playing with the redesign of journals which don't appear often enough to be useful, and the content of which does not justify either the expense or the typographic frills. A newsletter may be less satisfying to the ego of the editor or the association but, cheaply produced and frequently issued, it could get information to members and subscribers while it is needed and useful. A quarterly may be a handsome ornament but as a carrier of information in today's world it is a medieval device.

And now to another, and perhaps even worse, gaping hole in the library press. If the Negro, at the time of Ralph Ellison's marvelous novel in the 1950s, was still the invisible man, the library press, still at the end of the 1960s, is the personification of the invisible position—and not just on broader social issues (which many librarians still think it improper for a professional periodical to discuss) but even on basic professional matters. There are so few exceptions to this generalization that those which do exist are often regarded as either vaguely heretical or deliberately sensational.

It was this flat conformity and dullness, this lack of individuality and viewpoint that struck me as the most pervasive quality of the library press of North America when I took my first really solid look at it after being approached about the *LJ* editorship. My reaction was a mental echo of Jimmy Porter's anguished cry in *Look Back in Anger:* "How I long for a little ordinary human enthusiasm."

It was easy to confirm that *LJ* wasn't stirring up a whole lot of enthusiasm. My first check was one I had carried out on several other magazines I had been associated with. The Letters to the Editor file was virtually empty. This is a good test; if this file does not consistently contain more letters than can be used, it is a fair bet that the magazine is not getting through to its readers. Clearly, at the very least, it is not evoking much response from them. I think the most apparent current example of the relationship between a healthy Letters to the Editor column and the resurgence of a periodical is the *ALA Bulletin*—by far the most obviously improved library periodical in the United States.

So how does one set about stimulating some of Jimmy Porter's "ordinary human enthusiasm"? I don't know that I can give any standard recipe but I can tell briefly some of the elements of the program I set for myself when I took over *LJ*.

The first objective was to find some writers—other than the few good, well known, established and over-exposed ones—who had not only words (and perhaps style) but passion, writers who would express their ideas and convictions without equivocation. (Too many of those who appear in our literature are Lone Rangers—they never take the mask off.) Having found such authors, of course, one must give them their heads, not constrict them. My gambit was never to ask them to write on assigned topics but to try to find out what moved them. I'd ask: What do you get excited or angry or impatient about? What do you really care about? What's your thing? That's what I want you to write about. I've always regarded Dorothy Broderick, now well known and much in demand, as the first success of this policy. The first piece of hers I published in *LJ* was so successful that reader response was enough to fill a couple of subsequent issues. Another measure of success was that Ms. Broderick was fired by her university.

A second element in my program, and a major one, was to give *LJ* an identifiable editorial stance in relation to the library world. In broad terms this was an easy decision to make. Since the majority of the other periodicals were published by associations or institutions, they tended collectively to present a kind of party line, to be an establishment chorus, very middle of the road, timorous about criticism (of anything!). The way for me to use *LJ*'s independence, I felt, was to make the magazine an opposition voice. I meant opposition in a constructive sense, in Disraeli's terms ("No government can long survive without a forceful opposition"), though few people believed there was anything constructive in my approach.

It seemed to me essential to establish at least one outlet in our professional press where any established virtue could be questioned, where no cow was so sacred that its tail could not be pulled in public, where criticism was more welcome than self-congratulation. The editorial text, for those who wanted one, was Dana's Law: "Where there is a standard method of doing a thing which has been accepted and approved over a considerable period of time, it is safe to assume that it is wrong. Or at least that it is capable of being improved. It is no longer based on the intellect, but has become merely habit and imitation."

Third, since we already had a plethora of periodicals concerned principally with the furniture and techniques of librarianship, and because most of our worst problems seemed to me to derive from attitudes rather than faltering skills, I determined to reduce what Ralph Shaw christened the "how-I-run-my-library-good" articles, and to concentrate more on ideas, philosophies, and opinions than on facts or gimmicks. Like Mortimer Adler, who said "The telephone book is full of facts but it doesn't contain a single idea," I will trade a bagful of facts any day for one good idea. I wanted to get away from some of the too-pat answers and dig up some hard, relevant questions. Questions have a way of leading you on to something else; answers sometimes only stop you cold.

Another item on the editorial agenda was to crack the pervasive domesticity of the library periodicals and of the profession they served. It was all right to spend some of our time debating which classification scheme to adopt, or how to improve circulation control or the interlibrary loan system, but we had to get our eyes off our navels once in a while and take a look at the world and its changes and forces and what they were doing to libraries' relevance.

Librarians are people, too, and I was sure they couldn't be as unconcerned about the individuals, the communities, the society in which they and their institutions orbit as the library periodicals appeared to indicate. It was already, for example, in my first year at *LJ*, six years after the Supreme Court decision on school desegregation. It was nearly three years after Little Rock. And it was the year in which the sit-in movement really got under way in the lunch counters of the South. The air buzzed with public concern about equality of access to education, to lunch counters, to swimming pools, and to the front seats of buses, but there was scarcely a murmur about libraries. It was understandable that the Negro who was fighting for much more basic human rights would not put libraries at the top of his priority list, but it was incredible that librarians—and more particularly, the library periodical editors—should be exhibiting such a total lack of concern or interest in what all this meant for libraries and their services. It was with that issue that the involvement of library periodicals in public and social issues in the sixties really began, with the leadership coming from the *Wilson Library Bulletin* and *LJ*.

Why, then, are milk and water still the principal ingredients of the library press, why does all the fire and brimstone settle down into the slush of footnotes? One obvious reason, I think, is that ours is, overall, a notoriously timid profession (though that is changing somewhat, as Atlantic City made apparent) and the editors, mostly drawn from that profession, are not too unlike most of their colleagues.

Another reason is that too many of our periodicals are edited by committee or group decision, by consensus rather than out of individual conviction. Whether a periodical is published by a commercial concern or a professional association makes little difference: the editor *must* be left alone to do his own thing. At such time as that becomes unbearable to those who hired him, the option always remains of firing him. This at least has the virtue of bringing the policy differences into the open. But while he is on board, a group cannot control the editor's decisions and actions—not if it wants a periodical with any identity or individuality. Only the editor, operating freely and insisting on such freedom, can supply these qualities. John Berry did it with *The Bay State Librarian,* Bill Eshelman with *The California Librarian,* and Gerry Shields, surrounded by higher walls of bureaucracy than any of you at state or regional levels has to climb, is even managing, gradually, to do it with the *ALA Bulletin.*

Nevertheless, lack of viewpoint remains an obvious feature of most of the library press, and I believe there may be a deeper-seated reason for this. Reared from the first days in the library school womb to believe that the library should be a neutral place where all points of view should be housed and disseminated impartially and dispassionately, too many among us have come to believe that the same rules apply to the librarian as individual. The librarian operating without commitment seems unlikely to me to be much of a useful servant to his society. And the librarian-editor who believes that he should be faceless and neutral on all issues is the certain father of a stillborn periodical.

Total objectivity is death, so far as the editor is concerned. The editorial that states, with equal force, all sides of every question it raises leaves nothing for the reader to respond to. So rule number one for the editorial writer is, to take out all the ifs and buts and maybes and equivocations, come out from behind the shelter of objectivity and fairness and recognition of the "other" point of view, and state his case forcefully and even somewhat baldly. It does no harm for him to be a bit exposed. In this way, he may generate some response from his audience, both from those who are glad to see someone saying something they haven't had the nerve to utter publicly, and from those who profoundly disagree.

When the disagreement comes in, the editor can demonstrate his cherished objectivity. Providing that the other points of view are literate, or can be made so, he should publish them. There is, after all, a difference between the editorial page and all other pages of the magazine, and this difference must be abundantly clear to the readers. The editorial page should be the preserve of the editor (or the editorial staff) alone. It alone speaks *for* the magazine; it is the magazine's voice, its identity.

On one occasion during the year when Wyman Jones (now librarian at Fort Worth, Texas) was my invited guest columnist in *LJ,* he sent in a column which was about 180 degrees removed from an editorial which I had just completed for the same issue. I printed the conflicting pieces on facing pages. My point is that I don't believe many of our readers were confused about *LJ*'s position on the issue being discussed because it was clear by then that *LJ*'s position always appeared on the editorial page or over the byline of a staff writer. Wyman's position was his own and his position as guest columnist didn't mean *LJ* endorsed his views.

It is both surprising and annoying that a profession which discusses its own professionalism so insistently should be so tolerant of amateurism in its so-called professional periodicals. Now I don't really expect that all of our magazines can be manned by people who come equipped with training and experience in journalism, but it does seem reasonable to expect that those who take on jobs as editors should also undertake a little self-education in the processes of journalism, even if they do no more than read some of the professional practitioners with an editorial rather than a lay reader's eye.

Take the matter of headlining. In many of our periodicals the article titles read like catalog entries (or worse). Perhaps the worst offender in this respect, unless you count *American Documentation* as a library periodical, is *College and Research Libraries*. Such titles are *meant* to be helpful and informative but actually they become roadblocks, turning the reader away from the article. The title should be a sort of advertisement for the article. Like a low-cut dress it should make you interested in exploring what's underneath. The purpose of the title, and of its supporting deck or bank, is to lure the reader into the first paragraph of the article.

What journalists and many freelance writers do in the first paragraph is to present what they call a "hook"— either a teaser or further clue about what's to come, or a very tight summary of what they're going to expand and fill in for the next few paragraphs. But in the library press, the reader who is dogged enough to get past some of the titles is stopped cold in the first paragraph. Too many of our articles read like research reports in which you first have to wade through soggy pages of the writer's methodology. One paragraph from the end you finally reach the one small finding or startling conclusion which resulted from the mechanical processes so laboriously described. But the reader rarely reaches the meat because he is too stuffed by the indigestible appetizer. The author may not know any better, but the editor certainly should, and the article can be made more interesting by a little reshuffling, by re-titling, and generally by the application of a little journalistic know-how. Whatever its content, the author's article is going to serve little purpose unless people read it.

The medium may not *be* the message, but it has one hell of a lot to do with whether and how the message gets through.

Some of the flaws of our periodicals are not so much the result of amateurism as of editorial laziness. One obvious symptom of lazy editing is the parade of articles which are not articles but speeches—full of the rhetoric of the platform (such as the one you are reading now) and the cute asides from which a captive audience cannot escape but from which a reader can. It usually only requires the simplest surgery to remove the speech and audience aspects from such a paper, but in most of our periodicals you can bet, particularly if the speaker is fairly eminent, not a comma will be touched.

Finally, one flaw which is more annoying and frustrating than anything else. It results usually from an editor's overfamiliarity with his field and his material. An editor of a magazine inevitably gets to meet or correspond with a lot of people, to move to places and meetings more than most people, to see more printed material in his field than most. But he must never forget that his job is to *interpret* much of what he sees and hears for his audience. If he begins to assume that his audience starts from the same point as he does, he begins to look like one of those comedians who shares an in-joke with some of his colleagues who have turned up for the first night and are sitting in the front row. The rest of the audience is left out in the cold, and resents it. The detail must be spelled out, the people and places identified. A follow-up story on an event covered in its earlier development must repeat enough of the gist of the earlier story so that the reader knows what is being discussed. A page reference to an earlier issue is not enough.

To conclude on a more positive note, there are many areas where collaboration between the local and national periodicals might help.

The state and regional periodicals might produce some livelier and more interesting and useful material than they presently exhibit if they were to select some of the material in the national press to follow-up with local versions. For example, some years ago I did a survey of public library book selection practices as related to some of the more controversial novels then being published. One young man in Pennsylvania, recognizing that the results of the *LJ* survey might not be typical, since the concentration was upon the larger metropolitan libraries across the country, decided to check out the survey's findings against a sample of small to medium-sized libraries in one area of his own state. Both the contrasts and the similarities between the *LJ* and Pennsylvania surveys were interesting and revealing. The young man didn't send it to his state periodical but to *LJ,* and since it was good, I published it.

But this is the kind of material I am suggesting the state and regional periodical editors should be commissioning, and if more of them would do it we would begin to get a clearer picture of national practices and attitudes than the big three can hope to divine from Chicago and New York. If a dozen or more of the local periodicals were to follow up on the same theme, one of the national periodicals could then provide a useful service by synthesizing the results of all these efforts and presenting a story with a broader base than our present fragmentary efforts are likely to achieve.

The original lead for such a concentrated action doesn't have to appear in one of the national periodicals. One state might well produce something which would be worth following up in others. For example, I have always been puzzled and a bit disturbed that no other state ever decided to take up the *Fiske Report* and check whether its findings are accurate or valid outside California. Obviously, a state periodical editor wouldn't have the resources to do a study in the same depth as Fiske, but there is no barrier to taking one or two, half a dozen, of Fiske's more startling findings or charges, and checking them out against a representative group of libraries in one state.

The same kind of follow-up would be helpful when ALA or some other professional body publishes yet another of its multitude of standards documents. How real or relevant are some of these things? How real or relevant was the Access Study? Or Castagna's rush item on the personnel crisis?

I see other possible areas of useful collaboration between our periodicals at state and national levels, for example in news coverage. When a story breaks in one state which is obviously of broader than local interest, the state editors would be doing the profession a real service if they would act as news feeder sources for the national periodicals. Even if they did no more than provide a quick lead that the event had taken place, it would constitute a step forward. (From personal experience, I can tell you that the state libraries and extension agencies are virtually useless in this respect.)

On some of these local stories, also, the local periodicals should be providing the kind of in-depth coverage that the national periodicals, with their broader range, can rarely spare space for. Cooperation should be a two-way thing, of course, and the national periodicals in some cases might be able to lend a hand to the local editor, in the form of resources, advice or technique. For example, the national periodical might have pictures that would be relevant, or background information in its files on similar cases in other parts of the country, or knowledge of action being taken or contemplated by one or other of the professional associations which would be relevant to a story on the case.

By way of illustration, take the Ellis Hodgin case in Martinsville, Virginia, which got cover, editorial and front page news treatment in *LJ*. This isn't a very good—or rather not a very typical—case to illustrate my point, since news about it spread so fast that the details were available on the national scene almost as soon as the most alert local editor could hope to get them. But this is by no means the normal situation, and is unlikely to be until some national library periodical is rich enough to afford stringers in all parts of the country like the *New York Times*.

But disregard the fact that on this occasion *LJ* had a man on the spot almost as soon as the story broke. In the normal course of events the local editor would have heard about the story long before it reached New York or Chicago. He could have quickly assembled the bare bones of the story and contacted one or more of the national periodicals to alert them that something important had happened. The national editor could then have decided to follow up the story in depth, or he could have asked the local editor to feed him more material as the story developed. The local editor, in any case, should have pursued the story in depth for his own periodical, getting interviews with Hodgin and local officials, gathering factual background on those involved, and so on. If his deadline were longer than that of the national periodicals (which is likely) he could have continued to feed in the more important items while still putting together the complete story for his own magazine.

And again, the process could have been two-way. Shortly after the Hodgin story broke there was a meeting of the Social Responsibilities group in New York City. There, the Hodgin case was discussed, and various actions vis-à-vis ALA and other channels were considered. Also, a collection was taken up by the group as a sort of informal beginning of a defense or support fund for Hodgin. *LJ* had an editor at that meeting in New York, and she could easily have been assigned to relay the relevant information on the meeting to Dick Burns for whatever story he might be preparing for *The Virginia Librarian*.

At about the same time, or a little earlier, ALA, receiving the Hodgin news, finally decided it had better show some inclination to do something so far as a defense fund for librarians was concerned. Gerry Shields, if our editors were working as a network in the manner I am suggesting, could also have fed this information to Dick Burns for incorporation into his story in the local periodical.

My final suggestion is that the state and regional periodicals could do a good deal more than they are doing to supplement the efforts of the national periodicals in providing current information for the working librarian. For example (and this may sound like a note of self-interest), while some of the national periodicals do a reasonably good job of reviewing most of the books published for the professional librarian or the student of librarianship, many of these reviews appear six weeks to a year, or even more, after publication. The state periodicals could supplement this reviewing by publishing, say, monthly lists of new publications in librarianship. This sort of current awareness service would not be difficult to accomplish. Information on the majority of new publications could be obtained from little more than half a dozen publishers—ALA, Bowker, Wilson, Scarecrow, Shoe String, Gale, McGraw-Hill—and I have no doubt that these publishers would be only too willing to cooperate.

The state and regional periodicals, also, ought to make an effort to round up current data within their own territories; data such as salary levels, new buildings, central processing developments, use of teletype, and a dozen other things. The national periodicals attempt occasional summaries of information of this kind, but the results will be fragmentary until a more sustained effort is made at the state level.

This has been a long diagnosis and a short prescription. Both elements fall far short of any claim to comprehensiveness. There are other symptoms of illness—and surely other cures—along with plenty of material for more conjecture. I am off the news scene now, out of the periodical editor's chair. Perhaps some of what I've suggested has begun to happen. There are some hopeful signs of life despite the general malaise of the library press. I've named a few, you know of others. Perhaps the best advice is to suggest that you support, through your subscriptions and your response, the library periodicals you prefer. With luck, the others will fade from the scene.

The Journalist and the Writer

Once upon a time there was a young librarian who, ever since he had been knee-high to a charging desk, had dreamed of being one day a journalist. Like others before him, he traveled across the seas to the land of opportunity, and opportunity, as it is supposed to in that land, beckoned. He became indeed a journalist, with all the pages of the library Bible spread out before him at his command.

The fledgling journalist loved perhaps one American above all others, an Oriole called Mencken, and he cherished the muckrakers of earlier (pre-Agnew) days. He determined to try to bring some of this spirit to what is loosely known as the literature of librarianship. Under his command the library Bible began to take on a fiery earnestness and the smoke of many "causes" curled from its pages.

But the journalist had, also from those knee-high days, been reared on the words and irreverences of a red-headed Irishman named Shaw, despite that writer's assertion that people should not adopt him as their favorite author even if it was for their own good. While not exactly tiring of the crusades launched by the library Bible the journalist gradually began to become aware that many of the crusaders seemed deficient in one or other of the qualities he had come, through Shavian saturation, to expect of words assembled together on paper—notably wit and style and some sustained effort to make men take themselves less seriously (in short, perspective). He knew, of course, being older by then and a chauvinist to boot, that he could never hope to make women take themselves less seriously.

He began to search for such qualities in other, less biblical areas of the literature of librarianship and found, not these qualities but the language of Madison Avenue incongruously in bed with the frumpish

---

Reprinted with permission of R. R. Bowker, a division of Reed Publishing (USA) Inc. from *Tales of Melvil's Mouser*, by Paul Dunkin (Epilogue, pp. 179-182). Copyright © 1970.

footnote of academe. For a while he believed that the Americans had slaughtered wit and style and irreverence as they had slaughtered the Indians (and later the Vietnamese).

But crusaders, particularly English ones, do not give up easily, and our journalist pursued his quest even into the most incredibly unlikely realms, even into the literature of cataloging. In the pages of a publication with a ghastly, bifurcated, even schizophrenic title—*Library Resources and Technical Services*—he discovered at last what he was looking for. And he proposed. Surely a man who could write not just with wisdom but with wit about *cataloging* could bring his gifts to just about any topic. Come write for my library Bible, the journalist pleaded. Scintillate about the whole wide captivating world of library land. Reach out from your little 5x3 ghetto. You are too good to be left in the LRTS.

The scintillating writer about cataloging was modest and reluctant but he was wooed and seduced by the persistent journalist in the end, and for a whole year he became what the journalist called a columnist. He occupied, in solitary splendor, a page second in holiness to that temple among the library Bible's pages, the editorial page, which the journalist always kept for himself.

The columnist's year was divided into twenty-two parts (being a cataloger still at heart, he called them subdivisions). As the columns followed each other in a steady stream the journalist (and even a few of the library Bible's readers who could detect that words have a shape as well as a meaning) began to appreciate the new savor and flavor of wit and perspective that had entered the pages of this muckraking malcontent in the family of the literature of librarianship. And when the year ended, the journalist (as even were some of the readers) was sad. How often, he philosophized in the manner of his favorite philosopher, Lawrence F. Berra, can you hit a home run?

Even so, the journalist had not seen at the time (for though he was earnest he was not as perceptive as he should have been) that what the scintillating writer had wrought was something more than twenty-two isolated exercises in wit and wisdom about libraryland. These columns were in fact the beginning of a Grand Design. The scintillating writer had, by God, imperceptibly, fiendishly, started his own subtle crusade. There is some excuse for the journalist: a crusade-within-a-crusade is even harder to detect than a conference-within-a-conference.

Perhaps what he had done—or begun—was not even clear immediately to the scintillating writer. He returned to the LRTS and the land of the five-by-three, though now with status and power, controlling its destinies just as the journalist did the library Bible's. But still, his new throne at the LRTS was little better than a Procrustean bed, and it was scarcely visible from some of the far-out corners of libraryland. The scintillating writer began to yearn for the wide-open spaces again. Never again could he be restricted solely to the fifteen-square-inch dimension. Freedom of speech, as it ever was, is heady stuff.

This time *he* proposed to the journalist. What if the twenty-two parts (subdivisions) were to multiply and become forty-four, or more? What if the parts could be so structured, with the fiendish ingenuity of a man who knew classification, into a whole, and what was once a mere column could become a volume—A BOOK? Is a book not more biblical than the holiest of periodical publications?

Whoever heard of a librarian throwing away a book? A magazine is a now medium, but the book is the foundation stone of all media. The journalist was not modest and reluctant and he could not withstand the passion and logic of the scintillating writer's propaganda. Besides, if finding wit and perspective in the periodical literature is like looking for that proverbial needle in the haystack (who *does* sew in a haystack?), similar qualities in the books about libraryland are as rare as a woman at a meeting of the Melvil Dui Chowder and Marching Association. And so this book was born.

And now it is easy to see that the pieces do indeed fit together, and do form a design, grand or otherwise, depending which mousetrap you view it from. Our scintillating writer's message is whispered with a smile but its penetration is more deadly and insistent than the stridency of the journalist and his cohorts of crusaders. No lofty aims, the writer says he has. These little tales "do not pretend to be the truth, the whole truth, and nothing but." And yet . . . and yet . . . beneath the pleasant fancies there is the uncomfortable stench of an overriding truth. It is perhaps not, as another writer has told us, that truth is stranger than fiction. What this writer tells us, page after light-tripping page, is that truth (or the truth[s] we promulgate about ourselves and our profession) *is* fiction.

You were, dear librarians, better off, safer, with us simple muckrakers and journalists.

Hook, Line and Sinker or, Fishing for a Publisher

"Once upon a time only potato vines were debugged. You could do it with your fingers one bug at a time. Or you could do it with Paris green and a water sprinkler—a mass production job. From that age of innocence we have long since slipped into an age of sophistication and we have learned to debug anything: machines, systems, theories. Even poetry."

Does that make you want to read on? It's the opening paragraph of a chapter in *Tales of Melvil's Mouser,* written by the late Paul Dunkin, one of Rutgers' finest and one of the best writers I knew in the library profession. He could even write about cataloging and make it interesting. The title of the piece I just quoted is "The Debugging of Victor Hugo."

Here's the opening sentence of another chapter: "Bibliography belongs in a circus." The title of that one is "The Tabby Cat and the Elephant."

I start with these Dunkin gems because they demonstrate so well Lesson No. 1 for anybody who wants to write successfully (that is, with frequent acceptances). In my freelance writing days I learned that the pros called such opening paragraphs or sentences "the hook." It is more prevalent in the journal literature but it could be used more often, and profitably, in books.

The lesson here, in short, is the old adage, "first catch your hare." A good title will entice the reader to the first paragraph. A good paragraph will carry him/her into the text. The hook is in. And if it gets in deep enough, the reader may stay on the line.

An edited version of a paper delivered at a Rutgers University program for librarians on the basics of publishing. Entitled "Publishing—Not Perishing," the program was presented at the Hermann Labor Center, Rutgers University, New Brunswick, N. J., January 21, 1977.

This, as a Lesson No. 1 should be (for it too is a hook), is vital. Publishers, editors are among the most cynical, jaded, tired readers of all. Most of them read for most of their waking hours, and the worst part of all that reading is often the daily manuscript pile.

So, if you crave publication, first unlearn all you have been taught in college or library school about writing a term paper, dissertation, or what all. If your first paragraph is a series of dull disclaimers or a mere processional recounting of what is to emerge later in the manuscript, the odds are that the manuscript will be in Uncle Sam's charge and on its way back to you the next day.

This is not to say that a dissertation can never get published. Some do. But it is a rare one that can without massive re-working.

Lesson 2. If you want to write anything, the first thing to nail down is for whom you are writing it. There are two stages to this. The first, so obvious it shouldn't need mentioning, is the direct audience. Are your words aimed at beginning students or seasoned practitioners? Catalogers or media freaks? It makes a difference. If you do not get this fixed in your mind *before* you start writing, you may be somewhat like a person on a mountain top, shouting into the wind. *Someone* may hear you, but the odds against a rapt audience are immense.

Having decided that, you need then to investigate and decide on which publisher (a) is likely to entertain your proposed book, article or whatever, and (b) is likely to reach the audience you are setting out to address. Would you believe that Scarecrow Press receives a children's book every week or two, a collection of poems about once a month? It does. And it has never published one thing that could possibly lead an author to believe that it is a likely place to send such things. Authors like that will die unpublished. They are shouting into the wind. And they're wasting time and effort (theirs and ours), not to mention postage.

So, with topic, treatment and audience all firmly in mind, research your potential publishers. In library science, that's practically no trick at all. There aren't much more than half a dozen publishers who will go near library science. But even in this restricted field there are differences among the library science publishers, and one may be more appropriate than others for your book. How do you find out?

The best way I know is first to check their catalogs. See what they *have* published. Then check some of their books; look at the level at which they are written, what audience they are aimed at. If you were to do that you'd find, for example, that Scarecrow is not by any means just a publisher of library science materials. Sure, it's a publisher for libraries and, more than that, for librarians, but library science as a subject accounts for certainly no more than 20 percent of its list today.

If you're going beyond library science, that is, working in another subject field or perhaps compiling a reference book on a specific topic, then you need to start checking sources which will give you some selectivity, so that you don't wind up sending poetry to Scarecrow or a bibliography on acne to Doubleday. Among the key places to check first are: *Subject Guide to BIP,* which will show you which publishers tend to be active in your chosen subject or treatment area; *Literary Market Place* (and this is beginning to sound like a Bowker commercial), which has a list of publishers classified by the subject matter in which they are *primarily* interested (I stress *primarily* because publishers aren't automata—they break the mold occasionally, particularly when an untypical item catches some editor's fancy). But if you're starting out, stay with the odds. And then there is the battery of writers' books: *Writer's Handbook; Writer's and Artist's Yearbook; Writer's Market,* etc., all of which list potential markets in a variety of ways.

There is, of course, a major step to take before all that stuff under Lesson 2. It is to find out whether the book you have in mind is needed. Has it been done already? Back to *Subject Guide to BIP.* Can the subject stand a new treatment? How large is the potential audience for what you have in mind? (And try to be hardnosed and realistic about that—few authors are.) This last factor, incidentally, can influence your choice of publishers to approach. Many publishers won't touch a book if its apparent audience is less than 5,000 or 10,000. Others, if they like the book well enough and see a real need for it, may take it on even if they envisage, say, no more than 1,000 potential sales. Scarecrow is an example of the latter, though I must add that that does not mean it goes looking for books with limited potential. Many of its books sell much more than 1,000. Indeed, the best selling title is now somewhere up around 130,000 copies.

Okay, so you are now ready to query your publisher. Yes, *query.* Don't spend a couple of years researching and writing, and then start looking for a publisher. Remember Lesson 2. You may be lucky if you wing it the whole way, but I repeat, play the odds.

They are never so good in this business that you can afford to ignore them. And there's another reason for getting a query out early. All your bibliographic checking won't tell you, with any certainty, what else in your field may be in the works. You would be surprised how often one potential author will query a publisher about something which the publisher already has on contract, in production or—in the worst cases—has already published.

Now some query letters are skeleton in form (Scarecrowish, you might say). They simply ask: "Would you be interested in a book about ... " castration of kangaroos, or whatever. I do not altogether decry this kind of letter myself. It can help us weed out a lot of poor ideas early and without much effort. But such letters don't do much for the author's chances. Even if your one- or two-sentence letter has enough of a hook in it to entice a tentative nibble, the publisher won't be able to give you an answer that emits more than a vague interest. He or she will want to know more.

Let me here interject one of those really basic, ground zero points. Please, don't just type your name and address on the envelope. Put it on the letter inside. Silly point? The volume of mail coming into a publishing house in a day is often mind-boggling. If a letter gets to your desk without an address the probability of matching it up with the one envelope among hundreds in the round file are very slim, and few editors are likely to undertake such an information retrieval project. So you may never get a reply. And you'll blame the publisher for discourtesy.

What do publishers like to get in a query letter? What they like to receive includes the following:

1. A pretty complete outline of the proposed book—preferably more than just a Table of Contents. They want to know in some detail, or with some clarity, what's *in* each chapter or section, how it's arranged, etc.

2. If it's a reference book, they like some clear indication of sources the author has used; the types of material included (books, periodicals, multimedia, dissertations, whatever); the scope (chronologically—where does it start and stop; and in terms of languages, countries covered, etc.); whether or not it's annotated, and so on.

3. The estimated size of the project. It makes a difference whether it's likely to be 80 pages (which most book publishers won't look at) or 4000 (which most won't look at either).

4. A projected deadline. And this should be realistic. It will probably be built into the publishing contract, because a great many more projects start than finish.

5. And finally, a generous sample of the book you're preparing. In the case of a monograph, at least a chapter or two. In the case of a bibliography or other reference work, sample entries from various sections, including indexes.

Your ideal and perfect query letter is in. What happens next? If you're dealing with Scarecrow you will almost certainly have a full response within a week. If you are dealing with some other publishers, you may get an acknowledgment card; with yet others you need to be prepared to wait weeks or even months for any kind of reply. And some will never answer unless you enclose a stamped, addressed envelope.

In Scarecrow's case, the response is likely to take one of several forms:

1. They'll tell you the project is not for them. They usually don't spell out reasons because this just gets them into profitless debates and adds to the unproductive correspondence pile.

2. They'll tell you that they need more detail about some aspect or other.

3. They'll tell you that they like the manuscript basically, but will present several suggestions for alternative treatment or for revisions, and will wait to see how you react to those.

4. Or, they'll tell you that they are sold, in which case they will probably send you a contract immediately.

You, of course, are in that last, successful category. So you receive two copies of the contract, one for your records, one for the publisher's. When they're signed, you are in business together: author and publisher. Both parties' objectives are the same (though some authors don't understand that): to produce as good a book as possible, and to sell as many copies of it as possible.

Some contracts are extremely detailed and complicated, and you should read them very carefully. Some place what I regard as unwarranted restrictions upon an author, like ensuring the publisher the first option to the author's next book or next several books. Scarecrow's contract is fairly simple, barely more than one mimeographed page. Its very simplicity worries some people, but it has worked to the satisfaction of more than 1,000 authors for better than a quarter of a century. It spells out details of copyright (virtually always, at Scarecrow, copyright is registered in the name of the author); of royalties—how much they are, when they are paid and when you receive a royalty accounting; the division of income on subsidiary rights (translations, paperback rights, etc.)—very few bibliographies are made into movies. It stipulates conditions about proofreading, indexing, etc., and places some penalties on the author who wants to rewrite at late production stages. It tells you, if you have quoted liberally from others, that *you* must obtain the necessary permissions for this and must pay permission fees as required. And it reserves details of production, design, marketing, etc. to the publisher. You'd be surprised how many authors are not satisfied to be experts in their subject; they also feel they know better than the editor or publisher how to design their book and how to market it. In almost every case, such authors are wrong, so the contract tries to cut this sort of thing off at the pass.

Let's assume that you, being the perfect author, get your book completed by the contract deadline. There are many who don't. They will receive periodic prods and, if the delays are interminable, finally a cancellation. But here we're dealing with a good author and a good publisher.

Your manuscript arrives on time and the publisher responds immediately (that's a rarity with many publishers, a certainty with Scarecrow). We will usually take just a fast initial check of the manuscript and give you a general acknowledgment type of response. It may be enthusiastic or guarded, but it will most often say that we'll be back to you in more detail when we have had time to examine the manuscript thoroughly. We may spot some problems right away, though, in which case we'll immediately make specific suggestions for correcting them before we go further.

During the editing stage, which may be a month or two after your manuscript is submitted (and on schedule here, I'm talking about Scarecrow's; they vary a lot, and most publishers are slower than we are), there may be further correspondence. We will not return the manuscript to you unless major revisions are necessary. But we may well send you queries about a passage which doesn't make sense to us or appear to be supportable; about missing information, a blind reference, or a host of other details.

After all of the editorial problems have been solved, you will have another wait of perhaps a couple of months before proofs begin to arrive for you to read and correct. When the publisher gets these back, they are checked further in the publishing office and all corrections are made. You will have sent the necessary indexes back with the final proofs, and these will be set and proofread, often in house. What we have just skimmed through is the *composition* stage, the setting of the book. Now books may be composed in a variety of ways, but to keep it simple, the two main broad categories are *cold type* and *hot type*. Let us not mention computer composition—it has its uses, but they are restricted to certain kinds of material, and it is expensive. Cold type is composition by typewriter, and it comes in a number of varieties, some so sophisticated that you cannot easily tell the difference in the finished product from hot type. Hot type composition is from "hot" lead, that is on a linotype or monotype machine.

I don't want to get into technical matters here, but I mention this point because Scarecrow composes in cold type exclusively. We do so for economic reasons because many of our works have quite restricted audiences and, therefore, sales. Some people, however, criticize our books because they are "offset." Such people simply do not know what they are talking about. Offset is a manner of printing, as opposed to letterpress for example. It has nothing to do with composition. And perhaps 90% of everything you read today—from your newspaper to your professional journals to the books on your shelves—is printed by offset.

Well, your book has been composed and corrected and now it goes off to the printer, and from there to the binder. That process altogether, with the shipping involved, usually takes about another three months.

During this period, Scarecrow's promotion director will contact you for suggestions about promoting your book, which journals you think should receive review copies or announcements, and how *you* would like to see your book described. She'll also want some biographical details. We have some ideas of our own in this area, and a great deal of experience, but this is a partnership and certainly no one should have a better understanding of your book than you. Both the author and the publisher (to repeat) have a serious stake in doing the best they can for each book that comes off the press.

At this stage, then, the publisher begins the marketing process, seeing that it gets into the *Weekly Record,* into *BIP* et al., preparing and sending out flyers and catalogs to specific mailing lists, advertising, sending out review copies, and so on. One sure thing is that very few authors will ever be convinced that *their* books have been properly or adequately promoted. If they are librarians they may complain, on the other hand, about the number of times some publishers hit them with announcements. You can't win.

One other certainty I can state at this point is that nothing promotes a book better than a review (which the publisher, of course, cannot guarantee an author). And while I'd always prefer a good review, naturally, I'd much rather have a bad review than *no* review. Authors get terribly upset by bad reviews. I always tell them to learn what they can from critical reviews, but not to bother otherwise. Bad reviews still sell books.

Four questions were posed for this symposium to answer. I've concentrated on the first: what steps can you take to ease the way from typewriter to printed page? The second: What are editors looking for?—is easy: Good books that are needed by enough people so that they will not only make a contribution to knowledge, but also a contribution to profit, without which we disappear.

The third question—How long will it take before the material is in print?— has a lot of variables written into it. I've tried to indicate as I went along how Scarecrow's schedule works. If things go normally, it will take about a year from receipt of manuscript to get the finished book into your (and other readers') hands. With many publishers it will take rather, or much, longer.

The fourth question—Is money available for a research project?—is not generally a publisher's concern. Certainly, most publishers won't make such money available.

One more clean-up job: my title. I started out with the hook, and a lot of lines have followed. What's the sinker? The sinker is stark reality. Write if you must publish rather than perish. Write if you love to do it or can't resist it. But don't write for money. The sad truth is that very few authors, if they count all the time and effort involved in researching and writing and preparing the manuscript, ever earn much more than a buck an hour from such work. And that's a lot less than the minimum wage.

The Library Press and Eric Moon: An Interview Conducted by Frederick J. Stielow

Ever since Melvil Dewey and R. R. Bowker launched the *Library Journal* in 1876, the library press has played a significant role in the professionalization of the field. Yet never had the press involved itself in social and political issues to the extent it would in the Sixties. The press not only acted as a sounding board for the factions of the era but also expanded its scope of inquiry to include a variety of heretofore neglected problems. There emerged a new form of advocacy journalism for librarianship. This new variant was almost unprecedented for the press of such a profession—and its leader was Eric Moon.

To paraphrase Karl Nyren, the history of the library press in the Sixties was essentially the story of Eric Moon. In a manner unlike any editor before him, Moon was able to use his publication to catalyze action on social issues and bring the "skeletons out of the closet." Through his direction of the *Library Journal,* Moon served notice that the intellectual freedom and service orientation of librarianship demanded addressing such basic issues as racism and sexism.

The following text is excerpted from an interview at the 1984 American Library Association meeting in Dallas. Moon, a transplanted Englishman, was explaining how he came to this country and gained his editorship:

This article appeared in *Activism in American Librarianship, 1962-1973,* Mary Lee Bundy and Frederick J. Stielow, eds. (Greenwood Press, Westport, CT, 1987), pp. 99-111. Copyright © 1987 by the Estate of Mary Lee Bundy and Frederick J. Stielow. Reprinted with permission of Greenwood Publishing Group, Inc., and Frederick J. Stielow.

MOON: It was hard to make the transition. I had really wanted to come over to the States for some years, but one ran into some familiar problems such as nonrecognition of professional qualifications from other countries. So I couldn't get in here at any appropriate level. I was already pretty well up the ladder in Great Britain, and I even had some problems getting into Canada, except for the lucky fact that Newfoundland seemed still to regard itself as much a part of Great Britain as of Canada. And so I became the provincial librarian of Newfoundland and then, eventually, got the call from Bowker and was asked: "How would you like to be the editor of the *Library Journal*?"

STIELOW: Then you hadn't really tried for the job?

MOON: No, it arose out of some earlier connections. My assistant at a branch library in London in the early Fifties, a guy called John Wakeman, came over here for a year on exchange with a librarian from Brooklyn. When he returned to England I had gone on to another job. He seemed not to like much working with the new librarian there and wrote back to Frank St. John in Brooklyn and said, "If I come back, will you have a job for me?" St. John said there might be some problems, but we're really creative here in Brooklyn and we'll find something. And John became, I believe, the assistant public relations librarian for the Brooklyn Public Library. And then the editorships of both of the major library publications, the *Library Journal* and *Wilson Bulletin,* became available at roughly the same time so John applied for both of them. He was interviewed first at *Library Journal* and didn't get it. In fact, decided that he really didn't want it, in part because he felt that the internal political problems there were more than he could cope with. But he did get *Wilson*. And he was having dinner with some friends one night and said, you know, I know of only one guy who could handle that *Library Journal* job. He talked about me sitting up there in Newfoundland, and someone said: "Why don't you write the *Journal* about him." And he wrote this marvelous letter about me, claiming that I had been one of the leaders of the young library movement in England. Dan Melcher got interested and just picked up the phone, and out of the blue here's this voice from New York saying, how would you like to be editor of the *Library Journal*?

STIELOW: So you were actually hired for being part of the avant-garde?

MOON: Well, Dan Melcher is a progressive guy; he was much involved in the great democratic nightmare at the Chicago Democratic Convention. He was a pretty good guy to work for, and that was just as well, because once I started rolling in the *Library Journal* and with the

Civil Rights movement the protests from the field were loud and often rather dirty.

STIELOW: But Bowker stood behind you?

MOON: Yes. Well, the board would get a little nervous every now and then but Melcher was always very supportive. And whenever anyone would start to twitter, he'd say: "Well, let's look at the bottom line, what's happened to the *Library Journal* since Moon took over?" Fortunately circulation was well up, the advertising was well up, and how could you beat that?

One of the first things I did after taking over the job at the *Journal* was to look around at the scene, at the library literature. My feeling was that it was terribly boring, dull, ill . . . it seemed to me not to be looking at any issues of importance. It was cautious and had very little to do with reality, with real life. In fact when I was first interviewed for the job I said I thought it looked as though it had a bad middle-aged spread. (I wouldn't say that today, at my age, because anything middle-aged looks pretty good from my current perspective.)

I didn't really set out deliberately to deal with controversial issues, but I didn't see any real way to cure the pervasive dullness other than by trying to excite, to challenge, to create some enthusiasm. At least I felt I had to deal with some things I could get enthusiastic about. I wasn't the only one attempting to breathe life into the library periodical scene. My old friend John Wakeman was on deck at the same time as I was in the early Sixties and also was trying to do the same thing. But he was working at quite a disadvantage. At Bowker I had the support of a liberal board of directors; John was at the Wilson Company, which has always been stuffy, but despite that, he was in right at the beginning on the civil rights issues in the library field. Subsequently other editors began to pick up on this kind of real-life issue, and for a spell there we really did have a good lively library press. It was perhaps the beginning of what some here called advocacy journalism in librarianship. But I really don't think anything would have happened if these two national journals hadn't come about, gotten excited, and tried to relate what was happening in society to library services and our profession. I do think there were some results from what we did. One was, to use a current phrase, the trickle-down from that change in national press. Following a few of the editorials in *Library Journal* and *WLB* others began to appear in some of the state journals. Two of the first to pick up the ball [in January of 1961] were Bill Eshelman at the *California Librarian* and John Berry at the *Bay State Librarian*. It's no accident that those two later wound up as editors of the *Wilson Bulletin* and the *Library Journal*.

STIELOW: It is remarkable that the library journals were out there leading the way. I think library periodicals might be unique in that.[1]

MOON: Well, I think it's very important for a journalist to believe in people and to try to persuade them to do what must be done. What we were trying to do was not so much to specify what ought to be done but to insist that something *had* to be done. I outlined some possibilities in the first civil rights editorial I wrote in *LJ*. It was entitled "The Silent Subject."[2]

STIELOW: That was along with the Estes article at the same time?[3]

MOON: Yes, the Estes contribution was a deliberate gambit on my part. Remember, I had only been in the country for one year. I decided, since I'd already stirred up readers with some previous editorials, that for me to launch the civil rights issue alone, when it hadn't been touched in library literature with the single exception of the editorial by Stanley Kunitz in *WLB* in 1939 called "Spectre at Richmond," would not be very smart. What I ought to do was to lead off with an article from someone who had impeccable credentials, someone who had been born and reared in magnolia country, someone who had been brought up in the midst of that whole terrible racial struggle and could write about it first-hand. Rice is a hero, you know. He was subsequently ignored and vilified by friends, and that article took a lot of guts. If you look back at my editorial in that issue, it made many proposals that subsequently became reality. It was the first editorial, I think, to advocate the use of federal funds as a weapon. It was the first editorial to suggest a legal defense fund to help librarians who were out there on the front lines. And a variety of other things like that, they were all in that editorial.

STIELOW: Were there other key articles that you would pick out during your editorship?

MOON: Well, I can't remember, but many of them are I suppose in those two books that we published about the period.[4] I don't remember many specific articles, but a few stand out in my memory. For example, when John Berry started sounding off in the *Bay State Librarian*, he got over-enthusiastic, as John often does, and went to town with an editorial (April 1963) suggesting that ALA should stop giving awards to strengthen libraries that were still segregated. I'd done a little more research on this issue than John, and I wrote what he says is still the longest editorial in library literature attacking somebody,[5] reproving John Berry for not having done his homework. He was terribly wounded by this for a while, but a month or so later I went up to Boston, met with him, and he and I went on a two-day binge. At the end of it I asked him if he would like to be assistant editor of *Library Journal*. And he said, "Man, I don't understand you. You attack me like hell in the library press and then you come out and offer me a job."

STIELOW: Speaking of Berry, when Dr. Bundy and I were first talking about doing this book, it is remarkable how many people like Berry and E. J. Josey, Nyren, Pat Schuman have now done very well in the library world—although you have mentioned Estes and that some people have indeed been hurt.

MOON: Oh yeah, lots of people have been hurt. There were a number of librarians who lost their jobs, who were given a very, very hard time. Yet, those are risks that we have to take. I could well have lost my job because the pressures were very, very heavy, and they were coming from the top of the profession. They were writing to Bowker, to the president and the chairman of the board, letters saying that I had to be stopped because I was destroying all relationships between the profession and the company.

STIELOW: Did that ease off with the downturn in the segregation struggle?

MOON: Well, I think it eased off some but not until quite late in the Sixties. There was a kind of constant opposition, particularly from some of the state leaders in the South. And not only from them, from some of the people who were right up at the top in the ALA.

STIELOW: Yes, you had written in your editorials how this was almost a grass-roots movement, where Council had actually been more of a retrograde force in the push for segregation and had to be almost forcibly dragged toward this realization.

MOON: Yes. Of course another interesting aspect of the criticism of me was that not only was I presenting my views in the pages of *Library Journal*, but I was getting personally involved in the action, for example, as a member of the ALA Council. And a lot of people saw that as wrong, said that I couldn't report on the Council because I was so involved in it myself. But to me that's hogwash. Because, member or not, I couldn't report objectively—no one could report objectively—on the Council. What I was trying to do was report creatively, so that people got a flavor of what was happening—not just a mere set of committee notes. I never saw those conference reports as news but as commentary. I think it was Archie McNeal who once said that my conference reports were the longest editorials in library literature. Which in a way was true. They really were, and I was not going to let my being on Council influence that one way or the other. I think that it's nonsense to say that people who write shouldn't vote or voice their opinions in other forums.

STIELOW: What was the *Journal* like before you took over—what were the tendencies?

MOON: Well I came into a situation that was very much in limbo. Lee Ash had been the last editor and he had been gone for a while. In that interim period, Karl Brown from the New York Public Library was acting editor. But he was working in the library full-time and was trying to put the *Library Journal* together in his spare time. In the meantime many of the decisions about what was going into the *Journal* were being made by various people around the company. So it was a bit of a mess, and I made it very clear that I thought a magazine had to be controlled by the editor. Otherwise it can come out looking like another one of those horses designed by a committee, you know. Dan Melcher was extremely helpful in enabling me to get the kind of control I saw as necessary. Prior to my taking over, there was a lot of writing without much content, much rigor, or much style.

STIELOW: You talked about attacks. Did you ever have any really physical threats against you?

MOON: Threats yes, but none that really materialized except in one incident which had to do with Mary Lee [Dr. Mary Lee Bundy], but she can probably tell you about that.

STIELOW: Yes, she did mention some of that.

MOON: Well, she and I went to a cocktail party at a convention and we walked in, bought our drinks, and sat down on the couch. We're having sort of a quiet chat when the brigade of southern dragons, mostly lady librarians from high up in state activities, came marching into the room and launched their usual verbal attack on me. Mary Lee got rather bored with this and got up and made to leave the room. As she did, she said, "Eric, I'll see you later," and they picked her up and literally threw her out in the hallway.[6]

STIELOW: My impression from talking to her was that maybe this kind of thing had happened to you all the time.

MOON: Well, that was one example; I remember others. I remember going down to the deep South and speaking a couple of times. I was given the usual kind of nonsense there, telephone calls every hour on the hour throughout the night, saying get out of town, it's bad for your health here. But none of that really ever came to anything.

STIELOW: You did a number of articles, editorials rather, on Vietnam, yet when we started to do background research for this book, we found it very difficult, almost impossible to find Vietnam indexed in normal library literature. Do you remember running any specific articles on Vietnam?

MOON: Well, I'm fairly sure there has to be something; there was so much activity. I was involved in a number of the protest groups against Vietnam. There were several in New York alone, one with Norman Mailer and a variety of other people. Then there was the big *New York Times* advertisement, organized by Dick Bye at Bowker and paid for by concerned publishers and librarians. I'm sure I could not have failed to write about Vietnam.

STIELOW: Yes, you wrote editorials but I couldn't find articles and, also, Vietnam or anti-war protests hadn't been indexed for our literature.

MOON: Yes, that's probably the old subject heading disease Sandy Berman has written about for years.

STIELOW: What was your response to the ad?

MOON: It was pretty good. We raised certainly enough money to cover the ad, which was a lot, and what was over we used for some other related things. We certainly had demonstrations at ALA and concerted efforts on the floor at Council and membership meetings to get past the blockade that these problems were not library issues. To show you about how much things have changed there was a motion on the floor last night about U.S. involvement in South Africa which passed with no discussion. It didn't pass that easily on the vote, but no one spoke in opposition to that issue. That is a big change.

STIELOW: You mentioned that people from fairly high up in the library field had given you opposition. Did Council as a body ever come out and oppose some of the activities you were involved in as editor?

MOON: Not as a body, no. Individually, yes. And individual ALA staff members too. One—and I'm not going to name names—but one came to me after one of these meetings and said to me and to Wakeman (the other Limey), "Why don't you two go back to England where you both belong?"

STIELOW: You came in 1959, which is five years or so after the *Brown v. Board of Education* landmark desegregation decision. Yet you say nothing was being done in the library press in particular to fight against this issue?

MOON: Well, go back and look in the literature. I couldn't find anything really in the literature with that one exception I named earlier.

Of course, Blacks were mentioned a few times, but there were no suggestions that we should do anything about this racial problem. We started off clearly and very deliberately with an emphasis on dealing with libraries that were segregated, particularly in the South. But it very quickly became apparent to us that that wasn't the only problem. Our own profession was a problem. We had library associations that were segregated, and we had to deal with that too. E. J. Josey couldn't belong to the Georgia Library Association. Some of them didn't specifically exclude Blacks, but the conference situations were such that Blacks could not attend the conventions. So the effort began to move in that direction. We figured if we couldn't start cleaning our own house, how would we ever be able to move further out to the larger societal problems? E. J. was the person that I worked most closely with over the whole period. I figured I couldn't really find out what was going on unless I had a network of information about what was going on in the deep South, a network largely composed of Blacks who were intimate with the problem. E. J. was the principle one who helped build that up. He was also the first Black, I think, who came right out front and stuck his neck out the whole way on the issues. He got a lot of pain from it too. He's a very gutsy guy, and I have a tremendous amount of admiration for him. We've worked as closely as almost anybody I can think of for the past twenty-five years or so now. I think it's easy to see why I was one of his chief supporters for president.

STIELOW: How do you see the Black issue in relation to the other issues in the era?

MOON: I think the Black issue was really the first cause that became prominent in the library press and in ALA meetings. In fact it was the seed from which a lot of other things grew, the seed for the whole beginning of the social responsibility movement in ALA. The growth of the Social Responsibilities Round Table, in particular, the Gay Liberation movement, the women's movement. They all in some way could be said to have emerged from that initial impetus.

STIELOW: What about the women's movement and being a part of a feminine profession—did you find there was a consciousness about this prior to the Sixties?

MOON: No, I don't think there was. In fact, I think, like a lot of other people, I was rather insensitive to that. It was one of those things that I hadn't seen as clearly as I'd seen the Black problem. In fact, I mentioned in a speech that I gave to the Black Librarians Caucus in New Jersey a few weeks ago that when I came to the *Library Journal,* Dan and I thought it would be very helpful over the first year or two to have a group of advisors to whom I could turn for any help, advice, contacts. After all, I was a newcomer to the shores, a newcomer to the American library profession. So we involved a terrific group of people. But it wasn't until a few years later, when I got involved in the social movements, that I began to realize how little I had known at that time. Because on that board there wasn't one woman, there wasn't even one minority person. And no one even noticed. There wasn't enough consciousness then that would bring such an omission into focus, either on the part of the profession—or on my part, for that matter, I must confess. I don't think the women's movement really got any steam until rather late in the Sixties. It's now probably the most effective group of any, but it was sort of late in arriving.

STIELOW: Certainly the Black movement seems to have led the way in American history, especially in the Sixties, and the other movements followed it. But was the *Journal,* in addition to the women's movement, involved in any of the other ethnic minority struggles?

MOON: No, I don't think it really was significantly involved in any other minority movements until much later. I don't think that many of the other minority groups really emerged in the ALA until much later. Even now there doesn't appear to be much cohesion or identity.

STIELOW: We've mentioned Vietnam, the Black issue, and women's identification. Are there any other major issues that stick out in your mind during your editorship of the *Journal?* Perhaps unionization?

MOON: Yes, unionization was beginning to be an issue, but I don't think it ever got to be a really big one in the sense that the others did. Some of the other issues perhaps don't seem so important, but they had to do with the general democratization of the association, which I would say is not totally removed from these other struggles. It had to happen for the voices from below to get through. That whole movement growing out of the late Sixties, early Seventies, arising from the efforts of the Congress for Change, the emergence of the Social Responsibilities Round Table [SRRT], the formation of ACONDA and ANACONDA and Bill Dix's efforts to bring in younger people and newer voices onto those committees—which were set up to examine the total structure of ALA and how it should respond to change, among other things, to this new social responsibility—were all part of the same movement, the same fabric. I remember some of the younger people in the SRRT movement used to react to me with a certain frustration and constantly call me a structure freak, because I would say protests are fine, demonstrations are fine, digging up resolutions is fine. But if you really want to do something about this association, you have to get where the power is. The only way to get where the power is, is to organize.

STIELOW: The Kansas City meeting of ALA (1968) seemed to be a very pivotal point in the entire activist issue.

MOON: It was sort of like the Olympic trials before Atlantic City. I think that the organization for what occurred at Atlantic City began to emerge. But you couldn't tell even then, only one year before, you couldn't possibly have predicted what was going to happen in Atlantic City. Atlantic City was probably the greatest library convention in library history anywhere, any time. Anybody who was not there can't have any idea how different it was from anything that ever happened before (or since, I might add). The *Library Journal* suite was a sort of revolutionary and tactical headquarters. We had one of the largest suites in Atlantic City, and the Congress for Change people, mostly students and mostly broke, had been at a meeting in Washington previously to get organized. And they came down to Atlantic City with lots of fervor but not much money. I don't know how many of them we had sleeping on the floor, all over the *Library Journal* suite. We had sessions there at which people reported, and great tactical discussions on how were we going to go about this, what should we do about that. It went on for days and days and days. I don't know how long the membership meeting lasted, but it must have been some two and a half days. I found it particularly fascinating because I was in a role that I'd never been in before. I was sitting with the Congress for Change people, but I was the only one who knew most of the guys sitting up at the top table. And periodically the Congress for Change youngsters would say to me: "Well, what do they want?" Then the president or someone would call me up to the platform and ask: "What do they want?" So I was sort of translating and mediating between the two groups. It was an entirely unfamiliar role.

STIELOW: Had your suites always been open before, or was this the start of a pattern?

MOON: No, our suites were always wide open. In fact, through most of the Sixties the *LJ* suite was the place where most of the emerging activists gathered. If you didn't come by the *Library Journal* suite now and then, you weren't likely to be much involved in the action. It was a good thing, editorially as well as from the point of view of involvement. I knew a hell of a lot more about what was happening because so many people were coming by all the time. And for awhile at midwinter, when we were meeting at the Shoreham there, I established the first table inside the door of the bar as the *Library Journal* table. Everyone would stop by and tell me what was happening. I didn't have to cruise the convention quite so much. The *Library Journal* suite was a social center as well; we always had some kind of entertainment going.

STIELOW: In more general terms, while there is certainly enough precedent for activist journalists, still, how did you come about justifying your involvement as a journalist and the whole idea of sustaining of objectivity?

MOON: I never believed that objectivity is very good journalism. I think you have to report facts objectively, but for the rest of the *Journal* I didn't feel a need to be objective at all. The rest of the *Journal,* in my mind, was a way to open up discussion for the profession, a way to open up thinking. If you write an editorial that presents every view on an issue, you haven't left anybody anything to say. Whereas, if you write an editorial that represents one point of view, you're leaving room for others to come in; you're creating room for discussion and involvement. I can't think of anything that's more likely to kill discussion or response than the sentence that includes every "if," "and," or "but." It's hard to separate issues and views and commentary from facts, and I'm not so sure we were always totally successful in that. But we tried in the straight news columns to be factual In the rest of the *Journal* we weren't trying to be objective, and I still don't believe much in total objectivity. I don't think it gets us very far.

STIELOW: What about regrets? What do you feel about not coming out against Nixon in 1968?

MOON: I suppose I didn't come out against Nixon, did I? I think I didn't for several reasons and some of this has got to be guesswork now because I'm not really sure how I felt exactly in 1968, except that certainly I didn't like old Dick. I can hardly remember 1968 now. I was very divided about the Democratic campaign. I was very unhappy with the Democratic Party's selection of Hubert Humphrey because of his lack of support for Eugene McCarthy, when the police force raided McCarthy's headquarters in Chicago and Humphrey didn't protest or intervene. I guess I really didn't think that Nixon would win. I was also, I think, getting to the point where I wanted to hand over the *Library Journal.* I was afraid that I might start repeating myself, which I didn't much want to do. But I thought we had already made the point, when for the first time in library periodical history, we declared for a candidate in the Johnson/Goldwater contest in 1964. We didn't need to do it again to make the point. I didn't think there was anyone in the country at the time who would really think that we were for Nixon. In other words, we really didn't *have* to make the point.

STIELOW: Were there any issues that you now would have liked to have come out for?

MOON: I don't know. I think perhaps I was dealing with as much as I could cope with. There might have been others that we should have done something about, but I don't think anyone can do everything. I hope that what we did helped. The Goldwater thing, by the way, was one of my personal joys and highlights of the Sixties. We debated at some length whether or not we should do it. It was unprecedented. John Berry and I spent a whole day at the New York Public Library researching the votes of Johnson and Humphrey and Goldwater and Miller on everything that looked as though it was vaguely connected with libraries or education. The editorial was based on those research facts. We didn't have to talk about anything else. This was just on professional issues. And it was devastating; the case was made, we felt. And so we decided to go on those grounds alone, without getting into the other political issues. We tried to find a way to make sure that nobody missed that editorial, so I decided to run a gold cover with Goldwater's picture on the cover. All it had underneath was a little one-line quote from the editorial. The New York Library Association Conference was in New York just at the time the issue was coming off the press; and so we scurried over to the *Library Journal* booth with this great pile of gold journals with Goldwater's picture on them and put them on the table. I stood right down at the end of the aisle to watch and see what would happen. People would go strolling by, you know the way they do, they'd get about a yard or two past the booth, do a double take and come back. The people who were in the booth told me you wouldn't believe how many people said: "Do you think he's finally gone crazy?" And then they'd see the line from the editorial and open the journal and turn to it. And I said, "John, it worked!"

Later, we filled almost one whole issue with letters written in response to that editorial. We could have filled several.

STIELOW: What about some of the other features, your book reviews, some of the more traditional areas?

MOON: One of the early things that happened at the *Library Journal* was that I talked to our book review editor (Margaret Cooley) and said: "Look, we've really got to put some zip into those reviews. They wouldn't make me interested in reading the book, even when they recommend it. And the ones that review the controversial stuff, they make even those sound rather dull, because they're so cautious in their approach." I said: "I want to see all these caveats taken out at the end, you know, 'the librarian is advised to read before purchase,' and so on." I said: "That's no good, you review the book, tell them what it's about, get across its flavor and let them make their own decisions." So Margaret said: "Why don't you review a couple of the more controversial books?" And I said, "Gladly." So I became the principal erotica book reviewer for *Library Journal*. One result was that Grove Press regarded me as among their best friends in New York. I used to go to all the Grove Press parties, which is where I got to be friendly with the likes of Norman Mailer, Allen Ginsberg, LeRoi Jones, and the whole gang that hung around down there. That was one of the nice added perks of the job.

STIELOW: Beyond the perks, you'd mentioned before how the readership had actually increased in the *Journal*. Do you remember any statistics about this?

MOON: I think in a period of about three years we went up something like 60 to 70 percent. The *Library Journal* had been in existence for 80 years before I went there. It had always been a loser financially, the way library periodicals normally are. Within a few years, we were either number one or number two in earnings at Bowker. The money came not only from circulation, of course, but principally from advertising. We had great advertising salesmen and they were much helped by the fact that the magazine now was really widely read. Advertising just zoomed in those early years of the Sixties.

STIELOW: Did any of the advertisers ever attempt to put any pressures on you to control your editorial views?

MOON: Yes, they would balk occasionally at some things. More cared probably in regard to censorship because we were heavily involved in that area too. There's a whole other book to be written on that topic alone. As you know, I was doing a lot of quick and dirty surveys of libraries to find out about controversial books and what libraries were doing or not doing, and why.

STIELOW: Let me ask the obvious question. We're sitting here in the summer of 1984; how do you look back on that era of the Sixties?

MOON: Well, from a personal point of view, it was the period in my life when I worked the hardest and had the most fun. I never enjoyed anything as much as the Sixties, but I never want to do it again. By the end of the decade I felt strongly that I couldn't continue participating in that way and still maintain the same impact—that the *Journal* needed a change of direction. John Berry and I have differed frequently about the direction of the *Journal* under his editorship, but I think of all the library editors today, he is the only one who carries on that activist tradition to any extent at all.

STIELOW: You left, then, in part because you were afraid of getting too stale?

MOON: I left because I wanted to see new life injected into the *Journal*. The trouble with most organizations is that those in charge stay around too long. I've said the same thing about the ALA and other bureaucracies: when you perpetuate people you tend to concentrate power, and to some degree generate stagnation. I didn't want that to happen to the *Journal*. I didn't want to see it start to wind down slowly. I really wanted to give it another jolt.

Postscript—Eric Moon

I fear, after reading the transcript of this interview, which took place in a crowded cafeteria during the 1984 ALA convention, that it fails altogether to capture the excitement many of us felt during those years of the Sixties, or the dedication of at first a few and then many, many more who did in fact bring off a revolution of sorts. Even such an epic event as the emergence of a new cataloging code had to cede the headlines to the new insistence on focusing on people and their problems, the apparently new realization that library interests and societal events were not separable.

There are those who seem to feel that today we have sunk back into apathy and lack of concern, but I do not altogether accept that. Much of the sensitivity and consciousness that was brought to the surface in those embattled years remains, and our deliberations continue to benefit from the injections of awareness and humanity that were perhaps the principal benefits of all that turbulence.

I do worry, though, about the lack of fervor and the ignorance about this significant period of library history among some of the younger people emerging from library schools into the profession. Recently a friend of mine who teaches had each of her students read a couple of editorials or articles I had written in the Sixties. She sent me their reactions to the ones they had chosen. The majority seemed to see these writings as something out of another century, although a timid few felt the opinions to be too revolutionary even for today. Most disturbing, however, was the number who felt that all or most of the problems I was writing about, twenty or so years ago, had been solved, or were no longer relevant. If that attitude becomes pervasive we may well be headed toward the kind of insensitivity and apathy that made the Sixties revolution in librarianship necessary.

It is my hope that this volume, featuring many of the participants in those battles against prejudice, parochialism, and narrow professionalism, will help to revive some of the social spirit of those years. May it also heighten the alertness of those who have come along since and enable them to see that the enemy of discrimination is still among us, though wearing often a more subtle and apparently benign mask.

Notes

All notes and their commentary are from the editor. Let me interject a note of thanks to William Wilson, Librarian of the College of Library and Information Services at the University of Maryland, for the formal citations. [Frederick J. Stielow]

1. Readers may also be interested in the firing of Gordon Burke as editor for the American Library Association at this time.

2. *Library Journal* 85 (December 1960):4436-4437.

3. Rice Estes, "Segregated Libraries," *Library Journal* 85 (December 1960):4418-4421.

4. Eric Moon, ed., *Book Selection and Censorship in the Sixties* (New York: R. R. Bowker, 1969); Eric Moon and Karl Nyren, eds., *Library Issues: The Sixties* (New York: R. R. Bowker, 1970).

5. Eric Moon, "Editorial," *Library Journal* 88 (July 1963): 2644-2647.

6. Dr. Bundy's recollections of this occasion vary somewhat. She does remember such epithets as "dirty yellow journalist" being directed at Moon, but the assault was more of someone throwing a foreign object and hitting her. In a note of some historical irony, it was this incident that first prompted her to become involved in the Civil Rights movement.

PART VIII

GENERAL ARTICLES AND A REVIEW SAMPLER

Introduction

This final Part, which departs from the chronological order used in preceding sections, is something of a rag bag. I had wanted to include more here, if only to demonstrate that I did write on occasion about something other than library-related matters. My editor did not consider this an important objective, so the editorial knife was applied.

"The Province Nobody Knows" is the only product herein of my brief stay in Newfoundland as its director of libraries. It is a fairly true and perhaps mildly amusing account of my departure from the West End of London and arrival on the bleak and rocky shores of that North Atlantic island. This was the first of a series of articles I wrote during this period for an interesting magazine called *The Atlantic Advocate*. The other pieces were all products of research in the fascinating historical collections of the Gosling Memorial Library in St. John's.

The next item ("Blimey, a Limey . . . ") is an oddity I wrote for a small newsletter that the library department of a major New York publisher sent out to libraries in the sixties. I don't remember with any certainty how it came about, but it is possible that my friend Richard Brown, who later became *LJ*'s advertising manager, asked me to write it. I have included it for light relief.

The rest of Part VIII consists of book reviews, of which I have written hundreds. None of the many I wrote for *LJ* are included. Those that are represented here are arranged by source.

The two pieces from *Books and Bookmen,* on Steinbeck and Henry Miller, are not reviews so much as cover stories about authors whose latest works were about to be published. I got started with *B & B* because my friend Bill Smith, my co-hell raiser in the AAL, had become its editor. One day, the person assigned to do the cover story on Steinbeck had fallen ill. Knowing that I had done my Library Association thesis on Steinbeck, Bill called one afternoon and said: "I need x-thousand words on Steinbeck by tomorrow morning. Can you do it?" Well . . . as Jack Benny used to say.

I began as a reviewer for *Saturday Review* after meeting Norman Cousins at a publishing party (they occurred several times a week in those days). Somehow we got to talking about the forthcoming volume of Miller/Durrell correspondence. When Cousins found that I had read just about everything by both authors and also knew Larry Powell and the English bookseller Alan Thomas, who had preserved most of the letters, he asked if I would be interested in reviewing the volume. He explained, carefully—and as *LJ* editor I well understood—that he first had to check out the possibility with his Book Review Editor. Editors-in-chief do not mess with their Book Review Editors!

I don't know how I got started with *Book Week*, which was published as a supplement to the Sunday editions of *The Washington Post* and *The New York Herald Tribune*, but the Simenon review included here has a special place in my memory. When my son Alan was in school in New Jersey his English teacher asked each student what his father did (an apparent sexist, he asked not about mothers). Alan replied, shading things a bit, "My dad's a writer." He was sent home by the gung-ho teacher with a request that I come and speak to the class. I declined. Next week came a request that Alan take in something I had written, so I gave him the Simenon review, which had just been published. The teacher read it, then said to the class, "When I ask you for a book report, *this* is what I want." My son was sent to whatever the New Jersey equivalent of Coventry is, and with all the unreason of youth blamed me for the whole thing!

The final two items were reviews Judy Krug asked me to write for the *Newsletter on Intellectual Freedom* during the time when I was chair of the Intellectual Freedom Committee of ALA. Since she did not ask me again, I can only assume that she believed my ability and credibility as a reviewer on intellectual freedom topics were not likely to survive my departure from the IFC chair.

The Province Nobody Knows

A few months ago I said my goodbyes to London's West End. Today I live and work a few yards off Water Street, St. John's. This main street of Newfoundland's capital city is the oldest street in the Western Hemisphere, a thriving center of commerce when New York's Broadway was no more than a swamp.

Four hundred and fifty-one years ago John Cabot landed at Cape Bonavista and set up the flag of England on the New Founde Isle. In 1583 Sir Humphrey Gilbert took possession of the Island in the name of Queen Elizabeth and the cornerstone of the British Empire was laid. When I sailed in 1958 I felt every bit as much a pioneer as Cabot or Gilbert. A lot more than two thousand miles of water lies between London's Whitehall and Water Street, St. John's. Britain has still not discovered Newfoundland, and my journey was virtually a voyage into the unknown.

Is this an extravagant fancy? One of the first pamphlets I read after landing began: "It is true, unfortunately, that Newfoundland is indeed 'The Province Nobody Knows.' There is probably no other part of North America about which so little is known and concerning which so many misleading fallacies exist." My story is a confirmation of this sad comment, a way perhaps of committing some of the fallacies to the flames.

Having fought through the awkward preliminaries of getting a job by airmail, one fine spring day in London I announced my intended departure. There followed the plunge into the complicated rigmarole of resignations from accumulated commitments, of emigration formalities, of passports and vaccinations and the endless nightmare of form-filling. These weeks of frenzied scurrying around surprised and temporarily silenced my friends, and it was some time before a few of them reached the point of polite enquiry.

Reprinted by permission from *The Atlantic Advocate* 49, No. 8: 29-31, April 1959.

"*Where* did you say you were going?" they said, obeying the English convention of inflecting into a question the implication that you have already answered it. I had not said, but they knew the advertisement columns as well as I did and they hazarded a few guesses. "Manchester?" they asked, "Eastbourne? Hendon?" With the smug superiority of the prospective adventurer and traveler, I nursed a mild contempt for the unimaginative insularity of my friends.

"I'm going to . . ." Was it *Newf*'ndland or New*foundl*and? Or even Newf'nd*land*? Most British people put the accent on "found," favoring the rich, round, sandwiched vowel sound, but echoes of distant geography masters came down to me through the corridors of memory and I was inclined to settle for the first, though without assurance. "St. John's," I said, by way of clarification—and escape.

Some were kind: "charitable" might be a more accurate word. They murmured unconvincing congratulations, but at least managed to project the note of sheer incredulity somewhere into the background. Others were blunt and honest in the northern British manner. "What in hell would anyone go there for?" An old friend, himself an *emigré* to New York a few years previously, wrote offering numerous alternatives to what he called this Devil's Island prospect. "You will surely die there," he said. I replied, philosophically at that early stage, that I would surely die somewhere, and why not Newfoundland? But that was before the composite picture which follows had been drawn for me in analytical and terrible detail by friends, relatives, neighbors and professional colleagues. In case you should assume that in England I consorted only with morons, may I say on their behalf that my friends and others were averagely intelligent, middle-class, educated and normal people.

My wife and I, in common with the newspaper readers of the world, had spent a large part of the previous twelve months admiring the exploits of Fuchs and Hillary in Antarctica. Within a few weeks we were to become convinced that, by comparison with what we should shortly be facing, these two tough explorers had been leading a cushioned-parlor existence. "You are going," said my father-in-law, who as an ex-seaman spoke allegedly from experience,"to the land where they have nine months' winter and three months' cold weather."

Weather is a subject dear to English conversationalists of all classes, and there was a neat contrast between the universal knowledge of the notoriety of Newfoundland's weather and the over-all vagueness about its geography.

It emerged that this island is elastic in size and somewhat indeterminate in its location. It is roughly in the vicinity of Greenland, or Iceland—oh! on the edge of the Arctic Circle anyway. Wild laughter, as at a Perelman story, greeted my first few half-hearted attempts to point out that St. John's was actually south of London. Nothing could be said about its being on the same latitude as Paris: the mention of Paris at such moments might have led to hysterics. No reference, of course, was ever made to a map. They knew. They had heard.

My initial inquiries at the offices of a large shipping company in London produced equally unfortunate results. The understanding man behind the counter with infinite tact gave me everything he could find about Saint John, New Brunswick. I produced documentary evidence to prove that my future employers were waiting for me at a place called St. John's, Newfoundland. The patient tone in which I was told that "none of our ships has ever called there, sir" made me feel like the small boy who persisted in asking: "Daddy, how far is up?" Chance acquaintances who had heard of this wild escapade at second hand found another location and asked me a dozen times if I was going to like it in Nova Scotia. And Heinz, I thought, produces only 57 varieties.

Weather, too, was what the B.B.C. meteorological experts call rather variable. On this topic my London friends had a head start on anyone else. In England, the word London immediately conjures up visions in the mind of the determined weather-humorist. As surely as Manchester is a cue for any old music-hall joke about rain, London means smog—its own unique version of fog, black and dirty as midnight. "Fog!" they said, right on cue, "if you think we have fog . . ." One confirmed optimist found a note of consolation in this. "At least," he said, "if the place looks terrible you don't have to worry. Most of the time you won't see a thing."

My face and hopes darkened with the weather forecasts but the conversation became tenaciously lighter and unbearably brighter. Fog gave way to snow. Foolishly I had dropped a word somewhere about the possibility of my buying a car soon after I landed. Fuchs's sno-cats were thrust upon me as a more practical form of transport, and I was pictured as a latter-day Jack London character, spike-booted behind my team of savage huskies, forcing an occasional "Mush! Mush!" from my frozen larynx as I traveled the wild road to work.

Ice was the natural sequel to snow, and *the* most overworked line was the one about living in igloos. Of no avail was my acid defense that centrally-heated igloos were to be preferred to coal-fired, externally water-piped British houses with their guarantees of bursts each January or February. An alternative to the igloo, offered by some kindlier souls concerned for our future welfare, was the log cabin deep in the forest, with bears for boon companions. Only my eldest son found consolation in this prospect.

Fog apart, Newfoundland's best-known commodity, if one may judge by my English friends—and they were more accurate in this than some other fancies—is COD. Even as one who likes cod as well as the next man I began to regard it as a horror dreamed up by Charles Addams as the few variations which may be played on a cod joke were repeated more often than a pop tune on radio. Most popular was the theme of catching our breakfast in the back garden—through a hole in the ice. No fishermen, our friends, but they had seen and remembered their *Nanook of the North*.

The menus were varied from time to time and on occasion we were offered the possibility of whale meat or seal, or perhaps, returning to land food, a tasty slice of caribou or moose. Milk and eggs, butter, fresh fruit and vegetables as we knew them would never again form part of our diet, unless we could afford holidays abroad.

But of course this was the remotest of possibilities. No stone so gloomy could be left unturned, and these exponents of Commonwealth affairs passed to a brief *résumé* of the economic position. Not that any word of the McNair Royal Commission had reached their ears. A quarter of a century before, news had seeped through that Newfoundland was in dire economic straits: this information had taken root and for these observers time had since stood still. The place was dead broke, I was told, "always had been." Hand in hand with this went the slightly paradoxical conclusion that the cost of living was fantastic, and that my salary would be worth less than nothing. I should in fact be lucky to get *any* salary after the first month or two. Canada (there were a few up-to-date enough to realize that Newfoundland was a province of Canada) was, in any case, in the grip of a terrible recession. *Everybody* was unemployed. I might not even get relief.

There is not too much journalistic license in this account. All these things were said, some of them admittedly with a smile, but they *were* said. I met Newfoundlanders in London who were hardly more encouraging. Perhaps they were spoiled by London, their vision distorted by the neon splendors and atrocities of Piccadilly Circus, but they dwelt lovingly upon the worst aspects of life in Newfoundland. There are no roads, they told me (with what bitter truth I now know), schools are terribly overcrowded, there are no theatres, none of the facilities of city life. And the constant refrain: "You'll find it cold in St. John's." But never a mention that income-tax is a third what it is in England.

British mulishness saw me through and against all the odds I came. After six days of rock and roll, the North Atlantic's perpetual rhythm, came a moment, hardly morning, when my boys were roaring round the ship announcing land ahead to sleepy travelers who didn't yet want to know. Before us were what might have been the white cliffs of Dover, aged by a fiercer sea, browned, and greying at the temples. Then through the historic Narrows a shutter-eye view of a wooden town, strangely toylike to red brick-accustomed English eyes, like a shanty town sleeping in the sun. Untidy and unkempt it looked, certainly, with the houses facing every and which way, but there was a happy absence of the town planner's iron glove, an assertive freedom about it all. Authority seemed to be vested in the twin spires of the Basilica standing ramrod straight, high on the hill like a pair of sergeant-majors on the parade ground, and beyond, the houses stretched on up the slopes as though reaching for the skies and the promise above of better things than were to be found on the typical Skid Row of the waterfront.

A few weeks here taught me that in most things my friends back home were no more accurate than my youngest son, who before we left, lived through the golden glory of two months' unshakable conviction that Newfoundland was inhabited only by Red Indians and the legendary scarlet-coated Mounties. For a while he was the most disappointed member of my family. For Indians the best I could do for him was to show him the skeleton of a Beothuk Indian in the local museum, and he cannot yet regain faith in a country unromantic enough to place a Mountie behind the wheel of a modern car, with never a red coat nor a horse in sight.

Blimey, a Limey! or, Let's Not Be Beastly to the British

I got a letter a few weeks ago. The letterhead was impressive. The Edward L. Bernays Foundation Award, Cambridge, Massachusetts, Zip code, U.S.A., it said. Zeros spattered the first couple of paragraphs below like holes in the fabric of civilization. A lot of them appeared in a declaration about "the present communications gap between 200,000,000 Americans and 53,000,000 Britons." There were more zeros yet: $5000 was offered to anyone who could come up with some "practical" idea(s) "to further mutual understanding."

I put it down to the fact that those Bernays people are up near Boston somewhere. Isn't that where the *other* Cambridge is? That old tea-party brawl is probably floating still near the surface of their consciousness. Let's admit that things were a bit rough for a while after that fracas. That isolationism became an American way of life. That the British relegated the ex-colonials to that "foreigner" classification that merits no more recognition than the supercilious curve of an eyebrow beneath the bowler. But all that was a hell of a time ago. Where have those Bernays people been? *Communications* gap? Today?

Just ask yourself—who are the biggest box-office stars out there in Reagan-land? Two ample jugs of British Burton and that English sound of music, Julie *from* London—that's who. And the kings of the overpopulated spy ring? No other than a Scot bottled in Bond and an able cockney named Caine. What import outsells the Volkswagen?—those long-haired pop-tops, the Beatles. Now conquering the communication networks and shooting the American flyboys of "Twelve O'Clock High" off the idiot box screen are black-leathered Emma Peel and her bowlered Steed. And

---

Reprinted from *Owl Among the Colophons* 3, No. 2: 1-2, May 1967. This newsletter was published by Corporate Library Services, Holt, Rinehart and Winston, Inc. Copyright © 1967.

what does it take to rattle the Neilsen ratings of such Biblical Sunday-night fare as Ed Sullivan or the bachelors of the Ponderosa? Why, a British flick (admittedly from a French novel—credit where it's due!) featuring a stiff-upper-lipped British colonel named Guinness (funny how those booze references keep creeping in). Who fills the lecture halls and the test-tubes in the labs these days? Cut-price boffins from England—the brain drain, you know. And while they are still baring their topless wonders out on the Coast, here in the East Twiggy has arrived and the Carnaby Street tailors' knives and the miniskirt are taking us closer to the bottom of the matter.

Now, with all this evidence that American isolationism is dead, that a British cultural (?) invasion is already a fait accompli, I ask again: where do those Bernays people get off with their communications gap?

After intensive concentration, which a problem of this magnitude requires, I finally came up with a theory. The Bernays group has probably been looking at the book world—which allegedly has something to do with communications—and perhaps particularly at that battlefield of creative writing known as "the novel." There are ugly rumors emanating from this scene—which may just have reached Cambridge—that some publishers' salesmen and representatives still scream like dervishes when an editor brandishes a British book for the Spring list. The walls of sales meeting rooms are said to reverberate to the incantation: "Won't sell, Won't sell."

And the refrain, relentless rumor also has it, is taken up out there further in culture and communication land. Booksellers insist, "Nobody buys British novels." Librarians check the reviews in *Library Journal* or other Biblical (sorry, bibliographical) sources, watching always for that touch of international leprosy. "Our patrons," they patronize, "don't like British novels. Waste of money to buy them."

It's silly to even entertain the thought, but what if all this is not rumor? What if it's true? Could it be that Tolkien really isn't a legend in his own time? That *Lord of the Flies* isn't a rival to *Catcher in the Rye* as an American campus classic? Perhaps it is just that there is no quality left in the British novel; that writers like Doris Lessing, Graham Greene, Angus Wilson, Iris Murdoch, Muriel Spark, C. P. Snow, Kingsley Amis, Keith Waterhouse, David Storey don't really compare with any first half-dozen American novelists you like to pull out of the hat.

Or perhaps we're not talking about quality but in commercial terms. It's probably true that you can find, any day of the week, a number of American first novels that sell better than *The Collector, Room at the Top,* or *The Spy Who Came in from the Cold.* And I'm just gullible enough to believe it when one of these commercial wizards tells me that *no* British novelist really sells well here—not Ian Fleming, Mary Renault, Len Deighton, Rebecca West, Helen McInnes.

Back to that Bernays letter. It says: "Even history textbooks, used in schools of both countries (England and America) are biased and indoctrinate millions of people with national prejudices and false notions." Together with my own cogitating about the false notions either I or the said publishers' reps, booksellers and librarians entertain about the British novel's potential in the U.S., that sentence gave me an idea.

Clearly, somebody has been lying to one of us. Perhaps the reviewers? Or maybe the best-seller list? Anyway, I'm going for that Bernays Foundation Award and will search for truth and understanding in the book world. Questionnaires are in the mail. Publishers' reps, booksellers, librarians—be warned. I'm going to find out what you've been reading lately. A British novel, maybe?

Writer of the People

Not long ago the film world's current "gimmick" was the omnibus of short stories introduced and linked with commentaries by the author. The British film studios gambled, successfully, with the craggy countenance and readability of Somerset Maugham, the Americans countered with O. Henry. O. Henry, being dead, presented a problem. Looking for a writer who had the same immense appeal, the same contact with the American everyman, Hollywood chose John Steinbeck to fill in.

Looking every inch the tough itinerant farm laborer he so often writes about, Steinbeck came on to the screen, and announced solemnly to his plush-seated audience in the best American deadpan manner: "My name's John Steinbeck. I'm a writer." Mickey Spillane once made the same claim from the silver screen, but while it is legitimate to doubt Mr. Spillane's statement, few people would claim that John Steinbeck overstated his case.

This 55-year-old Californian was one of the big names of the thirties, one of that fabulous collection of novelists in America—Hemingway, Wolfe, Faulkner, Dos Passos, Sinclair Lewis—who made the English literary scene look like a desert. These writers are all big names still, but what is perhaps significant is that only Hemingway and Steinbeck among them remain truly popular with the reading public of today, on this [the British] side of the Atlantic at least. The cynical Sunday paper reviewer might attribute this to the fact that both write eminently filmable books. A fairer and more likely reason is that both write most of the time in a simple yet vivid prose, both present life in simple terms through the mouths of basically simple characters. Simplicity is a technique which worked for Mark Twain, it worked for Dickens and it may ensure a place in posterity for some of the Steinbeck novels.

The classic education for the American writer, apart from those of the "sensitivity" school, is that he shall throughout his adolescence and young

---

Reprinted by permission from *Books and Bookmen* 2, No. 8: 5, July 1957.

manhood have performed every menial and degrading job in society, from dish-washing to street corner paper-selling, with a period as a hobo "riding the rods" as an optional but desirable extra. Steinbeck ran true to this pattern, only maintaining his individuality by embroidering it with a touch of the exotic. Not every writer has worked in a trout hatchery or in the laboratory at a sugar refinery, nor been a winter watchman in a remote house in the Sierras. And when Steinbeck laid bricks they were for the Madison Square Building—bricks that were going to stay laid. Formal education ended with six rather vague years at Stanford University which left him without a degree but with the firm resolve to be a writer and nothing else.

There were no sensational early best-sellers. Not for Steinbeck the easy road of the postwar sex and violence fraternity of the James Joneses and Norman Mailers. He managed to sustain the role of struggling writer through three financial failures before *Tortilla Flat* took his name into the literary headlines. This book, and one of the earlier trio, *The Pastures of Heaven*, might have led Steinbeck into the deep rut now so comfortably occupied by Erskine Caldwell. His *paisanos* in the town of Monterey in California, loafing around, drinking wine, making love, trying to exist without working, behave in much the same way as Caldwell's poor whites of the South. The difference is that Steinbeck's *paisanos* are more amiable and picturesque, and they are helped along towards acceptance by a pleasant folksy sense of humor, something Steinbeck is rarely credited with possessing.

From this point on Steinbeck seemed to set out to prove that he was capable of as much variety in his books as in his prewriting life. His fourth book, *In Dubious Battle*, though among his best, has never been published in England and is little known over here. It is the story of a strike in the apple orchards of California, of communist organizers moving in on a district where the wage has been cut below a living standard and leading the men in a ruthless fight for higher pay. This gained Steinbeck a somewhat undeserved and unwelcome reputation as a proletarian writer, and his next venture was so different that it looked like an attempt to remove himself from the company of Farrell and other writers of this kind.

The result was a happy one, and *Of Mice and Men* remains one of his two great books. A tragic little story of the friendship between two migratory workers, George and Lennie, who have a secret dream to save up enough money to buy a small farm and live in peaceful and settled independence, this is the universal dream of peace and security told in the tragedy of two of the most lovable characters in fiction. There is no touching on the industrial and social problems here, and the book might have been ruined if there had been. The dramatic tension and the quality of the characterization probably explain why this novel also made such a successful play.

With *The Grapes of Wrath* Steinbeck reached a peak he has never been in sight of since. It won the Pulitzer Prize in 1940 but its publication in the previous year caused something of a furor in the United States. Maxwell Geismar said that the book was burned and banned, smuggled and borrowed, but above all, bought. The story is basically a simple and uncomplicated one of the journey of a family of tenant farmers, the Joads, forced off their land in Oklahoma by the dust storms and the machinations of a bankers' syndicate, to the promised land of California. But it is treated on an epic scale, with the author attempting to show the social forces at play and the slow and steady weaving of new social patterns for a people and a nation. Certainly it gained a great deal in emotional power because the social problems it dealt with were so urgent and so oppressive that they could not be ignored, but if it lasts as a great work of fiction it will be because these social problems are so effectively dramatized in individual characters and situations.

What do you do after you've climbed Everest? This seems to be John Steinbeck's problem since *The Grapes of Wrath*. *The Moon Is Down* was much lauded when it came out as a powerful piece of propaganda on the Quisling theme, but a re-reading fifteen years later shows it to be not much more than an opportunist hack-job. Since then there have been one or two despairing attempts to recapture the flavor of *Tortilla Flat* in books like *Cannery Row* and *Sweet Thursday,* and a couple of attempts at the long short story, *Burning Bright* (with a circus background) and *The Pearl,* an alleged Mexican folk-tale lost under layers of over-conscious symbolism. *The Wayward Bus* is just a wayward book, and a travel book on Russia about completes the post-war output.

There is one exception to this dismal tale. *East of Eden,* though now often regarded only as the vehicle for the much lamented James Dean, was greeted by Mark Shorer in the *New York Times* in these terms: "Through the exercise of a really rather remarkable freedom of his rights as a novelist, Mr. Steinbeck weaves in, and more particularly around, this story of prostitution a fantasia of history and of myth that results in a strange and original work of art."

It is not as successful a novel as *The Grapes of Wrath* because it has an artificiality and pretentiousness the earlier book had not. The clue lies perhaps in the biblical parallel with the story of Cain and Abel.

Steinbeck is at his most effective when he keeps it simple and uncomplicated, and is capable of many an excellent novel in direct terms. If he can throw off the influence of the Irish part of his ancestry, and with it the whimsy, we may look forward to a reincarnation of the Steinbeck of the thirties.

Meanwhile there is reason for trepidation. His new novel to be published in the summer by Heinemann is *The Short Reign of Pippin IV.* It is announced as an extravaganza dealing with the restoration of the monarchy in France in the person of a middle-aged amateur astronomer. It sounds a long way from the Okies and the dust bowl.

Too Hot to Handle

This Miller's tale is a strange one, in some ways a rude one—certainly one that Chaucer might have approved. The tired fictions of the artist living in Parisian bohemian squalor or exiling himself into the wilderness at the height of his fame are so perilously near to the truth in the case of Henry Miller that they cast a shadow of reality.

Who is Henry Miller? This would be an absurd question to put to almost any literate person on the continent of Europe, or even in most parts of the Orient. In Japan he is the third best-selling American novelist, yielding pride of place only to Hemingway and Steinbeck. But no man is a prophet in his own country, least of all Miller. In his homeland, America, and in Britain, the works on which his world-wide reputation has been founded are virtually unknown, and many serious readers have probably not heard of him.

Among those who do know him is Lawrence Durrell, a poet of sensitivity and skill, and the author of the best novel published in this country last year (*Justine*). Writing in *Horizon* in 1949 Durrell said of Miller: "Judged by his best work he is already among the great contemporary writers." There is the other view of Miller, which may be adequately illustrated from comments by a judge of the United States Court of Appeals: "Both books (the *Tropics*) are replete with long passages that are filthy, revolting and tend to excite lustful thoughts and desires," and "If this be important literature, then the dignity of the human person and the stability of the family unit, which are cornerstones of our system of society, are lost to us."

Those are both extreme views, but if you collected together all the people who have views about Miller most of them would be out toward the wings of one or other of those extremes and the center-stage would be pretty empty. Edwin Corle said: "There is no disputing the fact that with

---

Reprinted by permission from *Books and Bookmen* 3, No. 7: 25, April 1958.

James Joyce and D. H. Lawrence off the stage, Henry Miller assumes the mantle of the most controversial writer of our times." This is almost the only non-controversial statement that can be made about him. Miller always inspires either passionate admiration or acute antipathy, and those who take the latter view would probably consider either Joyce or Lawrence pure as driven snow by comparison.

Who then *is* Henry Miller? Of German ancestry—his grandfathers came to America, he says, to escape military service—he was born in New York, raised in Brooklyn. He struck the first blow for the Miller kind of freedom when his father gave him the money to go to Cornell University. He took the money and disappeared with his mistress, a woman old enough to be his mother. In his book, *The Cosmological Eye,* he lists something like fifty jobs he held—from grave-digger to gymnasium instructor. The only thing which can be learned from them is that he never believed in the slogans about the dignity of work. Work, he felt, was degrading and humiliating and killing—all except vocational work, that is.

He quit an important job as employment manager of a public utility corporation in New York City when the itch to write finally caught up with him in the early twenties. From then on, he says, "the real misery began." Articles and stories poured from his pen, but none were ever accepted.

Most of the thirties he spent in Paris, and there it was that his first book was published. *Tropic of Cancer* was an act of desperation. "I had little hope," he says, "when writing it, of ever seeing it published." But William Bradley, an American literary agent to whom he showed the book, knew Jack Kahane, founder of the Obelisk Press, publishers of what some have claimed to be the erotic, if not at times the strictly pornographic, but publishers too of such famous books as Frank Harris's *My Life And Loves,* Cyril Connolly's *Rock Pool,* and Lawrence Durrell's *Black Book.* "This book," said Bradley by way of recommendation, "is dynamite. It goes further than anything I've ever read. It doesn't *verge* on the obscene—it is obscenity incarnate. Dots and dashes won't help here. It's got to be printed as it is or not at all." It *was* printed, and Kahane sent it out to the booksellers with an injunction that "this volume must not be displayed in the window." Despite this he soon had a best-seller. and best-seller it has been ever since. Miller had arrived.

The rest of the thirties he spent writing the kind of books he had no hope of seeing published in America or England. They included *Aller Retour New York, Black Spring* and the other Tropic—*Tropic of Capricorn.* It was 1939 before *The Cosmological Eye* appeared, the first book which any American or English publisher dared handle without asbestos gloves. Miller's books had at last reached the Anglo-Saxon world.

After a tour of America in 1940, the record of which appeared as *The Air-Conditioned Nightmare,* he settled down in California, writing and painting atrocious water-colors, and again living near enough to the bone to have to publish an advertisement appealing for old clothes and water-coloring materials. Then in 1944 came the offer of a cabin in the mountain country of Big Sur, near Carmel, California. There he has been ever since, and out of Big Sur has come the material for Miller's new book, *Big Sur and the Oranges of Heironymus Bosch.*

Big Sur has changed since Miller first went there, and he recalls with obvious nostalgia the good primitive early days when, hitched to a little wooden cart like an old billy-goat, and dressed in nothing but a jock-strap, he would haul the mail and groceries up the hill, a fairly steep climb of about a mile and a half. "Today," says Miller, "Big Sur is no longer an outpost. The number of sightseers and visitors increases yearly. What was inaugurated with virginal modesty threatens to end as a bonanza."

This new book is autobiography in the Miller manner. For that matter, every book he has ever written is autobiography, but this is one of the kind where he uses the proper names and doesn't try to tell a story. It is a rag-bag of a book which doesn't conform to any kind of pattern or form, except perhaps his own. He can finish one chapter with "Signing off now. Time to eat," and start another with "Where was I?" Everything is casual, natural—and alive. People he knows, the books he reads, his water-colors, excursions into philosophy and reminiscence—they are all here. It is bitty, diffuse, infuriating and rewarding. Above all, Miller writes of life, and it's a pretty shapeless affair.

Publication of this new book does not mean that Miller is now a reformed or completely accepted character. He is still the author they love to ban. His only work in progress is *Nexus,* the final volume of a massive trilogy called *The Rosy Crucifixion.* The first two books, *Sexus* and *Plexus,* are of course banned in England and America, and *Sexus* is forbidden to be published in any language—even in France.

Why does he go on writing books like the *Tropics* and *The Rosy Crucifixion?* He claims to be actuated by an inner voice (like Blake?). For example, "And how it would come! I didn't have to think up so much as a comma or a semicolon; it was all given, straight from the celestial recording-room."

"Above all," he says, "I am for imagination, fantasy, for a liberty as yet undreamed of. I want to be read by fewer and fewer people." The censors of many countries—but particularly England and America—are doing their best to grant him this latter request. "As to how and where to get the banned books," Miller says, "the simplest way would be to make a raid on the customs house in any of our ports."

Those who do not want to take this chance, but who would like to read more *about* Miller and his background, cannot do better than read *My Friend, Henry Miller,* by Alfred Perlès (Spearman, 16s.).

From the Twosome, a Quartet

Aside from the sprinkling of exotic, esoteric words, which Lawrence Durrell has never been able to resist, little betrays the common authorship of his earliest and latest works. *Black Book* is rather like a gray carbon copy of *Tropic of Cancer,* more temperate and less powerful than the Henry Miller novel. On the other hand, the Alexandrian novels, with their voluptuous prose and sustained control, are a world apart from the steamroller rhetoric of Miller.

Some of the reasons both for the similarities and the differences between Miller and Durrell are to be seen in this correspondence, which gushes and ebbs and floods again through all the chaotic, destructive years of the past quarter century. Except for a few tedious spells of mutual admiration, it is a fascinating collection, and most of all the letters are interesting for what they tell us of Durrell and his growth as a man and a writer.

Miller remains throughout the supercharged man depicted in his own books and in Alfred Perlès's biography, *My Friend, Henry Miller.* "Action at any cost, that's my motto," he says in one letter. And it's true. He's a veritable factory, bristling with energy and enthusiasm, always in the midst of another 1,000-page opus, churning out essays and magazine articles, reading, painting, writing, corresponding with half the world, negotiating with his peculiar underground network for the publication in yet another language of his work, or Durrell's, or some other friend's, scheming, planning, organizing.

Only slightly less remarkable than his stamina and gusto is his generosity. Money, books, encouragement—all these he sends to Durrell in unrationed quantities. He's a warm man, Miller, a little cockeyed perhaps, but above all, as John Wain noted recently, "an enjoyer."

This review of *Lawrence Durrell and Henry Miller: A Private Correspondence,* edited by George Wickes (Dutton, 1962) appeared in *Saturday Review,* February 23, 1963, pp. 28-29.

Nevertheless, with all this busy involvement, Miller watches the world go by and rarely makes contact. His dreams are more powerful than reality. Buzzing like a bee in his hive, he writes meanwhile to Durrell constantly of plans for pilgrimages to distant places, of retreat from the frantic world he loves hating so much. Tibet is his fondest dream (and what does he think now that this mad world has caught up with that quiet place too? Perhaps a later collection of letters will tell us).

Durrell, actually more the solitary, is much more aware of the world he lives in. Writing and lounging in Corfu, teaching in Greece, mingling in the literary world of London, producing propaganda for the British Information Office in Cairo and Alexandria, editing three newspapers in three languages in Rhodes, working for the British Council in Argentina or the Foreign Office in Yugoslavia—wherever he is, he records and absorbs the people, the landscape, the atmosphere, and the relentless pressure of events on all of them.

While nothing fazes Miller, not even exile, Durrell knows the tug of his own country: "It's lonely being cut off from one's race. So much of England I loved and hated so much. The language clings. I try to wipe it off my tongue, but it clings." And while Miller airily prophesies "a world-wide revolution" and "the greatest change the earth has known," Durrell more accurately reflects the depression of the war years. "The poetry I exude these days is dark gray and streaky, like bad bacon," he says, and later, "I am in charge of a goodish sized office of war propaganda here, trying to usher in the new washboard world which our demented peoples are trying 'to forge in blood and iron.' It's tiring work."

In the postwar years too, Durrell, seeing the suffering of the Slavs, comments: "What a madhouse communism is. And how grateful we are to the USA for taking it seriously. Europe is a sheepfold full of bleating wooly socialists who simply *cannot* see that socialism prepares the ground for these fanatics."

But it is books and writing that are the major obsession of these two men and the major topic of their letters. In the welter of criticism and praise and swapped enthusiasm, one sees Durrell take on stature and confidence, gradually changing from the exuberant young fan of the early letters who apes the master a little, tries to impress, and hides from Miller the fact that he produces "potboilers" under a pseudonym. Within a few years, Durrell can write: "Been reading you again without so much fear of contamination. Growing up, I suppose."

By 1949 he has grown up and shaken off his awe of Miller to the point where he cables: "*Sexus* disgracefully bad. Will completely ruin reputation unless withdrawn revised." Later he has doubts and follows with a placating letter, trying to preserve a friendship he feels he may have endangered.

But it is not necessary; criticism rolls off Miller. He tells Durrell to publish his attack on *Sexus*: "Blast hell out of me."

By the end of the correspondence published here the roles have been reversed. It is Miller who has become the fan, admiring the skill and style of the new, assured Durrell. But he hasn't run out of steam, and closes the collection with the longest letter of all, writing for days and producing certainly the best Miller letter included here.

More readable than most novels, these letters are a sourcebook for our recent times, and some of its literature particularly. They are also the record of a great friendship between two men who rarely met, and immensely valuable as dual self-portraits of two of the great "outsiders" of contemporary writing.

The collection has been made possible by an antiquarian bookseller in England (Alan Thomas) and an American librarian (Lawrence Clark Powell), and has been enhanced by the careful and unobtrusive editing of George Wickes. They, as well as the authors, deserve credit for what, even this early, is surely one of the books of the year.

New Blacks in Notting Hill

How is it possible that Colin MacInnes has escaped the attention of American publishers and the American reading public for so long? While books by Amis, Murdoch, Spark, Sillitoe, and other (fashionable?) British novelists have appeared here with regularity, the fiction of Colin MacInnes has remained virtually unknown on this side of the Atlantic.

The three novels that make up this hefty volume, and which have taken about a decade to cross the big divide, may change all that. Many an American reader, discovering the humanity and vitality of these explorations of the London scene, will regret having had to wait so long for them. But the delay serves one useful purpose: The passage of time emphasizes the unusual quality of these novels. They read with the immediacy of newspaper reportage, yet they clearly have the added dimension of art, for not a word seems to have dated in the slightest over the years since their first appearance. They speak so vividly to today's concerns—concerns that are as real in New York or Chicago as in London—and with so much more balance and understanding than most writers have brought to the kind of territory MacInnes explores that one cannot but marvel that they were all written ten or more years ago.

Each of the novels is set in the rumbling subworld—not really the murky depths of the underworld, nor yet the manufactured veneer of so-called swinging London—and each focuses on the lives of the big city's "outsiders." *City of Spades* is about the blacks, West Indians and Africans, who poured into Brixton and Notting Hill, and entered the conscience and consciousness of England during the Fifties. *Absolute Beginners,* which also touches on England's color problems with, among other things, the best description in fiction of the Notting Hill riots, is primarily concerned with another contemporary malaise: the gulf in understanding and sympathy between the teenagers and those over twenty (yes, MacInnes sets

---

This review of *The London Novels of Colin MacInnes* (Farrar, Straus & Giroux, 1969) appeared in *Saturday Review,* February 8, 1969, p. 25.

the divide there, not at the commonly assigned thirty). And *Mr. Love and Justice,* an allegory about a seaman turned pimp and a cop elevated to plainclothesman (and thus given more opportunity to bend application of the law to his own purposes), seems to anticipate the fears about police behavior that have become the common text of newspaper editorials and commission reports in the 1960s.

What raises these novels far above many of today's excursions on the wild side is that they are not simply elemental explosions of anger or social protest. Not that these qualities are missing in MacInnes; few books contain more devastating condemnations of police practices and attitudes. But the novels also reflect an insistent realization of the joy of life and the process of discovery that is its bloodstream, a trait that surfaces doggedly in MacInnes's characters even when they are struggling down there in the darker depths of adversity. The most surprising elements in stories set in such a milieu are their romanticism, their humor, and their warmth.

These qualities are perhaps most easily seen in *City of Spades,* certainly the best of the three novels. It captures the tempo and the texture not just of the language but of the lives of black men in postwar London. In Johnny Fortune from Lagos, MacInnes has created an unforgettable, indomitable character who breathes the affirmation of life from every pore. "We Africans," he says, "are not a people who deposit our days in a savings bank. . . . Our notion is that the life is given us to be enjoyed." (The American concept of the pursuit of happiness?) Even at the end, returning to Africa after finding that the streets of London are no more paved with gold than those of Lagos, Johnny Fortune is untouched by defeat. "This is my city," he cries, "look at it now; look at it there—it has not killed me! There is my ship that takes me home to Africa; it will not kill me either! No. Nobody in the world will kill me ever until I die."

If in *City of Spades* MacInnes's identification and sympathy with the new blacks and his understanding of them are little short of miraculous, his feat in *Absolute Beginners* of seeing the world as teen-agers do is no less astonishing. Only the totally undiscerning could read these two books without having his comprehension enlarged.

Mr. Love and Justice seems to me the least successful of the three novels. While it plays skillfully with the title themes and their interrelationships, it too often sounds like a textbook for the beginner in the vice world. Frankie Love receives his basic instruction in the art of pimping from his prostitute girl friend, while Edward Justice is taught how the law is bent from the "right" side by a smart-aleck "star sleuth" and a tough, crooked detective sergeant.

What finally gives real depth and dimension to the "outsiders" who people these novels is their other, large hero: The trilogy is essentially a sustained poem to London, "the ugly old indifferent capital" that "encourages the presence of such people" and, "by its very incoherent indifference, enables them to discover one another more freely and happily than elsewhere..."

Nat Hentoff, who provides a perceptive introduction, says: "I have not lived in London, and, for all I know, a diligent London newsman or sociologist could write extensive corrections of *City of Spades* and *Absolute Beginners,* in terms of their accuracy as documentaries." This reviewer has worked or lived in many of the areas of London that these novels describe. No novelist I know, and, for that matter, no newsman or sociologist, more realistically captures the feel, the smell, the essence of that dirty, old, fascinating city and the impact it has on the people who live in it.

One doesn't read many novels these days—at least, not serious ones—that leave one feeling buoyed up with hope, despite all the odds. The last such I read was a little first novel, *Gumbo,* by Mack Thomas, a story of the Depression years in Texas. MacInnes's London is no happier a place than Thomas's Texas, but it has warmth and depth, and somehow you know that its people will fight and survive—and enjoy.

Simenon's Magic

Take a small boy—smaller than most, gentle, delicate, silent, apparently vulnerable in a rough world. Raise him with five brothers and sisters in one unsanitary, all-purpose room where the children sleep on mattresses which "lay side by side on the floor and smelled of mildewed hay." Only a hanging sheet separates the mattresses and the one real bed which at night is occupied by the children's mother and a fairly regular succession of itinerant males. A hole in the hanging sheet allows the children to learn what makes the springs creak, and the eldest son and senior daughter experiment with what they have seen. Our small boy, in turn, observes the lessons at even closer range.

Given this for starters, what a fine sociological fury some of our contemporary American writers might make of it. But Simenon's is a European and perhaps more sophisticated lexicon in which realism does not equate with hysteria, where judgment does not give way to judgments and prescription, where the lines between good and bad, the permissible and the forbidden, are not sharply drawn. His characters are people, not symbols of society's decadence or power. If the opening paragraph of this review suggests squalor, it is only because it does not present the whole picture. Simenon's virtue is that he does. Here, for example, is that apparently ghastly room as the little boy, Louis, sees it:

> Perhaps it was not so much that he refused to learn as that he refused to be taken away from the universe which he considered his own and in which he felt safe. He liked the room that was divided in half by the bedsheet which hung from a rod, he liked the smell of the mattresses lined up side by side, the portrait of his mother in a white veil and of a man with a blond mustache, the patches of wallpaper, particularly the one with the girl on a swing. He liked, above all, the warmth that the stove gave off in

---

Reprinted by permission from *Book Week* (*The Washington Post*) 3, No. 34: 12, May 1, 1966. Copyright © 1966, *The Washington Post*.

waves, in blasts, the way it roared at times, the glowing ashes that suddenly collapsed into the drawer at the bottom.

The atmosphere here is one of warmth. And so it is with the mother and her relationship with her children. She is not dismissed as a slut or a whore. She, too, is warm, working hard for her family but grasping also what she can get from life, caring for her children but without being desperately protective or shrill about it. Growing, the children follow no very predictable paths; some turn out badly, others dully respectable. And little Louis. whose nickname gives the book its title, although he is the "different" one, is shaped just as certainly by this room and his environment as he is by that undefinable spark inside which gives him his difference. He's secure in his home, his bond with his mother is strong and affectionate but never sentimental.

Simenon himself was pleased with this book. He wrote to William Jovanovich, Harcourt's president: "For the French edition, I wrote a short sentence: *Enfins, je l'ai ecrit!* It means that for years I tried, almost at the start of each novel, to attain some serenity, some little light coming from inside of my main character and giving to him a kind of 'aura'." He has done just that.

What is remarkable is that this book is both so like and so different from other Simenon novels. Like its predecessors, it displays the author's instinct for atmosphere, his deep understanding and sympathy for the human condition, a deceptive simplicity in structure and language, and the expected plot tension of the master novelist of detection. But over nearly all the other Simenon novels there hangs the certainty of tragedy. As Nicholas Blake said, "evil hangs over everything, as heavy, as concentrated, as real as a black fog. It is a raw wine, which must burst the old bottles." In *The Little Saint,* it is the serenity—and a touch of romanticism—that is new.

It is anyone's guess how many books, Simenon has produced, but since he began with pulp novels in the Twenties the total is certainly in the hundreds. On this side of the Atlantic, he remains little known and, in some quarters where he is known, considerably undervalued. There may be two reasons for this undeserved lack of reputation. One is the assumption, common in literary circles, that Simenon's kind of massive output is inconsistent with quality. The other is that he has been too often "typed" as just a mystery writer. Only an uncritical reader of even the Maigret novels could reach such an unperceptive evaluation.

The Little Saint, without a trace of a detective, may convince a larger audience that this fertile Frenchman is a novelist of stature, style, and serious purpose. Add to the warmth and subtlety of his characterization, his sense of time and place. Most novelists could not begin to convey all this in anything less than one of those giant family chronicles. Simenon does it in a typically short, spare book which stimulates and exacts response from the imagination. It is the work of an artist—a minor one perhaps, but a true and moving creation.

Interpretations of the First Amendment

This short review of several aspects of the First Amendment is one of those delightful exercises that leave many readers thinking hard and reaching out for answers, and some other readers, surely, agitated if not provoked.

The body of the book consists of three relatively brief chapters: "A Graphic Review of the Free Speech Clause," "The Controverted Uses of the Press Clause," and (delightful title) "Scarcity, Property and Government Policy: The First Amendment as a Mobius Strip." What is unusual is that the limbs attached to this body are at least as interesting, if not more so than the three central chapters.

The Introduction, entitled "Interpreting *This* Constitution" (and the italics are the author's), elicits the following comment in the Preface: "In some respects, it does not fit the balance of the book and many readers may do better to ignore it and to begin at once with chapter 1." (p. ix) Here is one place, certainly, where the author's advice should be ignored. The Introduction, which talks of "a greying of the Constitution" and "an uneasiness respecting the interpretive predilections of our own Supreme Court," is an absorbing review of the "'special' theories of constitutional interpretation [which] have competed for favor within our Supreme Court." (p. 5) Says Van Alstyne: "One's sense of the ill-fated equal rights amendment, for instance, is that it became a casualty to the apprehensions of persons who frankly feared not what it said but how it might be judicially construed." (p. 5)

The other arm attached to the main body of three chapters is a 36-page section of Notes. I have rarely felt compelled to urge readers to pore through hundreds of notes, but these are so lucid and lively, so full of apt

---

This review of *Interpretations of the First Amendment,* by William W. Van Alstyne (Durham, N. C.: Duke University Press, 1984) is reprinted from the *Newsletter on Intellectual Freedom* 34, No. 2: 39-40, March 1985, by permission of the American Library Association.

quotations, as well as providing a solid base for a good bibliography on this topic, that they just should not be overlooked.

Chapter I looks at 200 years of judicial doctrine concerning the free speech clause and sorts it out into what the author calls "the basic rival doctrines." The text is here accompanied, although not illuminated, by eleven graphics (recognized in the chapter title) which attempt to simplify these doctrines—but don't. For the most part rather textbookish and perhaps a bit contrived, the chapter does, however, have a sparkle or two, as in the following comment: "In public places, for instance, many will be offended by the studied vulgarity of crude expressions made in exception to some important policy. Still, neither more moderate nor more intellectual discourse may say the same thing, even half as well, as the bluntness of declaring: FUCK THE DRAFT." (p. 42)

The press clause chapter is considerably more interesting than its predecessor and examines such sensitive questions as the one posed in an opinion by Justice Brennan: "whether the media should enjoy greater access rights than the general public." (p. 56) The author's conclusion to this chapter is typically thought-provoking: "It would be a consummate irony were the press, in seeking new advantages framed in terms of serving 'the public's right to know,' and the press as an agent, surrogate, or fiduciary of the public interest, to embrace a perspective that historically trapped it in a spider web of accountability and regulation." (p. 67)

This sentence is an ideal lead into the third chapter, which essentially compares the First Amendment protection granted the printed press with the regulation of the broadcast press by the Federal Communications Commission. This, in view of the deregulation proposals of Senator Packwood and others, is a very timely topic, and it is good to be reminded of the words of that lion of the First Amendment, Justice William 0. Douglas: " ... the prospect of putting Government in a position of control over publishers is to me an appalling one, even to the extent of the Fairness Doctrine ... It is anathema to the First Amendment to allow Government any role of censorship over newspapers, magazines, books, art, music, TV, radio, or any other aspect of the press." (p. 79)

The author, William Van Alstyne, is William R. and Thomas C. Perkins Professor of Law at Duke University, and has served as a consultant to many U.S. House and Senate committees on constitutional matters involving the First Amendment. His prose lapses now and then into an unholy wedlock of legal obscurity and academese, but is clear for the most part, and occasionally sparkling.

For all who care about the First Amendment, which one assumes to include most librarians, here is a book to be read, pondered and enjoyed.

Emergence of a Free Press

When Leonard Levy's *Legacy of Suppression*, which he called revisionist history, was published in 1960 it evoked a storm of dissent. This history of the First Amendment and what "freedom of the press" meant to the framers of that amendment flatly contradicted liberal assumptions and such champions of them as Zechariah Chafee, Oliver Wendell Holmes, Louis Brandeis, Hugo Black and William O. Douglas. *Legacy of Suppression*, nevertheless, went on to become a classic, widely regarded as a definitive work on the First Amendment.

In this major revision, sixty per cent longer than the original work, it is therefore something of a surprise to find Levy declaring: "I have long had a dissident view of the 1960 book." In a fascinating Preface, he details his relations with Robert M. Hutchins and The Fund for the Republic, which had commissioned him to write a memorandum on the original meaning of the First Amendment. Hutchins and The Fund disapproved of Levy's views on the free speech-free press clause and refused to publish that part of his work. "Thus," says Levy, with disarming candor, "I wrote *Legacy of Suppression* to spite Hutchins and The Fund . . . . The title I chose and the rather strong theme I developed . . . reflected both my shock at discovering the neglected evidence and my indignation at Hutchins and The Fund for attempting to suppress my work. As a result I overdid it."

Does this mean that *Emergence of a Free Press* is a watered-down version of the earlier work? By no means. Levy has recanted on his earlier view that "the American experience with freedom of political expression was as slight as the conceptual and legal understanding was narrow," but he reinforces his original assertions "that the revolutionary government did not seek to wipe out the core idea of seditious libel (that the government may be criminally assaulted by mere words); that the legislatures

---

This review of *Emergence of a Free Press* by Leonard W. Levy (Oxford University Press, 1985) is reprinted from *Newsletter on Intellectual Freedom* 34, No. 4: 108, July 1985, by permission of the American Library Association.

were more suppressive than the courts; that the freedom of expression remained quite narrow until 1798, except for a few aberrant statements; that English libertarian theory was usually in the vanguard of the American; that the Bill of Rights in its immediate history was in large measure a lucky political accident; and that the First Amendment was as much an expression of federalism as of libertarianism."

The real difference in this imposing volume is that Levy has conducted very extensive research on press *practices* in the early American years, whereas in the earlier volume he had been concerned primarily with law and theory. As a result, he says, "I now know that the American experience with a free press was as broad as the theoretical inheritance was narrow."

Levy maintains, however, his myth-shattering views on many of the early proponents of liberty and their limitations when it came to freedom of expression of views they abhorred. His range of fire takes in such "untouchables" as Milton, Franklin and Jefferson. Says Levy: "If the Revolution produced any radical libertarians on the meaning of freedom of speech and press, they were not present at the Constitutional Convention or the First Congress, which drafted the Bill of Rights." But he sees no cause for distress in this exposure of the reality that underlies the mythic gloss of history, and reaches this hopeful conclusion: "We may miss the comforting assurance of having the past's original intentions coincide with present preferences. Yet the case for civil liberties is so powerfully grounded in political philosophy's wisest principles, as well as the wisest policies drawn from experience, that it need not be anchored to the past."

Levy, who won the Pulitzer Prize in history for his 1968 book on the *Origins of the Fifth Amendment,* may well be in line for another Pulitzer for this fine example of detailed, fascinating, muckraking "revisionist history." It is one of those rare volumes that truly deserve that over-applied label, "a basic work." And in today's political climate both his subject and his revelations are of huge importance.

Index

A. L. A. Bulletin [periodical] 126, 357, 360 *see also American Libraries*
Absolute Beginners (Colin MacInnes) 416-418
Access to information 13-15, 48-49, 50, 57-58, 64, 74, 104, 120, 130-131, 143-144, 149, 156, 160, 161, 333, 338-339, 340 *see also* Fees for Service
Access to Information (Library Association Report) 241
"Access to Public Libraries" (Access Study) 17, 85, 91-95, 97, 103, 115, 363
Ackerman, Page 291
ACONDA (ALA Committee on New Directions) 332, 385
Activism in American Librarianship, 1962-73 (Mary Lee Bundy and Fred Stielow) 85, 346
Adler, Mortimer 200, 359
Adult Services Division (ALA) 204, 236
Advancement of Learning (Francis Bacon) 206
Afro-American [newspaper] 261
The Air-Conditioned Nightmare (Henry Miller) 411
Alabama Library Association 114
"The Alchemy of Books" [speech] (L. C. Powell) 299
Alexandria Quartet (Lawrence Durrell) 413
Alexandrian Library 11, 55

Ali, Muhammad 261
Alternative Books in Print 330
"An Alternative Model of a Profession for Librarians" 280
America [journal] 87
American Arts Alliance 49, 50
American Association of School Librarians (ALA) 161
American Book Publishers Council 129
American Booksellers Association 129
American Civil Liberties Union (ACLU) 90, 101, 134
American Documentation [journal] 361
American Federation of State, County and Municipal Employees (AFSCME) 275
American Institute of Architects 229
American Libraries [periodical] 310 *see also A. L. A. Bulletin*
American Library Association [Divisions and Round Tables are entered under their individual names] 29, 32, 34, 35, 36, 37, 40, 53, 58, 64, 70, 71, 77, 79, 80, 81, 84, 88, 89, 90, 91, 95, 96, 99, 100, 101, 102, 103, 107, 108, 110-116, 128-129, 134, 138, 139, 143, 151, 153, 154, 159-163, 232, 235, 298-299, 302, 305-306, 309-319, 321-322, 325-333, 335-342, 347-348, 356, 363-365, 377, 381, 384-386 ALA Policy Manual 156, 160; Black

Caucus 115, 317, 330; Black Task Force on Librarians for Africa 115; Code of Ethics 151; Commission on Freedom and Equality of Access to Information 306, 335-342; Committee on Intellectual Freedom *see* Intellectual Freedom Committee; Committee on Mediation, Arbitration and Inquiry (SCAMI) 315; Committee on Professional Ethics 151, 154; COPES 316; Committee on the Status of Women 330; Coordinating Committee on Freedom and Equality of Access to Information 156; Council 37, 76, 80, 81, 96, 102, 103, 111-115, 129, 152, 154, 159, 313, 316, 317, 318, 332, 337, 339, 381-383; Executive Board 37, 92, 111-113, 115, 316, 317, 322, 330; Federal Legislative Policy 88, 156, 158; Goals for Action 88, 100; Handbook of Organization 329; Intellectual Freedom Committee (IFC) 88, 91, 111, 128, 154, 159, 161, 313, 317, 341, 396; International Relations Committee (IRC) 76, 115; International Relations Office 348; Legislation Committee 3, 37, 313, 335; Nominating Committee 316, 332-333; Office of Intellectual Freedom (OIF) 144; Planning Committee 160; Policy on Governmental Intimidation 158; Special Committee on Civil Liberties 111; Washington Office 3, 72, 74, 104, 312, 313, 339

American Libraries [journal] 310

American Society for Information Science (ASIS) 309

Amis, Kingsley 132, 403, 416

ANACONDA (ALA) 332, 385

Anglo-American Cataloging Rules 38, 334

Another Country (James Baldwin) 145

Apartheid 115

Areopagitica (John Milton) 122

Aristotle 56

Arksey, Laura 291

Arnold, Brian 329

Ash, Lee 382

Asheim, Lester 119, 134, 170, 201, 348

Assistant Librarian [journal] 175, 185, 305, 328, 331-333

Association for Library Collections and Technical Services *see* Library Resources and Technical Services Division

Association for Library Services to Children *see* Children's Services Division

Association of American Publishers 104

Association of Assistant Librarians 169, 185, 305, 308, 324, 325, 326, 329, 330, 331, 395

Association of College and Research Libraries (ALA) 236; College Libraries Section 28

Association of Research Libraries 27, 32, 238, 241, 242, 282

Association of Special Libraries and Information Bureaux (ASLIB) 227

Atlanta University. School of Library and Information Studies 94, 113

Atlantic Advocate [journal] 395

Atlantic Monthly [journal] 355

Auchter, Thomas G. 147

Austen, Jane 195

Bacon, Francis 206

Bagdikian, Benjamin 306, 336-338, 340

Baker, Russell 321-322

Baldwin, James 133-134, 145, 354

Index

Baltimore Reaches Out (Lowell Martin) 205
Baraka, Imamu Amiri (LeRoi Jones) 389
Bay State Librarian [journal] 101, 111, 134, 360, 379-380
Bearman, Toni Carbo 71, 73, 76, 78, 80
Beat writers 21
The Beatles 297, 402
Bellow, Saul 264, 268-269
Bendix, Dorothy 91, 92, 102
Benge, Ronald 296
Berger, Patricia 163
Berman, Sanford 383
Bernays (Edward L.) Foundation 402-404
Berra, Lawrence F. 367
Berry, John N. 1, 2, 14, 22, 72, 79, 80, 101, 152, 159, 163-164, 355, 360, 379-381, 388-389
Berry, Mary Frances 69
Bevan, Aneurin 139, 295
Big Sur and the Oranges of Hieronymus Bosch (Henry Miller) 411
Birch (John) Society 12, 21, 133-134
Birmingham (England) Reference Library 323
Bishop, Sarah G. 76-77
Black, Justice Hugo L. 97, 141, 425
Black Book (Lawrence Durrell) 410, 413
Black Boy (Richard Wright) 145
Black Muslims 21
Black Panthers 326
Black Spring (Henry Miller) 410
Blake, Nicholas 420
Blasingame, Ralph 14-15
Blume, Judy 145
Bodger, Joan 158
Book Manufacturers Institute 129
Book Selection and Censorship: ... California see Fiske Report

Book Selection and Censorship in the Sixties (Eric Moon) 119, 170, 202
Book Week [newspaper supplement] 396
Books and Bookmen [journal] 395
Books in Print 330, 375
Bookseller [journal] 176, 179
Boorstin, Daniel 72
Boston Public Library 16
Bowker, Richard Rogers 377
Bowker (R. R.) Company [publisher] 101, 140, 217, 297, 345, 356, 365, 371, 378-379, 381, 389
Bradley, William 410
Brahm, Walter 16, 28, 39, 242
Brandeis, Justice Louis 425
Brennan, Justice William J., Jr. 142, 423
British Broadcasting Corporation (BBC) 173, 237, 399
British Council 414
British Foreign Office 414
British Information Office 414
British Museum 55, 238
British Museum Catalogue 241
British National Bibliography 191, 241
Broderick, Dorothy 119, 121, 133, 140, 152, 164, 358
Brooklyn Public Library 180-181, 378; Park Slope Branch 47, 60
Brown, James Duff 296
Brown, Karl 382
Brown, Richard 395
Brown vs. the Board of Education 99, 327, 383
Browne Charging System 173
Browning, Robert 62
Bryan, Judge Frederick van Pelt 135
Bryon, J. F. W. 178
Buck, Pearl 132
Bundy, Mary Lee 216, 246-249, 255, 258, 262, 346, 381-382
Burchinal, Lee 67

Burkhardt, Frederick 70
Burning Bright (John Steinbeck) 407
Burns, Richard 364-365
Butler, Pierce 232
Bye, Richard E. 1, 383

Cabot, John 397
Caldwell, Erskine 132, 406
California Librarian [journal] 91, 101, 111, 215, 228, 360, 379
Callender, Thomas 191
Camus, Albert 252
Canadian Library Association 309, 310, 325
Cannery Row (John Steinbeck) 407
Capote, Truman 132, 354
Carlyle, Thomas 35
Carnegie Commission 284
Carroll, Lewis 350
Carter, James 175
Carter, Jimmy (James Earl) 37, 321, 333
Cartter, Alan 57
Cary, Joyce 132, 178
Cashmore, H. M. 331
Castagna, Edwin 10, 19, 25, 110, 363
Castagna, Rachel 110
Cataloging 190, 216, 236, 238-244, 251, 270-271, 348, 367
Catch-22 (Joseph Heller) 143
Catcher in the Rye (J. D. Salinger) 147, 403
Catholic Church 145
Cat's Cradle (Kurt Vonnegut) 143
Censorship 11-12, 21, 97, 103, 115, 119-165, 200-202, 222, 341, 389, 411-412
Censorship of Publications Act (Ireland) 132
Central Michigan University 292
Chafee, Zechariah 425
Chancellor, John 144
The Chapman Report (Irving Wallace) 269

Chaucer, Geoffrey 409
Chaucer House 138, 172, 185, 324
Children's Services Division (ALA) 236-237
Christie, Agatha 329
Churchill, Winston 139
Ciardi, John 11, 12, 199-200
City of Spades (Colin MacInnes) 416-418
City University of New York (CUNY) 292
Civil Rights 380, 385 *see also* Segregation
Civil Rights Act 16, 23, 112
Clark, Justice Tom C. 97
Clay, Cassius *see* Ali
Clearwater, Thomas [pseud.] 185
Cleaver, Eldridge 334
Clinton (LA) Public Library 96
Collective Bargaining and the Academic Librarian (John Weatherford) 292
The Collector (John Fowles) 403
College and Research Libraries [journal] 187, 280-281, 283, 286, 353, 361
Coming of Age in America (Edgar Friedenberg) 161
Committee for Economic Development 24
Conable, Gordon 159
Concord (NC) Public Library 95
Conference Board 45
Congress for Change 319, 326, 385-386
Congressional Quarterly [journal] 6
Connolly, Cyril 410
Constitutional Convention 426
Continuing Library Education Network and Exchange (CLENE) 39
Contracting Out (of library services) 74, 105
Cooke, Alistair 119, 351
Cooke, Eileen 80

Cooley, Margaret 388-389
Cooperation 59, 241, 248, 272, 350
Copyright 341
Corle, Edwin 409
Cornell University 410
Cors, Paul 162
The Cosmological Eye (Henry Miller) 410
Council on Library Resources 134, 249, 356
Cousins, Norman 396
Cozzens, James Gould 132
Crane, Stanley 180
Cuadra, Carlos 77
Curley, Arthur 41
Cutter, Charles Ami 296, 322

Dalhousie University. School of Library and Information Studies 305
d'Amboise, Jacques 98
Dana, John Cotton 235, 296
Dana's Law 358
Danville (VA) Public Library 13, 102, 159
Darling, Persis 249
Darling, Richard 250
Darwin, Charles 199
Davies, G. R. 176, 179
Davis, Angela 318
Davis, Marie 204
Day, Doris 269
Dean, James 407
"The Debugging of Victor Hugo" (Paul Dunkin) 369
A Decade of Censorship in America (L. B. Woods) 144
DeGaulle, Charles 237
Deiches Fund Studies 251, 272
Deighton, Len 404
DeLillo, Don 158
Dentler, Robert A. 4, 5, 6
deVoto, Bernard 132
Dewey, Melvil 222, 296, 322, 323, 377

Dickens, Charles 405
Disraeli, Benjamin 358
Dix, William 332, 385
Documentation 226-227
Domestic Council Committee on the Right to Privacy (Rockefeller Commission) 44, 48
Dos Passos, John 132, 405
Dostoievsky, Feodor 176, 194
Douglas, Justice William O. 141-142, 423, 425
Downs, Robert B. 296
Downs (Robert B.) Award 164
Dryden, John 194
Dudley, Edward 306
Dunkin, Paul 216, 235-237, 239, 345
Dunn, Donald A. 46
Durrell, Lawrence 396, 409, 410, 413-415

Eagle Forum 120
East of Eden (John Steinbeck) 407
Echo House (Baltimore) 249, 257
Economic Opportunity Act 5
Edinburgh University 53
Edwards, Edward 222
Edwards, James B. 147
Elliott, Carl 26
Ellison, Ralph 357
Ellsworth, Ralph 296
Emergence of a Free Press (Leonard W. Levy) 425
"The End of Free Library Service Is at Hand" (Eugene Jackson) 51, 64
Energy Consumer [journal] 147
English Social History (G. M. Trevelyan) 188
Enoch Pratt Free Library 205, 247, 251, 272
Equal Rights Amendment 145, 330
Equal Time Provision (Federal Communications Act) 337-338
Eshelman, William R. 40, 91, 101, 159, 217, 297, 360, 379

Estes, Rice 85, 88, 89, 90, 91, 100, 110, 380-381
Evans, Luther 98, 297, 299
Evergreen (WA) School District 341

Fader, Daniel 204, 252
Fairness Doctrine (Federal Communications Act) 336-338, 423
Falwell, Jerry 144
Farmington Plan 240
Farrell, James T. 132, 406
Faulkner, William 132, 405
Federal Communications Act 336
The Federal Role in Library and Information Services (Marilyn Gell Mason) 105
Fees for service 40, 51-52, 61-68, 77, 78, 79, 106-108, 160-161, 333, 336, 337, 339-340 *see also* Access to information; Nonresident fees)
Fey, Harold 146
Finchley (London, England) Public Library 101, 327
Finnerty, Ed (Vonnegut character) 293-294
First Amendment 140-143, 146-150, 152, 153, 158, 159, 162, 337, 422-424, 425-426
Fiske, Marjorie 137, 134, 164, 222, 363
Fiske Report (1959) 121-122, 127, 153, 164, 363
Fitzgerald, F. Scott 132
Fleishman, Stanley 146
Fleming, Ian 404
Florida Atlantic University 242
Foot, Michael 321
Ford, Gerald R. 36
The Forsyte Saga (John Galsworthy) 192
Fortune and Friendship (L.C. Powell) 217, 297, 300-301
Francis, Sir Frank 238, 297
Franklin, Benjamin 163, 426

"Free Access to Information" (ALA policy) 160
Free Library of Philadelphia 126
Freedom of Information Act 104, 105, 147
Freedom Schools (Mississippi) 12
"The Freedom to Read" (ALA) 109, 128, 140, 153, 158, 165, 314, 327
Freedom to Read Foundation 158, 314, 341
Fremont-Smith, Eliot 204
Freud, Sigmund 199
Friedenberg, Edgar 161
Frost, Robert 33
Fuchs, V. E. 398, 399
Fund for the Republic 425

Gaines, Ervin 161
Gale Research Inc. [publisher] 365
Galsworthy, John 192
Galvin, Thomas J. 340
Gambee, Budd 322, 323
Gandhi, Mohandas K. 282, 295
Gardner, Frank 296, 331
Gaver, Mary 238
Geismar, Maxwell 407
Geller, Evelyn 216
Gemel, I. M. (pseud.) 122
Georgia Library Association 102, 110, 113-116, 384
Gide, André 132
Gilbert, Sir Humphrey 397
Gillett, J. T. 185
Ginsberg, Allen 389
The Globe [newspaper] 323-324
Godfrey, Annie 322
Goldwater, Barry M. 1, 4, 5, 6, 7, 147, 231, 267, 387-388
Gollancz, Victor 173
Gosling Memorial Library (St. Johns, Newfoundland) 395
The Grapes of Wrath (John Steinbeck) 407

Great Society (Johnson administration) 18, 65
Green, Frederick Lawrence 178
Green, Henry 178
Green, Julien 178
Greenaway, Emerson 126, 272
Greene, Graham 178, 403
Grove Press [publisher] 124, 125, 126, 389
Guinness, Sir Alec 403
Gumbo (Mack Thomas) 418

Hall, G. K. [publisher] 243
Hall, R. Geraldine 247-248, 254, 256-258, 262
Ham, F. Gerald 293
Hamill, Pete 47, 52, 60
Hamlet (William Shakespeare) 200
Hard Times (Charles Dickens) 46
Hardy, Thomas 56, 195
Harlan, Justice John Marshall 97
Harlow, Neal 271
Harper's [journal] 355
Harris, Frank 410
Harrison, J. C. 187
Harvard University 57, 58
Hashim, Elinor 71, 73, 74, 75, 76, 78, 79, 80
Havel, Vaclav 164
Hawthorne, Nathaniel 145
Haycraft, Howard 298
Hayes, Robert 299
Heilprin, Laurence 249
Heller, Joseph 143
Helms, Senator Jesse 158
Hemingway, Ernest 132, 145, 405, 409
Henry, O. 405
Hentoff, Nat 418
High John 216, 245-263
Higher Education Act 27, 74, 241, 245, 247
Hillary, Sir Edmund P. 398

"Historic Occasion Fatigue" (Russell Baker) 321
Hodgin, Ellis 364
Holliday, S. C. 169
Holmes, Justice Oliver Wendell 425
Homer 56
Hooked on Books (Daniel Fader) 252
Horizon [journal] 409
Horn, Andrew 299, 300
Horn, Zoia 158
Horrocks, Norman 305, 330
"How Libraries and Schools Can Resist Censorship" (ALA statement) 129
How to Lie with Statistics (Darrell Huff) 93
Howe, Harold, II 23
Hudson, Rock 264, 268-269
Hugo, Victor 30
Hulme, Thomas E. 322
Humphrey, Hubert H. 5, 6, 387-388
Huntley, Chet 237
Huston, Tim 253-254, 261
Hutchins, Robert M. 425
Huxley, Aldous 132

Iacocca, Lee 297
Illinois Library Association 72
In Dubious Battle (John Steinbeck) 406
The Indian Librarian [journal] 356
Information Industry Association 336
"Information Technology: Its Social Potential" (Edwin Parker and Donald Dunn) 46
Information Technology: Some Critical Implications for Policy Makers (Conference Board) 45-46
Integration in Public Library Service in Thirteen Southern States, 1954-1962 93
Intellectual Freedom and the Teenager (ALA preconference) 161

Intellectual Freedom Manual (ALA) 162
Intellectual Freedom Round Table (ALA) 120
Interlibrary loan 161
International Research Associates 92-95
Isacco, Jeanne 338
Islam 163
It Can't Happen Here (Sinclair Lewis) 222

Jackson, Eugene 51, 64
Jefferson, Thomas 140, 145, 426
Jevons, William Stanley 32
Job Corps (Kennedy administration) 16
Johnson, Lyndon 1, 5, 6, 9, 16, 18, 22, 25, 63, 65, 112, 327, 354, 387-388
Johnson, Sonya 145
Jones, Clara 42, 71, 322, 332
Jones, James 132, 406
Jones, LeRoi *see* Baraka
Jones, Sarah 114
Jones, Virginia Lacy 102, 113
Jones, Wyman 360-361
Jordan, Peter 328
Josey, E. J. 2, 28, 79, 85, 86, 98, 102-103, 107-109, 110-116, 119, 159, 217, 286, 339, 381, 384
Journal of Academic Librarianship 57
Journal of Library History 322
Joyce, James 410
Junior Libraries [journal] 87
Junior Members Round Table (ALA) 301, 305, 307-308, 319, 325-326
Justine (Lawrence Durrell) 409

Kahane, Jack 410
Kee, Janice 19
Kennedy, John F. 16, 22, 136, 277
Kent State University 326

Khomeini, Ayatollah Ruhollah 163
Kilpatrick, James Jackson 13, 147
King, Martin Luther 69, 99, 326
Kister, Kenneth ix
Kluger, Richard 293
Koch, Edward 22
Koestler, Arthur 178
Krug, Judith 396
Küng, Hans 145
Kunitz, Stanley 99, 327, 380

"Labeling Library Materials" (ALA Policy) 129
Lacy, Dan 71, 164, 209, 306, 335-336, 338, 341
"The Lacy Commission Report" 306, 335-342
Ladd, Dwight 283
Lady Chatterley's Lover (D. H. Lawrence) 123, 128, 135
Lagerkvist, Pär 132
Laird, David 301
Lambeth (London, England) Public Library 169
"Large Scale Data Banks: Will People Be Treated as Machines?" (M. E. Maron) 267
Law Notes Library (England) 193
Lawrence, D. H. 410
Lawrence, William 249
Layton, Jeanne 158
Lear, Edward 350
Leeds [Public Library] *Book Guide* 183
Legacy of Suppression (Leonard W. Levy) 425
Leonard, John 55
Lerner, Max 130
Leroy Merritt Fund 314
"Less Access to Less Information By and About the U. S. Government" (ALA) 104, 339
Lessing, Doris 403

"Letter from America" (Alistair Cooke) 351
Levy, Leonard W. 425-426
Lewis, Sinclair 132, 222, 405
Lewis's Medical Library (London, England) 193
Leyh, George 187
Liaison [journal] 298, 331
"Librarians as Literature Experts" (Dorothy Broderick) 121
"Libraries and Information Skills in Elementary and Secondary Education" (NCLIS statement) 76
Library Association (UK) 129, 138, 169, 172, 184, 185, 238, 241, 298, 305-306, 308, 322, 329-331, 347-348, 395
The Library Association Record [journal] 171, 185, 238, 298, 306, 347
Library Awareness Program *see* U. S. Federal Bureau of Investigation
Library Bill of Rights 14, 21, 88, 111, 120, 122, 129, 155-157, 160-165, 206, 277; "Free Access to Libraries for Minors (interpretation) 143-144, 161
Library Education 35, 175-178, 183, 185-187, 222-223, 228-229, 232, 234, 239, 245-263, 295, 299, 3118, 349-350; Continuing Education 39, 183-184
Library Journal [journal] ix, x, 1, 2, 3, 9, 70, 72, 76-77, 84, 91, 98, 99, 100-101, 110, 111, 113-115, 119, 128, 139, 150, 152, 266, 298-299, 305, 322, 323, 325, 347-348, 353, 355, 357-364, 377-382, 384-391, 395-396, 403
Library Literature [index] 87
Library of Congress *see* U. S. Library of Congress
Library Quarterly [journal] 185, 348, 355

Library Resources and Technical Services [journal] 235, 367-368
Library Review [journal] 185
"Library Service in Mississippi" (Dorothy McAllister) 87
Library Services Act 18, 26, 90, 101, 224, 312
Library Services and Construction Act, 1964 5, 16, 22, 245, 248
Library Trends [journal] 286, 348
Library World [journal] 119, 187, 345, 347
"Libraryland" (*LA Record* column) 306
Life Goes On (L. C. Powell) 217, 297
Lincoln, Abraham 140
Lindbergh, Charles A. 295
Lindsay, John 22
Lippman, Walter 264
Literary Market Place 371
The Little Saint (Georges Simenon) 420-421
Lloyd George, David 295
Lolita (Vladimir Nabokov) 128
London, Jack 399
London Union Catalogue 194
Look Back in Anger (John Osborne) 357
Lord of the Flies (William Golding) 403
Los Angeles Public Library Librarians Guild 275
Louisiana Library Association 112, 114
Lubetsky, Seymour 216, 232, 299
Lyle, Guy 296

McAllister, Dorothy 87, 89
McCardle, Katherine 123
McCarthy, Eugene 387
McCarthy, Joseph 128, 140, 153, 165, 314, 327
McColvin, Kenneth 169

McColvin, Lionel 169, 180, 296
McColvin Report 180
McCoy, Cheryl 85
McGraw-Hill [publisher] 365
MacInnes, Colin 416-418
McInnes, Helen 404
McIntyre, Jennie 249
MacLeish, Archibald 266, 270, 278
McNair Royal Commission 400
McNaughton Plan 251
McNeal, Archie 91, 305, 381
McWilliams, Carey 147
Madden, Henry 215, 228-233
Mailer, Norman 123, 132, 204, 252, 354, 383, 389, 406
Malone, Dumas 33
Manchild in the Promised Land (Claude Brown) 252
Mandela, Nelson 164
"Manner of Speaking" (*Saturday Review* column) 199
Mao Tse-Tung 21
Marlborough (public house, London, England) 138
Maron, M. E. 267
Martin, Lowell 205, 251, 272
[Maryland] Metropolitan Cooperating Libraries project 248
Mason, Ellsworth 289-290
Mason, Marilyn Gell 75, 78, 105, 106
Mathieu, Jane 249, 257
Maugham, W. Somerset 132, 405
Maurois, André 132
Mead, Margaret 132
Medical Library Assistance Act 26
Medical Library Association 310
Melcher, Daniel 98, 207, 298, 378-379, 382, 384
Melvil Dui Chowder and Marching Association 368
Mencken, Henry L. 266, 366
Mercouri, Melina 131
Metropolitan Opera Association 49

Mill, John Stuart 141, 322
Miller, Arthur 209
Miller, Henry 124, 125, 133-134, 395-396, 409-412, 413-415
Miller, William E. (v-pres. candidate, 1964) 5, 6, 388
Milton, John 121-122, 208, 426
Minarcini vs. Strongville City School District 143
Mississippi Library Association 112, 114
Mississippi Summer Project 12
Missouri State Library 158
Mr. Love and Justice (Colin MacInnes) 417
Mitre Corporation 44, 45
Molz, Kathleen 10, 215, 355
Montclair (NJ) Public Library 85
Moon, Alan 396
Moon, Eric 11, 76, 103, 336, 377-390
Moon, Ilse 345
The Moon Is Down (John Steinbeck) 407
Moore, Everett 299, 300
Moral Majority 144-145, 147
Moravia, Alberto 132
Mormon Church 145
Moses, Richard 246-262
Mudge (Isadore Gilbert) Award (ALA) 113
Mumford, Quincy 298
Murdoch, Iris 132, 403, 416
Musil, Robert 183
My Friend Henry Miller (Alfred Perlès) 412, 413
My Life and Loves (Frank Harris) 410
Myra Breckenridge (Gore Vidal) 203

Naipaul, V. S. 49
Nanook of the North [film] 400
Nash, Ogden 183
National Association for the Advancement of Colored People (NAACP) 90, 101

A Nation at Risk (National Commission on Excellence in Education) 76
National Advisory Commission on Libraries 25, 27, 79
National Book League (UK) 185
National Commission on Excellence in Education 76
National Commission on Libraries and Information Science (NCLIS) 2, 36, 37, 38, 40, 44, 57, 70-81, 105, 107, 108, 163, 288; *Community Information and Referral Services* [report] 78; *National Information Policy* [report] 44, 106; *Public Sector/Private Sector Interaction in Providing Information Services* [report] 72, 77, 106, 338; *Report of the Task Force on Library and Information Services to Cultural Minorities* [report] 78-79, 107-108; *Toward a National Program for Library and Information Services: Goals for Action* [report] 71
National Commission on Obscenity and Pornography 37
National Defense Education Act 5, 16
National Education Association (NEA) 129, 283, 315
National information policy 2, 42-52, 67, 72, 333
National Inventory of Library Needs (ALA) 25
National Lending Library for Science and Technology (UK) 227
National Lending Right 75
National Library Week 112
National Science Foundation 44, 67
National Taiwan University 348
Nemeyer, Carol 335
Network [film]
Networks 38, 71
Never on Sunday [film] 130

New Federal City College (DC) 210
New Members Round Table *see* Junior Members Round Table
New Republic [journal] 122
New Statesman [journal] 173
New York (State) 3-R's program 30, 59
New York Daily News [newspaper] 47, 59
New York Herald Tribune [newspaper] 396
"New York Letter" (*Library World* column) 119, 351
New York Library Association 388
New York Library Club 49-50
New York Public Library 22, 58, 274, 382, 388
New York Times [newspaper] 9, 40, 113, 125, 321, 383; Book Review 206
New Yorker [journal] 123, 133
Newfoundland 378, 395, 397-401
Newman, Jerald 3
News of the World [newspaper] 265
Newsletter on Intellectual Freedom (ALA) 88, 125, 396
Nexus (Henry Miller) 411
Nixon, Richard M. 34, 36, 37, 39, 313, 387
"No Segregation Here" 87, 89
Nobel Prize for Literature 132
Nonresident fees 28, 96 *see also* Fees for service
Norris, Hoke 131
North-Western (London, England) Polytechnic School of Librarianship 169
"Not Censorship, But Selection" (Lester Asheim) 119, 170, 201
NPAC program (Library of Congress) 271
Nyquist, Ewald B. 29, 30
Nyren, Karl 377, 381

Obelisk Press [publisher] 410
Oboler, Eli 102
Observer [newspaper] 177
OCLC 288
Of Mice and Men (John Steinbeck) 406
"Off the Record" (J. F. W. Bryon) 178
Olivier, Sir Laurence 264, 268-269
"On the Grindstone" (*LJ* column) 221, 299
O'Neill, Eugene 176
Origins of the Fifth Amendment (Leonard W. Levy) 426
Orwell, George 58, 132, 157

Packwood, Senator Bob 423
Panizzi, Sir Anthony 222, 296
Parent Teacher Association (PTA) 124, 133
Parker, Edwin B. 46
The Pastures of Heaven (John Steinbeck) 406
Pauling, Linus 56
Paylore, Patricia 233
The Pearl (John Steinbeck) 407
Peel, Emma [TV character] 402
Pendleton, Clarence M., Jr. 69
Perez, Leander 12
Perlès, Alfred 412, 413
Peyton Place (Grace Metalious) 203
Phillips, Howard 322
Philolaus 56
Phinazee, Annette 102
Playboy [journal] 123, 239
Player Piano (Kurt Vonnegut) 294
Plexus (Henry Miller) 125, 411
PNLA Quarterly [journal] 291
Podhoretz, Norman 354
Poole, William Frederick 322
Porter, Jimmy [character] 357
Powell, Benjamin 88, 101
Powell, Enoch 328
Powell, Fay 301

Powell, Lawrence Clark 99, 108-109, 111, 215, 217, 228-229, 231, 295-302, 396, 415
Presidential Commission on Obscenity and Pornography 313
President's Committee on Libraries (Johnson administration) 25
Priestley, J. B. 180
Prince George's (MD) County Memorial Library 247, 251, 259; Sojourner Truth Room 260
Privacy Act of 1974 48, 104
Providence (RI) Public Library 126
Public Law 480 program 240
Public Library Association (ALA) 79
Public Library Inquiry 92
Public Sector/Private Sector Task Force Report (NCLIS) 338
Publishers' Weekly [journal] 87
Pulitzer Prize 407, 426
Punch [journal] 123
Putnam, Carleton 133
Putnam, Herbert 296

Quisling, Vidkun 407

Race and Reason (Carleton Putnam) 133
Racine, Jean 194
Racism 145, 312, 328-329, 416
Random House [publisher] 285
The Reader and the Bookish Manner (S. C. Holliday) 169
Readers' Digest [journal] 147
Ready, Will 296
Reagan, Ronald 70, 76, 78, 153
Recruitment 35, 274, 291, 328
Reference Services Division (ALA) 236-237
Regents of the State University of New York 56, 57, 98
Register of Prohibited Publications (Ireland) 132
Reining, Henry, Jr. 24

Remarque, Erich Maria 132
Rembar, Charles 149
Renault, Mary 404
Resources and Technical Services Division (ALA) 216, 235-238, 244
Rilke, Rainer Maria 194
Roberts, Don 205
Rockefeller, Nelson 44
Rockefeller Commission *see* Domestic Council Committee on the Right to Privacy
Rockefeller Foundation 348
Rock Pool (Cyril Connolly) 410
The Rolling Stones 297
Rom, Patricia 158
Room at the Top (John Braine) 403
Roosevelt, Eleanor 12
Roosevelt, Franklin Delano 12
Rosenberg, Betty 299, 300
Ross, Harold 354
Rosten, Leo 17, 136, 199, 218-219, 221-222
The Rosy Crucifixtion (Henry Miller) 411
Rushdie, Salman 163
Russell, Bertrand 56
Rutgers University. School of Communication, Information and Library Studies 237, 345, 369

Sagan, Françoise 132
St. John, Francis 378
St. John's University 121
St. Paul (MN) Public Library 203
Salinger, J. D. 132
Sartre, Jean-Paul 132, 252
Satanic Verses (Salman Rushdie) 163
Saturation buying 193-195
Saturday Review [journal] 11, 131, 199, 396
Savage, Ernest 169, 171-172, 296
Savannah (GA) State College Library Award 102
Sayers, Frances Clark 299

Sayers, W. C. Berwick 331
Scarecrow Press [publisher] 86, 217, 237, 292, 296-297, 365, 370-371, 373-376
Schmidt, Richard M., Jr. 104, 105
"School Library Bill of Rights" (ALA) 129
Schuman, Patricia 72, 381
Science [journal] 46
Scientific and Technical Information: Options for National Action (Mitre Corp) 44
Sci-Tech News [journal] 51
Seely, Pauline 237
"Segregated Libraries" (Rice Estes) 91, 110
Segregation 85, 87-90, 91-95, 96-97, 99-103, 111-115, 159, 312, 327-328, 359, 383-384 *see also* Civil rights
Sendak, Maurice 145
Severance, Robert 114
"Sex and Censorship in Literature and the Arts" (*Playboy*) 123
Sexus (Henry Miller) 411, 414, 415
Shaffer, Kenneth 289
Shakespeare, William 194, 209, 269
Shaughnessy, Tom 286
Shaw, George Bernard 54, 55, 68, 194, 209, 216, 235, 278, 281, 366
Shaw, Ralph 95, 152, 223, 237, 296, 297, 299, 358
Sheldon, Brooke 337, 340
Shera, Jesse 226-227, 296, 297
Sherman, Stuart 126-127
Shields, Gerald R. 360, 364
Shoe String Press [publisher] 365
Shorer, Mark 407
Shores, Louis 237
The Short Reign of Pippin IV (John Steinbeck) 408
Shriver, R. Sargent 16
Shubert, Joseph 22, 348

"The Silent Subject" (Eric Moon) 87-90, 100, 110, 380
Sillitoe, Alan 416
Simenon, Georges 396, 419-421
Simple Justice (Richard Kluger) 293
Smith, Representative Howard 6
Smith, Ray 135
Smith, William French 147
Smith, William G. (Bill) 138, 298, 331, 395
Smuts, Jan Christian 295
Snaith, Stanley 350
Snow, C. P. 192, 403
"Social Class, Race Relations and the Public Library" (Peter Jordan) 328
Social Responsibilities Round Table (ALA) 115, 317, 319, 326, 329-330, 364, 384-385; Gay Liberation Task Force 318, 384; Women's Liberation Task Force 318
Society of American Archivists 293
Sojourner Truth Room (Oxon Hill, MD) *see* Prince George's County
Soule, Gardner 259
South Africa 115, 383
South African Libraries [journal] 87
Spark, Muriel 403, 416
The Speaker [film] 328
Special Libraries [journal] 267
Special Libraries Association 113, 227, 309
"The Spectre at Richmond" (Stanley Kunitz) 99, 327, 380
Spillane, Mickey 405
The Spy Who Came in from the Cold (John LeCarré) 403
Stable, Justice Sir Wintringham 131
Stanford University 406
State libraries 16-17, 29
State University of New York, Albany. School of Information Science and Policy 215, 281
Steed, John [TV character] 402

Steinbeck, John 132, 145, 395, 405-408, 409
Stevens, Wallace 206
Stewart, Justice Potter 97
Stielow, Fred 346-391
Stokes, Roy 187, 221-223, 348
Storey, David 403
Stringer, Raymond [pseud.] 122
Strong, Gary 337, 340
Students to Dallas 318
Subject Guide to Books in Print 371
Sullivan, Ed 403
Sweet Thursday (John Steinbeck) 407
Sun newspapers (Baltimore, MD) 260
Swift, Jonathan 182, 269
Sylvestre, Guy 265-266

"The Tabby Cat and the Elephant" (Paul Dunkin) 369
Tales of Melvil's Mouser (Paul Dunkin) 345, 369
Tallman, Johanna 296
Tauer, Carol 72
Tauro, Judge Joseph 143
Taylor, General Maxwell 8
Terkel, Studs 149
Thomas, Alan 396, 415
Thomas, Dylan 183
Thomas, Mack 418
Thompson, Donald 148
Thurber, James 350, 354
Time [journal] 355
The Times (London) [newspaper] 323, 348
Times Literary Supplement 173, 243
Tolkien, J. R. R. 403
Tortilla Flat (John Steinbeck) 406
Trevelyan, George Macaulay 188
Trollope, Anthony 329
Tropic of Cancer (Henry Miller) 124, 125, 126, 127, 128, 132, 137, 409-411, 413

Tropic of Capricorn (Henry Miller) 125, 409-411
Tucker, Harold 137
Twain, Mark 405
Twiggy 403

UNESCO 76; Public Library Manifesto 40, 51, 64, 221, 334
Unions 103, 104, 115, 275-276, 283-284, 292, 315, 316, 385
United Federation of Teachers 315
United Nations 12, 133-134, 155, 328
U. S. Bill of Rights 140, 141, 143, 156-157, 426 *see also* First Amendment
U. S. Central Intelligence Agency (CIA) 326
U. S. Commission on Civil Rights 69, 70
U. S. Congress 104, 141-142, 312, 313, 423, 426
U. S. Constitution 143, 156-157, 330, 422
U. S. Dept. of Commerce 73
U. S. Dept. of Energy Library 105
U. S. Dept. of Housing and Urban Development 105
U. S. Dept. of Justice 44, 69, 125
U. S. Dept. of State 77
U. S. Federal Bureau of Investigation (FBI) 158-159, 326
U. S. Federal Communications Commission (FCC) 44, 423
U. S. Government 104, 146
United States Information Agency (USIA) 11, 15, 231, 341
U. S. Internal Revenue Service (IRS) 314
U. S. Library of Congress 11, 33, 58, 266, 271, 318; Jefferson Building 33
U. S. National Committee for the UNESCO General Information Program 76

U. S. National Security Agency (NSA) 341
U. S. Occupational Safety and Health Administration (OSHA) 147
U. S. Office of Economic Opportunity 245, 247, 249
U. S. Office of Education 17, 28, 71, 247
U. S. Office of Management and Budget (OMB) 73, 74, 105, 106
U. S. Post Office 125
U. S. Supreme Court 85, 96, 99, 141-143, 148-149, 327, 329, 359, 422
Universal Declaration of Human Rights (United Nations) 155
University of Alabama 119
University of California, Berkeley. Institute of Library Research 40, 267
University of California, Los Angeles. Graduate School of Library and Information Science 215, 228, 232, 234, 296; Library 291, 299
University of Chicago. Graduate Library School 348
University of Kentucky. College of Library and Information Science 345
University of Maryland. College of Library and Information Services 216, 245-249, 252, 255-259, 262
University of Pittsburgh. Conference on the On-Line Revolution in Libraries 67
University of Texas 240-241
University of the Philippines 348
Updike, John 203, 354
Urban Libraries Council 282
Urquhart, Donald 227
Usherwood, Robert 328, 329

Valley of the Dolls (Jacqueline Suzanne) 203
Van Alstyne, William W. 422-423
Vann, Sarah 237
Variety [newspaper] 332

Vertical Integration 13, 159
Vick, Nancy 140
Vietnam War 1, 8-9, 103, 115, 267, 318, 326-327, 383, 385
"A View From the Front" (Eric Moon) 208
Virginia Librarian [journal] 364
Vonnegut, Jr., Kurt 143, 293
Vosper, Robert 26, 29

Wain, John 413
Wakeman, John 89, 101, 139, 159, 181, 312, 327, 378-379, 383
Wallace, George C. 290, 328
Wallace, Irving 264, 268-269
Walling, Ruth 113
War on Poverty (Johnson administration) 16, 327
Warren, Robert Penn 132
Washington Post [newspaper] 97, 261, 396
Washington Redskins 261
Wasserman, Paul 216, 246-247, 249, 255, 258-259, 262
Watergate (Nixon administration) 63, 281
Waterhouse, Keith 403
The Wayward Bus (John Steinbeck) 407
Weatherford, John 292
Webster's Third New International Dictionary 229-230, 232
Wedgeworth, Robert 80, 322, 335, 340
Weekly Record 375
Wells, H. G. 55
West, Rebecca 404
Westchester (NY) Library Association 4, 119
Westchester Statement *see* "The Freedom to Read"
Wheeler, Joseph 296

White House Conference on Libraries (1979) 42, 75, 77, 78, 79, 106, 107
White House Conference on Library and Information Services (1991) 2
Whitman, Walt 176
Why Are We in Vietnam? (Norman Mailer) 204, 252
Wicker, Tom 165
Wickes, George 415
Wilde, Oscar 235
Williams, Tennessee 132
Wilson, Angus 132, 403
Wilson, Edmund 132
Wilson (H. W.) Company [publisher] 101, 298, 365, 379
Wilson Library Bulletin [journal] 10, 88, 99, 101, 139, 159, 327, 328, 355, 378-380
Winchell, Walter 178, 264, 268
Winsor, Justin 296, 322
Wodehouse, P. G. 183
Wolfe, Thomas 176, 208, 405
Women's issues 318, 330-331, 384-385
Woods, L. B. 144
Wright, Richard 145
Writer's and Artist's Yearbook 371
Writer's Handbook 371
Writer's Market 371

Yeats, William Butler 200
Young, Andrew 328
Young Adult Services Association *see* Young Adult Services Division
Young Adult Services Division (ALA) 161
Youngstown and Mahoning County (OH) Library 203
Yutang, Lin 132

Zeitlin, Jacob 300
Zola, Emile 132